THE BEAUTY PARADOX

THE BEAUTY PARADOX

Femininity in the Age of Selfies

Chiara Piazzesi

ROWMAN & LITTLEFIELD

Lanham • Boulder • New York • London

Published by Rowman & Littlefield
An imprint of The Rowman & Littlefield Publishing Group, Inc.
4501 Forbes Boulevard, Suite 200, Lanham, Maryland 20706
www.rowman.com

86-90 Paul Street, London EC2A 4NE

British Library Cataloguing in Publication Information available

Library of Congress Cataloging-in-Publication Data

Names: Piazzesi, Chiara, author.
Title: The beauty paradox : femininity in the age of selfies / Chiara Piazzesi.
Description: Lanham : Rowman & Littlefield, [2023] | Includes bibliographical
   references and index.
Identifiers: LCCN 2023003332 (print) | LCCN 2023003333 (ebook) |
   ISBN 9781538175736 (hardcover ; alk. paper) | ISBN 9781538175743
   (paperback ; alk. paper) | ISBN 9781538175750 (epub)
Subjects: LCSH: Feminine beauty (Aesthetics) | Femininity. |
   Women—Psychology.
Classification: LCC HQ1219 .P53 2023 (print) | LCC HQ1219 (ebook) |
   DDC 305.4—dc23/eng/20230126
LC record available at https://lccn.loc.gov/2023003332
LC ebook record available at https://lccn.loc.gov/2023003333

♾™ The paper used in this publication meets the minimum requirements of
American National Standard for Information Sciences—Permanence of Paper for
Printed Library Materials, ANSI/NISO Z39.48-1992.

CONTENTS

ACKNOWLEDGMENTS

This book, like the research project out of which it has grown, would not exist without the help and support of many people, groups, and organizations. I believe strongly that we should appreciate more fully the extent to which our ideas and analytical concepts, and the stories we tell through them, are shaped by our encounters with other people—by their suggestions, their readings of various texts, their life experiences, and above all their willingness to share these with others.

First and foremost, I am indebted to the eleven women who generously agreed to participate in my research project: their diverse reflections, backgrounds, and feelings have deeply informed not only my thoughts but also the language I used to express them, which is intended to reach as wide an audience as possible. Catherine Lavoie Mongrain, who at the time was completing her PhD dissertation at the Université du Québec à Montréal (UQAM) under my supervision, worked with me at every step of the research project on women's online self-presentation for which the data discussed in this book was gathered. I am grateful for her commitment and her insights, which helped to shape the preliminary steps of the wider theorization presented here. My gratitude also goes to the Fonds de recherche du Québec—Société et culture, from which I received a generous three-year grant to carry out my research project. Further funding for the completion and revision of the manuscript came from UQAM's Faculté des sciences humaines and Département de sociologie. In addition, I'm thankful for a year-long sabbatical leave granted by UQAM, which brought a much-needed change of pace and allowed me to concentrate on writing. It is worth noting, for the historical record, that the book was written during the first two years of the COVID-19 pandemic. The life changes that the pandemic brought about made me particularly aware of the challenges associated with reconciling one's often competing commitments to work and family; as we learn from the women interviewed for this study, this is something that many if not most parents experience in their everyday lives, but it can be especially acute when they lack child care or they have demanding work schedules. The pandemic was a time of sadness, loss, fear, boredom, and social dislocation for many, but it was also one of increased empathy, of gratitude, and of appreciation for the smaller things in life, and perhaps especially for the pleasure that human encounters can spark. In some ways, I believe the book reflects my efforts to embrace such complexity in all social things, and to do justice to their kaleidoscopic nature. Readers can of course judge the results.

My deepest gratitude goes to the librarians at UQAM, whose professionalism, competence, and indefatigable service were decisive in ensuring the scientific rigor of this book, and also in enabling swift additions and revisions as I worked on the final manuscript.

Many colleagues and friends provided insights, sources, and critical observations at different stages of the writing and revising processes. I am particularly grateful to Barbara Thériault, an amazing colleague and friend, for our many terrific discussions not only on beauty culture but also on the experience of being a woman in academia who cares about appearance. My dear friend Jennifer Welsh was among the first people to provide firsthand autobiographical evidence for my belief that beauty is a topic worthy of "serious" sociological research. I thank her not only for sharing her experience and insights but also for listening, asking all the right questions, and for baking the most delicious spanakopita. The attention, intelligence, and generosity with which Vanessa Molina read and commented on a preliminary version of the manuscript proved crucial as I worked to finalize the book. My late colleague and friend Jean-Sébastien Guy, whom I deeply miss, provided rigorous yet charitable criticism, expressing the utmost enthusiasm while raising knowledgeable questions: such is the compound of qualities through which this scholar wishes to be read. My editor, Ryan Perks, read and annotated my manuscript with rigor, attentiveness, and empathy, without leaving even the smallest stone unturned. I am living proof of the fact that being exposed to his thoroughness and intelligence can work magic: it made an unripe manuscript into a real book, and definitely made the writer a better person. Alyssa Palazzo, my editor at Rowman & Littlefield, was the fine reader and wise counselor who shepherded the book through all the delicate stages of production—and ultimately into the real world. Her enthusiasm, gentle criticism, and constructive suggestions made the work of revision pleasurable and stimulating. I am indebted to the whole team at Rowman & Littlefield for giving me the opportunity to circulate my work beyond the walls of academia, and for supporting and advising me throughout the process.

Amanda Fehlbaum (Youngstown State University), Megan Jewell (Case Western Reserve University), and two anonymous reviewers provided generous comments and suggestions on the manuscript. The criticism they formulated helped me greatly improve the final result and will certainly inform my future research on beauty norms and their impact on different social groups.

I am also very grateful to the different audiences to which I was able to present my views on beauty and online culture throughout the course of my work on the book, and particularly to the young people whom I met at the TEDx event in the lovely Tuscan town of Empoli in September 2019: their enthusiasm, probing questions, and encouragement convinced me that I might have something to say about what beauty means for women in contemporary Western societies. For their attention and questions, I also wish to thank the audiences at the following venues: the "Sexualités et technologies" conference organized by Les 3 sex★ in Montreal (2019); the RILES seminar held at the Università di Perugia (2020); the 1st Congress of the International Network of Sociology of Sensibilities (RedISS, online event, 2021); the workshop "Genres et Sexualités: Représentations en art, littérature et medias" held at UQAM (2022); the 89th ACFAS Congress (2022); the Annual Conference of the Canadian Sociological Association (2022); and the 11th European Feminist Research Conference held in Milan (2022).

My deep love and gratitude go to my friends and family, and in particular to my husband and daughter, who have been patient, supportive, and compassionate without ever taking me too seriously: this has gone a long way toward mitigating my very Italian proclivity for drama throughout the long months during which this book took form. In all honesty, my daughter's unshakable determination to grant me glittery reward stickers each time I completed a section is what kept me going some days.

This book presents original insights, though some of the ideas and interpretations developed in the chapters were earlier tested elsewhere. These were published as follows: Chiara Piazzesi and Catherine Lavoie Mongrain, "Women 'Doing Selfies': Reflexivity and Norm Negotiation in the Production and Circulation of Digital Self-Portraits," *Sociologia e Politiche sociali* 3 (2019): 95–111; Chiara Piazzesi and Catherine Lavoie Mongrain, "Selfies de femmes, négociation normative et production de culture visuelle sur Instagram et Facebook," *Recherches féministes* 33, no. 1 (2020): 135–51; Chiara Piazzesi and Catherine Lavoie Mongrain, "Épreuves de la beauté et paradoxes de la capacité de choix des femmes," *Recherches féministes* 34, no. 1 (2021): 47–64; Chiara Piazzesi, "Sentirsi bene, sentirsi bella: Emozioni e contraddizioni nell'esperienza femminile della bellezza," *SocietàMutamentoPolitica* 12, no. 24 (2021): 83–104; Chiara Piazzesi, "On the 'Female Gaze' in the Interview Setting: Methodological Insights from Fieldwork with Women," *Italian Sociological Review* (forthcoming).

INTRODUCTION

Walking the Tightrope

More than a decade ago, as a young postdoctoral scholar, I spent several months conducting research at the Bibliothèque Nationale de France–François Mitterrand. Library days were for the most part lonely days, so I looked forward to shared coffee and lunch breaks in the library's common areas (food in the cafeteria was too expensive, and most of us would just bring our own lunches). I knew a few regulars, including a young French scholar—in my opinion, a pretty girl—who was doing a PhD in literature. While I certainly had many interesting conversations with her, I have no specific memories of our talks, save for one exception. One day, while we were having lunch on the stairs of the library's main hallway, basking in the sunlight that streamed in through the tall windows, I casually asked how she was doing. To my surprise, instead of the conventional small talk I was expecting, she replied rather emphatically: "Today, I'm doing *much* better: I washed my hair, put nice makeup on, gave a lot of thought to my outfit. And I'm writing a chapter. Yesterday, I left the house in the first thing I could find, without any lipstick on, and I felt miserable all day." My colleague, it seemed, was not only telling me that looking good was making her *feel* good—she was also making a direct connection between the way she *knew* she looked and her productive day of writing, which provided an even greater satisfaction. I recall covertly but attentively scanning her outfit, along with her hair and makeup, as if trying to steal a glimpse of the secret to both female beauty and academic success. Her confidence, on such clear display that day, has stayed in my memory ever since.

Fast-forward to 2020. Quoted in an article by Angelique Serrano describing the seeming ubiquity of professional beauty tips during the COVID-19 pandemic, Sarah Gibson Tuttle, founder of the Olive & June

1

salons and nail-care line, provides a similar account: "In college, classes were a totally different experience when I wore sweats versus when I wore an outfit. . . . When I was dressed up, I took better notes and was more engaged. I felt present and ready." Serrano also reports that Gibson Tuttle surveyed more than two hundred women about their beauty rituals in 2019, of whom 98 percent "reported feeling better when their nails were done."[1]

These statements are entirely consistent with the accounts of eleven women whom I interviewed in Montreal between 2017 and 2019 as part of a research project on the role of beauty in women's everyday lives. They are consistent as well with language I've heard many of my girlfriends and female acquaintances, of all ages, use to describe the advantages that accrue when one puts effort into one's appearance. Finally, they are consistent with my own personal experience as a woman professor, scholar, intimate partner, parent, consumer, client, and patient: While performing these roles in front of others and for myself, I would feel better if I knew I was well-groomed and my physical appearance carefully thought through—in a word, if I was pleasant to look at. By feeling attractive, then, I would also feel better prepared for my social roles and performances.

Tell this to any woman, and she will simply reply, "Of course." However, scholarship tends either to belittle these statements, as if they were unworthy of proper sociological investigation, or to dismiss them as symptoms of a psychological issue on the part of women, a pathological need, or some form of "false consciousness." Women, and especially young women, who invest in their appearance are often characterized as superficial, narcissistic, as having succumbed to a "lack of confidence"—the latter a sort of trivial, one-size-fits-all explanation for (young) women's behaviors, particularly in the era of social media and the ubiquitous selfie.

This book, by contrast, seeks to take women's statements seriously[2]— to listen to them when they say that they feel better when they feel beautiful and that they need to feel beautiful in order to feel like legitimate actors in their social lives. I intend to consider these statements as sociologically relevant, insofar as they pinpoint the sociological dimension of women's beauty: women are universally rewarded for their beautiful appearance, just as they are (morally) blamed for not being beautiful; they are encouraged to value beauty and to generously invest resources (time, money, mental energy) to its pursuit, which also stirs up pre-existing socioeconomic inequalities; they feel that their social legitimacy depends a great deal on the way they look, no matter their age, what roles they perform, and what challenges they face. Thus, beauty is not only for the aesthetic eye: inasmuch as competent femininity must be visibly inscribed on the attractive female body, beauty means social acceptability, moral status, legitimacy, and reliability.

What women say about the importance of being well-groomed, well-dressed, and physically beautiful is of sociological importance for another reason. Women certainly affirm that beauty makes them feel *good*, that it enhances their well-being, that it gives them pleasant feelings, but this is not all they are saying. Their claims about beauty also relate to the social roles they perform in their everyday lives. Beauty works as a facilitator or lubricant for social processes in which women are involved and within which they are put to the test—whether carrying out a task at school or work, showing up for an important event, applying for a mortgage, or seeking medical advice. By providing an increased sense of legitimacy, beauty as a resource helps them successfully fulfill their social roles. Interestingly, older woman interviewees with successful careers and/or reputations in their fields explained to me that they felt they could allow themselves to skip aspects of the beautifying process to which they had subjected themselves in the past. At a certain point in life, these women drew a stronger sense of legitimacy from their accomplishments, and the legitimacy provided by a beautiful appearance came to play a secondary role in their social and professional lives.

The older women I interviewed also talked about a further lesson that age had taught them: they had come to learn that aging meant that you cannot please everybody and that you will always be criticized, no matter what you look like. This awareness points to a third, and likely the most important, sociological aspect of beauty, one that also lies at the theoretical heart of this book. Drawing on the work of psychology and fashion scholar Efrat Tseëlon, I will argue that women's experience of beauty is caught between a set of paradoxical injunctions and that this prevents them from succeeding at their attempts to fully, durably, consistently feel beautiful—and, as a consequence, to stop worrying about their appearance.

Generally speaking, a paradox is "a situation or statement that seems impossible or is difficult to understand because it contains two opposite facts or characteristics."[3] From childhood on, women are forced to undertake the seemingly impossible task of navigating contradictory instructions, obligations, and judgments concerning beautification, appearance, and femininity. For instance, we learn that a woman who cares for her appearance is shallow, but that a woman who does not care for her appearance is not really a woman. We learn that appearance should not be the criterion on which we are judged, but also that we are first and foremost judged for our attractiveness. We learn to perform beautification techniques as a necessary part of our daily routine ("cold water and moisturizer every morning for beautiful skin!" my grandma would say when I was a little girl), but we also learn that we should preferably appear "naturally" beautiful. We are not only told that we can always do more and better for our appearance, that we can always be fitter, buy better products, and improve our beautifying skills, but also that a woman who does too much to be beautiful is narcissistic, or lacks self-confidence, or might be too openly sexually available (to put it bluntly, a slut). This is the paradoxical logic in which virtually every woman is caught: Are both sides of these statements true, or are both false? Which side should we pick to feel competent and, ultimately, to be happy?[4]

In the words of one of my interview subjects, navigating these paradoxical injunctions can feel like walking a "tightrope." The image of the tightrope is a potent one because it points to the feeling of having to maintain an endlessly precarious balance, one that requires concentration and training, imitation and scrutiny, one that is attained through incessant work, creates deep anxieties, and is monitored by other people ready to judge whether or not the endeavor has failed. This experience is familiar to many (probably most) women in Western societies, who feel that they work hard to convey an acceptable appearance but who are nonetheless criticized if they fail—as most of us do, for one reason or another—to meet the standards of female beauty. But they know that they can also face disapproval for working too hard to achieve them. Women are blamed for overeating, for starving themselves, for foregoing makeup, for wearing makeup, for dressing too casually, for dressing up, for being too sexy, for not being sexy enough, for covering their gray hair, for not dying their gray hair—the list could go on and on. It is tempting to think that the solution would be picking one side of this tortured logic and sticking to it. As a matter of fact, one must pick neither and both at the same time to the extent that one must continuously renegotiate an impermanent, fleeting balance between paradoxical injunctions, the ultimate effect of which is to destabilize one's confidence in one's choices and indeed oneself.

This is why beauty is such a compelling phenomenon from a sociological point of view. Like many sociological problems, it can be pointed out and examined, but it cannot be "solved" in any traditional sense. Actually, beauty is a very good example of what Watzlawick, Weakland, and Fisch have described as a situation in which "the solution is the problem."[5] Embracing beauty standards or rejecting them is not a "solution" to the problem of beauty as either choice ends up feeding the problem it aims to solve, inasmuch as the problem is created by the articulation of paradoxical injunctions. Since there is no "right way" of dealing with the problem of beauty, then, it is sociologically fascinating to look at how women respond to this problem in their everyday lives, through their practices, their choices, their reflections, and also their production of self-representing visual culture—what in popular parlance we call selfies. But is beauty exclusively a concern for women? Schneickert, Steckermeier, and Brand, in their study of the association between perceived unattractiveness and social disadvantage in the acquisition of wealth, knowledge, and social relations, found that the price of unattractiveness appears to be high for men too.[6] They claim, furthermore, that there might be a gender bias in scholarship on attractiveness and that we might be collectively overestimating the value of attractiveness for women. However, I would argue that the discursive framework through which Western women experience beauty still places a greater emphasis on its importance for women compared to men; defines attractiveness as a necessary condition for women's social recognition; generates a number of social instances in which women are reduced to their appearance; and places the blame for unattractiveness on women as individuals. Such cultural framing has concrete consequences in terms of how women perceive, maintain, value, and also resent beauty, and this is especially true within what scholars define as a "postfeminist" cultural environment in the West. Stemming from an unlikely combination of traditional and late-modern definitions of proper femininity, Western postfeminist discourse is centered on a "defanged" understanding of feminist politics in which the edge has been taken off certain critical claims and demands in exchange for a reading of gender relations that privileges reconciliation. More specifically, gender relations are seen as no longer requiring resistance and opposition from women, as though feminism's job is already complete. Within such an understanding, as Angela McRobbie notes, women are encouraged to engage in practices, generally linked to their ability to participate in consumption activities, that can be characterized as "both progressive but also consummately and reassuringly feminine."[7] Hence, as Sarah Riley, Adrienne Evans, and Martine Robson argue, the concept of a postfeminist sensibility enables an understanding of "how a set of otherwise contradictory notions of femininity come together to form a cohesive way of making sense about what it means to be a woman and to have a good life."[8] Postfeminist culture is riven by contradictions and tensions inasmuch as it promotes a version of femininity that hinges simultaneously on the embrace of certain classic feminist themes (the promotion of women's empowerment, agency, their visibility in the public sphere) and the "disavowal" of feminism as a political force, as McRobbie notes.[9] As a consequence, postfeminism entails a discursive shift that seeks to bestow on women a dual status as objects of desire and the masters of their own choices, thereby reaffirming that feminism's demands are fulfilled and women can sit back (or "lean in"?) and enjoy their fully liberated agency. Echoing the work of many scholars who have come before me, I will also argue that the space available for women to exert such agency while maintaining their status as self-determining subjects is still severely restricted by the persistence of traditional normative frameworks, which women must negotiate in their everyday lives. In particular, I claim that a host of paradoxical norms regulate women's choices in matters of beauty, appearance, and visibility, thus continuously destabilizing their sense of social and personal legitimacy, both online and off.

This is the subject of this book. It is not about "what beauty is," so to speak; rather, it is about how beauty is discursively constructed in contemporary North American societies, and about the practical influence this has over women's daily choices, judgments, experiences, and feelings. The following chapters offer an exploration of women's practices and thoughts with regard to beauty as an ongoing test—one framed, as we've seen, by a multitude of paradoxical injunctions—of their abilities and competences as social actors. These paradoxical injunctions are part of a cultural framework in which, as Kristi Coulter writes in her 2018 memoir *Nothing Good Can Come from This*, "there's no easy way to be a woman, because there's no *acceptable* way to be a woman." To me, this is why it is so riveting to observe and document how women nevertheless persist in going about *being* women in their daily lives.

The first chapter of the book describes in greater detail the paradoxes created by the contradictory instructions women either receive directly (from family, peers, significant others, media) or draw from their sociocultural environment. In the last two decades of the twentieth century, Tseëlon and MacCannell and MacCannell have identified some of these paradoxical injunctions. The chapter organizes insights gleaned from their work, to which I add general observations, sociological analyses, and theoretical interpretations stemming from my fieldwork as well as my personal experience as a white woman in my forties working as an academic and living in North America in the early twenty-first century—which is to say in the age of the selfie and social media. The four paradoxes that I discuss are related to women's worth, authenticity, power, and commitment with regard to beauty. I argue that, as a result of these paradoxes, the conditions of possibility within which women make choices are themselves paradoxical: whatever women choose to do with regard to their appearance, they will be subject to scrutiny, criticism, and negative judgments. Such scrutiny is universal, but its harshness and its concrete formulations differ according to variables defining individual identity and, thus, social status. With regard to attractiveness, the most relevant variables are gender, race, age, social class, capability, and body size. As I will show in the following chapters, women's identities are situated at the intersection of these variables, a position that in turn affects their access to recognition based on appearance and femininity. Paradoxical injunctions are thus enhanced by power relations based on racial, gender, age, socioeconomic, and bodily differences. The political consequences are tremendous: at stake is nothing less than women's autonomy. Long described as a fundamental right by feminist movements, women's self-determination remains thwarted by the highly circumscribed social, cultural, and political spaces within which their choices are made.

My description and theorization of the four paradoxes of Western beauty culture provide the conceptual underpinnings for the following chapters. Drawing on this theoretical framework, chapters 2 through 6 present and discuss the results of a two-year qualitative research project aimed at documenting women's experience of beauty in the early twenty-first century. Since selfies are one of the principal vehicles for women's visual self-expression and self-presentation, I expected beauty and appearance to play a major role in their production and circulation. I recruited eleven women of different ages living in Montreal and sharing selfies on social media and invited them to share their thoughts and their pictures with me. We talked about beauty in general, beautification rituals and routines, the role of attractiveness in different spheres of life (such as working and parenting), the challenges of aging, the act of taking and sharing selfies, the experience of seeing other women's selfies, and of being seen and judged by other women, and so forth. In addition to giving me access to their Facebook and Instagram accounts, the participants also agreed to take a series of selfies according to my instructions: for each image they were asked to tailor their appearance to a specific situation, ranging from formal and public to private and personal, immortalize it in a picture, and share it with me. In subsequent interviews with each of them, we then discussed these selfies; this provided me with original insights into the reasoning, emotions, and expectations that structured the participants' relationship to the appearance and self-expression conveyed through their pictures.

As we will see in the following chapters, beauty injunctions do not target *all* women at the same time and in the same way. Depending on their ethnic background, socioeconomic status, sexual orientation, body size, and age, women experience the constraints and opportunities of beauty culture in different ways. An analysis of beauty as a daily experience in women's lives must take such diversity into account. The group of women I worked with was relatively diverse in terms of age, socioeconomic status, and even body size, but it was quite homogeneous in terms of ethnicity (ten women out of eleven being white) and sexual orientation (all heterosexual). Such homogeneity can represent a limitation for a research project aiming to document how beauty injunctions are experienced along these axes of inequality. As psychologist Sarah Riley and her colleagues highlight in their research on women's practices of looking at and judging each other's bodies within the context of a postfeminist culture (the "female gaze" that I will discuss in this book as well), in certain circumstances, sample homogeneity can actually reveal itself as an advantage. Since Western postfeminist beauty culture is still premised on an idealized notion of femininity that is white, upper middle class, heterosexual, and thin, it is relevant to document, claim Riley and colleagues, "how white heterosexual women respond to this address [i.e., this notion of femininity]"—and, I would add, how they respond to its intrinsic neglect of diversity.[10] What this book provides, then, is first a solid, pathbreaking theoretical framework in which to talk sociologically about how women experience beauty and its paradoxical normative framing in contemporary postfeminist culture. Having assembled this theoretical toolbox, it then offers the first application of these tools to data gathered from a small convenience sample of North American women (I provide a more thorough explanation of my methodology in appendix B). Due to the limitations stemming from my study's design, more research is certainly needed to determine if and how paradoxical normativity regarding appearance and attractiveness applies to different ethnic groups, gender identities, and sexual orientations, and the effects that it produces. Some of the theoretical findings and insights presented in this book, however, may well reflect the experiences of women around the globe, since the postfeminist sensibility, as Riley, Evans, and Robson observe, is spreading beyond the cultural environment of North America, the United Kingdom, Europe, and Australia to "inform . . . developments in gender subjectivities and practices" in other cultural spaces.[11]

In a manner already hinted at in the anecdote with which I opened this introduction, perhaps the most salient observation that participants shared with me relates to the connection they experience between feeling beautiful and feeling good. This connection unfolds in at least two ways. Traditionally, Western cultures have linked women's beauty to their health, physical (especially reproductive) as well as spiritual and/or moral. Women's putative ugliness has historically been framed as a mark of degeneration, illness, or either physical or moral corruption, while beauty has been understood as the outward manifestation of physiological health (which is also tied to one's suitability for biological reproduction) and moral rectitude. In this sense, female beauty is not simply an aesthetic feature radiating from the surface of the female body; it is an outward manifestation of something much deeper—namely, bodily and spiritual health. This link between female health and female beauty persists in Western culture, notwithstanding various discursive shifts throughout the centuries. The reader will certainly be familiar with contemporary marketing strategies touting cosmetic products based on the idea that beauty comes from within, that it must be nourished from the inside and that beauty treatments are really "wellness" treatments in that they heal the soul while beautifying the flesh. This primary connection between beauty and well-being is also entangled with the authenticity paradox: a "healthy" beauty, one that glows from within, is supposed to be "natural" and authentic; on the other hand, it is incumbent upon women to participate in beautification and the consumption practices seen as a necessary precondition for their attainment of such "natural beauty."

The second modality is related to women's self-perception, with participants seeing feeling good and feeling beautiful as mutually enhancing experiences. These women explained that they feel more confident and "ready" to face everyday challenges in their social lives when they feel they are sufficiently attractive. But they also understand their beauty as a consequence of their well-being, of being at the "right place" in their life. Hence, one's inner and outer states are regarded as being interrelated, and beauty is experienced as all but a superficial feature of the body. Hence, the second chapter illustrates how beauty is situated both inside and out. It also explores the entanglements of female beauty with nature (authenticity) and artifice (inauthenticity) as aesthetic and moral qualities.

In a sense, then, beauty appears and is culturally understood as a natural feature of the (female) body, radiating from the inside out. Historically, however, women's beauty has also been regarded as artificial, as constructed, and hence fake, inconstant, or covering up a natural deficit of beauty. Here we can easily observe the paradoxical nature of the Western cultural framing of women's appearances: this tension between natural and artificial permeates our understanding of beauty, as well as the categories that we use to differentiate beautification practices and women's looks. These categories also imply a moral judgment dividing authentic from fake. Consequently, such moral ambiguity surrounds beauty work in general, understood as the time, money, energy, and training that women invest throughout their lives in trying to look good, or to look better. This is another of the paradoxes that women have to navigate while taking care of their looks: they are expected to do enough—not too much, not too little—to look beautiful, but "enough" will never be enough, inasmuch as one can never attain beauty once and for all.

The work of beauty, in other words, is endless. Tomorrow morning, I will again have to fix my hair, moisturize my skin, remove unwanted body hair, trim my nails—but also exercise, watch my intake of food and alcohol, try to get enough sleep, and so on. None of these actions can be undertaken in any definitive sense; rather, they form a discipline, a habit, a daily commitment. The more inconstant beauty is, the more consistent must be the practice of beautification. Chapter 3 discusses these aspects and problems of beauty understood as work, as an endeavor and an investment for women. In doing so, it also deals with the entanglements of beauty and economic thinking. The last section of the chapter discusses the "day" as a temporal and psychological measure for beautification efforts. The twenty-four-hour day frames one's beauty routine, but it also structures the sequence of social situations and commitments that one has to engage with in order to get "through" the day. Such commitments demand specific planning with regard to appearance, and hence influence the amount of time and energy that need to be invested in looking the part. Finally, the day is subject to a large degree of emotional self-perception that changes every morning depending on one's energy level, personal situation, and even environmental factors (such as humidity in the air and its effect on one's hair). Again, such aesthetic and affective self-appraisal influences our assessment of the degree and type of beautification required for a given situation.

In matters of beauty, time plays a major role beyond the short-term temporality of the day. The unfolding of time in a biographical path, entailing life stages laden with their own symbolic value (puberty, maternity, menopause, etc.), was also a main topic of discussion during my interviews. For the most part, every woman is expected to be aware of the fact that beauty fades with time. Aging is considered the main threat to beauty, to the extent that Western cultures regard beauty and old age almost as opposites. This implies the adoption of strategies that conceal and even prevent aging for women. On the one hand, they are encouraged to hide exterior signs of aging (such as wrinkles, gray hair, age spots), so that a common, highly appreciated compliment to an aging woman is that she looks younger than she really is—in other words, that she does not look her age. On the other hand, women are also targeted by a commercial and social discourse that urges them to preserve their beauty, to capitalize on it while it is still fresh, "young," available. However, this does not mean that being young and good-looking is always an advantage, or easier, for women. Older participants highlighted the drawbacks of beauty and the visibility it often affords at a younger age. They also characterized time as both a learning process with regard to beauty, and as entailing a sort of "liberation" from the duty of looking good, since one becomes almost invisible as one ages. With this in mind, chapter 4 analyzes the passage of time and its influence on women's experiences with beauty, with biological and aesthetic changes entailing a shift in social recognition due to the way they affect the criteria by which we judge a woman's appearance.

My work is situated in what could be called a "renaissance" of sociological interest in attractiveness and its role as an individual resource in contemporary Western societies. Perception of one's physical traits appears to play an increasingly consequential role among social actors, inasmuch as it occurs through ideas and stereotypes, the social purpose of which is to "rank" individual status in a social hierarchy of worth and legitimacy. For instance, in ordinary life situations, we might comparatively assess our social standing and appraise our fellow social actors by inferring their moral qualities on the basis of their appearance—and undergo a similar assessment on the part of our interlocutors. Such inferences normally span the categories of competence, moral worth, legitimacy, trustworthiness, and the attribution of these qualities (or lack thereof) can strongly influence one's social trajectory. Looks can help determine one's opportunities in the labor market, one's marital prospects, and one's place in the economy of visibility on social media.

If this form of inference based on looks has a long history, and is therefore no secret either to scholars (Erving Goffman's seminal work comes to mind here) or to ordinary social actors, its salience might have increased as a result of what sociologists Chris Warhurst and Dennis Nickson define as the shift toward an aesthetic economy, and more generally to an aestheticization of social relations. In recent decades, aesthetics, here materialized in design and style, has become a central feature of the manufacture and service economies: appearance, and the feeling that an object or experience might convey, are part of what is traded in retail economic transactions. As a consequence, in the service economy, attractiveness, or at least a certain appearance, is a major asset when it comes to successfully navigating the labor market, and it is used by companies to promote their brands—as Arlie Hochschild already observed in her research on female flight attendants.[12] If attractiveness influences one's employability and career opportunities, it also contributes to producing and reproducing inequality, since attractiveness is in itself an unevenly distributed resource across gender, race, age, body size, and social class. In this respect, my work deepens our understanding of the individual experience of beauty as a personal asset and resource in women's everyday lives and self-presentation in highly aestheticized societies. In addition, I situate such experience at the intersection of multiple axes of inequality: attractiveness, age, social class, and race. This is especially relevant in chapter 5, where I discuss the impact of attractiveness—or lack thereof—on various aspects of women's lives, from everyday casual interactions to work and consumption practices. Attractiveness appears to serve as an enabler, facilitating interactions and boosting women's confidence in more challenging situations. Women are aware of the return they stand to gain on attractiveness and are willing to cash in on it while also wishing to avoid the drawbacks of female beauty and of being assessed purely on the basis of their appearance.

A second, crucial factor contributing to the increased salience of attractiveness and a stylized appearance in everyday social interactions is, in my opinion, the overwhelming visuality of online social networking platforms and of the content created by the users of these platforms. In a departure from the vast majority of scholarly work on beauty, my book discusses attractiveness in the era of digital photography, social media, and selfies. The affordances of connected devices equipped with digital cameras, combined with the ubiquity of social networking sites, places a specific emphasis on visual self-presentation—both as a method of showcasing one's identity online and as way to fashion a personalized narrative through visual content. Norms of feminine beauty, surveillance, and visibility are transposed and transformed within selfie-taking and selfie-sharing practices, yet the role of attractiveness in this context goes relatively undiscussed in the relevant sociological literature. Chapter 6 aims to fill this gap by examining the convergence of norms regulating women's visibility online and those that determine what is an appropriate appearance and what sort of participation in the act of beautification is acceptable. It shows that such convergence reproduces traditional paradoxical injunctions, even if these are now adapted to new interactional contexts—for instance, with regard to the tension between incitements to self-exposure online and the alleged "narcissism" of women who make themselves visible, or between self-editing practices (which serve to foster a culture of idealization and perfection) and the imperative to present an online persona that will come across as authentic and trustworthy.

As I mentioned earlier, selfies were used as research material in the project that led to this book. Hence, their methodological function, in my interviews with participants and later, as my research entered the analytical stage, was threefold. First, they served to illustrate what participants meant when they described feeling beautiful and talked about their desire to preserve a memory of that feeling within the specific framing of the quotidian moment captured in the typical selfie. Second, through their characteristics and modes of circulation, individual selfies manifested the norms and features of a larger selfie culture in which they are embedded and in which their producers willingly inscribed them.[13] Third, they served as specific visual examples of different instances of situated self-expression through the online circulation of digital self-portraits. Hence, I used selfies as a synecdoche for the larger cultural framework that I wished to understand, as "data for sociological analysis"[14] stemming from producers situated in different social positions, and as a fieldwork device to enhance participants' reflexivity on practices of visual self-expression. The centrality of visual self-expression, and of the reflexivity that this form carries and triggers, constitutes an innovative aspect of my research on women's experience of beauty.

Thanks to the women who generously participated in this study, who enthusiastically responded to my invitation to share their thoughts and their selfies with me, this book contributes to our understanding of women's lived, embodied experiences of beauty as both a resource and a challenge in everyday life, online as well as off. Throughout my fieldwork, analysis, and writing process, I have strived to tease out insights capable of acknowledging, as Claire Tanner, JaneMaree Maher, and Suzanne Fraser rightly call for in their book on twenty-first-century "vanity," "both the problems and *pleasures* associated with normalisation"—that is, with the effort of abiding by norms of acceptability and legitimacy.[15] My hope is that the chorus of voices that I have brought together in this book will serve to enlighten both scholarly readers as well as the merely curious. Interrogating the paradoxicality of the norms that regulate our experiences of the world, and of the demands that we face as a consequence, is in itself, I hope, a worthwhile endeavor. For it is only by putting such paradoxes in perspective that we might eventually overcome them.

Chapter 1

THE PARADOXES OF BEAUTY

In her short 2017 essay "Be a Lady They Said," feminist author Camille Rainville denounced the pressure women face from media discourse and cultural norms targeting their appearance, their sexuality, and their visibility. Of course, Rainville was not the first to do so: there is a long feminist tradition of criticizing beauty culture and the double standard framing men's and women's sexualities. What is new in Rainville's text, however, and what makes it particularly riveting, is the way she pins down an intrinsic, structural feature of Western beauty culture, what I will call its "paradoxicality."

According to the *Oxford English Dictionary*, the term "paradox" is "often applied to a proposition or statement that is actually self-contradictory, or contradictory to reason or ascertained truth, and so, essentially absurd and false."[1] As a simple example, I make a paradoxical statement when I claim simultaneously that something does and does not possess certain qualities—two assertions that contradict each other. In her essay, Rainville shows that women are targeted by a series of injunctions about beauty, beautification, and sexualization that are clearly contradictory. To produce the surprising, disconcerting effect of paradoxicality, Rainville constructs her text as a compendium of competing injunctions—media messages, commonplace moral lessons, advertising slogans—and stacks them in such a way that their cumulative absurdity becomes impossible to miss:

> Be a lady they said. Your skirt is too short. Your shirt is too low. Your pants are too tight. Don't show so much skin. . . . Cover up. Leave something to the imagination. . . . Show some skin. Look sexy. Look

hot. Don't be so provocative. You're asking for it. Wear black. Wear heels. You're too dressed up. You're too dressed down. . . .

Be a lady they said. Don't be too fat. Don't be too thin. Don't be too large. Don't be too small. Eat up. Slim down. Stop eating so much. Don't eat too fast. Order a salad. Don't eat carbs. Skip dessert. You need to lose weight. Fit into that dress. Go on a diet. Watch what you eat. Eat celery. Chew gum. Drink lots of water. You have to fit into those jeans. God, you look like a skeleton. Why don't you just eat? You look emaciated. You look sick. Eat a burger. Men like women with some meat on their bones.[2]

In Rainville's telling, being a "lady" is something of an impossible endeavor since women's beautification practices, self-discipline, and (sexual) self-expression are subject to myriad contradictory injunctions. Women are told to be or do one thing *and* its opposite, and to strike an impossible balance between the two.

After circulating in its original form as a blog post after 2017, Rainville's powerful essay received a second wave of media attention in February 2020 thanks to a short video directed by Paul McLean for the women's magazine *Girls Girls Girls*, founded by photographer Claire Rothstein.[3] In McLean's video—which bears the same title as the original essay—actress Cynthia Nixon delivers a captivating performance of Rainville's words, accompanied by images of women who embody the paradoxes that interest us here. According to Jo Chappel, thanks to its circulation on social networking sites, the video had already been watched twenty million times by March 5, 2020. Are we to gather from these numbers that Rainville's words struck a chord with a meaningful swathe of the general population?[4]

At the end of May 2020, as the world grappled with the immediate effects of the COVID-19 pandemic, the French edition of *Elle* magazine published a special issue on weight gain and weight loss during the early months of the lockdown, when exercise was reduced to a minimum thanks to school and gym closures and the widespread switch to working from home, and when many people embraced cooking (and more specifically baking[5]) as the ultimate form of self-care. The special issue garnered a huge amount of attention on social media, where it triggered numerous critical reactions from women.[6] Among other things, *Elle* was accused of reinforcing traditional injunctions encouraging women to watch their weight and be skinny, regardless of the extraordinary circumstances of the pandemic and its effect on people's well-being and mental health. In addition, the special issue was clearly organized by contradictory statements on weight and body size. As political adviser and feminist activist Laure

Botella vividly stated on Twitter, "Let's summarize. For @ELLEFrance, if you are a woman and you have: gained weight: it's not OK. Lost weight: it's not OK. Gained muscle: it's not OK. Eaten organic grains with no bra on: it's not OK. In short, if you are a woman and you have breathed, it's not OK."[7]

Voices like Botella's are converging on a new and rapidly spreading awareness of something that has been observed and remarked upon for decades, albeit in more inchoate forms: Whatever women do with their bodies and their looks, they will likely expose themselves to criticism or shaming. Women are encouraged to be beautiful, yet also sanctioned if they're *too* interested in beauty and beautification. They are enjoined to do *enough*—not too little, and not too much—to stay beautiful, sexy, young, and attractive, and yet enough never seems to be enough. They are encouraged to buy and use a panoply of products, techniques, and services, to develop skills and know-how to improve their looks; and they also have to appear natural, to stop trying too hard, to love themselves as they are—what French feminist journalist and author Jennifer Padjemi calls "the women magazine syndrome," according to which every article or advertisement contradicts the previous one.[8] Western cultural messages about female beauty put women in a paradoxical, indeed impossible situation.

Drawing on the findings from my own fieldwork as well as previous work by Kathy Peiss, Efrat Tseëlon, and Juliet Flower MacCannell and Dean MacCannell, this chapter discusses the four main paradoxes that structure women's experience of beauty: the worth paradox, the authenticity paradox, the power paradox, and the commitment paradox. This prepares the way for a more theoretical discussion of paradoxicality as a common feature of communicational and cultural frameworks. Finally, the last section of the chapter introduces the main scope of the book, which takes the form of an exploration of women's strategies for, and more general reflections on, coping with the paradoxical injunctions of Western beauty culture.

THE WORTH PARADOX

Zoe is a contract teacher, but she also works in the media sector as a freelance journalist. She is fifty years old at the time of our first interview. When she was younger and trying to build her career in the media industry, her good looks helped a lot, she says. Hence, she used her looks to be noticed, to stay visible, to be taken into consideration—and also to fit into a work environment that values aesthetics, style, and fashion. As a younger woman, her beautiful appearance was a very important component of her sense of worth. However, she describes a fundamental ambiguity when recalling the effect that her appearance had on coworkers or potential employers: she felt valued, she says, but not exactly for her professional skills. As a consequence, she started going to job interviews or showing up for new gigs without any makeup on and with an intentionally plain look; she felt that people would more readily perceive her competence and professional abilities that way. "I had the feeling that with loose hair and more makeup on [. . .] I was perceived as superficial," she recounts.[9] She felt that her personal and professional worth was somehow hidden behind her looks and that she would consequently be kept around and validated for the wrong reasons.

Many of the women I interviewed describe similar experiences. They report mixed feelings about the role of beauty in their lives, and they are aware of the drawbacks of the very qualities that facilitate their participation in many social and professional situations. Audrey, forty years old and self-employed, told me that she appreciates the validation she receives for the way she looks, and yet at the same time she does not like liking it because she resents being judged on the basis of her appearance:

> Yeah, absolutely, it still feels good to get the positive attention for your physical appearance, but I simultaneously resent it. I resent liking it, I resent that that's the way we function, I resent the fact that people are treated differently because of their appearance. I've also been a very thin girl and a very big girl, and it's amazing how differently you get treated.

Contradictory feelings like the ones described by Audrey are a consequence of paradoxical messages regarding the place of beauty in a woman's life, and its role in the collective assessment of her worth. Hence, the first paradox of Western beauty culture (though we could probably extend this to other cultures and societies) is the worth paradox, which can be formulated as follows: *A woman must care about her appearance. However, if she cares about her appearance, she is superficial, and thus unworthy; if she does not care about her appearance, and rejects beauty culture, she is not a woman, and thus, again, unworthy.*[10]

In Western societies, beauty has traditionally been framed as a woman's duty, one on which rests her acceptability and her worth as a woman: a woman without beauty is not completely a woman.[11] In many of the stories we still read to our children, women make their way through the world and climb the social ladder thanks to their beauty. Classic fairy-tale princesses such as Snow White or Sleeping Beauty are not particularly skilled at anything beyond looking good and being at the right place at the right time (which might be considered its own sort of skill, after all). Bad sisters, loveless mothers-in-law, perfidious witches—these women are usually depicted as ugly and evil, unworthy of both the prince's love and collective approval. Social expectations weighing on little girls from childhood on encourage them to be cute, graceful, well-dressed (possibly in pink and sequins), and to do all the things that a woman should do to count, to be worthy *as a woman*.[12]

But here comes the tricky part. As feminist thinker Colette Guillaumin has argued,[13] the work of beautification and feminization serve to materially inscribe a qualification on women's bodies, one that allows them to be identified as feminine. Hence, female bodies are "marked" as belonging to a special category, *different* from the general category of male (which in itself requires no characterization, being the reference for everything that is *not* masculine). Historically, women's difference was framed not only as "being different" or "being other than" but also as a form of inferiority entailing a restricted access to social recognition, resources, and opportunities—a cultural framing against which women's movements have fought and indeed continue to fight. This cultural marking has been naturalized, which means that its cultural and historical (and hence arbitrary) origins have been "forgotten," and the difference considered "natural," thus justifying the different arrangements, prescriptions, and expectations targeting women and men in Western societies. The female body—disciplined, groomed, beautified, adorned—bears the mark of such an allegedly natural state of affairs.[14]

The difference in worth, based on the naturalization of a cultural difference, also extends to the opposition between the feminine "realm" and the male "realm" in society (the kitchen vs. the garage, the beauty parlor vs. the football stadium, and so on). Not only women but all that concerns them is ratified by the hierarchical difference between men as a social group and women as a social group. Women's activities, too, and especially their beautification practices, are marked as feminine, hence regarded as less valuable and less worthy than masculine activities. With a twist that is typical of cultural constructs, those who devote themselves to feminine activities are also marked as less valuable than those who do not—which is why men who use cosmetics are often targeted with homophobic remarks. The result is a sort of tautology whereby women are deemed less worthy because their occupations are unimportant, and female occupations are judged as unimportant because women (themselves less worthy) undertake them. Of course, this dynamic extends to the realm of beautification. As feminist philosopher Sandra Lee Bartky writes, "A women's effort to master feminine body discipline will lack importance just because she does it: Her activity partakes of the general depreciation of everything female."[15]

In 1894, the British parodist Max Beerbohm published his famous satirical essay *In Defence of Cosmetics*, in which he depicted British women's lifestyles at the end of the Victorian age. Beerbohm, in an argument that echoed debates spreading in British society at the time, contrasted the increasing number of women using cosmetics, and especially makeup, or "paint" as it was often called, against the movement of progressive, liberated women who were taking up sports and other outdoor activities (riding bicycles, for example) and fighting to gain the right to vote and demanding political reforms in the areas of gender inclusiveness and equal rights. What Beerbohm describes was indeed a major shift in women's identities and lifestyles at the turn of the twentieth century, and yet he comforted his readers by telling them that there was no need to fear society's impending moral collapse: these "pioneers" were "doomed already," he said, because nobody would follow in their progressive path. Women would instead be the prisoners of their own natural vanity; they would care for their appearance more than the political cause of women's liberation, since the former would prove incompatible with the demands of the latter. As Beerbohm cheekily put it, "With bodily activity their powder will fly, their enamel crack. They are butterflies who must not flit, if they love their bloom."[16]

Historians Catherine Fouquet and Yvonne Knibiehler highlight a similar discursive strategy in their history of beauty in France between the seventeenth and twentieth centuries. Fouquet and Knibiehler observed that women's freedom and access to public life was progressively reduced across this four-hundred-year period and that women were increasingly subjected to male authorities (fathers, husbands) through legal, religious, and moral devices. Women's protests against such exclusion were cynically met with the semi-paternal reassurance that women would "rule" over men's souls and hearts through their beauty, grace, and "natural" composure. However, at the same time, women's interest and investment in beautification were publicly ridiculed, taken as evidence of their futility, and hence of their unfitness to participate in such "male" preserves as politics or science.[17]

In contemporary society, the worth paradox is especially evident when the duty to pursue beauty is combined with what is perhaps the other principal duty still imposed on women: maternity. As I will discuss in chapter 4, upon becoming a mother, a woman is expected to demonstrate her competence as a woman by showing that she still cares for her appearance (just think of the magazine covers portraying glamorous pregnant celebrities), but she is also expected to demonstrate her competence as a mother by placing the well-being of her child before all else. For instance, when a woman is pregnant, she is encouraged to eat more and gain weight so as to nourish her baby, but she should by no means let herself go and relinquish thinness and fitness. The reader will by now have recognized such contradictory advice from Camille Rainville's powerful essay on how to be a "lady" (to say nothing of their own life experiences).

Lena, who has two young children and is thirty-seven years old at the time of our first interview, recounts a similar paradox. She greatly enjoys working out; indeed, staying fit is one of her daily occupations. However, like many other women, she struggled a little to lose the pregnancy weight after giving birth to her first child. When she would talk about working out and compare exercise routines with other mums at the playground, she was sometimes asked if she was also "eating enough." After all, a mother, as sociologist Marion Braizaz notes, must not be perceived as a selfish woman who cares more for her looks than for her offspring.[18] However, at the same time, Lena felt the pressure to lose weight and rapidly return to what she perceives as her more attractive pre-pregnancy body:

> 'Cause when your belly was out there [*gestures with her hands*], and now it's in there, but it's still not where it was, I think it leads to a lot of insecurities, and your clothes don't fit [. . .] and, "Hey, she had a baby before me, and she's wearing pre-pregnancy jeans, and I can't even [. . .] get one leg in" [*sigh*]. [. . .] And then you always have the one mom who's like [*mimicking a girly voice*], "You know, I just bought new clothes and they're a size smaller than I was before."

Lena felt that her social recognition depended on her looks and her ability to live up to mainstream beauty ideals. At the same time, though, she felt judged for caring about this at all with a baby around.[19] The confusion that she experienced was the effect of the worth paradox.

THE AUTHENTICITY PARADOX

In 2011, the British-Irish boy band One Direction (or "1D," as their millions of fans know them) released the song "What Makes You Beautiful." The lyrics extol the appearance of their subject, a beloved girl who is insecure because she is unaware of her status as a "natural" beauty, and they offer some instruction on how she might preserve it. The song and its message were mocked by feminist stand-up comedian, actress, and author Amy Schumer in a 2015 episode of her show *Inside Amy Schumer*.[20] In this hilarious sketch, Schumer is getting ready to step out of her apartment in the morning, well-dressed and with light but visible makeup. Suddenly, a boy band starts singing, encouraging her to wash off her makeup and reveal her natural beauty; she does not need to cover up to be beautiful, they say. Elated, Schumer returns to the bathroom, enthusiastically removes her makeup, and, with a dramatic gesture, throws all her cosmetics in the garbage. When she proudly shows up in front of the boy band again wearing her "natural" look and a big smile, the young men appear frightened, almost disgusted, and quickly withdraw their initial advice: she better put her makeup back on, they say—better yet, *more* makeup. It turns out she really does need it.

Schumer's smart takedown points to the contradictions surrounding the idea as well as the *ideal* of natural beauty for women. These contradictions have a long history, rooted as they are in an age-old moral prejudice against women's beauty that still pervades the cultural landmarks through which Western societies understand women in general. Traditional tales and myths, like more modern literary and media narratives, often depict beautiful women as two-faced beings, fascinating yet dangerous, enticing yet deceitful. As Efrat Tseëlon and other feminist thinkers point out, this fundamental fear is triggered, more generally, by women's sexuality, a quality that patriarchal society has systematically attempted to harness, discipline, and confine within certain boundaries. The seductiveness that is associated with beauty represents a threat to this order, and it has therefore undergone the same cultural harnessing and the same moral blame. In several religious traditions, for instance, women are depicted as deceitful and fake,[21] masters of dissimulation and artifice who threaten—mostly through their beauty, wittingly or unwittingly—to lure men toward the path of sin and damnation (the "slippery slope").

As Bruno Remaury shows in his cultural history of women's representations in Western societies, femininity and masculinity are understood through a series of oppositions, of which the polarity of inauthenticity and authenticity is an omnipresent feature. Early Christian theologians of the second and third century, such as Clemens of Alexandria and Tertullianus, already condemned women as skilled in falsehood and artifice, as experts in the dangerous arts of deception. The main culprit—then as now—is makeup, together with hair dye and self-adornment (clothing, jewelry).

From late antiquity onward, cosmetics were identified as both the symbol and the material expression of women's fundamental inauthenticity, whereas "nature" or a "natural appearance" symbolized authenticity, trustworthiness, and accountability. This opposition between nature and artifice is a constant feature of Western cultural understandings of beauty, and it reiterates the fundamental mistrust in which women have for millennia been held as practitioners of artifice who are naturally inclined to inauthenticity. In her social history of beauty culture in the United States, Kathy Peiss reports that "in 1915, a Kansas legislator proposed to make it a misdemeanor for women under the age of forty-four to wear cosmetics 'for the purpose of creating a false impression.'"[22]

Rather than translating into an opposition between the use of cosmetics and the rejection of beauty treatments in general, however, the nature-artifice polarity was historically understood, as Remaury points out, as the antithesis between cosmetics as artifice—which covers up, conceals, and creates an illusion—and cosmetics as skillful enhancement of natural beauty. The acceptable beauty treatment, the morally tolerable cosmetic or makeup, is that which helps "*express* the natural (enhance, sublimate, and so on . . .)."[23] The injunction to display one's authenticity qualifies and discriminates against cosmetic treatments and uses more than it bans them completely. In other words, the moral and cultural praise of authenticity does not encourage women to relinquish beautification and self-transformation outright; rather, it insists that they fashion their appearance so that they *express* authenticity and perform what is understood, at various points throughout history, to fall within the category of "natural beauty." Authenticity becomes a moral and aesthetic performance through which women qualify themselves as competent, self-controlled, and morally respectable—inasmuch as the too-visible display of makeup, the excessive use of cosmetics, and the indulgence in artifice have signified and still signify an inclination to sexual deregulation, vice, vanity, and corruption.[24]

The link between aesthetics, morals, and politics in the celebration of authenticity is a very strong one. In eighteenth-century France, for instance, the rising bourgeoisie distinguished itself from the nobility through a moral discourse oriented toward simplicity, authenticity, and truthfulness, which implied a praise of natural beauty and "natural makeup" and a corresponding distrust of the artifice, mendacity, and excess that was thought to characterize aristocratic appearances.[25] The same obsession with natural beauty was present throughout the Victorian era, during which makeup ("paint," in Beerbohm's essay) was the subject of increasing social anxiety. According to Kathy Peiss, one of the main causes of the unease surrounding women's appearances was the growing financial and personal independence that resulted as women entered the labor force, formed social movements, and demanded political reforms.[26] Makeup, hence, became the symbol of a shift in identities that was rapidly undermining the available social mechanisms for disciplining women and keeping them in their place. Interestingly, if face paint was condemned by Victorian moralists, the corset still was largely prescribed as an indispensable tool for achieving beauty.

It is thus clear that the cultural injunction to adopt a natural beauty never really meant abandoning self-discipline and beauty work for women. Drawing on the work of Efrat Tseëlon,[27] I call this the authenticity paradox, which I define as follows: *If women work to embody an idealized version of feminine beauty, they are inauthentic, and yet if they relinquish all beautification to embody a "natural beauty," they are ugly.* In other words, women must perform beauty work to stay beautiful, young, and fit, but they must conceal this work so that their beauty can be perceived as "natural."[28] Behind this paradox emerges an even more disquieting feature of Western culture's representation of women's "nature." As Remaury demonstrates, from late antiquity onward, the female body has always been regarded as somehow physiologically and anatomically flawed, defective, unstable, and unreliable. This is why, Remaury continues, not only women's appearance but also women's health was historically governed by a panoply of prescriptions to prevent or at least slow a decay that is regarded as "natural," inscribed in women's essence itself. Centuries of medical discourse have constructed women's bodies as naturally fragile, more subject to illness, weakness, and exhaustion than men's, and hence requiring specific and detailed regimens regulating all aspects of their lives (hygiene, nutrition, self-care, sleep, etc.).

As Remaury's account shows, the fundamental concern was clearly with women's ability to carry children and fulfill their main social and moral function as mothers.[29] A beautiful appearance might certainly be the sign of a healthy body, but women's inferiority cannot be permanently corrected: women's physiology is always considered, if not "repulsive," as was still the case in the seventeenth and eighteenth centuries, then somehow prone to malfunction—in need of ongoing correction (nicely marketed as "cleansing" or "purification" in current parlance). Behind the illusion of beauty looms what Dean MacCannell and Janet F. MacCannell call "the originally 'hidden ugliness.'"[30] For centuries, women have been encouraged to correct and cover up their natural bodily appearances—too redolent of their natural impurity—through cosmetics and beautifying techniques. The message that they receive from childhood is that the best way of showing their worth is by hiding what is naturally unpleasant in the way they look. A woman cannot and must not trust her body, the flaws of which will naturally reappear despite her best efforts. Rooted as it is in historical representations of women's "nature," the tension between natural beauty and concealment acquires a specific salience in twenty-first-century celebrations of authentic beauty online, as I will also discuss in chapter 6.[31] Being one's best self and realizing one's full potential are contemporary imperatives of self-actualization that cosmetic products and services are allegedly crafted to enable and online networking platforms allegedly created to showcase.

As I sit and write these pages—it is the fall of 2020, during the second wave of COVID-19 here in Canada—the Montreal cosmetic manufacturer Marcelle targets me with an advertisement in the form of a blog post entitled "How to Simplify Your Beauty Routine." The virtues of a "minimalist" routine, the post claims, have been driven home by the unusual life conditions brought on by the pandemic. It assures me that I could have a perfect look and "achieve a radiant glow" and "flawless complexion" with just one product—in this case, Marcelle's tinted moisturizer. To Marcelle, it goes without saying that I'd be interested in "unifying the complexion or correcting skin imperfections," in "minimiz[ing] the appearance of blemishes, minor scars and uneven skin tone."[32] Who wouldn't want to be radiant and look natural—that is, without a visible layer of makeup—while also concealing their natural ugliness? My skin, the ad tells me, can *look* healthy and beautiful, but it most certainly *is* not either of these things.

THE POWER PARADOX

As in the case of the authenticity paradox, there is a long tradition in Western culture associating women's beauty with a form of power. According to the lore, women's beauty and desirability could entice men not only into sexual contact but also into courses of action and decisions that would be profitable for women and beneficial for their ambitions. Indeed, in Western tradition and beyond, beauty is regarded as women's power par excellence—especially in those contexts in which women are barred from acquiring any other form of power. An attempt to understand and describe the way women themselves perceive this alleged female power was indeed the starting point of my fieldwork on beauty. In this chapter, I will not go into a full discussion of other scholars' accounts of beauty as a female power (I'll return to that in chapter 5). Instead, I wish to point out that conceiving of beauty as power is itself dependent on a sort of paradoxical logic. We can therefore add the power paradox to the worth and authenticity paradoxes detailed above.

When asked whether or not they felt that looking good endowed them with some kind of power, the women I interviewed were able to report as many disadvantages as advantages. While reflecting on how she perceived beauty back in her twenties, Audrey, whom we met earlier when discussing the worth paradox, stated—not without a certain amount of emotion in her voice—that

> Youth and beauty is a double-edged sword. [. . .] It is [. . .] simultaneously powerful, and very much a gilded cage, if I can use a whole bunch of clichés at one time, and certainly myself, growing up when I did, where I did, as an attractive, able-bodied white lady, it's hard not to cave into certain expectations. [. . .] I was certainly aware of the power I could have [. . .], but it's almost a false power because you know young beautiful women, in many ways, they can get the door held open for them, they can get men to pay attention to them, they can get whatever, but it's such a narrow little box that they have to live in in order to benefit from that youth and beauty, and it's not like we're getting paid the same or anything, so it's a false power, it's not real power. [. . .] Yeah, it's more like, I guess, approval than anything, which goes a long way, but it's still currency.

Whereas filling the gender wage gap would mean that women have acquired a *real* power—that of being paid as much as men for the same kind and amount of labor—the power provided by beauty, especially when coupled with youth, is "false," according to Audrey. In order to wield it, women have to accept all the restrictions that come with it, and especially the most costly one: to be reduced to their appearance. In addition, it is a power that does not actually accomplish much, because it fails to influence decisions where it really counts. As Audrey notes later in our conversation, the advantages provided by a beautiful appearance are also strongly conditioned by one's conformity to general, approved standards of female beauty: it follows, then, that bodily changes such as weight gain or aging substantially reduce a woman's visibility, and therefore all the benefits that she could expect to draw from a social approval based on her looks. The insight that Zoe shared with me regarding her experience in the workplace during her youth reinforces Audrey's observations on the limitations of a pleasant appearance: in work environments characterized by intense "power games," she says, "young women investing a lot in their appearance would have jobs from which not much power could be extracted."

As I claimed when outlining the worth paradox, women's credibility, competence, and value are commonly assessed on the basis of their appearance. And while appearance may not be the sole criterion, it generally plays a crucial role in the way a woman is perceived. Not only are the stakes high—so, too, are the standards and social expectations to which women are held, especially those who ascend to powerful positions in Western societies, and whose visibility is therefore greater. Interestingly, Zoe cites Hillary Clinton as an example of this phenomenon:

> She was harshly criticized, you see, when she first appeared after losing the election—you know, with flat hair, in a suit—even though she triggered way more positive feelings among women when she looked tired, whereas all throughout the campaign, when her hair was done and she wore expensive clothes, people would perceive her as cold and distant. And then I'm like, you know [. . .] you can't win on any front.

Further examples of this phenomenon are seemingly countless. When Emmanuel Macron was elected president of the French Republic, media in France and around the world subjected his wife, Brigitte Macron, to intensive scrutiny over her age and her looks. Little was reported, however, about her professional competence or her role in her husband's political success. Her reduction to her appearance was completed by US president Donald Trump during an official visit to Paris in July 2017. Welcomed by the Macrons in front of the press, President Trump's first words upon greeting Brigitte Macron were, "You're in such good shape." Trump then turned to the French president and repeated, "She's in such good physical shape," before adding, "Beautiful."[33] The second "compliment," directed to the husband as if President Trump were congratulating him on the qualities of a voiceless piece of property, was likely more humiliating than the first.

US representative Alexandria Ocasio-Cortez, who is a strong advocate of working-class people and ethnic minorities, is also very vocal about her interest in beauty, providing beauty tips, sharing her favorite lipstick brand, and unveiling her skin-care routine over Twitter and especially Instagram. Public interest in her appearance has taken different forms: she was called "a bright, shiny object" by Democratic senator Claire McCaskill, criticized for wearing clothes that are too expensive for someone who supports the rights of working-class and marginalized people, and praised for being a feminist role model who can talk politics without neglecting her looks.[34] According to Sangeeta Singh-Kurtz, Alexandria Ocasio-Cortez is an exemplar of a new kind of woman politician, one who can embrace femininity, feminine beauty, and interests that are traditionally considered feminine (hence intrinsically vain) while also being a competent congresswoman making a meaningful difference in her constituents' lives.[35]

Be it in praise or judgment, Ocasio-Cortez's appearance garners a level of attention that has no equivalent among male politicians. Beauty is at the core of women's social recognition: public women's appearance is constantly under scrutiny; they have to publicly justify their interest or lack thereof in beauty and/or supposedly feminine activities (having children, cooking); their good or less good looks are weighed against their fitness for office, the more severely, the more power they (might) have. Consider a further example. As reported in a 2015 *Rolling Stone* article, Donald Trump, then campaigning for the Republican Party's presidential nomination, dismisses his opponent Carly Fiorina solely on the basis of her looks:

> When the anchor throws to Carly Fiorina for her reaction to Trump's momentum [in the polls], Trump's expression sours in schoolboy disgust as the camera bores in on Fiorina. "*Look* at that face!" he cries. "Would anyone *vote* for that? Can you imagine that, the face of our next *president*?!" The laughter grows halting and faint behind him. "I mean, she's a woman, and I'm not s'posedta say bad things, but really, folks, come on. Are we *serious*?"[36]

According to President Trump, Fiorina's face is simply unsuitable for the presidential office. The casualness with which the remark is made speaks to the fact that judging a woman's competence or worth by the way she looks is common—indeed, it is taken for granted, at least in certain social circles (think of Trump's later invocation of "locker room talk"[37]). In this same utterance, Trump makes another interesting semantic leap. He states his awareness of the fact that he is not supposed to "say bad things" about a woman—political correctness demands that women be treated fairly and given equal opportunities—"but really, folks, come on": if we are "serious" (as only men can be?), we cannot but acknowledge that a woman with *that* look could not be taken seriously in a key political position.

In sum, it is common for women in the public sphere to be summarily dismissed for not corresponding to standards of female beauty; however, even when they try to integrate a mainstream understanding of beauty and beautification into their self-presentation (as we saw in the case of Representative Ocasio-Cortez), this can and will be used to question their competence and cast doubt on their suitability for office. Hence, drawing again on Efrat Tseëlon's observations,[38] I offer the following definition of the power paradox: *A woman's power is powerless as long as her legitimacy and worth are assessed on the basis of her physical appearance.*

My claim is that any power that is contingent on the social appreciation of its bearer's aesthetic qualities is all the more easily undermined as the appreciation of that aesthetic quality diminishes or is contested. A beautiful appearance and a manifest interest in beautification are easily labeled as superficial, thus disqualifying and silencing the woman who expresses such an interest. The fragility of women's power depends on the fact that beauty is, as sociologist Maxine Leeds Craig argued, a "contested symbolic resource":[39] the assessment of its value as either an asset or a liability depends on the power relations that structure the context in which it is appraised. At any given moment, in a patriarchal society, appearance can be turned against a woman to disempower and discredit her.

However, it could also be argued, as postfeminists often do, that beauty in itself can be empowering. Since the late 1990s, popular culture and media discourse have promoted the idea of a "girl power" premised on independence, individual self-fulfillment, agency, and above all beauty and sexiness. In the following decades, accordingly, female success in Western societies has been depicted as being in control, being powerful, having a fulfilling career, often a lovely family, and a perfect, sexy body. We commonly see this version of femininity marketed as an updated, more glamorous form of feminism, as opposed to the popularized view of "traditional" feminist activists and theorists as anti-beauty (which often authorizes their dismissal as "ugly," and hence as losers). It is for this reason that, as I discussed in the Introduction, scholars have defined such a stance "postfeminist."[40] On the one hand, the "postness" invoked here points to the popular discourse claiming that feminism is obsolete because women have by now conquered the upper echelons of power; on the other, it highlights the individualization and depoliticization of women's struggles that the postfeminist sensibility promotes by its reduction of feminism to mere individual self-accomplishment—which more often than not are equated with visible feminine beauty and expressive sexiness.

Traces of this discourse merging beauty and power are everywhere apparent in popular culture. On January 28, 2019, retweeting Amanda Litman's praise of her ability to merge skin-care tips with oratorical advice drawn from Martin Luther King Jr. and Angela Davis, Alexandria Ocasio-Cortez wrote, "Be a fierce woman who can do both."[41] A "fierce woman" is able to make a social and political difference while also using makeup and cosmetics: beautified empowerment becomes then the ground for a new form of female solidarity and mutual support. In a 2016 interview with Cheryl Wischhover about her decision to serve as the brand ambassador for No7, a line of beauty products from the British retailer Boots, the Nigerian feminist and writer Chimamanda Ngozi Adichie said that "in the larger sense I wanted to be part of the message that women who like makeup also have important and serious things that they're doing in their lives. And that those can co-exist, that women are a multiplicity of things. I think it's time to really stop that ridiculous idea that somehow if you're a serious woman you can't and should not care about how you look."[42]

We can agree that it would be difficult to sell beauty products if women thought that being serious did in fact entail relinquishing makeup. And Adichie and Ocasio-Cortez surely have a point when they demand respect for their interest in beauty, fighting the old rhetoric denigrating it as a sign of worthlessness. However, this demand is far from politically neutral in a culture that still belittles and disqualifies women for *not* being interested in beauty, and, more damningly, for *not* being beautiful. Women's power appears to be acceptable only as long as they remain the gatekeepers of acceptable femininity, do not relinquish self-surveillance, and participate in disciplining other women's individual expressions of feminine identity. Hence, the power of beauty is in reality no power at all when it can only be exercised within the narrow boundaries set by a society that still assesses women's worth on the basis of their appearance.

In September 2020, the Italian city of Verona played host to a "Beauty Festival" (in Italian, "Festival della bellezza"). The event's organizers were harshly criticized for their decision to convene a "manel"—that is, a panel composed (almost) exclusively of men.[43] Out of a total of twenty-two invited speakers, twenty-one (or 95.5 percent) were men, while just one woman had been asked to attend. "Manels" have long been denounced in the academic world as a reflection of gendered power relations among scholars. As a simple rule of thumb, many critics have called for the organizers of similar events—academic and non-academic alike—to ensure that the percentage of women in their programs more closely mirrors the proportion of women in society at large (in Italy, that was about 51.3 percent at the beginning of 2020).[44] In the case of the Verona conference, historians, sociologists, economists, psychologists, entrepreneurs, and advertisers would all probably agree that "beauty" is a particularly salient topic for women in Western societies and that women might therefore have a thing or two to say about it. It is also worth noting that the image that graced the festival's poster is *Girl with a Bee Dress* by American artist Maggie Taylor (in an instance of copyright infringement, to boot, according to the artist): it pictures a young girl, in the prime of her beauty, holding a white and pink flower. A beautiful woman.

THE COMMITMENT PARADOX

As should be clear by now, beauty has a moral dimension for women.

On the May 19, 2020, episode of *Everything Is Fine*, Tally Abecassis and Kim France's podcast for "women over forty," the two hosts sat down with Jane Larkworthy, a beauty editor and columnist at *The Cut*. Their discussion starts on the topic of an alleged makeup rule for women over forty (a rule about which I must plead prior ignorance, despite my belonging to the show's target demographic): you either do your lips *or* your eyes, but you don't do both. After explaining that she herself doesn't particularly believe in this diktat, Larkworthy pleads instead for a sort of "gut rule" for makeup after forty: if you think (or feel) a certain application is too much, it probably is.

Where to begin? We might first observe the rigid threshold that the age of forty appears to represent in a woman's aesthetic (and not only aesthetic) biography. Where does this number come from, and why is it treated as if it represented some fatal boundary for women? After all, when showbiz celebrities reach the age of forty, they are often praised for their ability to stay beautiful, fit, and employed as if this is some sort of miraculous accomplishment (and given the dynamics we've explored thus far, perhaps it is). But let us focus on the more relevant idea of "too much." When I listened to Larkworthy's statement, I had the feeling that determining the line between an appropriate and an excessive level of makeup was nothing short of a moral question. And indeed, the idea that errors or excesses in beautification are about more than just aesthetics is by no means new. As I mentioned when describing the authenticity paradox, the "painted face" has long been considered a sign of immorality, sexual promiscuity, and low social standing.[45]

Even if nowadays the use of makeup is widely accepted as a standard beautification practice, and even regarded as evidence of competent feminine self-care, Larkworthy's claim shows that the boundaries of its application are still closely guarded: women can by no means do whatever they want with blush, mascara, and lipstick. Historian Kathy Peiss reports that, beginning in the 1920s, as social disapproval for makeup was weakening, more specific regulations for its use were formulated by beauty experts, columnists, and cosmetics producers. These "subtle distinctions" held, for instance, that "coloring the eyelids and beading lashes were fun in the evening but bad taste in daylight; acceptable for adults but not for girls under eighteen; lovely on the dance floor but not in the office." Such rules are easy to find in current beauty advice as well—so much so that we could say, drawing again on Peiss's historical work, that "delineating appropriate makeup based on time of day, activity, age, and circumstances" is still "a commonplace of beauty reporting."[46] As a result of our socialization to proper self-presentation, women inherit, reproduce, and give concrete form to a detailed body of knowledge that prescribes not only what to choose but also what to avoid in beauty matters.

However, beauty reporting, and especially beauty advertising, is also mainly about instructing women on how much they can (still) do to improve their looks.[47] Embodied beauty, as opposed to idealized beauty, is always imperfect and flawed. In addition, as we saw in the previous sections, women's nature is regarded as unstable, and so, as a consequence, is beauty. Women are considered particularly vulnerable to physical deterioration due to hormonal changes, aging, pollution, sunlight—the list goes on. They have to protect, preserve, and capitalize on their beauty. They must foresee, and with their consumption practices hedge against, the ravages of time: adopt the right skin-care regime while also covering their gray roots; treat their wrinkles without neglecting their cellulitis; peel the dead skin off their elbows while also keeping those cuticles in check. There is always something more that one can do, something more that one could buy, and something else that one could (and should) focus on.

While I was writing this chapter, I was targeted—be it the cunning of karma or that of algorithms—by an advertisement on Instagram from Lise Watier, another Montreal-based cosmetics producer. The ad informed me that I might have fatally neglected my "tech neck," and it instructed me on how to rectify my mistake before it's too late. The "tech neck"[48] is a Y-shaped patch of skin, situated between the jawline and the base of the neck, that is apparently particularly affected by our habit of bending our heads down as we look at our screens. Premature aging, loss of elasticity, deeper skinfolds—Lise Watier has the right product to tackle all of this. I can ignore this particular ad, of course, but its underlying message nevertheless leads me to wonder: Am I seriously considering the consequences of neglecting the effects of looking at my phone fifty times a day?

On the other hand, as I highlighted above, women are still severely policed in their recourse to beautification procedures and cosmetics. Women, and especially older women, who are judged to have overdone it with cosmetic surgery, makeup, clothes, or hair, are routinely shamed, whether in media, popular culture, or on social media. Journalists, psychologists, and laypersons engage in the seemingly perennial debate over the appropriate age for a girl to get a nose job or start collagen injections, and on the psychopathological motivations behind the choice to have cosmetic surgery "too" soon (is it narcissism or a deep-seated need for attention?). Indeed, as I will discuss in chapter 6 with regard to selfies, women's transgressions of these unwritten rules governing female propriety are commonly attributed to psychological disorders ("lack of self-confidence" is a media favorite).[49]

Accordingly, we might define the commitment paradox like this: *A woman will always do either too little or too much to beautify her appearance. If she feels she has done enough, she can always do more. If she does more, she has likely done too much.*

Audrey, who was very vocal about the detrimental effects of beauty standards throughout our two interviews, provides a gloss for the commitment paradox in her own powerful words:

> No matter how fit you are, how perfect your hair is, no matter what makeup style, what clothes you wear, somebody is going to disapprove. [. . .] If your skirt is too short or too long, you know, no matter what, you're under scrutiny and you're going to have a fan club and you're going to have the haters.

Echoing the concept of "slut-shaming"—the stigmatization of women who engage in sexual behavior that is considered immoral or excessive—Audrey concludes that the disapproval women inevitably receive on their appearance is "like choice-shaming." What Audrey is referring to is the moral dimension of the ubiquitous surveillance of women's appearances—the scrutiny, the criticism, the judgment: in essence, these are used to question women's competence as autonomous subjects able to make choices and act without guidance, to make good use of their "freedom."

Before summarizing this chapter's exploration of the four paradoxes of Western beauty culture, let me briefly return to the idea, expressed by Jane Larkworthy, of a "gut feeling" for what is right and wrong in matters of makeup and grooming. Since at least the late seventies, when French sociologist Pierre Bourdieu published his work on the social mechanisms of aesthetic judgment (epitomized in his 1979 book *Distinction: A Social Critique of the Judgement of Taste*), social science scholars have known that the notion of a "gut" sense, which in this case stands for aesthetic taste, is not only socially constructed but also hierarchically organized and unequally distributed across social classes.[50] Because taste is socially constructed, we learn, through our specific socialization and the interactions punctuating our daily lives, the culturally specific criteria of aesthetic judgment that apply to our gender, age, social class, race, and even body shape. Such embodied criteria inform our very perceptions of the objects and people around us: by choosing what we "like," we immediately "know" what is (already) meant for us and what is not. In this way, we learn to assess beauty by observing our relatives and teachers, friends and colleagues while they pronounce aesthetic judgments on objects and bodies situated in different environments and settings. Such judgments are far from natural or universal, of course; their object is not some kind of general ideal of beauty. Indeed, different social groups, as do different cultures, apply different aesthetic criteria to tell the beautiful from the ugly, the tasteful from the distasteful, and the refined from the vulgar. Bourdieu argues, for instance, that members of the working class will, generally speaking, appreciate and choose goods differently than members of the upper class—and each choice will also "rank" the chooser accordingly.

Bourdieu's idea of distinction, however, holds that goods and looks chosen and displayed by the upper class are in themselves considered "of good taste" for the simple reason that they are owned or displayed by people whose "good taste" is guaranteed by dint of their social status. According to Bourdieu, a hierarchy of aesthetic preferences exists in every society, where the upper class's aesthetic taste usually constitutes the principal reference point in determining what is refined and what is vulgar. Thus, aesthetic taste, that useful "gut feeling" that might tell us how much makeup would be too much, is not ingrained in us from birth—even if it functions without any conscious reflection on our part—and it is unequally distributed among social strata. To state the problem plainly: it is a privilege of the upper class, and it can easily turn into a device of oppression when the "distinction" entails shaming the apparent vulgarity of those whose judgment is deemed to be less refined.

In the early 2000s, Angela McRobbie analyzed popular British TV shows in which "experts" advise women on how to improve their looks, teach them how to shop, and help them adopt suitable self-grooming techniques. In keeping with the standard format, the experts tend to overtly denigrate, mock, and humiliate their victim (in front of an audience, of course) for her vulgar taste, her poor choices, her shabby looks. Indeed, these shows oppose the experts, whose higher social status is obvious thanks to their displays of affluence and especially their recognized competence, to the victim, whose presence on the stage already testifies to her obvious lack of aesthetic taste.

McRobbie interprets the "snobbiness" and "bitchiness" of the upper-middle-class (female) experts as cultural devices that mark class differences within a society where women's standing is now defined less by marriage or family background (as it once was) than by education, affluence, and body image.[51] Appearance thus becomes one of the main sites of contemporary class conflict for women: if education and career are the paths toward social distinction, good taste in appearance and body image are its corresponding outward signs. For women, this entails conforming to beauty standards that express taste, competence, status—and, I would add, navigating the paradoxes framing women's commitment to beauty culture.

"Sadly," McRobbie concludes, "it seems there is little space for the resolutely unimproved woman to stake a political claim to remaining shabby."[52] Although it is structured by inequalities and power relations—in essence, by politics—beauty remains a rather depoliticized sphere of experience and self-expression for women. In other words, despite the abundant (feminist) literature and the denunciations of countless critics, beauty is generally cordoned off from legal, political, and social fights for equality and justice, which makes its injunctions so pervasive and difficult to outmaneuver, especially since women's social worth increasingly hinges on the expectation that they will display a competently groomed appearance. How do you frame beauty in terms of equality and justice if women not only appear to take pleasure in looking good but also stand to gain considerable advantage from being perceived as good-looking? How do you convince the general public that beauty is one of the primary devices of social control for women if the popular narrative—also shared by some men and women who are vocal in championing women's rights and emancipation—simultaneously maintains that beauty is superficial, vain, and not at all important for assessing someone's value?

WHAT IS A PRAGMATIC PARADOX?

This overview of the four paradoxes of beauty culture has no doubt left some readers with myriad questions about my use of the paradox concept—where it comes from, whether similar paradoxes exist outside of beauty culture, and why we should even be invoking this concept at all. In answering these questions, I'd like to draw on the work of Paul Watzlawick and Niklas Luhmann, as well as other scholars. I will begin with a general discussion of pragmatic paradoxes before turning to the question of "re-entry." Readers wishing to forego what is admittedly a somewhat technical presentation of these concepts can feel free to skip this section without compromising their understanding of the following chapters.

Logical and mathematical paradoxes have played an important role in the Western philosophical tradition since its founding in ancient Greece.[53] The most popular of these paradoxes is likely the so-called liar paradox, in which a person says, "I am lying." The question of whether this person is lying or telling the truth results in an irreducible logical impasse: should the person be telling the truth, then she is lying; but if she is lying, she is telling the truth—and yet she is also *not* telling the truth. A more recent example is Russel's paradoxical definition of "the set of all sets that are not members of themselves,"[54] formulated at the beginning of the twentieth century. This, too, leads us down a logical cul-de-sac when we try to determine whether or not the set of all the sets that are not members of themselves is—well, a member of itself.

In addition to mathematical and linguistic paradoxes, Gregory Bateson, Paul Watzlawick, and their respective research teams highlighted the centrality of paradoxes in ordinary human communication. Paradoxes are built into everyday utterances and interactions, but also into larger relational patterns and cultural frameworks, including political ideologies.[55] In some cases—as claimed, for instance, in Bateson's famous "double bind" theory[56]—paradoxical injunctions structure pathological relationships and contribute to the appearance of mental health issues in some individuals. The ordinary contradictory instructions that emerge in human speech and actions are defined by Watzlawick as "pragmatic paradoxes." These arise when an individual faces contradictory demands within a relationship and attempts to respond to them in such a way that would allow them either to preserve the relationship, avoid losing face or prove their worth. Hence, pragmatic paradoxes are not hypothetical or merely formal exercises; rather, they are concrete and charged with meaning for the individuals involved.

Since the psychosocial stakes are high, pragmatic paradoxical injunctions can trigger strong emotional reactions from those who feel themselves caught within them. Being "caught" within a paradoxical injunction is tantamount to being logically and practically confined to a particular view of reality that does not otherwise admit of the paradox as such. One instead experiences feelings of frustration, a sense of impotence, of having arrived at an impasse. (If only they could *see* the paradox for what it is, they could find a way out of this impasse.) The most common example of this type of paradox, according to Watzlawick, is the injunction to "be spontaneous."[57]

A certain behavior is demanded as authentic and spontaneous, and yet, inasmuch as the behavior originates in an explicit request (one might say *an order*) from the other member of the relationship, the spontaneity/authenticity of this behavior is no longer possible. Should someone demand of her partner that he "spontaneously" take on more household chores, neither could perceive the fulfillment of such a demand as spontaneous. Unable to observe the paradox, the partner could then feel stuck between his desire for autonomy within the domestic sphere and a fear that he might damage the relationship. He might resent his partner for criticizing his lack of involvement, feel anxious about his ability to make the right decision, lash out in anger toward his partner or himself, and so forth.

According to Watzlawick and colleagues, and following the theory of logical types, a pragmatic paradox can really only be understood from an external (or "meta") perspective. Only then can one view such contradictory injunctions together, at once, and thereby understand the emotional effects of their clash as stemming from their "impossibility." Such insight would enable what Bateson, Waltzlawick, and their research teams call "metacommunication"—that is, a form of communication *about communication* that takes place at the first level of observation (i.e., where paradoxical injunctions are nothing more than equally valid contradictory demands). The partner would then be able to say (imagining, for argument's sake, a world in which domestic frustrations are conveyed in perfectly lucid speech), "You demand of me spontaneous involvement, but in so doing you prevent me from being spontaneously involved! Your request makes me feel guilty, angry, and does not motivate me to take on more responsibility around the house." Having made this observation, the members of the relationship could then change the terms of their communication and make a conscious effort to avoid putting each other in a similar bind. Adopting a "meta" perspective on a relationship structured by paradoxes can have positive effect on its members and their interactions, which is why the therapeutic impact of metacommunication is at the core of Watzlawick's approach to psychotherapy and psychological change.

However, the ability to step out of a pragmatic paradox, understand it as such, and then bring about its transformation is not universally accessible: it often requires time and experience, some training, and sometimes even professional help. Things get even more complicated when we take into account pragmatic paradoxes that are inscribed into hegemonic cultural frameworks, as is the case with beauty culture. The ability to see these paradoxes and to truly critique them on an individual level depends on a form of social awareness, the development of which is conditional on a variety of specific factors. More to the point, those who would seek to disentangle themselves from such paradoxes must acquire the ability to recognize and thereby jettison a vision of the world that, through a lifetime of socialization, they have largely accepted as their own. Necessary preconditions for such an awareness include the recognition of social arrangements as contingent and historical rather than necessary and "natural," and the understanding that cultural blueprints intersect with power relations and thereby abet the reproduction of various forms of inequality. As Luhmann puts it, "the communication of paradoxes fixes attention on the frames of common sense, frames that normally go unattended."[58] Historically speaking, widespread access to a constructivist approach to reality is a relatively recent development, and only in the last couple of centuries has such a view allowed for a generalized critique of hierarchical structures (whether of race, gender, colonial domination, etc.) within Western societies and beyond their boundaries. Moreover, social structures and cultural frameworks can themselves prevent individuals and groups from accessing a higher plane of social awareness, and from questioning what is otherwise taken for granted as "common sense."[59]

Luhmann presents us with another, complementary definition of the role of paradox (both logical and empirical) in social matters. Drawing on the work of Bateson as well as mathematician George Spencer Brown, Luhmann describes a paradox as the unity of a difference. "Difference" in this sense arises from observation—that is, from each cognitive and communicational act of qualifying something as *something*: it is a distinction between *that* something and everything else. In ordinary communication, this "everything else" is not named. For instance, we do not need to list all the objects of the world that are not a dog while pointing at a four-legged animal and saying, "Look, a dog!" However, this unattended side of the difference (everything that is *not* a dog) must exist for the observation to be successful—in other words, to emphasize the difference and distinguish something (the dog) from "everything else." If we step out of the first-order observation ("Look, a dog!") and observe its frame, what we see is paradoxical: we observe the unity of the two sides of the difference between what is the case (which is identical with itself) and everything else (which is different from it) in the world, a unity that the differentiating operation momentarily "breaks" in two.[60]

Let us take the example, drawn from the authenticity paradox, of the difference between natural and artificial beauty. When we identify someone's beauty as "natural," we draw a distinction—thanks to culturally specific criteria—between beauty that is natural and beauty that is unnatural.

This is an observation. Now, if we step out of this first-order perspective, we can qualify the observation *itself* as the emergence, from a certain point of view, of a difference that was not there before. We can see that the difference is contingent: for instance, we can recognize that standards of beauty change over time and that what is considered "artificial" today would therefore not have been understood as such a couple of centuries ago. We can observe the drawing of the distinction and thereby become aware of the paradox: the difference between what we see as artificial and what we see as natural is merely a (culturally informed) way of seeing, in the absence of which the distinction collapses.

Inspired again by Spencer Brown's theory of form, Luhmann highlights a further aspect of the paradoxicality of observations and differences. Let us return to the difference between natural and artificial, and the moment when we come to question this difference as contingent and arbitrary. By doing so, we *re-enter* the difference between natural and artificial into the first difference: we claim that the difference itself is *artificial*—that it is unnatural. "Re-entry," hence, is the operation of replicating the first difference and entering it into one side of the difference: through this operation, what we identify as "natural" in matters of beauty is acknowledged as rather artificial. Clearly, re-entry works as a source of paradoxicality.

Now, to get back to how all this applies to beauty culture. As I've tried to show in this chapter, the first, somewhat superficial paradoxical form we encounter in contemporary Western beauty culture is the host of contradictory injunctions we face in our daily lives. For instance, according to the worth paradox, a woman must care about her appearance, but if she cares too much, she will be deemed unworthy; if she does not care about her appearance at all, rejecting beauty culture outright, she will also be deemed unworthy. Performing a first-level observation, she will (more or less intuitively) apprehend that she is in a very tricky situation, since her social standing is at risk no matter what she decides to do with her looks. She will feel as though she was *walking a tightrope* in matters of appearance (as one of the interviewees aptly put it). Were she to manage to step out of these contradictory injunctions and consider them in their entirety, she might observe the paradox for what it is and shift the blame for her problems onto beauty culture and away from herself as an individual.

As I will explain in the conclusion to this chapter, just such an awareness is currently developing among a meaningful portion of the general population (and not only among intellectuals); indeed, we have some evidence of this from the cultural productions that I discussed at the beginning of this chapter. However, such awareness has not yet translated into a compelling explanation of the untenable paradoxes underlying Western beauty culture. More specifically, following Luhmann's conceptual framework, we have yet to identify the primary difference at the heart of these paradoxes. It is certainly not that of beautiful and ugly, or beauty and non-beauty. This is because the paradoxes hinge not on objective criteria that determine beauty (or lack thereof), but rather on the value that beauty represents in the determination of women's worth in society.

My claim is that the paradoxes of beauty culture arise from the re-entry of the difference between men and women *into* the difference between men and women. Let me explain. Sociologically speaking, beauty is relevant for women not just as a set of qualities that can be quantified or measured: it is relevant as evidence of one's competent participation in beautification. By bearing the signs of beautification, a woman shows that she is a competent player in the game of "being a woman." To put this in more technical terms, she shows (no matter how unwittingly) her commitment to upholding the difference between men and women, or between feminine and masculine, which is a structuring difference in most societies.[61] With regard to beauty, people who are interested in being beautiful, or feel compelled to show such an interest, are generally recognized as feminine in Western societies (and beyond). Beautification inscribes the signs of this difference onto individual bodies, hence "marking"[62] them as belonging to persons who can be situated on one side of the male-female binary.

By qualifying themselves as women, as different from men, women secure for themselves the social, moral, and political benefits that come with being a woman. At the same time, however, their status as feminine, as non-men, disqualifies them as nothing more than women.[63] As a robust body of scholarship has shown, the difference between men and women is not like the difference between coffee and tea: it also contains an appraisal on which hinges historical hierarchies, structures of inequality, and power relationships. The *feminine* is traditionally qualified as lesser, as inferior to the *masculine*. As a consequence, women's activities, interests, abilities, spaces, jobs—you name it—are considered less worthy than men's. And women, as unworthy beings, tend to be structurally excluded from masculine activities, endeavors, environments, jobs, and so forth. This is why we still need special programs aimed at fostering girls' interest in STEM, why children's toys are often coded as either kinetic and hands-on (qualities usually associated with boys) or dainty and "girly," and why in most Western countries women are excluded from top management positions in both the private and public sectors. Saying that a product, a service, a television show targets or caters to "girls" is already tantamount to disqualifying it in the eyes of "men." (Consider the stigma targeting selfies inasmuch as they are perceived as a feminine pastime.)

When women devote themselves to beautification, then, they are qualifying themselves as women, differentiating themselves from men, and upholding the difference between masculine and feminine. As a consequence, if they relinquish beauty work, they threaten that difference, and expose themselves to the risk of losing social recognition as women. The difference between men and women is preserved, among other actions and social processes, by the investment that women make in looking "good." However, the difference between men and women is also re-entered on one side of that difference, that of women, hence the paradox: identified as women thanks to their beautification practices, women are recognized as "not men," and hence as unworthy of the consideration, privileges, and social benefits linked to masculinity. Praised and celebrated as capable of the highest form of beauty in the world, women are at the same time viewed as naturally flawed, in need of constant correction in order to discipline their essential deficiencies. Women's beautification practices are therefore at once rewarding and disqualifying. Even women's "power" remains relatively powerless compared to men's.

CONCLUSION: NEGOTIATING THE PARADOXES OF BEAUTY

Thus far, we have learned that Western beauty culture is structurally ambiguous, both empowering and disempowering for women and that the stakes are not merely aesthetic but also moral, symbolic, and political: hence, women cannot altogether eschew the paradoxical injunctions of beauty culture in their everyday lives.

For over two centuries, Western feminist thinkers have criticized the injunction to be beautiful. Since at least the late eighteenth century, when the British philosopher and writer Mary Wollstonecraft blazed her pioneering trail as a staunch advocate of women's autonomy, successive generations of feminists have denounced beauty culture as an oppressive system that keeps women in a condition of inferiority, disciplining their bodies, desires, and aspirations and preventing them from realizing their full potential. Countless authors have also denounced beauty culture's entrenchment within capitalism, especially its contemporary neoliberal form, with its emphasis on individual consumption.[64] In recent years, however, scholars in the social sciences have also presented more nuanced interpretations of the role of beauty in women's lives. While recognizing that beautification serves to prescribe a very narrow view of acceptable femininity, these scholars show that it can still be a source of genuine pleasure, of sociability between women, and can help foster a sense of one's personal dignity.[65]

Based on my theorization of the paradoxicality of beauty injunctions, I argue that both interpretations are valid: beautification allows women to express their identities, receive social recognition, push the boundaries of their self-image, experience pleasure and gratification, bond with other women, indulge in self-care in social contexts in which they are expected to be fully available to others (partners, children, other family members, employers, coworkers, etc.); and at the same time, we cannot rightfully describe the choice to commit to beauty culture as "free," since one's failure to comply with the injunctions of beauty culture can result in a loss of legitimacy and invalidate one's recognition as a "woman."

This ambiguity is particularly salient in contemporary Western societies. As Bruno Remaury notes, the norms regulating women's relationship to beauty are not only linked to the duty to be beautiful (*You have to be beautiful*), as has long been the case; they also demand a display of willpower on the part of individual women (*You can be beautiful if you want to be beautiful*).[66] Being beautiful therefore becomes a sign of commitment, of self-discipline, but also of competence, of knowledge—to say nothing of disposable income. Being beautiful and in palpably good physical shape is the expression of one's status as a social agent capable of embodying the neoliberal values of self-control, individual self-fulfillment, and a commitment to exercising one's consumer power—in short, the very prerequisites of social recognition and upward mobility. There is a strong moral dimension to beauty, then, inasmuch as it expresses the modern feminine subject's ability to choose and commit to a specific set of chosen values. But what happens when these virtues are framed by a set of paradoxical injunctions? What happens when the Western female subject fails the test of competence in negotiating her appearance, as she is at some point bound to do?

The paradoxical injunctions explored in this chapter exert an objective influence on women's ability to make choices. They define contradictory repertoires of action for women situated in specific contexts, facing social, political, professional, and personal challenges, and bearing individual identities (not only gender but also ethnicity, class, age, body size, etc.). These paradoxical injunctions are obviously spread through discourse (popular as well as specialized), but they are also materialized in objects, images, and services, and inscribed in our social interactions. (We'll explore this in more depth in chapter 6, which looks at the role of social networking sites like Instagram.) As Ori Schwarz notes,[67] cultural frameworks also include "folk sociologies" of choice, which is to say personal and collective ideas about who can choose what and how, whose choices are free and whose are "determined" by economic considerations, various forms of oppression, psychological issues, and so forth.

This adds another layer to the analysis of beauty paradoxes, for two main reasons. First, seeking guidance from a set of paradoxical injunctions when defining our identities already induces a sense that our ability to make choices is flawed (as is true with pragmatic paradoxes in general). Hence, I was able to observe the hesitations, second-guesses, and self-criticism in matters of beauty and appearance on the part of the women I interviewed. Second, feminist critiques have been widely integrated into Western social reflexivity, meaning that women now have a much wider sense of the options before (in matters of beauty and beyond). A feminist posture implies a specific vision of the world in which women's ability to choose is understood to be limited by systemic inequalities and cultural hindrances. Hence, a feminist awareness influences the layperson's ideas about her own or other women's freedom to choose. More specifically, acknowledging the paradoxicality of beauty culture can induce women to adopt a wider view of who or what is to blame, be it "society" or "the system." This has the effect of politicizing women's struggles with the paradoxical injunctions of beauty culture, as is apparent in the words of some of my interviewees.[68]

As Bourdieu rightly noted,[69] scholars and intellectuals tend to generalize their privileged, theoretical view of the world, in what he called "the scholastic habitus." Looking down at the "messiness" of sociocultural practices, they are inclined to label these as contradictory, disorganized, or even irrational, inasmuch as they appear inconsistent when observed through the lens of "rational" analysis. The scholastic habitus depends on power relations organized around a series of oppositions, according to which "theory" is nobler than "practice," the "rational" is more valuable than the "irrational," and the "spiritual" dimensions of our existence are elevated above "material" or even "bodily" concerns. By reifying these distinctions, the scholastic habitus becomes complicit with the underlying power relations, and in this way exerts a form of violence on the "observed" social actors. I am deeply aware of the risks of this professional deformation, as well as the power relations that enable it and that render me an involuntary bearer of scholastic biases with regard to non-scholarly interlocutors. For the entirety of the study on which this book is based, I therefore made a conscious effort to maintain this awareness and avoid observing participants' practices and discourses through the lens of this intellectual bias. And what's more, my interviewees deserve credit for their ability to give voice to the dilemmas they have confronted in their own lives. It's in large part because of them that I allow myself to employ the "paradox" concept, and to point out the contradictions inherent in the logic and practices of beauty culture, for it is they who singled these out as worthy of analysis, albeit in their own idioms.

It's worth underlining here that the ability to observe the paradoxes of beauty is no longer limited to scholars and intellectuals studying beauty culture[70]—indeed, it is increasingly a theme of more mainstream discussions about the burdens that beauty places on women. More and more voices in popular media—like Camille Rainville and Amy Schumer, whom we encountered earlier—are defining their experiences with beauty culture in terms of contradiction and absurdity, and these voices are not confined to the ranks of progressive feminists. In an op-ed published in the *New York Times* in the summer 2018 on the subject of recent changes to the Miss America contests, Bari Weiss points out the hypocrisy of American culture when it comes to women's beauty and its importance in society. Noting that this hypocrisy is especially noticeable in productions like Miss America, Weiss nonetheless widens her lens to argue that it is equally shared by "us" all, inasmuch as we, for example, "lie under fluorescent lights and hold our thighs open for strips of burning hot wax while we chat about the new season of 'The Handmaid's Tale.'"[71] As Weiss shows, we willingly subject ourselves to the very same practices we understand as oppressive and that we are often so quick to criticize.

In attempting to manage the paradoxical injunctions of Western beauty culture, ordinary women oscillate between the two sides of the larger paradox that frames their experience. Beyond the boundaries of beautification, our everyday practices are organized by principles, values, and habits that may appear inconsistent if scrutinized in a vacuum—that is, outside of the various conditional contexts in which these practices normally take place, and which make their application pragmatically reasonable. What is remarkable, however, is that most of the women I talked to are also able to observe the paradoxicality of their positions, and to spell these contradictions out in their own words. None of the interviewees spoke explicitly of "paradox": that concept comes from the scholarly literature, as I've explained, and was chosen inductively during data analysis. Participants were nevertheless vocal about the contradictions, the inconsistent constraints, and the absurdities to which they are subjected in the pursuit of beauty culture. It is to Eva, a twenty-nine-year-old master's student who works part-time, that I owe the most striking formulation of this state of affairs: when asked about what she considers the biggest challenge for women in matters of beauty, Eva says that the high level of societal surveillance of women's appearance "creates [. . .] a tightrope on which we are constantly walking." With this powerful metaphor, Eva gives us a vivid expression of the "paradox" concept, and her words suggest that this is something women experience regularly in their everyday lives, rather than just a theoretical abstraction.

In the following chapters, we will see some of the many ways that women try to strike a balance while "walking the tightrope" of beauty culture. We will see them hesitating and oscillating between various conflicting impulses and desires and negotiating the paradoxical framework within which they are invited to choose and commit with regard to beauty and appearance. And we will read their struggles, uncertainties, fears, self-criticism, and conflicting feelings of well-being and inadequacy through a sociological lens.[72] Rather than being the symptoms of psychological fragility, lack of self-confidence, narcissism, or alienation, women's experiences with beauty deserve to be situated in a sociocultural setting in which they can be taken seriously. For nothing less than women's social and political legitimacy is at stake when they make choices regarding their looks and their self-presentation.

Chapter 2

BEAUTY, WELLNESS, AND AUTHENTICITY

WHERE IS BEAUTY SITUATED?

Is beauty on the outside, on the surface of the body? Or does it radiate from the inside, intertwined with one's bodily functions, emotions, and thoughts—in a word, the *self*?

These sorts of questions are crucial if we want to understand how, when, and why women feel beautiful. It follows that such a discussion is key to understanding the forms and logics of women's individual commitments to beautification practices and beauty-related self-discipline—including the consumer choices and judgments that women express on their own. This will also help us situate beauty within women's practices of visual self-expression, and selfies more specifically, to which we'll return in greater detail in chapter 6.

As we saw in the previous chapter, beauty has historically been framed through the opposition between surface—and hence futility, vanity, deceit—and depth—hence authenticity, purity, and truth. Whereas outward beauty can be fascinating and enticing, it is ephemeral and false if the "inside" does not sustain and nourish it: real female beauty, then, radiates outward, from a healthy body, and especially from a healthy moral self. However, beauty must be seen on the surface to be appreciated; good intentions and a strong physiological constitution mean little if a woman's appearance is deprived of recognizable beauty. In this sense, the opposition between artifice and authenticity is rendered paradoxical within the development of Western beauty discourse: natural beauty is in itself the result of beautification and self-discipline, which involves exploiting "artifice" in the form of techniques and materials.

Current Western discourse on the link between beauty and wellness reproduces and rephrases this long-standing opposition. Natural beauty is situated on the inside, framed through the language of cleanliness, purity, and health—a general well-being that requires self-discipline, good choices, and a series of rituals involving specific products, recipes, and services. At the same time, accomplished wellness must be visible on the outside, with flawless skin, a radiant complexion, a well-shaped figure, and so on.

My interviewees drew a strong connection between feeling good and feeling beautiful, between self-care, wellness, and a beautiful appearance. But how is this "feeling good" to be understood? Mainly revolving around the different forms taken by the authenticity paradox, this chapter will discuss contemporary wellness and beauty discourses, the way they are experienced by women, and the contradictions organizing the idea of natural beauty, before suggesting a sociological reading of the feeling of well-being that women link with beauty.

TRADITIONAL DISCOURSES ON
BEAUTY, HEALTH, AND MORALS

The connection between beauty, health, and femininity has a long history, one that also includes medicine, morals, and politics. A brief historical and cultural overview can help us situate current practices and thinking about this connection.

As mentioned in chapter 1, ancient philosophical and medical conceptions of women's nature argued for the inherent weakness, instability, and fragility of women's physiology. Women's health, so this thinking went, therefore requires more attention in the form of an ongoing adherence to a more specific regimen; this was all the more important because of women's roles as the guarantors of successful biological reproduction, and hence the health of the general population. In the ancient and medieval Christian traditions, moreover, women's natural inferiority was also understood to be rooted in their inherent disposition toward sin: essentially inclined to immorality, a woman's body harbors the sexual temptation that deflects man's attention from more righteous concerns. Hence, as Remaury notes, in religious and early medical discourse, women's instability is understood as physical, psychological, and moral:[1] easily fatigued, they are inclined to idleness, inactivity, and a lack of self-discipline, which in turn increases their physical vulnerability and facilitates their exposure to moral excess and loss of control.

Beauty has an ambiguous place in this picture. On the one hand, the beautiful woman is seen as dangerous, sinful, irresistible, and her beauty is therefore understood as constitutive of her proclivity for immorality and temptation. But on the other hand, beauty and health as feminine duties are conflated through the common connection to the biological functions of the female body, through which beauty is read as a sign of fertility, prosperity, and health. Beauty is ambiguously situated both on the side of imbalance, the lack of control that female nature is said to embody, and on the side of balance and self-discipline, here defined by women's social role as mothers. It therefore follows that, historically, the discourse around the link between women's beauty and health has helped establish and maintain women's subordinate role and inferior place in society, be it through their devaluation or through the widespread praise of female beauty.[2]

More generally, beauty has also served eugenic political purposes at different times and places, and never more so than when the "quality" of the population's health, or that of a specific hegemonic "race," was seen as in need of fostering or improvement. In late nineteenth-century Europe and North America, for example, there was a growing fear that the acceleration, complexity, and overwhelming stimulations of modern life would entail a generalized fatigue, and especially a physiological exhaustion among the population that could have alarming consequences for biological reproduction, and with it the health of nations.[3] Due to their natural inferiority, women were viewed as constitutionally more exposed to these threats.[4] Exhaustion and weakness were seen as endangering not only physiological well-being (by increasing one's vulnerability to illness) but also psychological strength and, as a consequence, morality. The well-known Italian criminal anthropologist Cesare Lombroso drew a connection between some individuals' propensity for criminality or immorality and their specific physical and facial features.[5] He was by no means alone in believing that physical appearance could be used as a key to predict people's behavior. Ugliness was considered as much a symptom of moral failure as it was a mark of physical decay, and it was believed that only concerted political action could curb this worrying trend. The growing scientific interest in physiology, psychology, and medicine in the second half of the nineteenth century reinforced the illusion of a scientific basis for national health policies aimed at improving the robustness and resilience of the population. Governing the population, and consolidating the nation-state, increasingly meant providing scientifically grounded organizational, biological, and disciplinary guidance for intellectual as well as bodily hygiene, an idea that Foucault conceptualized through his use of the concept of "biopower."[6]

In her study of the historical development of a normative definition of the female Black body, Sabrina Strings shows how, beginning in the late seventeenth century with early race theorists such as François Bernier, standards for female Black beauty were constructed in direct opposition to the dominant notion of white, European beauty represented by the "neo-classical ideal of Venus."[7] Any departure from that ideal would not only entail a negative aesthetic judgment, but would also be regarded as a sign of the subject's moral failure. In this way, a natural racial hierarchy was constructed whereby plumpness—to take one example—was read as a sign of laziness and inclination to excess, and never more so than when detected in the bodies of Black people. As a consequence, Strings observes, contrasting what was assumed to be a typically "Black" form of female beauty with that displayed by white women served the purpose of establishing "racial superiority, or inferiority," as the case may be.[8]

With this convergence of knowledge and social control, beauty played a major role in the biomedical discourse that came to permeate politics, in terms of both institutions and policies, in the late nineteenth and early twentieth centuries. As historian George L. Mosse showed in his study of the historical evolution of the masculine ideal, physical beauty is a main feature of the new masculine type that dominated nationalist politics in early twentieth-century Europe, and that subsequently played a crucial role in the rise of fascism.[9] Physical traits deviating from the ideal were considered abnormal, signs of biological inferiority as well as of a questionable morality, and as such were to be fought and eradicated. "As the ideal of beauty reflected the needs of society," writes Mosse, "so ugliness served to characterize its enemies."[10] In Germany, for instance, the anti-stereotype was constructed with the physical traits associated with Jewish ethnic origins, and especially the "Jewish nose." Echoing Strings's argument, beauty became a racist device,[11] one aimed at "normalizing" the population through correcting, and even eliminating, "inferior" ethnicities that could prevent the nation from thriving and increasing its strength and power.

Starting in the second half of the nineteenth century, the specialization of aesthetic surgery as a medical branch contributed greatly to this discriminatory normalization, with most "corrective" surgical procedures aiming to reduce "ethnic" facial traits that were thought to deviate from the national ideal, hence allowing the patient to "pass" as a member of the hegemonic group. The self-defining discourse developed by aesthetic surgeons also included humanitarian justifications, such as the patient's happiness and overall well-being.[12] Scholars have emphasized a similar entanglement of racism, national status, eugenics, wellness, and beauty as a patriotic project in recent studies on aesthetic surgery in other times and places—for instance, in contemporary Brazil.[13] During the first half of the twentieth century, when racial discrimination and its eugenic underpinnings were hardly criticized and treated as unjust, the cosmetic advertising industry exploited the socially constructed need for some people to "pass" as members of the hegemonic (in this case white) group in order to sell "normalizing" products, such as skin whiteners for Black people, in Europe as well as in the United States.

As feminist historians have demonstrated, the female body underwent increasing medicalization and normalization in Western societies beginning in the eighteenth century. This took the form of a gradual consolidation of medical knowledge, on the one hand, and the rise of a faith in science as the key to social progress, on the other. The result, as Yvonne Knibiehler and Catherine Fouquet show, was a shift in the general comprehension of female physiology from the "sinner stereotype" to the "reproductor stereotype."[14] In other words, if biological reproduction is the sole function of the female body, maternity becomes a woman's sole, inborn role, one through which every aspect of her life must be interpreted and organized, beginning with her health regime. In this respect, biology (already interpreted through a specific cultural and political lens, as is now clear) becomes the organizing principle of social relationships. This medical conception of gender difference served as an exclusionary device to keep women within the private realm, and outside of the political sphere, throughout much of the nineteenth and twentieth centuries,[15] and it has continued, albeit in more subtle ways, into our own century.

But the cultural discourse about women's physical fragility, instability, neediness, and tendency toward disease and disequilibrium excluded them from the male sphere, especially when it came to politics and education, in a second, more insidious way—one famously denounced by Simone de Beauvoir in her seminal work on the cultural construction of women's inferiority.[16] When, in the late nineteenth century, more and more women began seeking higher education and enrolling in American colleges, physicians, politicians, and male students made use of the whole repertoire of traditional arguments to disqualify their ambitions. As Carroll Smith-Rosenberg explains, these men argued that, by cultivating their intellect, women would subvert the natural order that destined them to reproduction and domesticity. They claimed that "the woman who favored her mind at the expense of her ovaries . . . would disorder a delicate physiological balance,"[17] thereby inviting mental and physical disorder. Of course, these women were also dismissed by way of less subtle arguments; for instance, they were called disgraceful, unladylike, and told that their interest in knowledge and academic study would make them ugly, that they would lose their femininity. More interestingly, their male critics would also appeal to racial and eugenic arguments to dissuade women from acquiring a degree: "society, late-nineteenth century physicians warned, must protect the higher good of racial health by avoiding situations in which adolescent girls taxed their intellectual faculties in academic competition,"[18] writes Smith-Rosenberg.

There is a circular logic at work here: Female beauty becomes a synonym for women's health, and women's health the precondition for the successful reproduction of a healthy population—which in turn justifies the social order in which women's roles and positions take on a markedly gender-specific cast, one that is also stratified based on race and social class. Hence, beauty and health come to be seen as women's social and moral responsibility, and the organizing principles of their lives as weak, dependent, and unstable beings (rendered as such by their physiology). Refusing to organize one's life around the accomplishment of female biological functions would result in ugliness and a loss of femininity—such is the anti-feminist argument by which doctors, politicians, and media sought to delegitimize women's attempts to emancipate themselves from the private sphere and maternal duties well into the second half of the twentieth century. The new "flapper" (*garçonne* in French) beauty ideal of the first few decades of the century, which saw the emergence of a slender and androgynous ideal figure, in contrast to the more generous curves extolled during the Victorian era, can indeed be read as a sign of the decreased centrality of the "maternal function" among (principally younger) women.[19]

Understood as social and moral responsibilities, beauty and health require self-discipline and self-surveillance. The need for self-discipline and policing one's body and appearance are reinforced by the traditional idea that female nature must be met with perpetual suspicion on account of its constitutional instability. It follows that the insistence on self-scrutiny and the implementation of bodily routines and regimes are a common feature of medical advice from the late nineteenth century onward; this is also apparent in the burgeoning cosmetic industry, to say nothing of the intergenerational transmission of lifestyles and ideals within the confines of the family and among friends.[20] "Balance" becomes a key term to indicate moral as well as physiological health, and the fact that both are (must be) reflected in a woman's glowing, naturally beautiful appearance.[21] Far from disappearing as a result of women's progressive emancipation and increasing participation in social, political, and professional activities, this insistence on self-discipline as the key to health and beauty remains a defining feature of female identity in the twentieth century.

If we see a weakening of the link with the maternal function in the first decades of the century, beauty still carries its moral stature as the outward reflection of a competent feminine self that is able to take charge of its health and achieve a personal balance.[22] In this sense, the idea of self-care is full of ambiguities for women, as Kathy Peiss observes in her history of American beauty culture. For suffragettes and women's rights activists, as well as "women who wrote cosmetics advertisements," beauty as self-care and self-expression was certainly associated with the ideals of "dignity" and "social participation" for women.[23] Peiss features a 1924 advertisement from the American cosmetics company Pond's, in which Alva Belmont, famous socialite and champion of women's rights, is interviewed about her skin-care routine. Touting the virtues of good skin care, Belmont at one point asks her interviewer, "Don't you know . . . how often the woman with an unattractive face fails in the most reasonable undertaking? Nothing is so distressing. Neglect of one's personal attractions generally comes from ignorance and as I am greatly interested in the success of women in every possible way, I urge them not to neglect themselves."[24]

What Belmont is saying here is that entering the public sphere (from which women had long been excluded) requires a visible allegiance to an idealized notion of competent, respectable femininity.[25] But as I argued in chapter 1, the connection between a woman's appearance and her personal worth gives rise to a paradox (the worth paradox, as I've called it): if she is deemed worthy exclusively on the condition that she displays the outward signs of competent self-care, her appearance ends up being the decisive criterion by which her worth is assessed. In addition, as Peiss notes, in the first half of the twentieth century, the discourse of advertising, especially as it related to self-care, gradually came to portray beauty as an end in itself. The link between individual expression and beautifying self-care, on the one hand, and the political goals of inclusion and participation in the public sphere, on the other, came to be seen as increasingly tenuous, with the result that self-care became utterly depoliticized. Self-care and well-being have instead been gradually framed as entrepreneurial individual endeavors in the late twentieth and early twenty-first centuries. As such, they have been placed at the core of a growing industry of services (including counseling) and consumer products; as author Leigh Stein puts it in her riveting novel about the wellness industry, self-care is a concept that can now be marketed and sold.[26] It requires self-control, commitment, and organization, certainly, but also affluence, participation in consumer practices, and an awareness of the ever-evolving trends and codes that define what successful femininity looks like.

THE PARADOXES OF WELLNESS AND SELF-CARE

Among the women I talked to, Cassandra, a forty-nine-year-old Black woman, is the most vocal about her choice to adopt a healthy lifestyle as what she calls her main "beauty recipe." When I ask her to be more specific about what self-care means to her, she offers the following clarification:

> From the inside out, from the inside out. I'm not about creams and lotions, I'm not about, like, all those money pits that people fall into, things like that. It's just inside out: good food, no bad toxins, keeping active, keeping happy, keeping stress low—that's, to me, my beauty recipe.

At first glance, it is clear the extent to which this "beauty recipe" buys into the current (yet historically long-lived) rhetoric surrounding well-being, which as we've seen hinges on the imperative to maintain an interior balance, cleanse one's body,[27] and protect oneself from the irritants of modern life. Coming from a low-income household and therefore lacking in disposable income (at least at the time of our interview), and with friends "back home" who struggle with money and poor health habits (she moved to Montreal from another province five years before we first spoke), Cassandra also has a strong sense of how economic inequalities can influence a person's ability to access a healthy lifestyle. Through her numerous selfies on Instagram and Facebook, she wants to show her friends and acquaintances that it is possible to stay healthy (and beautiful) without wasting money on useless beautifying products. By doing so, Cassandra also shows a certain degree of consumer savvy, which is a central feature of contemporary entrepreneurial femininity, as I will discuss in chapter 3.

Indeed, Cassandra's selfies can sometimes seem more like staged public-service messages encouraging the affordable pursuit of well-being and healthy habits such as exercising and eating fresh produce (in one, she and her boyfriend are pictured on their bikes; in another, she stands, beaming, in front of the produce department at her local grocery store). She feels responsible for her community back home because she does not "see anybody from my own neighbourhood" communicating about lifestyle changes and health. She wants to convey the right message to people who might not have the chance to learn from their peers, to set an example. And in so doing, Cassandra is perpetuating a politics of solidarity with a long tradition in the Black community in North America. As Brianna Wiens and Shana MacDonald remind us, "self-care" has been a key theme among Black women since the civil rights movements of the 1960s, when advocates started denouncing the correlation between marginalization, poverty, and bad health.[28]

However, Cassandra also tells me that her efforts to maintain a healthy and balanced lifestyle really come down to her desire to preserve her beauty, her looks. She is conscious of her age, and she wants to keep looking young by "staying" young (remember: "from the inside out"). To accomplish this, she believes she must focus on the important things—to make the right choices before it's too late. For instance, she harshly criticizes a friend who obsesses over false lashes while being overweight and exposing herself to the risk of heart disease. When I casually note that her efforts to preserve her looks sound to me like a lot of work, Cassandra's answer is categorical:

> Well, it's not a lot of work, it's *the* work. You have to decide—when you're young, hopefully—that you want to. But you don't have to decide that it's important to you, it doesn't have to be important to everybody. [For some people what is important is] . . . their educational level, and that's great. Some people think it's important to just be whatever you want to be. . . . For me, I'm very vain, so I decided it's my looks, you know? I mean, my looks on a very natural level, and healthy level. So I decided that, and Pamela Anderson decided it was going to be on a different level. It's a decision you make, and sometimes you're halfway through life and you can't really backtrack. You can never go back. Some mistakes are very permanent.

It's worth unpacking Cassandra's statement. Clearly, she draws a strong connection between beauty and general health, a connection we'll recognize from the historical overview of previous sections. However, Cassandra frames health in terms of choice and individual commitment; there is a discursive aspect to her framing that taps—unwittingly, perhaps—into a very contemporary definition of neoliberal subjectivity. Preserving one's beauty depends on taking care of oneself in a holistic way, which in turn depends on a series of critical choices to which one commits oneself over and over, day in and day out. Cassandra strongly believes in willpower as the key to achieving her individual goals: one has to make the decision, work hard, and carefully avoid the fatal mistakes that could compromise the whole endeavor. Wellness may be for everybody on a hypothetical level, but its achievement depends on individual qualities rather than on social, structural, or institutional transformations.

In addition, Cassandra assesses the role of choice in determining one's appearance on a qualitative level, depending on whether or not they focus on health and nature or artifice, surface, and technology. The model and actress Pamela Anderson, whose global success started with the hit television show *Baywatch* (1992–1997), represents for Cassandra the opposite of "natural," and therefore of hard work. At the time, Anderson's most discussed bodily feature was her large breasts, which were the result of silicone implants (these have since been surgically removed).[29] Right before she mentioned Anderson, Cassandra had been harshly critical of cosmetic surgery, which she sees as the wrong path to youth and beauty. She dislikes that so many women—including her sister—have turned to facelifts and nose jobs in a vain attempt to prevent aging. In avoiding the sheer hard work of achieving health and wellness, Cassandra says that these women are buying into the illusions of the beauty industry.

With her "stay healthy" message, we can see that Cassandra is not immune to two types of normative pressure: on the one hand, the injunction to assume individual responsibility for one's health and well-being and to commit to a form of self-discipline, the results of which will be displayed by your glowing appearance; on the other, the injunction to avoid artifice and stay as natural as possible, artifice and technology being tantamount to laziness, inauthenticity, and self-deception. In addition, the normative tensions of beauty culture are apparent in Cassandra's words despite her strong moral stance: when she reveals that her main reason for practicing self-discipline is the attainment of a beautiful appearance, she announces herself in pursuit of a goal that she herself considers morally unworthy (though even here she is not without self-awareness: "I'm very vain, you know"). Beauty, resurfacing as an end in itself, thereby threatens to discredit the whole endeavor as futile, as feminine.

Cassandra's ideas about wellness and beauty resonate with current discourses on self-care and health in Western societies. Wellness is treated as an overarching endeavor for which the individual must take responsibility. Poor health, which is to say a general absence of well-being, can be corrected by engaging in healthy personal habits. But this requires a total commitment to a regime that spans all aspects of one's life (sleep, exercise, eating, drinking, self-grooming, relationships, one's inner emotional life, and even home decor).[30] One's commitment to the regime is of critical importance: at stake is nothing less than the (moral) subject's ability to respond to vulnerability and impermanence with a sustained display of will-power. Indeed, as sociologist Peter Conrad has argued, wellness practices are nowadays increasingly framed in ethical terms: healthy habits are *good*, unhealthy ones are *bad*; we *should* do what is good and *should not* do what is bad; departing from this righteous path qualifies us as *lazy*, engenders a sense of *guilt*, and requires *reparation* and *restitution* (most obviously, in the form of exercise).[31] Furthermore, as Rachel O'Neill observes, wellness entrepreneurship and discourse are seen by some critics as abetting neo-liberal austerity policies aimed at shrinking the welfare state and rendering health and well-being an individual responsibility, especially with regard to people and groups identified on an ideological level as too dependent on public resources. As O'Neill writes, "the rise of wellness thus coincides—temporally but also ideologically—with the decline of welfare."[32]

If Cassandra is closer to where she wishes to be in terms of self-control, aesthetic discipline, and looks, Melissa, a fifty-year-old self-employed mother of two teenagers, acknowledges during our first conversation—with evident sadness—that she is far from achieving her personal aims. Like Cassandra, her main concern is aging and its consequences for her looks and especially her health, which she understands as her capacity to keep doing the things she likes to do (such as running and cycling) and the things she has to do (such as getting up early in the morning to feed her children a nutritious breakfast and prepare their school lunches).

Having recently started a second career as an artist, Melissa also struggles with professional uncertainties, in addition to facing the physical and physiological changes triggered by menopause. After a leg injury prevented her from exercising at her usual pace, she gained weight, and she has had a hard time shedding these unwanted extra pounds. She is discouraged by her inability to maintain her usual pace in life; she feels tired, heavy, and unwell. But at the same time, Melissa feels attracted to what we might call a "body positive" discourse that tells us we should feel comfortable and serene in our skin, no matter our individual shape, size, or features. She wants to stay young and preserve the beautiful appearance that in the past won her praise. What's more, she knows what to do to achieve this: sleep more, eat healthy, keep exercising, use a little (more) makeup, and keep her hair blond (she considers gray hair ugly and unacceptable, and she apologizes profusely for this natural shortcoming).[33] Melissa tells me that this self-discipline is key to her feeling good and, as a consequence, feeling beautiful. But she also resents becoming too focused on it, not loving herself enough—which is also part of wellness discourse—and she worries that she is sending the wrong message to her daughter about how much a woman should fret about her looks (I will get back to this last point in chapters 3 and 4).

Like many women, Melissa is aware of the contradictions built into the discursive connection between wellness, health, and physical beauty. Struggling with a bodily appearance that does not correspond to her ideal, she feels compelled on the one hand to act and change her lifestyle, and on the other to express self-criticism for desiring that kind of change for the sake of her appearance. Melissa finds herself caught in the clash between a body-positive-oriented discourse on wellness, which attempts to divest self-esteem from stereotypical expressions of beauty (especially as they relate to age and weight), and mainstream, consumption-oriented wellness culture, which ties well-being and health above all to appearance. As scholar Laura Martínez-Jiménez highlights, current Western self-care discourse targeting women is itself paradoxical, since it is simultaneously tied to the promotion of a compassionate and tolerant attitude to oneself, on the one hand, and the injunction to engage in relentless aesthetic work and self-improving routines and rituals on the other.[34] Although this is certainly not the intention of body-positive activists, in trying to follow what she sees as the more balanced path, Melissa is confronted with yet another instantiation of the worth paradox: inasmuch as it can take the form of a reproach for caring too much about appearance and trying too hard to comply with standard definitions of beauty and wellness, body-positive discourse can be challenging for many of the women who try to follow its dictates.

The following example will clarify my concern. In one of her Facebook posts, Lena (thirty-seven years old, self-employed,) wonders whether body positivity necessarily entails giving up once and for all on aesthetic self-improvement—whether the need to love one's body implies an unconditional self-acceptance with regard to one's looks. Body positivity is all about *"feeling good,"* writes Lena in her post, but what do we do with our desire to "look good" or to want our "clothes to fit nicely?" When it becomes an ideology, with all the moral injunctions that can come with that term, the "body positive" attitude can transform itself into its opposite: a source of guilt and self-contempt, and hence of disempowerment.

NATURAL BEAUTY AND THE AUTHENTICITY PARADOX

Healthy beauty is first and foremost *natural* beauty. "Natural," here, has different connotations. First, it gestures toward the traditional idea that women are somehow closer to nature than men are, a notion sustained by popular beliefs about the parallels between female physiological rhythms and the pace of the seasons or the march of the lunar cycle.[35] Second, it refers to the absence, or sometimes the rejection, of artifice or sleight of hand in improving one's appearance. In this sense, "natural" implies a sort of moral value that reproduces the long-lived traditional opposition between authenticity and inauthenticity. Natural beauty comes from within. Finally, there is a third, ethical connotation in that "natural" qualifies the person who displays this type of beauty: this person *does not need* artifice; she has achieved wellness, balance, and thus is "naturally" good-looking. This discursive compound of themes and injunctions, according to Martínez-Jiménez, accomplishes "the identification of self-care with consumption practices, especially aesthetic-related ones, which intimately link women's integral wellbeing to the reproduction of beauty canons."[36]

These different aspects of "natural beauty" are reflected in Eva's remarks about recent trends in selfie-posting on social media. Eva, as readers may recall, is twenty-nine years old at the time of our first interview and completing her master's degree while working part-time in the service industry. She has noticed in her social media feeds an increasing number of users sharing "more authentic" images of themselves. In these pictures, she points out, people still try to display the best possible version of themselves, but they now seem to be doing this in a way that signifies the sort of authentic, natural wellness that this chapter focuses on. They seem, as Eva puts it, to want to "radiate well-being." What's more, in addition to the poster's bodily comportment, this well-being is also reflected more subtly in their choice of mis-en-scène: pastel colors, minimalist decor, nutritious foods ("smoothies and chia seeds," Eva says), equipment or attire indicating involvement in specific wellness activities, rituals (yoga, meditation).[37] Eva's observations address the link between authenticity (as a moral quality), simplicity (as a rejection of artifice and technology), self-discipline, self-management, and consumer choices that are at the core of the idea of natural beauty. In this sense, natural beauty is about natural wellness, which means adopting the right—which is to say, a balanced—lifestyle. Clearly, this conception of "the natural" is already very much informed by contemporary cultural norms.

A similar unfolding of the authenticity paradox can be observed in Cassandra's self-narrative. The "natural" glow that she wants to embody requires, in her telling, a great deal of work, and this is especially true of her efforts to maintain the weight that she considers ideal in order to look beautiful and younger. Montreal's famously long and punishing winters cause her to decrease her level of physical activity and gain extra weight, which, in a sort of seasonal cycle, she then strenuously works to shed in preparation for the spring. During our first interview, which takes place at the end of March, Cassandra explains that she has just resumed going to the gym and watching her food intake, and she expresses full confidence as to her ability to be "ten pounds lighter by May." She adds that her aversion to her current body size has also impacted the frequency with which she usually shares selfies online: Cassandra feels that she is currently in the "cocoon stage," toiling as it were toward the future revelation of her new, spring beauty. But while her narrative might suggest that she see her yearly weight gain as the result of some natural process, and therefore as a completely understandable submission to life's usual ups and downs, this is not quite true: in fact, she frames it as a failure on her part, the result of her having guiltily surrendered her usual self-discipline, and this lapse demands reparation. Cassandra specifically describes her state of agitation when acknowledging the size of her breasts at the end of the winter:

> My boobs were like a forty; I know, I measured them, they were forty [. . .] I measured them a couple of weeks, and they were way out here, and it wasn't, like, sexy, hot boobs, it was, like, old-woman boobs, and I was like, "That's not okay," so I've been working out for about a month now, and they've come down to a very easy-to-work-with situation.

Aside from the assumed connection between slenderness and beauty in mainstream discourse, Cassandra's self-surveillance in terms of body size might also be rooted in the specific, historical stigma targeting plumpness in the Black female body. As shown by Sabrina Strings, norms regarding body size and food intake came to play a major part in the discursive construction of racialized subjectivities and bodies from the early eighteenth century, both in Europe and in the African and American territories colonized by the European powers. Strings states that, as of the late seventeenth century, "indulging in food . . . became evidence of actual low breeding."[38] Conversely, racial, social, and moral superiority was signaled by slenderness, which in turn demonstrated one's ability to exercise self-restraint in matters of consumption, an ability that Black people were assumed to lack. In addition to reinforcing the embodiment of the racial and social hierarchy, self-restraint formed the needle of a new moral compass, which, according to Strings, was a moderating factor vis-a-vis the wealth and material accumulation triggered by colonial conquest.[39] By providing such an enlightening intersectional reading of the historical construction of white women's slenderness as a normative ideal, Strings shows that the "fear" of the plump Black body as a marker of inferior social standing and low morality lies at the core of white and Black women's struggle to stay thin throughout the twentieth century and into the twenty-first.

In addition to being brought about through work and self-discipline, natural beauty, for all its emphasis on nature, is also about achieving a felicitous synthesis between the idea of the "natural" and available human technologies. This is especially clear when we look at so-called natural makeup. This is a recent but fast-growing trend in the makeup industry (which, by definition, uses science, research, and technology to craft new products). In a 2018 interview with *Forbes* magazine, Jennifer Hessel, a successful cosmetics entrepreneur, included natural beauty products (what she called "Skin Care from the Earth") among that year's top industry and consumer trends.[40] These sorts of natural products are marketed as "clean" (which carries a positive moral value), as derived from nature and the earth (as opposed to technology and harmful chemicals), and as working "deeply" on the skin, from the inside out, in order to achieve a general, authentic well-being (as opposed to cosmetics that act on the surface, thereby producing only the *impression* of wellness).[41]

When talking about makeup and beautification practices, the women I interviewed use the "natural" qualifier to mean good, harmless, reliable, morally acceptable, and better-looking in aesthetic terms. "Natural" evokes freedom, individualization, and unmediated self-expression. "Unnatural," by contrast, is that which goes against one's innate bodily processes (with hair removal frequently invoked as an example of an unnatural normative injunction). To prevent contact with the unnatural, with the artificial, the interviewees describe the choices, skills, techniques, and products by which they aim to replicate a "natural look." For all the references to an unmediated expression of individual selfhood, natural beauty is in fact scrupulously policed: the point is not to do away with grooming entirely, to reject all normative injunctions, to attain a sort of absolute liberty.

When I interviewed Jeanne, a twenty-six-year-old who works as an educator with young children, the subject of body hair came up. Though she prizes natural beauty and an authentic look, she nevertheless expresses disappointment at her relentless compliance with the norm prescribing a hairless body for a woman.[42] "Why should you look like a child?" she asks rhetorically. She admires women who ignore the pressure to remove their body hair,[43] yet she feels she cannot make that choice herself: she believes that she has internalized this normative injunction and that it prevents her from accepting what is otherwise an inevitable bodily process. And of course Jeanne is not alone in this; the idea of showing hairy legs or armpits is equally unacceptable to other interviewees, including those who enthusiastically recount embracing natural cosmetics for a more "natural" look. As I mentioned earlier, natural beauty products are seen as cleaner and more reliable: they are to the skin what food is to the body.[44] Indeed, Elsie Rutterford and Dominika Minarovic, founders of the company Clean Beauty, make just such a connection in their book of the same name. (The book's subtitle is telling: *Recipes to Manage Your Beauty Routine, Naturally.*) We should pay attention, they write, to "questionable ingredients that don't benefit our bodies in any way," and not only with regard to the food we eat but also what we put on the surface of our bodies.[45] The clean beauty trend is driven by consumer awareness and skepticism of the (often toxic) composition of drugstore cosmetics and other industrial beauty products, and, by extension, of the cunning and deceitfulness of commercial cosmetics brands.

For Juliette (thirty-five, working toward her doctorate), drugstore cosmetics, regardless of any marketing to the contrary, are bad for one's skin, for one's bank account, and for the environment.[46] In order to reject the industrial approach, then, one must develop a healthy skepticism, and even more importantly a new set of consumer skills and a more refined body of knowledge. Juliette explains that she made just such an effort to learn about clean beauty alternatives, and eventually came to privilege options that are both effective and less expensive. The age-old notion of the homemade "beauty recipe,"[47] developed according to ancestral wisdom and made with all-natural ingredients, resurfaces in the current vogue for wellness as a rejection of a consumer culture that serves the interests of big corporations over those of individuals. However, the rejection is often partial and contingent. If Juliette expresses her contempt for industrial cosmetics when it comes to skin care, she trusts these products implicitly when it comes time to pick a shampoo for her unruly hair. Likewise, Cassandra, with her deep commitment to a healthy lifestyle as a recipe for physical beauty, hides her gray hair with a cheap dye from the dollar store. In doing so, she even claims to be "fight[ing] the fight [against aging] in the most natural way."

A paradox would appear to link natural beauty with nature (inasmuch as technology, commercial strategies, normative injunctions, and consumer choices play a significant role in the pursuit of the former), and authentic beauty with authenticity (inasmuch as this type of beauty, at least as it's understood in popular discourse, does not entail a total rejection of artifice, let alone of cultural norms regulating the aesthetic appreciation of female bodies). In addition, natural or clean beauty requires an impressive amount of work, the investment of considerable financial resources,[48] time, and planning.

Staying with the "natural" makeup trend for a moment, let's consider a concrete example. After doing a bit of quick online research on natural makeup tutorials[49] (what is often marketed as "no-makeup makeup"), I chose a sample of five. After comparing each tutorial, I calculated that they include an average of 8.4 steps (most of which are reproduced across the various tutorials, from moisturizing to brow definition to applying lipstick) and recommend an average of 12.4 products—this to achieve a "natural" look. Ironically, that last number is quite close to the "fifteen layers" of makeup that one of the interviewees, Melissa, considers ridiculous and exaggerated, and obviously antithetical to the idea of natural beauty, especially for younger women.[50]

Of course, it's worth remembering that most makeup tutorials circulating online are specifically tailored to advertise cosmetics—hence the high number of products featured in these textual productions. But you could also say that consumer practices and products are at the very core of the natural beauty trend. Beauty columnists and advertisers are aware of this paradox and draw on it to create a sense of complicity with their readers, as well as inevitability: there is simply no point, they seem to be saying, in pretending that a natural look can be achieved without work. In one tutorial published on the *Cosmopolitan* website, the author states candidly: "In theory, natural makeup should be oh-so easy—it's minimal, which means minimal effort, right? I wish."[51] Another opens her tutorial in an almost philosophical mode: "Isn't it weird that we want to apply makeup . . . that looks like we're not wearing makeup? Existential beauty crisis aside, the off-duty model, no makeup vibes are here to stay."[52] It becomes clear that the authenticity paradox structures the whole discourse around natural beauty.

Zoe is used to dealing with professional makeup artists in her line of work. When she is interviewed on the national broadcaster in her capacity as a journalist, she undergoes professional, TV-specific makeup and hair styling. Sometimes she looks at herself in the mirror before going on air and thinks it is really "too much." But there is one makeup artist in particular whom she praises for his ability to give her a perfectly "natural" look. She tells me that, once, when getting started on her makeup, he said, "Look, it's going to take very long, but it will look super natural on TV." "And," she adds, "it was true."

WHERE DOES "FEELING BEAUTIFUL"
REALLY COME FROM?

Most of the women I interviewed told me that "feeling beautiful," for them, means "feeling good": their feeling beautiful is linked to a more general sense of well-being. They did not say that one causes the other, but they did describe the coincidence of these two feelings. At first glance, this connection could be considered an endorsement of wellness rhetoric—the claim that wellness radiates from the inside out, with beauty as its visible expression, and that one has to work on one's body and mind in order to look good. However, when we unpack what these women say about well-being and beauty, the picture looks quite different. Well-being appears less like an interior, solipsistic state of mind, achieved through meditation and green smoothies, and more like a feeling related to one's place in society and one's assessment of one's competence as a social agent. When the interviewees talk about feeling good, they evoke complex situations, interactions with people, performances of social roles, cultural gestures, rituals and objects, the materiality of the social world and of one's body situated within it. Hence, their lived experience of feeling beautiful contradicts the rhetoric of wellness and "natural" beauty discussed in the previous sections: feeling beautiful appears to be a collective achievement (other people's feedback is often an important consideration) and a social experience of competence and of being at the right place with the right look.

Like the French colleague whom I mentioned at the start of the introduction, who would feel empowered by appearing more put together for a day in the library, many women report positive feelings as a result of the effort they put into looking good, or looking better than they "naturally" would. This effort is sometimes made in response to a specific endeavor (a professional situation, a social gathering, a special celebration), but it often occupies a more quotidian place in women's lives, as part of the preparations that women must undertake in the course of a day. From what I gather, making an effort—as opposed to, say, simply putting on the first thing that they find in the morning—gives them a feeling of increased competence, of adequacy with regard to the social expectations that they perceive in connection with their different social roles. Often, complying at least partially with dominant standards of feminine appearance enhances this feeling of competence, of being at the right place—what women sometimes describe as "feeling good" in their own skin. Quoting Beverly Skeggs' insightful research on the performance of respectable femininity, we could say that feeling good about one's looks is indeed a feeling of being at a suitable place *socially*, of having and demonstrating the "right knowledge," of "getting it [right]."[53] Hence, several interviewees affirm that when they feel well-rested, when their skin looks good and their hair is cooperating, their outlook on the day is more positive and encouraging.

In addition, the positive feelings that stem from one's sense of being beautiful are often aroused by felicitous social encounters. For example, the women I interviewed described feeling particularly beautiful on "good days," which is to say the types of days when they have positive interactions with others, or when they go the extra mile to be friendly to their interlocutors and they get a favorable response in return. This positive feedback can sometimes take the form of a compliment on one's appearance, for instance, with the obvious effect of increasing one's confidence, of contributing to one's feeling of being in one's proper place—sociologically speaking, a very important self-appraisal for any social actor.[54]

Drawing on the work of Canadian sociologist Erving Goffman, Pierre Bourdieu developed a rich sociological understanding of the feeling of being in one's place. Through actions and choices, Bourdieu argues, people tend to maintain their social position, their "right place," since they have an intuitive "sense" that such a position is unlikely to threaten or devalue their competence, abilities, ideas, and manners (what Bourdieu calls "habitus").[55] Rather than being a merely deterministic principle, this sense of place is transmitted through affinities and positive reinforcement: people experience sympathies and compatibilities with others who, through positive feedback, increase their sense of belonging (which, generally speaking, *feels good*). Practices and rituals related to self-presentation, according to Bourdieu, are meant to reflect "the image of one's position in the social space."[56] Interestingly, Goffman used the idea of a "sense of one's place" to explain the moral self-restraint of individuals against "misinterpreting themselves," or offering an image or self-presentation that goes against social expectations related to one's status. To illustrate the idea, Goffman gives the following example: "in Western societies, women feel that it is seemly to refrain from using symbols of sexual attractiveness before reaching a given age and to abstain from using them after attaining a certain age."[57] Hence, appearance plays an important role not only in one's self-presentation—that's obvious enough—but also in the quality of feedback that one receives vis-à-vis one's situated, contextual legitimacy. As we saw in chapter 1, women are judged, qualified, or disqualified on the basis of their appearance more than men are.

Participating in "meaningful" activities can also boost one's feeling of being beautiful. Melissa, for example, reports feeling beautiful when she plays sports with other people; it allows her to prove her strength and ability, but also to feel a connection with other participants for whom the event is equally important and exhilarating. Melissa attributes these good feelings to the release of "endorphins," those pain-inhibiting hormones that are liberated during physical activity. But when she describes the situations in which this physiological process allegedly occurs for her, she talks just as much about positive interactions, about being with other people and sharing in a pleasant communal vibe. Again, she feels that she is in the right place. When I ask for a more specific memory of an occasion when she felt beautiful, Melissa recalls a formal event that she attended with a friend. The event, she explains, was linked to her ethnic background, which, for her, meant that it already carried a certain positive charge. She had put some effort into choosing the right outfit, a simple black dress, both comfortable and elegant, that would cover what she considers physical flaws; her hair (which has a specific salience for her) was beautiful; her weight was "okay"—in short, she says she "felt good and things were going well." Excited and well-prepared, she went on to receive positive feedback from the people around her that night, and had an easier time meeting new people; she felt bolder, even "flirtatious."

Many women also mention certain self-referential measures of their feeling good or bad, beautiful or ugly. This usually takes the form of a physical feature (often hair) that informs one's standing in terms of beauty and one's compliance with standards of commitment and discipline. For Lena, it is her "abs," which is to say the more or less athletic appearance of her abdomen. When she sees a muscular abdomen (a leaner, more defined shape), she feels good, empowered, and beautiful. When she sees fat (in her words, "belly flab"), she feels down, dislikes herself, and assumes she'll have a bad day. These divergences are evident in the selfies she takes and shares on Instagram. In many of these pictures, which she takes mostly at home, she lifts her top with one hand to uncover her belly. We discuss one in particular, posted at the end of the Christmas holidays, in which she wears a disgusted expression on her face while showing her abdomen. The caption amounts to a long confession, full of self-loathing, in which she admits her lack of self-restraint during the holidays and her embrace of certain unhealthy, self-destructive habits (eating too much, snacking on chocolate, eating without even being hungry, not having enough vegetables, not drinking enough water, having wine with every meal, etc.). She describes herself as "physically sick" from all the poor choices she has made. Now, invoking the symbolism of the New Year's resolution, she says it's time to turn a new leaf.

As with every conversion, Lena's begins with a confession of her moral failure to follow the right path, and in so doing she is following the unwritten dictates of modern communication in the age of Instagram and Facebook.[58] Indeed, social media is nowadays the most appropriate platform for this sort of modern atonement ritual. The repenting subject publicly shares her truth with an audience who witnesses her will to change and who, in the future, can testify to her ability (or her failure, as the case may be) to honor her commitment. (Incidentally, we can appreciate the contrast between Lena's strategy, which above all conveys a sense of atonement, and Cassandra's, discussed above: Cassandra instead simply chooses to refrain from posting selfies when she dislikes her looks and the shape of her body.) To feel better about herself and her social media persona—that is, to reinforce her status as a fit woman in pursuit of a healthy lifestyle and an ever more athletic body—Lena enacts her remorse in front of her community. The shape and size of her abdomen is a material reflection of her progress and failures. As she puts it,

> That's where I personally feel the most if I'm feeling okay or not. Because I always have muscles in my arms, that just doesn't go away, but seriously, I think about food and my abs go away, so for me it's the measure of how am I feeling, how fit I feel. [. . .] After eating all this, I was like, "Oh God," you know. Yeah, so for me that's just [. . .] you know, how do I feel, how do I feel about myself physically? I look at my abs: "Er . . . not there—not a good day."

Lena is obviously aware of the fact that her abdomen is not changing from one day to the next, or even from one week to the next. She not only has sufficient knowledge of exercise and nutrition to temper her expectations as well as her despair; she also knows that what she sees when she takes a selfie is not "real": "it's probably not even reflecting what's actually happening in the mirror, it is a state of mind," she herself admits. Nevertheless, her feelings about her body are connected to the appearance of a specific body part that materializes her status as a moral subject, to the point that "liking my abs" becomes a synonym for "liking my looks," and indeed for "liking myself."[59]

Healthy eating, a strict exercise routine, and a general balance between her professional and private life as a working mom are the main components of the self-presentation Lena aims to show through her social media posts. By performing commitment and willpower, she also wants to encourage other women to follow her path—even if this encouragement can take the form of the occasional confession of moral failure. In this performance, as

I've argued, a beautiful appearance serves as a stand-in not just for physical health but for *moral* health as well.[60] Lena's sense of her own body is filtered through the lens of the social expectations that she perceives with regard to her position in the larger social firmament. As sociologists Kathy Charmaz and Dana Rosenfeld write, the "felt, experienced body becomes a looking glass through which the person gains and interprets images of the self."[61] The social norms governing what is considered an appropriate appearance do not require the same level of self-consciousness from all social actors: Charmaz and Rosenfeld show how visible and invisible chronic illness, for instance, foster a state of increased individual self-awareness, since people perceive their bodily appearance and aptitude as already at odds with social expectations of "normalcy."

The same increased self-consciousness appears to characterize women's embodied experiences. A focus on bodily self-scrutiny has surrounded Western womanhood for the longest time, and women could aspire to an even greater degree of self-scrutiny with the increasing affordability of full-size mirrors and the popularization of photography during the twentieth century,[62] with the proliferation of advertising images and representations of the female body, and now with selfies. In his study of female body standards in France from the seventeenth to the nineteenth centuries, Philippe Perrot presents a reproduction of a 1931 painting by Albert Guillaume entitled *Inquiétude* (concern or worry). It depicts a woman, naked except for her high-heeled shoes, examining her body, and her buttocks in particular, in a full-size mirror.[63] Her right hand is on her right buttock, to which the viewer's attention is also drawn by the painting's framing. The title leaves no doubt as to the nature of the self-examination that she is conducting. To Perrot, *Inquiétude* epitomized Western women's relationship with their appearance in the early twentieth century. In North America, the main focus of women's aesthetic self-assessment shifted from the breasts in the 1950s to the lower body during the late 1970s and the 1980s.[64] Judging by the number of articles, tutorials, workout programs, cookbooks, meal plans, meal substitutes, herbal teas, and gadgets and devices that claimed to reduce belly fat, as well as the number of images featuring sculpted abs on social media and in popular magazines, the abdomen may well be the main focus of women's *inquiétude* in recent years. In her 2004 play *The Good Body*, Eve Ensler, author of *The Vagina Monologues*, shares her (almost obsessional) worries about the size of her stomach, and explores cultures and techniques of self-scrutiny among women from around the world.

Finally, beautification practices in themselves can be a source of good feelings and well-being. Clarisse, who is thirty-five years old at the time of our first interview, works full-time and has three young children. She explains that self-care services saved her at a time when she was struggling with depression and burnout. Work, family, household responsibilities, and the demands of a busy urban life had caused her to "neglect [her]self." Having taken a leave of absence from work, and with the children finally in daycare, she felt she could finally take care of herself: "only me, you know." That's when she started getting professional manicures, getting her eyebrows shaped, unwanted body hair removed—all of which she enjoys enormously. She also visits the hairdresser regularly (she complains about her unruly hair), and has fun shopping online for clothes, shoes, and accessories. Taking care of herself is purely "aesthetic," she says—no exercising (she doesn't like it, and she can find neither the time nor the motivation), only beautification to foster a sense of wellness and bring the focus back on herself.

And for Clarisse, it has everything to do with shifting the focus: beautification practices are pleasurable to her because they allow her to carve moments out of the day in which she can shed all her other roles and responsibilities.[65] These time slots, brief though they are, are also confined to material and symbolic spaces (the nail parlor, the hair salon) that demarcate "me time," during which her attention is not required by anyone or anything else. Hence, practices and places that are exclusively focused on making the body beautiful provide feelings of well-being by enabling or suspending specific identities that women carry in their everyday lives. As sociologist Miliann Kang observes in her ethnographic study of nail parlors, for example, self-care services, and especially manicures, are invested with expectations about their power to magically fix the problems that women encounter in their day-to-day lives.[66] As a consequence, these services are also often advertised with reference to the same discourse that treats self-care as a sort of self-cure, as wellness.

There are obviously times when things go wrong and one cannot feel beautiful, or good, at all. One tries everything, all the gestures and rituals that usually work, but nothing changes. Lena cannot feel beautiful when she is overwhelmed with worries (e.g., about a family member's illness), when she has had unpleasant interactions with loved ones (e.g., an argument with her husband), or when her choices go against her idea of health (e.g., by "binge eating"). She feels that, in those cases, going the extra mile to improve her appearance is no use: "'cause there's not enough makeup to cover up when you feel like shit, you know? Everybody's always gonna know." Audrey, for her part, says that even when she chooses not to reveal her negative feelings about herself to others, those around her could tell her that she is beautiful, but it wouldn't have any positive effect. Emma, a twenty-two-year-old student who works part-time to support herself, feels very vulnerable to the contingent effect of the external gaze on her sense of beauty; she feels that her "feeling beautiful," far from an internal, subjective process, is actually a power that other people, and especially men, have over her, and that this power can affect her self-esteem positively or negatively. For Fanny, a thirty-five-year-old self-employed mother of two young kids, the days when she finds herself locked in the "grind" of preparing meals, packing school lunches, dropping the kids off at school, driving here and there for errands, groceries, and so on, are days that leave no room for beautification, or even for basic self-care. On those days, she does not want to be looked at: she feels that there is nothing beautiful in her.

CONCLUSION: NORMATIVE AUTHENTICITY

In this chapter, I've discussed different ideas about where beauty is situated and where "feeling beautiful" comes from. I've outlined traditional and contemporary Western conceptions of the link between beauty, health, and morality, all of which revolve around the idea of a fundamentally unstable and fragile female "nature." The female body, as we've seen, is understood as requiring constant work, both inside and out, in order to be kept healthy and to appear beautiful.

More recently, the discursive framing of the link between health and beauty has hinged on the idea of cleansing, of purifying, of striking a *balance* between the mind and the body. Living "clean" is regarded as a full-time pursuit—and sold as exactly that. The aspirational concept of "natural beauty" embraces the idea of purity and frames beauty as the result of the successful realization of inner and outer balance. As Rachel O'Neill observes, for many contemporary health and wellness entrepreneurs, "health is understood not simply as freedom from disease, but a preternatural exuberance and luminous vitality, often denoted through references to 'glow.'"[67] "Natural beauty" is thus regarded as authentic, real, because it radiates from the inside: it is not *superficial* but *deep*, not *fake* but *genuine* (unlike the kind of beauty obtained through surgery, chemical applications, or "dirty" cosmetics). What is remarkable is that this is not only an aesthetic judgment: this language also gives voice to our moral appraisal of the subject who commits herself to being real, authentic, clean, and profound.

The link between aesthetics and morality is as clear in self-help materials as it is in the words of the women whom I interviewed: the naturally beautiful woman displays her moral (and social) status as much as her good looks, and this comes above all from embracing an "honest" lifestyle. One "wears" her hard-working, righteous, compliant self on the surface of her body. In the beauty and wellness industry, as in popular culture writ large, this compound of authenticity and cleanliness, and the natural beauty that is thought to emerge from it, is marketed as a form of empowerment for women. In this genuinely postfeminist narrative, beauty and spirituality are intertwined, with both stemming from one's commitment to pursuing self-enrichment and adopting the necessary consumer practices.[68]

For example, in her foreword to Habib Sadeghi's book *The Clarity Cleanse*, Gwyneth Paltrow, founder of the highly successful beauty and wellness company Goop,[69] describes an "honest" lifestyle as one that is free from the sort of emotional obstructions that come from not speaking one's emotional truth. Recalling how Dr. Sadeghi once helped her overcome a health problem, Paltrow writes that "he traced what was happening in my ovaries to my thyroid, otherwise known as the throat chakra—a common source of affliction for many women who do not feel empowered to speak, who stuff and stifle emotional pain rather than speaking the truth of their mouth."[70] So much for fighting the cultural and political structures silencing the voices of women in a patriarchal society! Here, disempowerment is strictly personal, and can be fixed through a healthy, "natural" lifestyle (premised on the appropriate consumption practices, of course).

What I gather from Paltrow's words is indeed that clarity and wellness rituals—the main objects of Sadeghi's book—can have an empowering effect on women (who are obviously Goop's main target audience) by boosting their confidence and their access to their spiritual selves.[71] What Goop and Sadeghi sell, in other words, is a truly postfeminist package. However, there would be no market for their services without the belief that women have to be fixed, or, better yet, that women have to fix *themselves*, and that the path starts with acknowledging all the ways in which they could do better.[72] This is why wellness and natural beauty are highly prescriptive and normative. Your body and mind can do wonders, we are told, but you need constant, daily (and hence endless) micro-fixing in order to express your "natural" potential. The work is not necessarily unpleasant, but it will require moral commitment and a considerable amount of personal resources. The authenticity paradox is clearly at work.

However, this chapter has also shown us that, if we look closely at what women say about "feeling beautiful," this feeling appears to emerge from a combination of factors and circumstances, among which wellness rituals and "natural beauty" prescriptions play only limited roles. Rather than simply emanating from some inner "purity" insulated from cultural prescriptions and social processes,[73] "feeling beautiful" and "feeling good" mainly arise from practices, interactions, and contexts that are intrinsically social, cultural, and intersubjective. As we've seen, the additional effort that one puts into looking good in anticipation of certain social situations can conjure good feelings about oneself, and the validation that such situations tend to generate can at the same time increase one's self-confidence about one's appearance. "Feeling beautiful" is also linked to one's general self-image, which often materializes in the look of a specific bodily feature (rather than in a "holistic" wellness) as a sort of mirror of the self. Finally, beautification and wellness practices can also play a meaningful role in women's lives, especially when they take the form of "me time," during which they temporarily suspend their other obligations and social roles—something that can otherwise be extremely challenging for women with busy professional and family lives.

Beauty, then, appears to be a multisite experience in which one's personal feelings and self-image are situated within the intersubjectivity of larger social and cultural contexts. Feeling beautiful is connected to the appraisal, both personal and communal, of one's moral and social status, which entails a set of criteria that are not purely aesthetic. Moreover, beauty's connection to nature and authenticity is heavily mediated by cultural prescriptions, commercial discourses, technologies, and by inequalities in the access to certain lifestyle choices and resources. Although commercial strategies and mainstream cultural representations depict beauty and well-being as individual endeavors instrumentally supported by products and services, "feeling beautiful" and "feeling good" are embedded within complex, situated social processes

Chapter 3

COMMITMENT AND INVESTMENT

In a 1928 cartoon drawn by Denis Wortman and published in the *New York World*, we view three ladies from behind while they stare at the window of a chic hair salon. Posted on the glass is a long price list detailing the salon's services, and a sign announcing "Colors hair as NATURE does." In the caption, one of the ladies says, "I'll tell you, Gladys, it's an expensive affair nowadays for a girl to be a natural beauty."[1] The cartoon, reproduced in Kathy Peiss's history of American beauty culture, provides a cheeky illustration of some of the paradoxical logics I discussed in chapters 1 and 2. But it also points to an aspect of beautification of which the women I interviewed are very well aware: namely, its demands in terms of personal commitment—that is, of mental space, financial resources, and time.

Beautification requires a certain level of consumer skill, information, and ability to choose in order to navigate the panoply of services, techniques, and products available to contemporary Western women. Not only must one learn what mascara is and how to properly apply it; one must also know which mascara is suited to which type of eyelash, how to use it to obtain a specific effect, and so on. This applies to every step of the daily beautification routine, the notion of which can be extended to encompass a seemingly ever-growing number of aspects of one's appearance.[2] By navigating the paradoxical injunctions that tell them to commit wholly to beautification, but without caring *too* much, women are left to their own devices when it comes to managing the amount of room they allow beauty to take up in their lives and in their identities. Here, again, women must also negotiate the commitment paradox in deciding which of the apparently endless calls to self-improvement—from media, from advertising, from employers, colleagues, peers, family members, and so on—they are willing to answer.

Translating such injunctions into practice means investing financial means, personal time, and psychic energy into thinking, planning, and performing beauty. Since these are all finite resources, each woman must develop her own decision-making criteria and strategies for allotting what she deems the appropriate amount of time, money, and energy to beautification, while also negotiating the paradoxes we've identified in previous chapters.[3] The challenge, as always, is knowing how much is enough—and answering this question in the face of a generalized paradoxical discourse that tells you that it is simultaneously *never* enough, and that, regardless, you might have "overdone" it already. This chapter discusses some of these criteria in an attempt to show how personal strategies are embedded in social processes and inequalities that define the conditions of possibility when it comes to individual involvement in beauty culture.

INVESTING MONEY AND TIME

When I ask Clarisse what the biggest challenge is for women in the areas of beauty and appearance, she doesn't start by talking about aging, as many of the other participants do. Clarisse says that the main problem is that beauty demands a considerable amount of time and especially money. When she was a child, her father would ridicule her mother's regular purchase of a particularly expensive face cream.[4] Clarisse remembers his dismissive attitude, but she also recalls her mother insisting that such a product was exactly what she needed and that a cheaper alternative simply wouldn't do. Now, in adulthood, Clarisse is learning from her own experience that beautification does indeed exact a high financial cost for women—even more so when she considers that these are mostly recurring financial commitments. What I gather from Clarisse's story is that she now understands that her mother's purchases weren't just made on a whim: rather, this is the way beauty works. Contrary to the perennial myth of natural, maintenance-free, almost incidental attractiveness—embodied by whichever Disney princesses happens to be in vogue at any given moment—beauty does not come easily (as we saw in chapter 2), and it certainly does not come for free. Indeed, participating in the consumption of beauty-related products and services is not simply utilitarian but also a sign of one's competent involvement in beauty culture.

The interviews that I conducted for this book provide rich data on the ways women grapple with the investments that beauty requires. Each person hopes to reach an individual arrangement in which their resources are perceived as sufficiently well-allocated; the goal is to feel that the costs related to one's specific priorities feel reasonable, the results are for the most part satisfying (on most days), and the budget does not exceed one's means. Notwithstanding their idiosyncratic nature, these personal arrangements are organized by various logics, criteria, values, and constraints that are, at least to a certain extent, shared by the participants, as this section will show. The most notable of these takes the form of skepticism toward the messages of advertising and expert advice related to cosmetics. Such distrust is mainly voiced to justify the resistance against excessive spending on makeup or skin care, a resistance that nonetheless depends on different factors in the interviewees' lives.

When Zoe talks about buying cosmetics, she conveys the aesthetic pleasure she takes in handling and storing "all the little cream jars," the makeup, and the hair sprays. As author and life coach Marie Kondo would put it, this really sparks joy. Zoe is nevertheless careful not to overspend on cosmetics. She refuses to splurge on, say, face lotion, like some women she knows. "I understand," she says, "that a good lotion need not be a three-hundred-dollar lotion." Notwithstanding ads and media messages that try to lure women into unnecessary spending, Zoe has worked to develop the ability to choose good quality for a fair price; in so doing, she feels that her critical capacity distinguishes her from some of the other women in her life, who still believe that good quality must necessarily mean a higher price. Zoe admits, however, that she buys more cosmetics than she needs, for the sheer pleasure of collecting the various products and following her inspiration when it comes to choosing one each morning or on special occasions. All things considered, her consumer behaviors do not appear to be entirely immune to marketing messages, but she has found an acceptable balance between her political values and her material desires.

The resistance to what one considers "excessive investments" takes different discursive forms depending on the socioeconomic status of the interviewee. Melissa is relatively affluent and does not express any worry related to her financial situation during our conversations. Nevertheless, she describes a certain level of anxiety when it comes to shopping for cosmetics and having to determine the appropriate amount of money she should invest in them. At our second interview, she tells me about a conundrum she recently faced: Her daughter wanted some special makeup for her birthday, and so they went together to buy it. But when it came time to choose a specific product, Melissa did not know how to behave. When it comes to makeup prices, she says, "the sky is the limit." What kind of message, she wondered, would her choice send to her daughter? (I'll get back to this question in the next chapter.) Spend less, maybe buy lesser quality, and she risks telling her daughter that beauty is of only secondary importance; spend much more than she considers appropriate in order to get the best for her girl, and she risks conveying the message that beauty trumps all else.

While consciously trying not to place an undue focus on appearance as a female asset in front of her children, Melissa is very sensitive to the question of a product's composition and ingredients, and she fears that cheaper options will go against her dictum of "not putting bad things on your face." Since she does not have to watch her budget, she can consider more expensive products. On the other hand, her dermatologist tells her that good sunscreen and a decent moisturizer are all a woman needs to achieve healthy, glowing skin (avoiding smoking and getting a good night's sleep are also part of the recipe, she adds). Not only does Melissa believe that good cosmetics should not cost a fortune, but after receiving this advice from her dermatologist, she finds herself increasingly skeptical of the marketing used to justify the astronomical prices charged for cosmetics. Her preferred way out of this quandary would be to take control of the things she puts on her skin. To this end, she would like to take a class on natural cosmetics so she can make her own at home. At the moment, though, she lacks the time, and so she feels it's even more important that she make wise consumer choices that align with her principles.

Melissa is not alone: thanks to price and product diversification, but also to a generalized critical discourse that nowadays places greater scrutiny on branding and marketing in cosmetics, the informed consumer does not believe—as perhaps she did in the past—that spending more always gets you better quality. Generally speaking, consumer choices appear to be guided by a combination of marketing cues, personal beliefs, and third-party information that affects our perceptions of the products we buy.[5] As a matter of fact, the interviewees bring critical and informed decision-making to bear in their buying of cosmetics, relying as they do on a combination of advice from peers and experts and their own personal experience. They develop strategies and habits based on their financial and personal situations, their willingness to invest time and energy in information gathering, their political stances with regard to beauty culture and its paradoxical injunctions, and their sense of self-worth. Indeed, Melissa's hesitations and reflections reveal the tensions between different logics regulating the aesthetic and moral performance of respectable femininity, some of which I discussed in chapter 2: the injunction to disciplined self-care and aesthetic self-surveillance; the imperative of moderation in the use of cosmetics, and especially morally dubious "bad" cosmetics; and the normative blueprint for women's "balanced" consumption.

Based on these observations, it is abundantly clear that not all of us can afford what we want, want what we are told we need, or are willing to do (or avoid) what we are told we should do (or avoid). This is particularly salient in the postfeminist economy of beautification, where the definition of women's sense of self and personal worth is increasingly tied to appearance,[6] and to the competencies required to maintain it. In twenty-first-century Western sociocultural contexts, critical consumption is also regarded as a "competent" feminine quality, and is deeply entangled with different histories: that of social criticism toward women's consumption as vain and excessive, as Claire Tanner and colleagues note; and that of an industry that, for decades, marketed harmful goods with little consideration of the consequences on consumers' health. As Brooke E. Duffy discusses in her work on online "aspirational labor," we can observe in Western consumer culture the emergence, beginning in the twentieth century and continuing into the twenty-first, of discursive devices directed at regulating women's consumption practices.[7] But if women have overwhelmingly been targeted by advertisers as the main drivers of domestic and family consumption, their own access to this consumption was (and still is) regarded as potentially disruptive to their mental and moral equilibrium—as leading to vanity and excess, especially in the form of immoderate and irresponsible spending. Hence, demonstrating consumer savvy as the ability to choose, criticize, and manage resources is a crucial feminine competence, even more so within the postfeminist construction of femininity as agency, autonomy, and (consumer) power. I will get back to the question of "balance" in the concluding section of this chapter. In addition, as Geoffrey Jones shows in his history of the global beauty industry, distrust toward cosmetic companies has a long tradition in North America, one that was especially well justified before the cosmetic sector came under formal public regulation in the 1970s, when companies were banned from including harmful chemicals in their products.[8] As has been observed in other spheres of activity, women develop justificatory narratives in which they can integrate material constraints, personal beliefs, individual habits, and perceived social expectations so as to preserve an image of themselves as socially desirable and sufficiently attuned to normative injunctions.[9] These narratives often combine apparently contradictory decision-making criteria. The sociological salience of such narratives is linked to the way they process cultural references defining femininity, as well as the effects that stem from the unequal access to its ful-fillment. Things get even more complex when women are also concerned about feminist issues, and are aware of the detrimental impact of beauty consumption on gender equality and dignity. Hence, they must reconcile a diversity of desires, values, beliefs, and material constraints to negotiate their aesthetic identity.

Eva has a limited budget for clothing—she can only afford to buy second-hand—and for beautification in general. Thrift stores (*friperies* in French) are very popular in Montreal, often offering a wide choice of clothing styles and sizes. That said, since the inventory consists of other people's discarded objects, one rarely finds the clothing items and accesso-ries that are fashionable at the moment. With a rather dismissive tone, Eva claims that she neither likes nor follows "fashion," which she experiences as a limit on her self-expression. At any rate, she also makes a virtue of necessity, as she cannot afford to follow current fashion trends anyway. Her clothing style revolves around a simple palette of black and white: restrict-ing her wardrobe in this way allows her to enjoy a greater degree of choice at the thrift store, while also developing a cool personal style in which she can distinguish herself with the creative use of patterns and shapes.[10]

Through Eva's example, we can appreciate the extent to which socio-economic status shapes women's personal appearance and the identities they project. This influence, however, is at once restrictive and enabling. Eva positively crafts her aesthetic identity to respond to the challenge of show-ing competence in a culture where beauty/fashion consumption is mar-keted as the main key to women's social validation.[11] Or recall Cassandra's "natural beauty" regime from chapter 2. Cassandra is adamant about her belonging to a low-income bracket, and, similar to Eva, she draws a strong discursive contrast between her consumer choices and the rules of the more rarified "beauty world," which she dismisses entirely. For Cassandra, too, limited budget plays a major role: her choice to buy makeup at the dol-lar store is not just a personal preference. Nevertheless, she makes sense of the material restrictions to which she must adhere through the language of priority and choice—she frames her not supporting the beauty system "money-wise" more as a matter of personal conviction than as a fact of life.

These observations are particularly important when we consider that beauty and social status are connected, as we'll see in more detail in chapter 5. A beautiful, well-groomed person is perceived as having a higher social status than a plain-looking one.[12] Aware of this collective bias, Eva tries to look cool and classy with what she can afford, as does Cassandra, as we'll see later in this chapter. Audrey, however, does not even try. This is partly due, she says, to her being "lazy," but it also depends on her "low-income" status. At our first interview, she tells me that her last haircut was eighteen months ago. She has no skin-care routine, although she believes that her sensitive skin would greatly benefit from specific protection. On the one hand, she is usually "too tired" to bother; on the other, due to her economic situation, she says that "spending money on something like a skin-care product is *not* an option, unless it's on sale, or at the dollar store."

Audrey is the only breadwinner in a family of three, and the big tax refund that they are entitled to receive due to her husband's disability will be a huge financial relief. She anticipates receiving this money shortly after our first conversation; she looks forward to some respite from the burden she normally carries, and maybe even allowing herself to spend a little extra on discretionary items. More specifically, Audrey looks forward to visiting a local branch of the cosmetic chain Sephora and putting herself in the hands of an expert there. She'd love to just say, "This is my situation [i.e., her skin problem]—can you help me out?" Audrey thinks that she would feel more self-confident with better-looking skin, that this would increase her sense of self-worth. (In this, she is not alone among the interviewees. Emma, for instance, buys the "cheapest" makeup but invests more in "natural" face lotions because of her sensitive skin—a choice that would seem to suggest the particular salience of this bodily feature in the current hierarchy of beauty and status.) But perhaps more than anything else, what Audrey aspires to is a sense of normalcy: the ability to partake in beautification, and in the consumption that it demands, like so many other women. The fact that she can't afford a visit to the cosmetics store fosters in her a sense of inadequacy. When she describes her relationship to beauty, she repeatedly characterizes herself as an outlier. Also, access to professional beauty advice or services involves the promise of an experience of pampering and of being taken care of that, thanks to at least a century of advertising, is perceived as a form of therapy for the female soul.[13] Investments in beautification and the prospect of wellness (or even happiness) are deeply, solidly entwined. (I'll return to this in the following sections.)

If money is a crucial factor with which women must reckon when defining their beautification needs, this is no less true of time. Simply put, one's time investment has to make sense.

For Zoe, who doesn't have much spare time to spend on makeup and hair, this is only on special occasions. And here there is a performative element at play, since often one of the things that makes an occasion "special" is the very beautification work that she decides to put in beforehand. A pleasurable energy builds up while she anticipates a situation and the appropriate matching look. After working full-time all week, Zoe makes time on weekends (a couple of hours in the afternoon, right before going out) to create an appearance that, while it would be unthinkable during her busy workweek, reflects how she would really like to look if she had the time and energy. This is why Zoe takes a selfie of her rare and ephemeral accomplishment: that ideal yet extraordinary look will serve her well on a digital curriculum vitae or on social media. It is through such selfies that she is able to give her ideal aesthetic self-material form. They are to Zoe a reminder of how she can look, and they give her a pleasurable feeling of competence. Such pleasure, however, is not enough to motivate Zoe to fit a lengthy makeup and hairstyle routine into her daily schedule, which is usually confined to a little moisturizer and a touch of mascara; better, she feels, to invest the time in making a second coffee or handling some other practical need.

Like money, available time is also unequally distributed across social groups and life stages. When she describes the reasons why taking selfies for my study was a challenge (more on this in chapter 6), Lena explains that some of the situations that I asked the participants to simulate or immortalize simply do not occur anymore in her life—at least, not in the way they once did in the past. The best example, to her, is getting ready for an evening out. Now that she is married and has two daughters, the time Lena might have spent going out has been sacrificed to other priorities. A decade ago, before she became a mother, Lena would spend an hour putting makeup on, trying on "three outfits," fixing her hair, maybe having a drink with friends before going out. Now, preparation involves all but beautification: "Life has changed, you know, and now with kids it's like, 'Okay, we want to go out, the babysitter is here, does the babysitter have food? Does the babysitter know where the diapers are? Okay, no, we have to go, let me just . . .' Whatever, you know. [. . .] The process is just so different. Not in a bad way, but it's just so different."

For a working mother of two children under ten, even an affluent one, time is a scarce resource, and beautification cannot be a priority when other responsibilities must take pride of place. Despite the marketing rhetoric of efficacy and velocity, in contemporary Western beauty culture, beautification routines, treatments, and know-how become increasingly elaborate and specific, and hence time-consuming. Exclusion from competent consumption and self-care certainly occurs for economic reasons, as we've seen, but one's amount of available personal time—which is statistically lower for women, and especially for women with children[14]—also plays a critical role.

THE SALIENCE OF HAIR AND MAKEUP

In trying to understand which body parts or beautification practices receive the highest investments of personal resources, I was confronted with a set of statements from my interviewees that I found at once predictable and completely surprising. I had expected, after all, to hear that makeup takes up a lot of women's mental space and personal time; this is completely consistent with the history explored in chapter 2, where we learned of makeup's centuries-old status as a sort of synonym for beautification. But I was surprised by the special emphasis that most of the interviewees placed on hair: not only did they claim that it requires the most thought and time, but for them, "good hair" is itself a synonym for "good looks."

When I ask Melissa, for example, what makes for a good selfie, she replies without hesitation: "My hair." To her, a "good hair day" is a day on which she can feel beautiful. When she wants to hide part of her face in a selfie—you'll recall that Melissa is highly conscious of any signs of aging or fatigue—she'll retreat behind her lush, curly hair. For Melissa, it is her hair that really defines her "beauty identity"; it is the "go-to thing" that, once in place, will help everything else to make sense. Her hair, however, is not "easy"—it can be rather capricious, in fact, depending on a myriad of variables (the humidity in the air, whether or not it's been freshly washed, the amount—and type—of product she has applied, etc.). If hair can make a woman's day, then, it can also ruin it. This is a recurring theme among the participants. Indeed, when they talk about their hair, they sound almost as though they're referring to some mercurial long-term companion whose unpredictable moods they can't change but can only endure. As Melissa puts it with a laugh, it all depends on "whatever nature has in store for me that day." Listening to her, though, I can't help but think the influence travels in the other direction too. In order to maintain harmony, Melissa and her hair have reliable rituals: using a comb, applying a softening product, and avoiding the hair dryer. Should her hair still refuse to cooperate, she must sometimes turn to more drastic means, such as the flat iron. Despite this challenging cohabitation, Melissa would not opt for an alternative arrangement involving less maintenance. When I note that, having short hair since the age of fifteen, I know nothing about brushing and blow-drying, Melissa replies,

> You want to know a secret? If I had no hair or short hair, I don't know what I would do because it's such a part of me, it's always been a part of me to have bigger hair or that sort of statement thing. My look has been my hair.

Clearly, hair is a crucial component of Melissa's embodied identity.

The same can be said about Fanny, who since childhood has always been complimented on her hair, and who has therefore always kept it long. Fanny says that she is like "a lion": the "bigger" her hair, the "sexier" she feels. Wearing a "big" head of long hair makes her feel different from other people, truly special—herself. When she is busy "doing stuff" (such as working and taking care of her young children) and has little time, she puts her hair in a bun, thus diminishing its volume and, consequently, its visibility. On days when she does "stuff that's a bit nicer," she takes the time to blow-dry her hair or do something "different" with it.

For Emma, bleaching her hair is extremely important: she wants it "almost white," and she also places a special emphasis on its softness and beauty, which for her requires additional work and products (masks, natural recipes, etc.), in conjunction with regular dyeing. She draws a stark contrast between her attention to her hair, including the pleasure that she takes in caring for it, and the "almost nothing" she does for her skin. For Emma, her hair's significance is enhanced by her occasional work as a model for hairdressers. Increasing the visibility of one's work on social media is usually part of the hairdresser's gig, hence it has become customary for Emma to shoot selfies showcasing her hair. It is nevertheless clear that Emma happily gives hair a special place both in self-care and selfie-taking for its own sake, regardless of the financial rewards this work brings her.

Juliette, for her part, says that she is "obsessed" with her hair. While trying to save money on most other forms of self-care, she buys expensive shampoos and goes to the hairdresser's as often as possible (less often now than in the past, however, when her monthly budget was higher). The obsession comes from her perception of her hair as a "problem," from her permanent discontent with it. Hence, going to the hairdresser or caring for her hair makes her feel "good." This feeling is particularly apparent during our first interview, when Juliette describes some of the issues she has had with her bodily appearance: a health problem caused her to slow down her exercise routine, which resulted in weight gain that is particularly distressing for someone who had always been skinny—and who had grown accustomed to being complimented on her slenderness. Juliette believes that this added weight has had profound effects on her sense of herself as a beautiful woman, something she hopes to rectify by ensuring that she has manicured hands and beautiful hair.

As we will see in more detail in chapter 6, Cassandra is passionate about staging selfie-shooting sessions; these allow her an opportunity to experiment broadly with her looks, to go from sexy to casual, from stereotypically feminine to "natural" and authentic. While she uses a variety of clothing items and accessories to assemble her visual palette, a carefully planned hairstyle plays a major part in her effort to obtain different aesthetic impressions. Indeed, while discussing with me some of her selfies, Cassandra draws a stark contrast between the well-coifed, chiseled identity that she projects when her hair is done up, and what she considers the more authentic self-presentation that she achieves when she wears "natural" hair. More specifically, for a long time Cassandra enjoyed buying and wearing wigs, which allowed her to explore the many possibilities of aesthetic self-expression, almost to play a variety of characters, both in her selfies and her daily life: she is so attached to every single item in her collection of wigs, which she usually acquires while traveling, that she can "always tell how old the pictures are by the wig." While looking at images in which she wears her hair loose—"natural," as she would say—Cassandra refers instead to ideas of authenticity, openness, self-disclosure, freedom from artifice and from (playful) make-believe. She also reflects on how, as she grows older, she has also grown fonder of her natural hair, which is now longer and "bigger" than it used to be.

In addition to being a key factor in women's sense of personal identity and impression management, Black women's hair is by no means neutral with regard to questions of power, marginalization, and anti-Black racism—all of which are particularly salient in North America. As Cheryl Thompson smartly puts it, "after centuries of condemnation, Black hair is inextricably laden with social, class, sexual, and cultural implications."[15] Indeed, as Kristin Denise Rowe writes, "the stakes of having their hair 'done' in a 'proper' way" are extremely high for Black women, as they are still likely to be severely penalized for wearing their hair "undone" (natural) in the public sphere, notably at school and at work.[16] Traditionally, "doing" one's hair often entails, for Black women, the use of chemicals, extensions, head coverings, and wigs, which serve the purpose of hiding, dissimulating, or "taming" the natural texture and volume of Black hair, to the point where the use of artifice to style one's hair might be seen, Thompson argues, as tantamount to performing a respectable heterosexual femininity for Black women.[17] This is why, as Rowe explains, in contemporary filmic productions featuring Black women the gesture of removing one's wig mainly symbolizes a self-revealing act of intimacy, the disclosure of a more authentic self, or a "shift in [the character's] self-concept."[18] These observations resonate deeply with Cassandra's experience, specifically with regard to the role that the opposition between natural and artificial, or authenticity and artifice, plays in her perception of her identity and her appearance in selfies. They might also explain why she feels confident wearing a more natural hairstyle now that she is in her fifties and enjoys a greater sense of personal stability.

Hair, and especially long hair, is one of the principal symbols of femininity and sex appeal.[19] Such imagery figures explicitly in Audrey's reflections on why she has never cut her hair short. Looking at my rather short haircut (what Melissa, in a separate conversation, calls my "pixie cut"), Audrey hastens to add that short hair is gorgeous—nothing wrong with it at all, it just isn't for her. When I ask why, she hesitates a little before answering that long hair is perhaps her way of "balancing out [her] femininity." Starting with her job in a male-dominated field, Audrey is "involved in so many conventionally masculine things," and her hair helps her to "retain some of that femininity" that she feels she has otherwise ceded in her day-to-day life.[20]

Having considered herself an attractive person in the past, Audrey is very acquainted with the "pressure" good-looking women feel to cultivate their attractiveness as an asset—especially in the mating game. For this reason, she admires younger women who reject a conventionally feminine identity through the obliteration of its most conspicuous signs; she looks approvingly, for instance, at those young women she sees with shaved heads, wearing "overalls all the time," deciding that "they don't want to have children" or "get married." This sort of individual and collective self-distancing from traditionally feminine roles and presentations through aesthetic work has a long history, and it is still relevant in a postfeminist culture where "girl power" is increasingly associated with hyper-femininity.[21] Audrey knows that, by abandoning the visible signs of femininity, such as hair, young women are doing their best to juggle the paradoxes of beauty culture. They dismiss a form of "female" power that comes with (and from) compliance with a restrained, stereotypical pattern of self-presentation and identity definition (to which I'll return in chapter 5). At the same time, they expose themselves, as many have in the past, to the social stigma that attaches to what Margaret Attwood memorably described as the figure of the "unwoman."[22] As psychologist Rita Freedman writes, "what's *on* a woman's head may be judged as critically as what's *in* it."[23] This is especially true in the case of visible minorities, as I have discussed earlier.

In the time between our first and second interviews, Jeanne went on to embrace a less conventional feminine appearance. Like Audrey, Jeanne always had long hair and lacked the courage to cut it short, despite her interest in doing so; "a girl must have long hair," the world told her from childhood on. When she was a little girl, she looked up to her father and admired his shaved head, wishing to emulate it. Shortly before our second interview, she finally decided to go for it, telling herself, "I can do what I want." This realization came at the end of a long period of questioning the ideals and stereotypes of femininity with which she grew up. An unsuccessful audition for an artistic performance triggered the change: upon receiving the rejection, Jeanne gave herself permission to once and for all stop pretending to be who she is not. She shaved half of her hair and dyed the rest pink, proudly showcasing her new look in several subsequent selfies (some of which she sent me as part of her "homework" for this project). To Jeanne, refusing a conventional hairstyle meant embracing a freer self-expression, beyond the more traditional boundaries set by a professional environment that was rejecting her and those she carried from her upbringing.

Not every woman I interviewed maintains a comprehensive lifestyle regime (sleep, food, exercise, skin care, etc.) aimed at preserving or enhancing beauty. But makeup nevertheless plays a role in every participant's life. More than just a specific beautification routine, for most interviewees, makeup is a necessary part of the daily process of getting ready and out the door. Even if it is just a touch of mascara, it must be done. Fanny does not care for exercise and has inconsistent eating habits, but she rarely leaves the house without makeup. The basics are foundation (to conceal a "reddish" complexion, she says) and mascara; some days, if she's feeling a little daring, she might try something more conspicuous. Similarly, most interviewees occasionally carry out a more elaborate makeup routine for parties, work-related events, or special days. As we saw in the previous section, where we noted the performative aspect of Zoe's decision to devote time to the work of beautification, a fully made-up appearance can itself be a sign of an event's extraordinary character. More generally, however, the choice to go beyond one's quotidian routine and to do something "more" can also be an attempt to boost one's mood, to feel special, and to look different from one's routine self-presentation. For example, Lena says that "lipstick always makes [her] feel better" on those occasions when she's having a hard time feeling beautiful: she says it helps her feel "more awake" to the people and circumstances around her. Other participants have a similar relationship to makeup, and lipstick in particular.

Makeup's mood-boosting, quasi-therapeutic function has been constructed by way of a long tradition of advertising promoting beauty and self-care products as a remedy for a woman's problems, big and small (I'll return to this in the next section too). The impact of this discourse is visible in women's consumer behaviors. It has been observed, for example, that women's beauty spending tends to be unaffected by, and even to increase during, times of economic hardship and social crisis—a seemingly counterintuitive phenomenon, observed since the 1930s, that has entered economic jargon by way of the term "the lipstick effect."[24] In a widely cited article, psychologist Sarah Hill and her colleagues explain the "lipstick effect" as the result of our natural imperative to mate: in times of economic recession, a woman's investment in beautification aims at increasing her attractiveness in order to secure a mate with more resources, and thus a degree of prospective economic stability.[25]

Hill et al.'s theory has only been tested with a sample of young (eighteen- to twenty-four-year-old) unmarried women, and it can hardly be generalized beyond this demographic. So it would seem that the mating strategies theory leaves us without a comprehensive explanation for why married women with children, such as Lena, turn to beautification in times of distress. Interestingly, data on consumer spending during the COVID-19 pandemic seem to give us further reason to question Hill et al.'s interpretation. During the first six months of the pandemic (March to August 2020), makeup sales took a big hit in the United States, whereas spending on skin-care products and even at-home spa equipment shot up significantly. This observation led some experts and journalists to question the "lipstick effect" and its translation into an economic index by which we might assess consumer confidence in times of economic hardship.[26] Notwithstanding the reduced social contact, generalized lockdowns, and mandatory face coverings that have characterized pandemic life in many if not most locales, beautification is still high on people's list of priorities. It's just that home-based self-care and other "therapeutic" products have been foregrounded, and makeup sidelined.[27]

And then there is the issue of skill: engaging with any of this requires a certain amount of technical competence. And yet many participants lament what they see as their inability to go beyond the basics and their desire to master a body of knowledge whose increasing complexity seems to belie the claims of advertisers that beauty is within everyone's reach.

Back in the 1990s, while I was navigating my teenage years without the Internet or social media, I would faithfully buy weekly installments of a self-help publication called *New You*, which featured hairstyling and makeup tutorials along with dieting and micro-targeted exercise routines (the "sculpt your calves!" kind of routines that claim to allow you to perfect particular areas of the body). Notwithstanding goodwill, ambition, and a serious desire for self-improvement, I never learned a single makeup technique—indeed, I remain almost clueless to this day. Clarisse relates a similar experience and says that a lack of know-how is the reason why her makeup is always simple; despite years of trying old and new things, even the most basic use of eyeliner remains out of her grasp. Audrey too: she is fascinated by an art that she believes she is unable to master. She loves makeup and tries experimenting with it, but she "always feel[s] clumsy about it."

The impulse to give it yet another try comes from the omnipresence on social media of peer and expert advice on beautification through cosmetics. Audrey, for her part, follows some makeup artists on Instagram, and their work gives her a genuine experience of aesthetic pleasure. Unable to emulate the results, though, and feeling her sense of herself as a competent woman capable of practicing these more technical feminine skills undermined, she responds with humor. Before our first interview, she took a picture with a construction face mask, which leaves only her forehead and eyes visible, and gave it an ironic caption to the effect that she was getting "the hang" of makeup. Through humor, Audrey tries to bypass the gatekeeping function of social media and its perpetuation of the notion of conventional beauty as the surest sign of one's legitimate involvement in feminine identity production.

COMMITTING TO THINKING, PLANNING, AND JUDGING

From the time I was very young until the age of fifteen, my hair was quite long and required daily care. I had neither the patience nor the organizational skills to carry out such a duty (a lacuna I resolved only later by adopting a minimalist, low-maintenance hairstyle). Brushing my hair after a day of playing outdoors, swimming in the Mediterranean Sea, and tending the chickens with my grandfather could result in an excruciating challenge. On such nights, or while waiting with disgust for the occasional egg yolk and rum hair mask to soak in, my grandmother would repeat the well-known Italian proverb "she who wants to be beautiful must endure some pain" (also known in its English shorthand as "beauty requires sacrifice"). Beauty, as we've seen, has long been framed as—and severely criticized by feminist voices for—entailing the suffering, sacrifice, and oppression of women.[28]

In recent decades, however, the rhetoric of cosmetic advertising has moved toward discursive patterns that could not be more distant from these ideas of pain and misery. Women's necessary involvement in beauty culture is generally recast in the language of commitment and individual entrepreneurship, anchored in a more broadly encompassing definition of neoliberal subjectivity. In this view, according to sociologist Christina Scharff, the self is regarded as a business, and its owner must productively manage time as a scarce resource, maintain a "positive attitude," hide her vulnerability, and constantly pursue self-improvement.[29] Beauty is the reward promised to the woman who commits herself to self-care and self-entrepreneurship, wisely managing her resources to maximize her investments and get the "best" results. Commitment, sure, but there is no talk of sacrifice here; rather, the beautifying self-surveillance, which penetrates every sphere of life (food, sleep, work, shopping, exercise, sexuality, etc.), is formulated as pleasure, as self-pampering, as "fun."[30]

As we saw with the authenticity paradox, the commitment to beautification and self-improvement, the promised results of which are premised on the micromanagement of one's actions and desires, is clearly at odds with the idea of the primacy of natural beauty. But it is the commitment paradox that more deeply informs the doubts, hesitations, and reasoning of the women I interviewed when it comes to negotiating the extent of their involvement in beautification as a form of self-fulfillment. They know that the amount of planning, buying, consuming, and assessing demanded of women is virtually endless, and is continuously brought to bear on new flaws, problems, and failures of the female body. They process information on beautification techniques and trends and integrate this into their daily lives by continuously reassessing the criteria by which they determine whether, when, and how often they need to invest time, money, and energy, and on what (a given treatment, a specific body part). They resent the seeming unavoidability of such commitment, at all stages of life, and they perceive that the injunction to police themselves has increased through mass participation in the production and consumption of visual culture on social media—especially with regard to selfies.

Two factors appear to play a particularly salient role in women's individual negotiation of their commitments to beauty: the increasing specificity and bespoke character of beauty marketing, on the one hand, and what psychologist Sarah Riley and colleagues call the "post-feminist female gaze" and media scholar Alison Winch calls the "gynaeopticon,"[31] on the other.

The diversification of cosmetic products, services, and techniques began a long time ago, while marketing discourse simultaneously began urging every woman to maintain an appearance appropriate to her age, social class, ethnic background, body size, and features, and to police her participation in beauty consumption accordingly. The goal of diversified individual commitment, however, has mostly been defined by a hierarchy of looks, at the top of which sits white, young, thin, upper-class, heterosexual beauty: most cosmetic treatments aim at normalizing "deviant" appearances—their supposed deviance being measured against this dominant (which is to say white) standard. Since the early 1900s, for instance, makers and sellers of cosmetics targeted Black women with specific products tailored to darker skin and curly hair. But notwithstanding the goodwill of entrepreneurs like Madam C. J. Walker and Annie Turnbo Malone, who refused to envisage Black beautification as a narrow effort to reduce anomaly (through such practices as skin bleaching or hair straightening), the early Black beauty market mostly capitalized on the desire of members of the Black community to avoid social stigma for their appearance, and thus fostered overtly racist social expectations.[32] To this day, in a multicultural urban agglomeration like Montreal, members of the Black community continue to lament the lack of services and products aimed specifically at celebrating their natural features.[33]

Diversification and specificity, then, do not necessarily lead to a general increase in free individual expression (as certain advertisers and beauty experts claim); what does increase, however, is the number of variables that every woman must take into account while estimating her assets and her flaws with the goal of "normalizing" her appearance. This is clear when Juliette tells me about the "facial" that she had just days before our second interview. She claims that her skin "needed it" after her six-month internship in a very polluted European city: the dirt had completely clogged her pores and she wanted the aesthetician to "suck it out" of her skin.

Indeed, as we saw in the previous chapters, beauty advice encourages women to envisage modern life (pollution, technology, UV rays, etc.) as a series of ongoing threats to beauty, especially to the health of our skin. To counter these generalized risks, women must opt for specific treatments, organize their daily routines ("You're not telling me you leave the house without sunscreen?!" I was recently told by the apparently scandalized skin-care expert at my local pharmacy), and stock up on dedicated products to "protect" their beauty from such perils. Advanced beauty treatments are certainly increasingly accessible across social classes (due to the variety of offerings and more affordable pricing), but they are also *recommended* to an increasingly larger public as necessary self-maintenance.[34] Aging is framed in a similar way: unavoidable decay could be slowed down through careful planning and spending, and by consistent discipline. The same reasoning applies to acne, puffy eyelids, unruly hair, excessively thin eyebrows, uneven complexion, sensitive skin, dry skin, perspiration, facial hair—you name it.

When she went for her facial, Juliette also had a specific lotion recommended to her by her aesthetician, who claimed that it would work to "get rid" of the little wrinkles around her eyes; she bought it right away and continues to use it regularly. Juliette also tells me that she should stop smoking in order to improve the appearance of her skin, and that she tries to drink a lot of water, which, she learned, is also good for one's skin and hair. As is generally the case, Juliette's commitment to maintaining a beautiful appearance depends on her being sufficiently knowledgeable about the specific challenges she faces, the identification of which depends, in turn, on her regularly scrutinizing her body for signs of "problems": Do I live in a polluted environment? Are my pores clogged? Is my complexion uneven? Am I neglecting my little wrinkles? Am I at risk of the infamous "tech neck"?

If women feel the pressure to maintain the right engagement with beautification, they are also sensitive to the promise of salvation contained within beauty culture. In old and new fairy tales, the myth of beauty as a life-changing force is subject to endless variation, whereas a lack of beauty is normally understood to entail social rejection. In Western postfeminist culture, beauty is a synonym for social success. The women I interviewed, for all their intelligence and self-awareness, and their evident ability to criticize the more clearly aspirational aspects of beauty culture, are nonetheless sensitive to the idea of beautification as self-improvement, as an endeavor that will bring them rewards in the form of better mental health and more satisfying social lives. After all, the tendency to change oneself in order to solve one's problems is a central feature of neoliberal subjectivity.[35]

Along with being part of an overall self-improvement strategy, thinking and planning is also situational, and aims at modulating one's investment of time and effort while preparing the right appearance for the different contexts and occasions that occur in the course of one's day (I will get back to this in the next chapter). Cassandra, for example, explains that putting together the "right look" means envisaging a situation, imagining the version of herself she wants to showcase therein (Does she want to stand out? To blend in?), and then putting together the right look to embody that persona. The work consists in choosing and applying makeup (often accompanied by fake lashes), matching hairstyle, clothing, and accessories such as earrings, hat, gloves, and scarf. When she browses her well-equipped wardrobe for the right combination of accessories, Cassandra says she is "like Barbie with all her shit." An appreciation of context, however, also depends on a sense of one's sociocultural environment and of the standards of appropriateness recognized therein. Cassandra likes dressing formally: it allows her to stand out in an urban context—in her case, Montreal—where, compared to her smaller hometown, "everybody is at a higher level of fashion." But here again, we see that a certain type of empirical knowledge is key to the realization of an appropriate standard of beauty. For Cassandra, the goal of appearing sufficiently beautiful requires observing and assessing other women, measuring her look against theirs, and accepting the reciprocal nature of this exchange—that in doing so, she will be exposed to their gaze and their judgment. This is the second factor in the negotiation of one's commitment, what Riley and colleagues call the "post-feminist female gaze" and Winch calls the "gynaeopticon."

With this term, Riley and colleagues indicate the centrality of women's looking practices in the creation of postfeminist subjectivity. The self-regulation required to aptly perform a gendered identity hinges not only on the "male gaze,"[36] or the dominant, objectifying masculine perspective that dominates in media production and becomes integrated into the way women perceive and visually shape themselves. Rather, according to sociologist Rosalind Gill, in a contemporary postfeminist sensibility, we can observe a discursive trend emphasizing women's ability to render themselves subjects through individual choice and mutual empowerment.[37] Once oriented by feminist movements toward social change and political resistance, the ideas of individual choice and mutual empowerment assume a vernacular position in postfeminist culture: both are depoliticized and progressively turned into forms of self-surveillance attuned mainly, if not exactly exclusively, to appearance and aesthetic self-possession, as I mentioned in the Introduction.

At the heart of this self-surveillance lies a broader dispositive (in Foucault's sense)—namely, the female gaze. Indeed, women's habit of looking at each other, and of seeing themselves through one another's eyes, plays a crucial role in reinforcing the rules and standards of self-regulation. Notwithstanding the emphasis on girl power, mutual validation, and female intimacy (I will get back to this later), such looking is only superficially benign. According to the women interviewed by Riley and colleagues, "looking between women" is essentially "judgemental, comparative, and pervasive."[38] In this sense, I argue that the "female gaze" helps to structure the reasoning and emotions underlying women's engagement in beautification; the modes and degree of their individual commitment are shaped by looking at other women, comparing themselves to them, listening to their advice, pondering their experiences, and assessing their results.

Likewise, Winch has shown that the pervasiveness of women's mutual surveillance in contemporary postfeminist discourse is intertwined with an emphasis on female friendship and intimacy. Looking at and scrutinizing one another's appearance seems to be so central in networks of female friendship that Winch suggests the metaphor of the "gynaeopticon" to describe them.[39] The term is of course inspired by Michel Foucault's account of Jeremy Bentham's famous "panopticon,"[40] a prison in which inmates would be subjected to uninterrupted, centralized surveillance. The idea of such a device, according to Foucault, symbolically marks the emergence of a disciplinary society, in which control, previously exterior and punitive, is displaced onto the subject himself, where it becomes embodied and takes the form of self-surveillance. For Winch, the notion of a "gynaeopticon" stands for the omnipresence, pervasiveness, and disciplinary effect of the female gaze as rooted in networks of intimacy and friendship. Women are always visible to other women, and their appearance is the main locus of the disciplinary, comparative, and assessing gazes that they are socialized to exchange.

Winch's description resonates with the accounts of the women I interviewed. Unsurprisingly, girlfriends are the number one source of beauty advice for these women: they provide tips on how to do things, what to buy, and where to go for the best, or the cheapest, service. The latter consideration is especially important for the low-income members of the group, for whom peer advice also serves the purpose of maximizing one's otherwise narrow financial investment in beautification. This can take the form of "do-it-yourself" beauty treatments (for instance, Jeanne and her friends dye each other's hair at home) or keeping each other apprised of deals for a given service or product. For the more affluent ones, peer networks provide a forum for mutual encouragement when it comes to trying new things, shopping together, or getting each other's advice on what to buy. Zoe shops for makeup with a friend who has a similar complexion, and who therefore entirely emulates Zoe's choices, knowing that they will be right for her too. Aware of Clarisse's interest and expertise in shopping for clothes, some of her friends seek her advice before investing their money: they text her selfies with different outfits directly from the store and ask her for guidance. Clarisse herself does the same with one of her best friends, who lives in a different town. At the heart of all these exchanges is visibility and the practice of looking, both of which are crucially important for aesthetic self-regulation, and hence strongly influence decision-making, self-assessment, and engagement in beauty culture.[41]

Consumption—of beautification products and treatments, among other things—is itself a highly visible practice that generates mutual admiration, emulation, and bonding among women. Because it is a mechanism for reinforcing a sense of belonging through aesthetic validation, however, the female gaze also works as an exclusionary device for those who cannot participate in the consumption required for an appropriate display of their commitment to beauty culture. Think of Audrey's love of makeup and her recurring sense of incompetence: looking at other women's skillful use of cosmetics can produce in her a feeling of inadequacy, along with a frustrated desire to belong. Clarisse, who is so afflicted by her unruly hair that she likens her attempts to style it to "a battle," looks for inspiration online and always imagines that she, too, could be "super beautiful." The results, however, are "always" disappointing, as what she sees in the mirror never corresponds to what she sees online. Remarkably, Clarisse even submits several post-hairdresser selfies to close examination after each visit—the results of which invariably fail to meet her expectations—in an effort to understand what went right and what went wrong. Together with self-surveillance apps,[42] then, selfies, too, serve to reproduce a culture of self-discipline in which attractiveness is seen as the key measure of a woman's competence and worth.

As a matter of fact, social media is overtly marketed as a source of "friendly" peer advice, which, as Winch observes, also renders it a locus of peer surveillance.[43] While scrolling through one's feed, one sees styles and looks that one desires to imitate—like Audrey with the makeup artists she follows and whose work she admires. Fanny follows a local beauty parlor specializing in brows and lashes, and she consults their Instagram profile for inspiration on what to try out or buy. But she also carefully inspects friends' selfies in order to get a sense of the makeup they use or to ask what they are wearing and where to find it. An important element in Jeanne's decision to shave her hair and dye it flamboyant colors was the social media accounts of celebrities she follows with similar looks. All the women whom I interviewed reported scrutinizing other women's physical appearance in detail, and either imitating or rejecting them, whole or in part, accordingly. And all placed special emphasis on their own and other women's selfies as a fundamental component of this engagement. As I will discuss in further detail in chapter 6, and as feminist scholar Mardi Schmeichel and her colleagues note, selfies function as a form of visual pedagogy for women in their quest for aesthetic self-improvement and validation as competent feminine subjects.[44]

Interestingly, the female gaze also played a role in the relationship between researcher and participants, as I was myself the object of the interviewees' scrutiny while conversing with them. During several interviews, especially with women of my age group, I felt that my appearance was clearly being judged, if only superficially. And the numerous comments I received on my hair, skin, signs of aging or lack thereof, makeup or lack thereof, clothing style, body size, and level of fitness are proof of the discriminating character of the gaze that participants directed at my body while talking to me about theirs.

Even more fascinating, as far as I was concerned, was the fact that the power of the female gaze had a tangible impact on my self-perception, notwithstanding my efforts to keep my own aesthetic concerns as an embodied female person out of the research setting. This attempt, which in retrospect appears rather naive from a methodological perspective, backfired when I realized that being looked at, assessed, and given recommendations triggered in me a degree of self-questioning, curiosity, and a reconsideration of my level of commitment to beautification. After Fanny mentioned the beauty parlor specializing in eyebrows, I inspected mine for shape and cleanliness, and I resolved to visit an aesthetician more often to get them done. The same thing happened when she talked about softening hairsprays—I promptly went to the pharmacy and acquired a bottle of my own. Looking at the selfies in which Eva sports a bold red lipstick, I fancied wearing a similar shade myself. When I finally did, I happened to cross paths with Juliette, and she complimented me profusely on it. When Audrey and Melissa compared their long hair with my "pixie cut," I couldn't help feeling like an outlier and reconsidering my decision to renounce long hair. When Cassandra asked whether I was wearing makeup and observed that my skin was "perfect" without it, I felt proud, as if she was confirming that I belonged to the right team. However, after that conversation, I also came to see my complexion as possibly one of my assets, and so resolved to follow more consistently a daily three-step skin-care routine. This sense of validation, mixed with an awareness of the need for continuous work, was even stronger when Lena, who is a fitness lover, said that she considered me to be someone who is in good shape. Even in a research setting, and notwithstanding my theoretical knowledge of the paradoxes of beauty culture, the female gaze altered my self-image, spurred in me a desire to adopt what I perceived as a more competent performance of femininity, and reshaped my material and affective involvement in beauty culture.

THE DAY AS A MEASURE OF BEAUTY

If resources must be managed over the long run—for instance, by preserving a youthful look and preventing the effects of aging (more on this in the next chapter)—the participants often describe an additional aspect of beauty's temporal segmentation, here measured in terms of "the day."

It is a dimension of beauty's inscription in time that often goes undiscussed in the literature, but beautification is a daily affair, for at least three reasons. First, the work of beautification starts over each morning, when skin must be moisturized, makeup applied, hair tamed, outfit chosen, and accessories matched. As such—and here is the second reason—daily beautification also depends on the specific, social temporality of the day—in other words, on one's schedule and plans for the day ahead. Accordingly, our attempts at beautification are guided each day by our anticipation of the particular activities, events, and planned or unplanned encounters that will occur within the space of the day. Appropriate appearance, adequate degree, and "style" of attractiveness (sexier, more elegant, etc.) must be calibrated to the *specificities* of each day. Third, each new day sees us grapple with an emotionally inflected self-perception that affects (positively or negatively) our ability to feel beautiful, as we've seen throughout this chapter. We wake up with bad hair, or after a restless sleep, something is worrying us, we are under particular stress, we feel tired, we are acutely mindful of the bags under our eyes—all of this can influence our self-perception and our outlook on the day. As a consequence, our daily, even hourly, changes in mood can shift the criteria by which we judge whether or not our appearance is "acceptable." In this way, the day becomes the measure of beauty in three respects: as the materiality of the beautifying gestures of a daily routine; as the schedule or plan that structures one's aesthetic and affective anticipation of the coming hours; and as the main emotional nuance affecting one's aesthetic self-perception.

According to the interviewees, one's morning mood and self-perception can play a key role in determining whether one embarks on the day with either a positive or a negative outlook. All of the women cite fatigue, anxiety, poor sleep, or rough patches in their relationships or inner lives as possible reasons for why they could start their day on the wrong foot. But a day can also be "bad" for no apparent reason: one can simply feel unattractive, even if the reasons are opaque. For instance, humidity in the air can result in an intractable head of hair, which, if unresolved, can affect one's conscious self-perception for the rest of the day. Eva even speaks of entire "weeks" during which her self-criticism spikes, making it impossible for her to feel attractive. As a consequence, a negative self-perception might trigger a modification of one's beautifying routine in the morning: since all the routine challenges of the day are dramatized by a basic sense of inadequacy, having the right appearance can seem especially important.

Perceiving one's appearance as appropriate, participants say, can help overcome the vulnerability that one experiences in the course of a "bad" day. The lower Clarisse's morale, for instance, the bigger the effort she invests in looking more put together. However, some interviewees reported that on some days, nothing can make them feel better and that they've learned to just let go and meet their commitments without fixating too much on their appearance. When possible, some of them will simply avoid going out altogether. When that isn't an option, they try their best not to draw too much attention to themselves. Fanny, for example, explains that on such occasions, she just tries *not* to be noticed:

> I think it depends a lot on [. . .] what my day is gonna be like. If [it's . . .] this grind of, like, making lunches, dropping [the kids] off, driving there, picking [them] up, doing groceries [. . .] then probably I first of all won't put that much effort into how I look, which is then going to reflect how I feel going about my day, you know. Sometimes I'll drop off my kids in the morning, and literally I don't want anyone to see me—I'm like, "Don't look at me," 'cause, like, I haven't even washed my face, I'm wearing my glasses [. . .] you know, yoga pants and a sweatshirt with no bra, I'm running in, like, "Bye!" and running out. Obviously, on that type of day I'm not gonna be like, "I feel beautiful." [. . .] No!

Hence, a busy day can impact the daily routine by which one might arrive at an "appropriate" appearance through negative self-perception. The results can sometime set in motion a sort of vicious cycle as one's negative self-perception can in turn induce a withdrawal from commitments, especially from the exposure to the omnipresence of other people's gaze (as discussed in the previous section).

For Emma, the daily ritual of applying makeup is a response to the basic expectation of being seen: for her, being watched, scrutinized, and judged is simply part of being a woman. Makeup is her way of negotiating that exposure—it makes her feel ready for whatever the day has in store for her. Hence, Emma's makeup routine affords her a level of protection inasmuch as it prepares her to meet her commitments. Lipstick, you might recall, makes Lena feel better on days when she does not feel beautiful. Or consider the anecdote with which I opened the introduction, the one about my French colleague at the Bibliothèque Nationale: feeling attractive and therefore prepared to be observed by others bestowed on her an invigorating sense of competence, of belonging, of poise.

An anticipation of one's daily activities and commitments also influences one's planning. When the participants have to face a specific "test"—a professional challenge, say, or a special social event—they put additional effort into creating an appropriate "presence." This extra care thus manifests their commitment to adequately responding to the social gaze: it is a ritual that proves—to themselves as much as to those around them—that they take the social test seriously.

A key aspect of anticipating one's day, as we've seen, is thinking about the encounters and interactions that will occur (or might occur) in the hours ahead, and thus about the identity that one intends to project within this framework. The daily negotiation of beauty, then, is not just a self-reflexive, interior process—it is fundamentally a social one. To be sure, it raises a series of highly subjective questions (How do I feel today? Do I have time for makeup? How is my hair?), but it also asks us to grapple with the normative injunctions, values, expectations, and cultural patterns embedded in our existence as social beings. Hence, the anticipatory relation to temporality (forecasting certain situations and the expectations to be found therein) is always contextual, specific, and material, inasmuch as it entails a more or less vague representation of how, where, and by whom one will be gazed upon.

CONCLUSION: HOW MUCH IS ENOUGH?

Women's participation in beauty culture is framed by paradoxical injunctions concerning the size and frequency of their investments in beautification. In chapter 1, I called this "the commitment paradox," which in part can be stated as follows: women are expected to do enough to be attractive on a daily basis, but it is unlikely that they will ever be allowed to feel that "enough" is truly enough. Advertising, expert recommendations, advice from peers, and involvement in the "female gaze" (to say nothing of its male counterpart) encourage women to believe that there is always more they can do and that they can do it better.

But the same discursive framing of women's beautification practices also demands that they refrain from doing "too much," which would expose them to the charge of superficiality, of only being interested in appearances. Women are thus expected not only to invest their time, energy, and money in beautification; they must also determine how much, how often, and on what they should invest these finite resources. Showing the exterior signs of one's adequate and knowledgeable participation in beauty culture is regarded as a marker of competent femininity.

Sociologists Kate Cairns and Josée Johnston use the term "calibration" to describe women's efforts to adopt a set of consumer behaviors with regard to food that will be deemed "reasonable, informed, and moderate" by those around them. Calibration, they explain, refers not just to the effort to remain within some "middle ground" but also to the careful negotiation of a competent postfeminist femininity that eschews the "feminized pathologies" "characterized by irrationality and loss of control."[45] Similarly, my interviewees talk about the strategies they use to attain optimal investments in beautification, which implies a negotiation of what I've characterized as contradictory injunctions. If a woman should do neither too little nor too much to be beautiful, how much is *enough* for her to be considered competently attractive, feminine?

To begin with, finding the optimal investment involves determining the place that beauty should have in one's life and everyday activities. Depending on the answer to that question, each woman must then manage her outlay of time, money, and energy accordingly. Such resources are unequally distributed across social profiles, and determining the appropriate investment depends on such variables as one's socioeconomic status and age, or more specifically, one's individual life stage. One's personal political values also play a role in the decision-making process, as women may choose to reduce their compliance with mainstream femininity and reject the consumer pressures by which it is materialized. Finally, two aspects of beautification have particular salience for the interviewees. Like many women, hair plays a central role in their "beauty identity," but it also presents specific challenges due both to its symbolic value within mainstream definitions of femininity and its intrinsic unruliness; simply put, unlike some other physical traits, a woman's hair is often resistant to control. Makeup, on the other hand, while it also occupies a central place in female beautification practices, demands a set of skills and a level of financial commitment that are simply beyond the reach of many people.

Looking at, and being looked at by, other women is a crucial dispositive that pushes women to re-evaluate their investments in beautification with an eye to maximizing their returns. The "female gaze," as a kind of mutual surveillance, motivates women to do more and better, but at the same time it serves a gatekeeping role insofar as it enforces certain physical and stylistic standards. Hence, participating in beauty culture also requires an ability to judge the appearances of other women, and a corresponding willingness to be judged by other women. The female gaze is such a fundamental aspect of women-to-women interactions that it even came to influence the relationship between myself and the women whom I interviewed—inducing, for me, unexpected aesthetic self-criticism together with deeper methodological reflections. The central role of selfies in social media today not only increases this mutual surveillance but also provides additional tools that augment the traditional aesthetic self-surveillance that women are expected to perform.

The planning of, thinking about, and investing in beautification is directed toward the general, long-term goal of "preserving" beauty, as well as the more immediate objective of adopting an appropriate appearance for "the day." Interviewees clearly see this as a temporal measure of beauty; for them, beautification is a daily endeavor to be carried out in accordance with one's resources, commitments, and mood on that specific day. Routine beautifying gestures are ideally performed every day (at its beginning as well as its end), but specific thought must also be put into managing aesthetic self-presentation so that it results in an appearance that suits the particular social contexts one expects to encounter on a given day. Finally, our mood can fluctuate and change, and this can impact the way we see ourselves and determine the amount of work we believe is needed to fashion an appearance with which we can confidently meet the day.

Chapter 4

TIME, AGING, AND MOTHERHOOD

After hearing from the interviewees about how they see the day as a temporal measure of beauty, and having listened to them characterize their own personal commitments to self-improvement in terms of money and effort but above all time, I began to contemplate the inherent temporality of attractiveness. If an idealized beauty is timeless, unaffected by change, embodied beauty is by definition constantly changing; in time, it fades.

"Preserving" beauty from the decay caused by the inexorable march of biological time has for centuries been the main imperative of female beautification. Implicit in this process is the notion of youth as the epitome of beauty and bodily perfection. Time, on the other hand, has always been—and as we've seen, still is—considered beauty's archenemy. Contemporary beauty culture reinforces these ideas and translates them into a pervasive push to consume goods and services marketed as age-preventing (or youth-preserving, depending on the particular offering). However, the celebration of youth does not mean that younger women are shielded from the challenges and contradictions linked to feminine attractiveness. Regardless of their age, the women I interviewed depicted youth as a time of enormous social pressure to conform to a mainstream definition of attractiveness. For them, youth entails a high degree of self-scrutiny and a lack of self-confidence about one's appearance, which in turn reflects a set of larger doubts regarding one's place in society.

The current popularity of "self-confidence" discourse, with its postfeminist allure, does not improve younger women's position in Western culture in any meaningful sense, but merely contributes to the individuation of young women's struggles with discriminating, misogynist standards of legitimacy based on feminine appearance. In accordance with the worth paradox, when it comes to beauty duty, younger women must travel the razor's edge separating reward from sanction. In later life stages (maternity, middle age, and so on), women might enjoy greater leeway with regard to their appearance, but this is accompanied by the new challenge of managing a set of physical transformations that are normally regarded as highly undesirable from an aesthetic point of view. The older a woman gets, the less she corresponds to mainstream standards of attractiveness—and the more she is encouraged by consumer culture and mainstream social media discourse to minimize, manage, or conceal the impact of time on her body. Here, the commitment paradox and the authenticity paradox threaten the very credibility of women's self-presentation: one must do enough, but not *too* much, in order to slow, if not halt, the aging process while also avoiding the stigma of the "fake."

And as we saw in the previous chapter, here, too, the female gaze plays an operative role. At every stage of their temporal relationship to beauty, women also look to each other, and especially across generations, to better evaluate the options and resources at their disposal when it comes to facing their respective challenges. In the era of selfie-taking and -sharing, their gaze is also more insistently turned to their own image as immortalized in their pictures, and, as a consequence, to the historicity of beauty as a biographical, embodied experience.

BEING YOUNG

For younger participants such as Emma, who is twenty-two, youth is literally all they know; putting it into perspective is nearly impossible. Talking to them, it almost feels as if they exist outside of time, in fact, in a realm where aging is merely imagined as a prolongation of what they already know. Intellectually, they can anticipate the appearance of an aging body, but they cannot fully appreciate the embodied experience of inhabiting one: the feelings, the perceptions, the limitations, and other people's looks. Still, young women know for a fact that youth and beauty are as important in a woman's life as they are ephemeral; young women are aware of the temporality of beauty, of the risk that it entails, and of the work that is required to successfully manage the inevitability of change.

In both Emma's and Jeanne's cases, high school was the time when they first realized that their appearance was a principal source of social acceptance or rejection, and that it was therefore highly scrutinized by both peers and adults. Both women remember those years as difficult and characterized by an enormous sense of pressure, something that older participants like Eva and Lena also clearly recall.

For as long as she can remember, Emma has been interested in clothing and makeup. During high school, she styled her appearance in what she calls a "hyper-feminine" way, and she enjoyed the attention that this attracted. Later on, while coming into contact with feminist ideas through education and peer interactions, she started wondering how she could reconcile her rather mainstream preferences in self-presentation with the urge to be "subversive" and to reclaim dignity for women's choices. Likely implied in Emma's reflections is the fact that feminist voices are generally quite critical toward beauty culture, and sometimes toward women's participation in it.[1] Emma found a way out of this conundrum by embracing, albeit largely unwittingly, a conspicuously postfeminist rhetoric that recognizes the possibility that women might indeed empower themselves through aesthetic self-fashioning. Though unsure at times about how to precisely describe her understanding of her hyper-femininity as "subversive," Emma explains that her feminist stance is expressed in the fact of her being beautiful and sexy "for herself" instead of others—namely, men. Dressing to impress, often in what she considers an "eccentric" way, and generously using makeup brings Emma good feelings, self-confidence, and pleasure, because she does it for her own sake.

As Rosalind Gill noted in her analysis of the postfeminist landscape, "the notion that all our practices are freely chosen is central to postfeminist discourse."[2] And yet, such an understanding of beautification can only be sustained if we disregard the power relations, economic interests, and discriminating standards that structure beauty culture and its normative injunctions. As such, this stance is hardly "subversive" of socioeconomic and cultural processes that reduce women to their appearance and judge them accordingly. Postfeminist discourse nonetheless promotes beautification and femininity as paths to increased self-confidence for women, and there is no doubt that Emma appears to find solace in such ideas, even if they come with the unintended consequence of defeating the underlying purpose of her declared feminist goals.

Emma's experience points to the intersection of current social anxieties regarding women's alleged lack of self-confidence and the injunction to undergo the sort of self-transformative work that consists mainly of aesthetic self-care practices whose ultimate aim is bodily acceptance. In popular discourse, unattainable standards of beauty and slenderness, which are often also reproduced by that very discourse, are deemed directly responsible for young women's lack of self-confidence and self-acceptance in contemporary Western societies.[3] This has generated a considerable degree of unease in North America since at least the 1990s. Although the "confidence gap," to use Facebook COO Sheryl Sandberg's term,[4] is considered in most self-help literature to extend beyond bodily self-acceptance, today women's relationship with their appearance is likely the main battleground in the fight for improved female confidence. Young women represent the principal targets of a generalized discourse aimed at promoting a healthier relationship with one's looks. By motivating girls and young women to embrace their appearance and to stop assuming that there is something wrong with it, the "love your body" discourse aims above all to "empower" them.

At a first glance, there is nothing wrong with the goal of improved self-confidence: Would not an increase in self-love strengthen young women and enable them to enjoy greater freedom of action in the world? The problem, as many feminist scholars have argued, is that this discourse depends on a distorted view of the problem's underlying causes, which in turn results in the adoption of certain dubious solutions.

Working with fellow sociologist Shani Orgad, Rosalind Gill showed that this discourse tends to attribute women's limited agency to individual psychological flaws, thereby obscuring the structural obstacles to women's participation in the public sphere and the labor force and their enjoyment of a more positive self-image.[5] For instance, it is noteworthy that many of the same companies that employ a discourse of self-love to advertise their products (such as Kellogg's, or the Unilever subsidiary Dove) also help, through some of their other activities, to reinforce normative ideals of female slenderness, agelessness, and standardized beauty.[6] They contribute, in other words, to the reproduction of the very same idea of femininity as fundamentally flawed (which you'll recall from the second chapter) that they otherwise invite women to eradicate from their minds.

"Love your body" discourse is indeed based on the idea that insufficient self-acceptance is a personal flaw that each woman must rectify individually. I believe that this deformed perspective explains why the younger women I interviewed feel that "working" on themselves is their surest path to increased self-confidence. For Emma, this work takes the form of embracing her passion for beautification and feminine looks and framing it as a form of self-love. She seems not to question whether there could be anything wrong with this approach in the first place.

Emma remembers being regularly reprimanded by her high school principal (a man) for the way she dressed and being told that she would not be allowed back into the school until she changed her style. This was only resolved when Emma's father, himself a teacher at the same school, interceded in her favor. It is fair to say that her acceptance as a worthy female subject was a subject of negotiation between men. Still, Emma does not directly question a cultural framework that shames women for their appearance—be it hyper-feminine or unfeminine or something in-between. On the contrary, she started worrying about her preference for hyper-feminine beautification *after* perceiving that it could be judged as somehow "superficial" (a fear that I interpret as clearly related to the pressures stemming from the worth paradox). Convincing herself that there could be something deeply political about her aesthetic preferences calmed her anxieties, which shows that the problem lies precisely in how some bodily features are more broadly interpreted and valued within a given social context. Even when, as in Jeanne's case, young women are more aware of the negative influence of social expectations and cultural codes on their self-image, they see themselves as the appropriate object of change, which mainly takes the form of a liberation from false ideas about what a woman should be and do. These young women regard resisting social pressure as a personal endeavor, and they appeal to individual willpower and determination to make their journey toward greater self-acceptance.

Jeanne, who is twenty-six at the time of our second interview, strongly resents the pressure that cultural codes dictating appropriate femininity exert on girls from childhood on, when they wear t-shirts praising their daintiness and are expected to align themselves with that image. Why don't you see t-shirts praising girls' strength or determination? asks Jeanne. Why can't you be a "strong princess" rather than a beautiful one? Although representations of girlhood are shifting, the pace of change is still too slow for Jeanne's taste. When she was young, she was taught—whether explicitly or implicitly—that there is something wrong with the female body, that it must be kept in check through ongoing surveillance and intervention. Later, she began questioning such ideas and realized that her self-image was in fact strongly distorted by them. That was when her deconditioning journey began. She gradually learned to think differently about beauty and appearance (her shaved pink hair, which I mentioned in chapter 3, is a tangible sign of this shift). Through reading, listening, and reflecting, Jeanne aims to disentangle her self-esteem from sociocultural pressure and narrow standards of femininity; her goal is to "express" who she really is.

In part, this depends on cultivating an acceptance of the inevitable physical changes induced by aging; "that's going to be my little fight against what I've interiorized," Jeanne says. In the last couple of years alone, her body has already been subtly transformed by "adult things" such as a shift in the distribution of body fat ("I have bigger hips") and the onset of stretch marks. Rejecting the cultural pressures encouraging women to invest in an ageless (which is to say "childish") appearance, Jeanne wishes to invert the trend and positively celebrate these transformations, and those yet to come. However, she still believes that these so-called natural changes need to be controlled and steered in a direction that corresponds to a general representation of successful aging (an idea to which I'll return in the next section). To age "well," one needs a certain amount of self-discipline—enough, in fact, that the benefits will extend into the future. To this end, Jeanne intends to exercise a lot, to apply sunscreen so as to prevent premature aging, and to eat well. She sees this as a necessary part of a full life, and the work she undertakes with regard to her self-acceptance goes hand in hand with the (aesthetic) work that she feels is necessary for her body to be *acceptable*.

When we are young, we can sometimes idealize the aging process, with the attendant consequences that we potentially overestimate our ability to cope with it or—and perhaps this is a distinction without a difference—misjudge other (older) women's concerns about the bodily transformations brought on by age. Clarisse remembers being quite judgmental, in her younger years, of older women who would worry about wrinkles, stretch marks, and uneven complexion. She would tell herself that she would not fall into the same trap as she aged, that she would embrace these aesthetic changes as they came. Things didn't work out the way she expected. When the first deep wrinkles appeared, when dark spots started showing up on her skin, when gray hairs became more visible, she was deeply disturbed, to the point that she wondered whether she might have actually delayed the aging process somewhat had she been less naive and neglectful. "When it happens, you have no choice but to do what everybody does and get on board," she now says. Interestingly, however, her participation in the production and circulation of selfies has made her even more aware of the "imperfections" that keep appearing on her face, and this has caused her to be hyper-conscious of aging and the effort she must undertake to manage it.

As Audrey puts it, the difficult part of aging is understanding, not just theoretically but practically and emotionally, that youth and beauty are temporary and will fade, together with the "power" that they bestow on women.

BEING NO LONGER YOUNG

For Zoe, the main contrast between her experience of beauty at a younger age and that of later decades revolves around the degree to which her appearance once represented a source of concern and self-scrutiny. At fifty, she still takes pleasure in beautification and related consumer practices, but she no longer cares as much about achieving the kind of idealized beauty she worked so hard to attain in the past. As a younger woman, she used to work as a model, which caused her to focus obsessively on the pursuit of bodily perfection: staying thin, looking flawless in a bikini, having impeccable hair (sometimes even styling her hair twice in one hour, she says). Today, Zoe has so many more important things going on in her life, and her everyday beautification routine aims at presentability rather than perfection. If her hair does not look good, she just puts it in a bun, and she's no longer bothered if she looks down while wearing a bathing suit and sees skinfolds—rather the opposite, in fact. Talking with girlfriends of the same age, she notices that many of them report a similar evolution: they seem to say that aging entails a sort of relief from the duty of perfection, from the severe self-discipline required of younger women and girls. This is why Zoe imagines her fifties and sixties as a time of great opportunity and fun, when she hopes to be appreciated for her competence and to give herself permission to adopt an even "funkier" look.

Sociologist Abigail Brooks interviewed a large sample of women aged forty-seven and up about the physical changes caused by aging. She observed that the interviewees tended to split into two general categories: those who saw aging as a force to be resisted through a careful lifestyle regime, and even through cosmetic interventions; and those who saw aging as an inevitable natural process to be accepted, perhaps even embraced. With some exceptions, the women I talked to situated themselves in relation to a similar divide. Zoe belongs to the latter group, and even offers an additional observation echoed by some of Brook's interviewees when she says she considers aging a liberation from the injunctions of conventional femininity, and especially from the obligation to garner male attention and admiration.[7]

Some participants clearly regard aging with more ambivalence.[8] Take Audrey, for example. Like Zoe, she also experienced a feeling of liberation as she left her thirties behind; but as we'll see later with Melissa, she also mourns what has been lost. Audrey says that she went from being a young, attractive woman, and thus hyper-visible and exposed to male attention (both wanted and unwanted), to being a bigger, older woman—and thus practically invisible. Though she misses being appreciated for her looks, she values the easiness of social interactions once they are divested of that layer of meaning: "It's so much less noisy—that's what it is, so much less stressful."

While younger than Zoe, Eva (who is twenty-nine at the time of our first interview) has undergone another type of big change in the last ten years: she has relinquished most of her former makeup routine, something she sees as an act of "self-love." In the past, she would perform a laborious beautification routine each day, including straightening her hair and applying a full face of makeup (in describing this regimen she stresses the eyeliner, which was particularly tricky to pull off). Later, she began what she calls "a progression through reduction," gradually abandoning elements of the routine and embracing a more natural look. What she let go of, she observes, was more than a certain amount of makeup; it was also the feeling that she was performing an identity that wasn't really hers. Before, she would refuse to leave the house without makeup, whereas now she strives to reject the idea that her appearance is unacceptable as it is. When she tries to anticipate aging, this is indeed the change she looks forward to the most—a gradual freedom from the desire "to be liked by people for whom I don't much care."

For Eva, then, aging has brought a degree of clarity: it has enabled her to reduce the emphasis she once placed on the performance of a stereotypical femininity, and to adopt an appearance that she feels reflects who she really is. She says that "things are falling into place," and this gives her a positive outlook on the decades to come—her forties, fifties, sixties. Her gray hair plays a big role in this. Like her mother's, Eva's hair began turning gray in her early twenties. She now considers this a visible sign of her maturation. She takes selfies celebrating her gray hair (one we discuss bears the caption "my hair, as grey as the sky"), and speaks of it as if it announced a future full of opportunity, free from useless worries about how to please others and comply with social expectations. Eva's pride in her hair also expresses her rejection of the mainstream beauty standards that weigh on women and make them feel that aging must be prevented and/or concealed.

However, Eva's interest in what is commonly referred to as "successful aging"[9] is perhaps also evidence of the fact that aging nevertheless remains a sensitive topic. Her goal, after all, has more to do with embracing a different conception of aging than not caring about it at all. In North America, the sociocultural imperative of "successful aging" has been promoted by mainstream media, an extensive self-help literature, and even public health institutions over the last four decades. It prescribes an array of early lifestyle changes that, if implemented, are said to lay the groundwork for a successful old age, one free from illness, loss of autonomy, or physical and/or intellectual decay. As anthropologist Sarah Lamb and her colleagues explain, this paradigm rests on values like individual agency and personal control (as necessary to achieve physical and mental health); the merit of productive activity (encouraging elderly people to stay perpetually active and engaged); avoiding dependence (with illness, frailty, and lack of autonomy considered moral faults); and a vision of ageless, "permanent personhood" immune to change.[10] But while the anti-aging crusade is at the core of cosmetic marketing targeting aging women, it also aims to reach an increasingly younger audience. Regardless of their age, women are constantly confronted by a discourse that says that the passage of time, and its effects on their bodies, is a problem, a challenge, a nuisance that they must successfully confront— which means aging as little, as slowly, as invisibly as possible.

When questioned about such expectations, some of the women I interviewed show a concern for fighting the signs of age by way of these tactics; their goal might be described as an ageless aging. In other cases, such as Eva's, we can observe a rejection of the most misogynist aspects of mainstream discourse, but the resistance is nevertheless coupled with an attendance to the seemingly inescapable pressure to age successfully. Eva's embrace of certain exterior signs of aging, like her gray hair, can be read as a strategy whose aim is the cultivation of a balanced attitude toward the passage of time. Such a strategy revolves around the ideas of willpower, autonomy, and self-improvement, as well as the conception of a "permanent personhood": Eva's idealized representation of the coming decades is predicated on the unbroken continuity of her current way of life. Across the next thirty years, she wants to remain exactly who she is today, to keep doing what she currently likes to do, to be engaged in as many projects as she is now. At the core of this belief lies a fantasy, albeit one whose articulation is more often than not subconscious. After all, aging as a changeless prolongation of the here and now is no aging at all, but rather an idealization of time as a worry-less process of maturation, an uninterrupted path to well-being, balance, and wisdom.

As Sarah Lamb and colleagues argue,[11] behind the idea of successful aging lies a great deal of ageism—the negative bias against older age and older people. This might explain why signs of aging, and especially naturally occurring changes in the female body (gray hair, wrinkles, uneven complexion, weight gain, sagging), tend to trigger larger reflections on how we might steer the aging process to our advantage. After all, there is much in aging that must be disciplined, prevented, avoided, and, in the worst-case scenario, (surgically) concealed. Although none of the participants use these exact words, their claims betray a fear of the fading of beauty and youth as part of an irreversible descent toward ugliness and social invisibility. Hence, once physical changes are apprehended, their progression is carefully monitored, and a not insignificant amount of thought is devoted to determining the most fruitful attitude toward them within our current cultural and political framework. Such reflections involve grappling with social expectations, political questions (especially feminist critiques of the stereotypes concerning youth and beauty), cultural norms, peer interactions, and personal judgments (as we saw in chapter 3). However, the dominance of visual culture on social media and the concomitant emphasis on self-representation also compel women who engage in online discourse to negotiate the place of selfies in their attitude to aging.

Melissa saw her turning fifty as a symbolic milestone on the succession of irreversible aesthetic changes caused by aging: she now observes wrinkles in new places, is more conscious of the fluctuations in her weight, and feels that validation based on her appearance has become scarcer. Interestingly, selfies have acquired a greater importance in her life as a result, and she posts them with notably raised expectations about the good feelings that positive feedback might trigger. Although Melissa does not count the number of "likes" each picture gets, she is eager to read flattering comments, which she takes as reassurance that her looks can still garner positive attention. In this respect, too, she enacts a response to the paradoxical injunctions of beauty culture, which say that women must worry about aging without succumbing entirely to dissatisfaction with one's aging appearance. She tries, in other words, to care without caring too much—which of course causes her to grapple with her own desire to be validated.

Melissa is by no means an outlier in this regard. Generally speaking, women of her age have a difficult time determining the most socially desirable attitude that they should have toward aging: Fight it or embrace it? Conceal it or wear it proudly? Should women work to maintain a youthful look in an attempt to dodge invisibility and uphold their full participation in social and political life? Or should they reject the cultural imperative of youth and promote women's visibility based on all but physical appearance? As we'll see in more detail in chapter 6, Audrey also finds herself oscillating between these two positions—and nowhere is this duality more apparent than in those times when she must choose whether to display her body in a selfie on social media. Eschewing the enormous scrutiny to which younger women are routinely subjected, Audrey experiences a heightened freedom in visual self-expression due to the greater control she exercises over her own image. But she is under no illusion about the source of that freedom, knowing that it really comes from belonging to another category of women: those who, because of their age, are no longer valued for their appearance.[12]

Selfies have a complex relation to aging. They are intrinsically ethereal: shot at a specific moment in one's life, they immortalize a look that will certainly change, and possibly deteriorate, over time. As such, taken one after another across a certain time span and archived on a device or a social media account, they constitute a journal of one's appearance and, necessarily, of its transformation, reminding the photographer of her beauty (or lack thereof) in the past while capturing her beauty (or lack thereof) in the present.

Launched in 2019, the so-called Ten-Year Challenge asked social media users—principally of Facebook—to post a picture of themselves taken in 2009 beside one from 2019.[13] Also known as the "How Hard Did Aging Hit You Challenge," this sharing trend highlighted something compelling about the temporality of visual data on social networking sites: like any other photograph, selfies stored online are in essence historical documents since they capture a specific moment in a person's biological, psychological, and social life. In particular, selfies constitute a record of the ways time and life events progressively affect one's looks. Thus, a person's ability to participate gamefully in the Ten-Year Challenge also depended on whether they had the courage to face and make public the physical effects of time's passage. As I argue in chapter 6, selfies shared on social media very often are about showcasing a beautiful (or beautified) appearance—an aspect of selfie culture that the relevant literature has tended to neglect. Because of the temporal, archival nature of selfies, taking the Ten-Year Challenge meant facing the risk that one would never again appear as young or as beautiful as one did in previous selfies.

In this respect, selfies taken by aging women can serve the dual purpose of boosting the taker's self-esteem and encouraging self-discipline and self-surveillance. Cassandra, for instance, is less worried about wrinkles and sagging, which she says Black women are less affected by (I'll get back to this later in this section), but she perceives weight fluctuations as a major challenge of aging. She therefore uses her past pictures as a benchmark; she wants to be reminded of how lean and beautiful she can be, and to be motivated to work hard each day in order to achieve that standard of attractiveness. "It's a guideline to what my perfect self is," she says while showing me a selfie. "I want to always look like this." And here again we're reminded of the notion of a permanent personhood at the core of "successful aging": an idea that normally refers to one's mental abilities, but which, I argue, also concerns the material features of embodied personhood. Cassandra's experience points to the fact that, for many aging women, it is crucial that an unchanging personhood be embodied in an unchanging vessel; this "perfect self," then, is not only an inner achievement—it must register on the outside as well, as a demonstration of one's ability to manage aging and retain recognizably feminine qualities over time. Although Cassandra does feel beautiful every day ("I always do," she tells me), her digital archive of selfies is her way of urging herself to never lower the bar when it comes to attractiveness. Instead of undermining her self-confidence, Cassandra says that selfies boost it, by showing her how attractive and youthful she *can* be.

Lena has a different relationship with the temporality of selfies: to her, looking at her recent pictures has involved a journey toward a greater acceptance of how she looks in the present. After struggling for years with a conspicuous C-section scar, she decided to display it in a selfie, which she posted on Instagram along with a long caption modelling self-acceptance (we'll hear more about this in chapter 6). The amount of positive feedback she received helped her reckon with the bodily changes she has undergone after (and as a result of) having two children and "not being twenty-five anymore." And she felt an additional pleasure knowing that she was helping to foster a similar acceptance in other women who had undergone similar physical changes. Selfies can represent a space for self-discipline as well as self-acceptance—and they can even be both things at once.

A third aspect of the relationship between selfies and aging, however, is the now virtually universal circulation of "good" pictures. Through learning (the Internet offers endless tutorials on how to shoot the best selfie), practice, or simply by chance, a selfie can serve as a particularly flattering portrait of one's appearance (and thanks to the digital format, those pictures that aren't flattering are usually simply deleted). To put this in more straightforward terms: often our selfies make us look younger, more attractive, less tired or troubled by life than we tend to see ourselves on a daily basis. Lena, who is thirty-eight at the time of our second interview and who tries, as we've seen, to embrace aging as a process of maturation and self-acceptance, nevertheless loves a series of selfies shot outdoors, during the winter, because in such a setting she says she does not "look so old." These images therefore recur from time to time on her public, professionally oriented Instagram profile.

The last aspect of aging that I wish to discuss is the more direct impact of shifting cultural norms in some cases, and of specific normative frameworks in others, on women's appreciation of the changes brought about by aging. Fanny, thirty-five at the time of our first interview, remembers that in her younger years she was often told that her thirties would be "the prime of [her] life." Back then, she felt that this was obviously nonsense: as a thirtysomething, she would just be old. Now that she is in the middle of that decade, however, she does indeed feel more confident, free from some of the pressures weighing on younger women with regard to appearance. In her twenties, not yet sure who she "really" was and what she was doing, she would avoid standing out "too much," but now she is willing to show her body more, to be vocal about issues she cares about, and to challenge the status quo.

Particularly interesting is the fact that Fanny believes she's benefited from shifting cultural norms around female beauty—and above all the greater social acceptance and visibility, especially on social media, of "fuller" female bodies. Crudely put, in this changed context, Fanny's body type has gained more currency than was the case in her youth, and this influences the way she assesses her appearance and the leeway she grants herself when choosing to share a selfie. Cassandra expresses a similar confidence as a result of the diversification of beauty standards, which now tend to target specific communities or identities. Cassandra considers aging unproblematic for two reasons. We touched on the first in chapter 2: her strict self-care regime, which for Cassandra bears the promise of preserving her youthful looks. The second, however, is linked to her ethnic background. After a moment of hesitation ("you don't want to say that, but . . ."), Cassandra explains "that the whole aging and Black women thing, it's a real thing." When I ask for clarifications, she adds: "Well I mean, we don't wrinkle. We don't take all the harshness of life on our face. You can see a well-preserved Black woman who is seventy and looks forty. My mum, you know."

The "whole aging and Black women thing" likely refers to the "Black don't crack" discourse that spread through the media, and which reverberated across social media through the #blackdontcrack hashtag that circulated in the mid-2010s and at the time of my conversation with Cassandra.[14] This discourse emphasizes the differential impact of aging on people of African descent, and especially women, compared to white people. At the intersection of relations of gender, race, and age, Black women are regarded as "naturally" favored in the fight against the stigma of aging. In this way, racial discrimination is apparently turned upside down, with a racialized identity seen as an asset for aging women in the Black community. As psychologist Tamara Baker and her colleagues show with respect to another popular stereotype of Black femininity—that of the "strong Black woman"—the "Black don't crack" rhetoric can be considered, and experienced, as both a hindrance and a form of empowerment.[15] They argue that the "strong Black woman" trope puts African American women under particular strain by emphasizing social expectations and by limiting women's ability to express identities and emotions that diverge from this idealized stereotype. And yet, they show that it can also work to empower Black women to face the aging process with a sense of self-confidence.

The same contradictory impact has been highlighted with regard to other hashtags celebrating Black women, such as #BlackGirlMagic, which circulated online starting in 2015. As Maria S. Johnson reports, the hashtag was meant as a form of "empowerment and self-affirmation for Black women and girls,"[16] and it rapidly assumed a vernacular status in the media and advertising world. However, #BlackGirlMagic has also been criticized as enforcing normative expectations around the "proper" comportment of Black women, and especially for its undue emphasis on toughness, strength, and exceptionality, on the one hand, and on style, glamour, and certain stereotypical notions of Black beauty (light-skinned, made-up) on the other. Hence, #BlackGirlMagic exemplifies what Johnson describes as the risk of "reinforcing narrow definitions of success and beauty."[17]

As Cassandra's comments show, the "Black don't crack" discourse, by similarly essentializes ethnicity, even if promoting as an asset, has the effect of also reinforcing stereotypes and normative injunctions targeting Black women with regard to their "natural" physical appearance. Cassandra herself claims that her racial identity is what allows her to look the same today as she did twenty years ago. She also cites her own firsthand observations ("my mum, you know") as proof of the claim. But the "whole aging and Black women thing" also adds a greater salience to the work that Cassandra considers necessary for successful aging, which for her, as you might remember, is primarily an aesthetic endeavor: Cassandra wants to maintain her physical beauty. The "Black don't crack" discourse becomes fused with an idealized agelessness, and hence it is a source of social pressure that specifically targets Black women. Instead of weakening the social norms regulating attractiveness, then, such rhetoric promotes a beautiful appearance as a mandatory prerequisite of successful aging for Black women. As such, the "Black don't crack" discourse represents yet another iteration of the authenticity paradox, this one situated squarely at the intersection of gender, race, and age. Since the stereotype says that the aging process is less visible on Black women's bodies, those assumed lucky enough to possess this "natural" advantage must do whatever it takes to reap the maximum benefit. Once again, Cassandra offers a tangible example of how this tension is experienced by women: notwithstanding her confidence in her "natural" assets, she still thinks that aging is the most difficult time in a woman's life, and she fights its exterior manifestations with an unshakable determination.

MOTHERHOOD

A symbolic rupture with the time of youth, a sudden leap toward a different category of womanhood, becoming a mother represents a major transformation in the life of any woman. As regards our purpose here, three main changes triggered by motherhood affect one's relationship with attractiveness and beautification. First, there are the bodily changes that a pregnant woman undergoes, and which usually persist for some time (perhaps years, perhaps for the rest of one's life) after the baby's birth. Weight gain is probably the most common—and probably the most lamented—transformation,[18] but it is by no means the only one. Lena, for instance, complains about the negative impact that breastfeeding her two daughters had on the size and shape of her breasts: they shrank to such an extent that Lena thinks "they would have gone inwards had I had a third child."[19] As we will see, the bodily changes brought on by motherhood are treated in much the same way as those that result from aging: generally undesirable, they must be addressed and, when possible, reversed, if one is to avoid being rendered socially invisible and thereby excluded from the hierarchy of sexiness and attractiveness.

The second big change of motherhood is the sheer amount of time, energy, and attention demanded of a new mother. Caring for a newborn, and then for an older baby, requires a reconfiguration of a woman's priorities and schedule, and it often leaves her with little or no time to engage in anything else (the presence of more than one young child serves to further reduce one's spare time).[20] For Fanny, however, the material reality of early motherhood—the severe lack of time and energy that one can devote to oneself—is dramatized by the social expectations heaped upon new mothers, especially the assumption that they will display an unconditional commitment to their children. In Fanny's experience, not only are mothers expected to show heroic selflessness vis-à-vis their children—they must also feel guilty for even *considering* putting themselves first, even briefly.

This is exactly what Clarisse describes when she recounts the "burnout" she experienced after having her twin sons and returning to paid work (and it's worth mentioning that she already had a young son by the time the twins came along). Caught in the overwhelming pace of life as a full-time worker and mother of three, she felt that she had "forgotten" herself. Outside of her job, Clarisse was constantly available to her family, with the result that time spent on herself felt like a neglect of her duties. As we saw in previous chapters, she dealt with her subsequent mental health struggles by reorganizing both her outlook and her daily schedule; helped by the fact that her children are a little older, she now regularly gives herself permission to devote personal time to aesthetic self-care. This "me time" has helped her overcome the feelings of guilt that she once experienced.

Working with new mothers, Fanny has witnessed this process over and over again. To her, a woman's relationship to her attractiveness and her body is deeply affected by the cultural emphasis on motherhood as a process of self-obliteration. Speaking about her commitment to encouraging mothers to maintain time and space for themselves, Fanny explains that women are socially encouraged to relinquish sexiness and attractiveness while transitioning to their new role as mothers:

> Society kind of says, like, "No, you're a mom now, you have to be quiet, you have to be [. . .] under the radar, because that's weird, that's not how you're supposed to act. You're finished with that, you moved on to the next stage." [. . . And] I'm like, "No, I don't have to be on one side or the other."

Fanny is describing here a well-documented Western cultural framework for motherhood, through which women are deprived of their status as sexual beings upon becoming mothers.[21] Motivated by a feminist concern, Fanny multiplies her efforts to persuade women to think differently about the relationship between motherhood and their interest in beautification, attractiveness, and sexiness—to see these as coexisting rather than in a state of constant tension. Clearly, Fanny attempts to offer solutions to a version of the worth paradox that applies specifically to motherhood, whereby a woman is thought to be worthy of attention if she is attractive and feminine, but deserving of moral reprimand if she seeks to cultivate these qualities while also being a mother. This brings us to a third major change brought about by motherhood: a woman must carefully negotiate her new identity as a mother, *aesthetically* no less than physically or emotionally, within the framework of the worth paradox, the reach of which extends well beyond the first months of the baby's life. In recent decades, new cultural norms concerning the intersection of beauty and motherhood have increased the paradoxicality of this framework. On the one hand, mothers are traditionally divested of their sexiness and attractiveness, labeled as selfless caregivers and discouraged from engaging in self-expression through feminine beautification. On the other hand, the rise of a postfeminist sensibility in Western societies has contributed to an expansion of the pressure women feel to be beautiful that first included the pregnant body (since the 1990s) and later (since the late 2000s) motherhood writ large.[22]

Through cultural representations of the "MILF" in North America and of the "Yummy Mummy" in the United Kingdom and Australia, spread by

TV, the Internet, and self-help literature,[23] sexuality, attractiveness, and sexualized femininity have been reintroduced into motherhood. It didn't take long, however, for this apparently liberating cultural shift to turn into an additional injunction governing women's transition to motherhood. As sociologist Jo Littler observes, the "Yummy Mummy" has to be "well-groomed," wear fashionable clothes, and be "very slim."[24] Indeed, mothers are now targeted by a host of new social expectations regarding their looks, the aesthetic expression of their identities, and their involvement in beautification practices—combined, of course, with the traditional expectations regarding a mother's dedication to her offspring. As Christina Malatzky puts it in her work on the "Yummy Mummy" ideal, "attaining a particular body 'look' is now part of being a good mother, but the work that goes into this must remain unseen or this image of successful maternity risks disrupting other dominant ideals about the good mother."[25]

The imperative to quickly return to one's pre-pregnancy weight is probably the best example.[26] Lena remembers being caught in this very paradox: while supervising her daughters at the playground (and hence acting as a good, selfless mother, deeply invested in her role), she would feel judged by other moms (remember the female gaze?) for her choice of casual, comfortable, not particularly stylish clothing. Moreover, she would often hear other moms brag about how quickly they had returned to their pre-pregnancy weight, or even leaner than before, whereas Lena's weight loss path was definitely bumpier. At the same time, she also felt criticized by other mothers for her interest in fitness and for her toned muscles; she was asked, for instance, whether she was "eating enough" while working out as much she was—a question that made her feel deeply judged. Lena also had interactions with other moms that left her feeling as though she had unwittingly entered some undeclared competition over who was doing the "best job" at mothering (measured by whose baby was sleeping better, eating more, growing faster, etc.). However, she felt that such competition and peer surveillance were also clearly about physical appearance. Not only was she expected to learn to (selflessly) care for her young children, she also had to simultaneously perform a normative ideal of attractiveness and femininity, the realization of which demanded time and resources that were often impossible to spare.

THE INTERGENERATIONAL GAZE

If peer surveillance covers one's youth and extends through motherhood and aging, the "female gaze" has an additional temporal dimension, one that informs intergenerational relations in matters of beauty and appropriate feminine appearance. Women of older generations look at younger women in order to assess, criticize, support, and foster—and younger women can look up to older ones or they can reject their choices completely. The intergenerational gaze plays a role in shaping individual styles, prioritizing certain goals, reproducing or undermining perceived social expectations. For instance, a woman can revere her mother or grandmother as a positive role model, but she can also resent their choices in matters of appearance, and, more generally, their invocation of certain normative references in the performance of femininity. Younger women can feel empowered by older female family members, but also feel judged and rejected specifically on the basis of their aesthetic self-presentation. Juliette, for example, admires her grandmother for her ability to stay beautiful and up-to-date with fashion and style into her seventies. Juliette's mother, by contrast, has never invested in her appearance and, as Juliette puts it, "never took good care of herself." Not feeling close to her mother—and not only in matters of self-care—Juliette looks up to her grandmother and her almost intact beauty.

For her part, Eva used to feel uncomfortable during family gatherings at her grandmother's house because of the formal dress code enforced on such occasions, a rule with which Eva and her brother often refused to comply. When both siblings were younger, the grandmother reprimanded Eva's brother for wearing jeans on Easter Sunday, a look she deemed entirely inappropriate for such a solemn occasion.[27] Eva still resents her grandmother for her negative comments, and for putting pressure on her to dress in a way she feels did not correspond to her identity. When she visits her grandmother today, however, Eva purposefully wears clothing that allows her to feel comfortable with herself; she hopes that this subtle effort at education will help her grandma learn to appreciate her for who she is.

By observing the older women in their families, and especially mothers and grandmothers, the women I interviewed also anticipate their older years and come to derive certain expectations about them. As we saw in the previous section, Cassandra admires her mother for her beauty, and considers her the strongest influence on her appearance and self-care. Indeed, more than her friends and peers, it is from her mother that Cassandra learns about beauty routines and products:

> My mum keeps giving me her scraps, and I make use of them and stuff, 'cause my mum is very high-end. [. . .] She's had the eyelashes put in [. . .] she's got cream on every minute—you can always touch her face and it's gonna be nice and lubricated and stuff, and she's seventy-five.

Not only is her mother's skin barely wrinkled, something that Cassandra describes with apparent admiration, but she also recently decided to stop dying her hair in favor of her natural silver ("with a slice of blue in it"). Although this is not a choice that Cassandra is yet ready to make for herself, her mother's self-confidence helps her to ease into the idea of one day embracing a more "natural" aging process.

The intergenerational gaze clearly operates also as a critical device that allows for self-distancing. To continue with Cassandra's example, while she admires certain of her mother's qualities, others are the object of a negative comparison. For example, looking at herself in the mirror, Cassandra, at forty-nine, says that she already sees "my mother's neck," among other bodily features, and she resents aging's role in bringing about an increasing resemblance between her and her mother. As much as she is a positive example of aging, then, Cassandra's mother also embodies the inevitability of that process. The intergenerational exchange operates in multiple directions too. Participants who have daughters are anxious about the role that beauty plays (and will continue to play) in young women's lives, and they question how they, as mothers, can best promote a healthy attitude in matters of appearance and attractiveness. Melissa, for example, is proud of her teenage daughter's balanced relationship with femininity: she "enjoys girly stuff," but she can also leave the house without makeup on or go three weeks without household amenities while camping in the summer.[28] As a mother, Melissa wants nothing more than to help her daughter love herself "the way she is," and especially to counter the outlook that instills in young women the constant need to edit, correct, and improve themselves.

And yet, Melissa finds it increasingly hard to lead by example. Her awareness of the undesirable physical changes brought about by aging fuels her dissatisfaction with her appearance, and she sometimes catches herself complaining about it in front of her daughter, who tries to step up and comfort her ("Don't say that, mummy!"). Knowing that this is the wrong message to send to a young woman, Melissa filters these expressions so as to "appear positive, no matter what,"[29] and to avoid undermining her daughter's self-confidence. In other words, Melissa does not want to pass her own dwindling self-love on to the next generation. Audrey, whose daughter is almost ten years younger than Melissa's, adopts similar strategies in an attempt to strengthen her girl's self-esteem and to shield her from the influence of mainstream notions of what a girl can or cannot do. Having been bullied during high school about the size of her nose, the color of her hair, her clothing style, or whatever other vulnerabilities her tormentors could alight on, Lena is also very aware of the importance of reinforcing positive messages when giving feedback to her daughters. She chooses her words carefully; in her family, she says, they insist on the value of being "strong" and "healthy" (instead of "cute" or "attractive," I infer). Interestingly, neither of the mothers of young boys in my sample voiced any concerns about their sons' self-esteem. As we saw earlier in this chapter, it appears that self-confidence (and perhaps especially the lack thereof) is generally considered a girl's issue.

In addition to encouraging her daughter to develop what she considers a healthy body image,[30] Melissa wants her to further disentangle her self-confidence from her physical appearance so that she will be a "strong person" no matter what she looks like. This rather nuanced point is relevant, Melissa explains, because her girl has "been blessed with . . . you know [. . .], she is a very beautiful young girl, but I don't think she lets that get to her head." Melissa wants her daughter to love her body *and* herself, and while being attractive surely helps, she nonetheless hopes that she will avoid placing too much emphasis on physical beauty. In this sense, Melissa negotiates the worth paradox on behalf of her daughter. Being beautiful is a blessing for a woman, she realizes, but she feels it would be wrong to "let that get to your head." In trying to resolve this tension, Melissa seeks also to answer a fundamental question that many women in her position ask themselves: How does one learn to achieve the delicate balance between feeling confidently beautiful (no matter what) and maintaining one's modesty and moderation while expressing such confidence?

A similar pedagogical intent can be observed in intergenerational relationships that take place beyond the confines of the family, within which women gaze at each other from a greater distance. Zoe, who experienced in her younger years an enormous pressure to appear attractive and to correspond to the mainstream ideal of femininity, pities younger women in their twenties. She sees her students making themselves uncomfortable with high heels or revealing clothing that they must constantly readjust in order to stay within the bounds of institutional propriety and respectable femininity. As far as she is concerned, they are unable to resist the pressures that weigh on them—indeed, they are increasing that pressure by scrutinizing, criticizing, and diminishing themselves for what they perceive as a lack of attractiveness. Having been there herself, Zoe tries to affect a shift of perspective in her students, as well as her younger colleagues and acquaintances; she tells them how beautiful they really are, and that they don't need to be so hard on themselves. At the same time, Zoe looks up to older women—she mentions one fancy-looking keynote speaker whose talk she had the pleasure of attending—to find examples that might reinforce her choice to dismiss mainstream standards of feminine beauty and the social expectations of what an older woman should look like.

CONCLUSION: THE TEMPORALITY OF BEAUTY

Beauty presents women with specific challenges at different stages of their lives, and it also brings them face to face with discursive frameworks that have shaped our understanding of the relationship between beauty and aging throughout history. For many women, youth brings a struggle to find the right balance between individual self-expression, the desire to win social recognition, and the pressure to comply with outside expectations. The paradoxes of beauty culture weigh heavily on younger women, then, since they are both rewarded and reprimanded for their attractiveness. Having experienced this for themselves, the mothers of girls particularly are self-conscious of the messages they send to their offspring in matters of attractiveness and beautification. However, they often oscillate themselves between the two sides of the worth paradox, and as a consequence, the messages they impart are often characterized by a certain ambiguity.

The encounter between a generalized social anxiety about young women's self-confidence and the wide application in contemporary Western societies of various postfeminist discursive themes has produced the perfect storm: the kind of self-assurance that young girls are encouraged to achieve is increasingly phrased in the language of conscious sexiness, fitness, and attractiveness (I'll return to this convergence in chapter 6). Instead of empowering young women by relieving some of these pressures, such discursive framing puts additional emphasis on the body, on beautification, and on consumer participation in beauty culture as a form of self-affirmation and sociability. Moreover, it transforms self-acceptance into a personal, primarily psychic endeavor that leaves oppressive standards and expectations largely undisturbed. This dynamic extends to the anticipation of the aging process and its impact on women's individual aesthetic self-expression. The authenticity paradox resurfaces in younger participants' discourse as their expectations regarding self-acceptance in later life are coupled with their commitment to doing the necessary work to belong among those whose bodies are deemed acceptable. In other words, the "successful aging" paradigm, despite some variations, replicates the idea that natural changes can be embraced only if they remain within the bounds of "good" aging. Although understandings of the latter may differ, none imply the unconditional acceptance of the sorts of bodily transformations that "naturally" result from aging.

Some older women, however, appear to be better able to disconnect from these idealized standards of beauty, and to tie their sense of legitimacy to criteria of their own choosing. A certain loosening of the injunctions implied by the worth paradox allows them to develop, for the first time in their lives, a more harmonious relationship to beautification and to expose themselves to the female and male gazes with a sense of playfulness. If they feel relieved when they receive less attention, thereby escaping a certain amount of scrutiny, some women also mourn that very loss of visibility that bestows on them a greater freedom. Because it still is a path toward social invisibility, aging forces older women to renegotiate the terms of the worth paradox: for them, appearance represents an increasingly unstable ground on which to secure social validation. In my view, this is why older interviewees seem more anxious to renegotiate their relationship to aging in a way that would allow them to create the conditions for happiness, self-respect, and competent participation in their social lives

Together with what I've called the "intergenerational gaze," selfies also play a role in this renegotiation. For one thing, visual self-presentation on social media can garner the sort of attention that for older women is often found lacking in embodied social encounters, if for no other reason than selfies are usually shared with the explicit intent of eliciting appreciation (which happens, according to interviewees, most of the time). For another, selfies, because they are intrinsically temporal, immortalize the exhilarating effect of one's present beauty (or the distressing lack thereof) while also constituting a visual journal of one's gradual bodily transformation, hence entailing a materialization of the fading of beauty over time. Lastly, the cultivation of certain selfie skills might bring about more flattering self-portraits, which in turn help women cope with aging and improve their self-perception.

Culturally specific frameworks can have a similarly positive impact. However, some discursive patterns—like the "Black don't crack" discourse that idealizes Black women's ability to resist aging, or the "MILF" trope that bestows sexiness and attractiveness on mothers—can break some stereotypical barriers associated with specific models of femininity, while also resulting in additional prescriptions tied to attractiveness. In other words, they can enhance the specific application of the worth paradox to identities situated at the intersection of age, gender, and race, for which they posit mainstream (ageless, sexualized) beauty as a precondition for social acceptance.

In her critical discussion of the challenges women face in aging, Martha Holstein describes this as the time when "the once taken-for-granted body is infused with new risks and uncertainties."[31] Holstein refers mainly to the diminishing physical abilities of the aging body, to the pains associated with movement and posture, to the loss of muscle mass (a process otherwise known as sarcopenia), flexibility, and balance. These hindrances to the free, assured, and painless use of one's body are generally unknown to the younger female embodied subject. However, the interviewees' experiences point to a further observation: even at the youthful peak of its physiological functioning, the female body can hardly be "taken for granted." Even if a younger body does not draw its owner's attention by way of pain and limits to movement, that is not to say it can enjoy the luxury of going unnoticed (and thus unattended), especially in social contexts. Women learn from a young age indeed that their bodies require surveillance, attention, strategical thinking, planning, reflection, and action. Younger women, then, can hardly "forget" their bodies, as their social worth depends on the way their bodies inhabit social space. Although the aging female body engenders additional, and different, risks and uncertainties over time, inhabiting a female body is a risky endeavor at every stage of a woman's life.

Chapter 5

WORK AND SOCIAL LIFE

In an insightful journal article published in 2011, my colleague Martina Cvajner, an associate professor at the University of Trento, Italy, relates a surprising experience she had while conducting ethnographic fieldwork in a northern Italian town with immigrant women from several former Soviet republics (mainly Ukraine and Moldova) employed as live-in maids or care workers. In what little free time these women had to themselves, they would often parade up and down the main street—the goal being maximum visibility—in what Martina, who took part in this ritual herself, calls in her fieldnotes "our usual 'look-at-us' stroll." What was peculiar about these walks was the women's appearance: they would systematically exhibit a hyper-feminine look, obtained through heavy makeup, tight and colorful clothes that left little to the imagination, high heels, and platinum blond hair. Martina's surprise stemmed from the fact that these same women, whom Italians would dismissively identify as "Russians" or "Slavs," were already subjected to severe social scrutiny on account of their reputations as alleged "husband-stealers," or more specifically, seducers of old Italian men whose wealth these women were apparently contriving to steal. Hence, Martina understood that the women's overtly sexualized appearance would logically serve only to reinforce the stigma, and thus feed into the collective mistrust that had already attached to them as a group and as individuals. What reason, she wondered, would these women have to engage in such obviously self-damaging conduct? Why didn't they instead try to downplay their sex appeal by adopting a less conspicuous look, thereby performatively defeating this harmful stereotype?

Intrigued, Martina decided to dig deeper into these questions in an attempt to unveil the women's underlying motives. What she discovered,

in her words, is that hyper-feminine beauty "may actually come to constitute an important resource for some groups of migrant women, as a way
to compensate for the damages that emigration has caused to their sense of
decency and moral worth." To begin with, these migrant women would
put a significant amount of money, time, and thought into beauty work in
order to retain their sense of identity as "real women,"—that is, as women
who care about their appearance and manage it appropriately. As a consequence, through beauty work, and of course through their public performance of what they considered proper femininity, these women could
empower themselves to, at least temporarily, shake off the stigmatized
identity that they were assumed by the townsfolk to embody during working hours; in this way, they were able to enjoy "not being a careworker
for a while." Being well-groomed and beautiful, strolling around downtown with friends and peers, afforded them a pleasurable respite from the
often degrading and dehumanizing work conditions they were expected
to endure day in and day out. Finally, feeling (and appearing) beautiful
and hyper-feminine would grant these women a sense of empowerment
vis-à-vis their women employers: contrasting their own looks to those of
the locals, they would dismiss Italian women as sloppy, lazy, unable to take
care of their bodies, and unwilling to perform the necessary beauty work
that allows a person to feel like a *real* woman. Through their aesthetic performance and verbal statements, the care workers would place themselves
higher than their Italian employers in the hierarchy of proper womanhood.
Martina also reads this gesture as an attempt to invert the prevailing social
order by turning the stigma to which these women were normally linked
on its head: if Italian wives needed to shield their husbands and male relatives from the care workers' charms, the immigrant women would often
claim, this was due to these wives' own lack of femininity, their careless-
ness, their inability to perform proper beauty work—a critique, Martina
notes, that was not only "aesthetic" but also "moral."[1]

These observations point to the crucial role played by beautification
work and by the performance of mainstream femininity in women's social
and professional lives. In addition, they point to the ambiguities of beauty
as a local, situated resource for women's status, a resource that is differently
valued depending on the sociodemographic characteristics of its bearer and
on the social position of the observer who assesses its value. This chapter
seeks to understand whether physical attractiveness can provide women
with social advantages, under what conditions, and at what cost. Beauty
is believed to generate interactions, structure forms of sociability, provide
opportunities, and bestow a higher social status. The women I interviewed

share this belief,[2] act upon it, and retrospectively interpret their life trajectories accordingly. However, they are also aware of the drawbacks of beauty's capacity to act as a social enabler, and many of them have direct experiences of beauty's limitations in this regard. Beauty provides a form of power that in turn is framed by paradox: it remains a *feminine* power, defined by an ambiguous relationship to various feminine qualities, interests, and abilities, and to those who control access to such power—namely, men. As MacCannell and MacCannell note,[3] one's subjective experience and sense of self can be disrupted by the awareness that one's power depends on one's appearance and that others' appreciation of that appearance is beyond one's control.[4]

I will begin by discussing how women describe using their beauty and their charm to bond with people and to reach certain personal goals. On a basic level, a woman's aim can be simple: to be liked, acknowledged, and validated. Further, beauty and charm can serve social purposes connected to one's professional activities. Finally, they can be wielded to obtain more general advantages in everyday interactions—for example, preferential treatment as a patron or customer.

BEAUTY AND SOCIABILITY

Many are the social interactions in which beauty acts as a helpful lubricant. Attractiveness is a social enabler inasmuch as beautiful people are perceived as more likeable, preferred, from childhood on, over average-looking people, considered to be morally good, and receive better treatment in an array of contexts.[5] This is no secret to the women I interviewed. When asked whether a pleasant appearance brought them advantages or better treatment in the past, all answered in the affirmative. Each can report at least one example of a social situation in which they felt that being more put together, better groomed, or simply more physically attractive produced some gains in terms of social acceptance and access to people, material goods, or opportunities. In addition to their experience (and to some extent, thanks to it), several interviewees formulate a general sociopsychological theory about the effects of attractiveness: they maintain that, overall, good-looking people are treated better, enjoy certain privileges, that others respond more positively to them, that beauty is rewarded and helps you move forward (or up) in society, and so forth. As a consequence—and as this chapter will show—the interviewees acknowledge consciously using their attractiveness to obtain certain social advantages.

In this first section, I will discuss how women describe the association between their appearance and these easier social interactions. But first, it is worth clarifying that when I talk about the participants' attractiveness, I am referring only to their self-reported feelings of being attractive or having been attractive in the past. I do not base my claim on any other assessment of their level of physical attractiveness according to some set of allegedly objective criteria. Similarly, I refrain from discussing their bodily features unless they are mentioned by the interviewees themselves, either in conversation or while presenting their selfies. What counts for my argument is women's subjective experience of being or not being attractive in specific situations or life stages, and the connection that they establish between these perceptions and their short- and long-term social trajectories.

Interestingly, participants claimed that, although attractiveness clearly functions as a social enabler, looks alone are insufficient. A pleasant, even beautiful appearance is clearly an asset, but absent personality, it is of little use. Being charming—a quality that might be said to represent a merger of the attractive and the personable—can open doors, entice people, and fix situations.[6] Jeanne, who is twenty-six years old and works in the performing arts, considers a certain amount of seductiveness one of the main skills that women in her field have to develop; enticing the spectators and giving them a pleasurable experience is, so to speak, part of the job description. For Jeanne and her colleagues, then, "charming" the audience becomes an everyday accomplishment. You search for cues about what makes people react positively, and you exploit them by enhancing certain aspects of your overall "presence," says Jeanne. If beauty plays a role, it is more of a general strategy of self-presentation by which the performer seduces others and encourages them to "open up." Emma, who is completing an arts-related BA, describes a similar connection between her artistic practice and her enhanced sensitivity to other people's expectations and perceptions. She also supplements her income by taking gigs and temporary jobs as a waitress or bartender, and like Eva (whom we'll hear from in the next section), Emma feels that working in the service industry has taught her how to make people comfortable and receptive. This, more than just her good looks, is the asset that allows her to positively influence others—sometimes to her advantage. For Zoe, too, being attractive triggers positive reactions in other people, and in that sense, her good looks serve as a social and professional enabler, but they do not function in a vacuum. Zoe believes that she secured gigs, contracts, TV appearances, and, while working as a teacher, highly positive ratings from her students by being a charming person with a pleasurable appearance (she tells me that her face displays certain "classic traits").

Juliette explains that a flirtatious attitude is her ordinary way of interacting with others—friends and colleagues, for instance—and that this does not differ much from the way one would seduce a sexual or intimate partner. It is a matter of attracting and retaining attention, she says, of establishing a connection, of making someone want to interact with you longer, more often. Mostly, it works with men. She recalls becoming aware of this "power" in her youth, when her looks would garner men's attention on the street and other public places and she would feel strongly desired, sometimes to the point of being uncomfortable. Juliette describes this realization as exhilarating: "You're under the impression that you can do whatever you want," she explains. However, that power faded with "aging," and it no longer happens to Juliette that a man's gaze lingers on her body while she passes by. She is very nostalgic for that powerful visibility, and the lack of attention in recent years makes her feel less attractive than she did in the past. In her mind, beauty amounts to a sort of currency when associated with the impermanence of youth in that it enables one to capitalize on one's fleeting—and because fleeting, finite, precious—physical qualities. What remains later is flirting, which is nevertheless central to her self-presentation. Juliette believes that subtle attempts at seduction can open doors in all social contexts.

Zoe reports a similar experience: being flirtatious facilitates sociability in many situations, especially when two people feel some sort of "connection" (in French, *complicité*), as coworkers or friends, without aiming for a more advanced form of intimacy. To Zoe, flirting happens when people feel a bond, whether expressed through ideas or through compatible body language, and not only when they desire each other sexually; it is an "energy" flowing between them, something special and rewarding. David Henningsen and colleagues echo this notion when they write that "flirting is a ubiquitous human activity."[7] For Zoe, flirting entails a form of bodily communication, the main object of which is mutual appreciation, especially of the pleasure of being in another's close presence. However, Zoe observes, something else must also be communicated—namely, that one is aware of the boundaries of informal flirting and does not intend to cross them. Entering the other's "bubble" breaks the spell, especially if done carelessly and with an express purpose (such as sex) other than the enjoyment of the flirtatious exchange. In other words, it is the clearly expressed (which does not necessarily mean *verbally* communicated) harmlessness of the flirt that makes it pleasurable for Zoe, who is in a committed long-term relationship. In this sense, her description of flirtatious connection partially contradicts a common definition of flirting, such as that put forth by Henningsen and colleagues, as always implying a sexual ambiguity that cannot be resolved by the person who receives the flirtatious attention.

Fanny knows that being pretty, pleasant, and slightly flirtatious can take a woman a long way. The interactions that she mentions, however, and the benefits that accrue from them, are so ephemeral that they do not allow us to think of flirting as anything more than a simple social lubricant: receiving prompt and attentive service when buying a coffee, being served a drink before other customers in a bar, a friendlier interaction with the bus driver. Again, it is a matter of looks, but it is just as much about impression management and self-presentation—what Fanny describes as "having a brighter, more polite personality." Clarisse states the opposite: she generally refrains from being flirtatious because she lacks self-confidence; she is shy and private and does not believe that her looks are sufficiently attractive. In a certain sense, this is consistent with Fanny's claim that, regardless of appearance, one has to be in the mood to flirt. When she is, a virtuous circle is set in motion: good interactions improve your good mood and that of your interlocutor, making the contact effortless and smooth. When she is having a bad day, when she is feeling somewhat grumpier, this personal, and in a sense collective, gain cannot be triggered. To be especially friendly, Fanny depends on a certain degree of correspondence between how she feels and what she wishes to express. Not so for other women, she says. While considering herself very different from her, and being sometimes embarrassed by her self-presentation, Fanny describes her mother as someone who strongly believes in flirting as a universally applicable social enabler:

> She'd be more flirtatious with, you know, men, whether there's a romantic thing or not, 'cause I think that she feels, like, "Oh, something will be improved by this behavior," whatever it is. Whether this will be more fun, or this will be an easier interaction, or whatever it is. [. . .] I think she's always been like that. But she also [. . . tends to practice] a more damsel-in-distress kind of thing, where, like, you know, she could go to a gas station and go, like [*in a high-pitched voice*], "Oh, I don't know how to do this [. . .]" [*laughs*]. Whereas I'm more like, "No, I'm fine, I've got this." Yeah, yeah [*laughs*].

The way Fanny describes the difference between her behavior and her mother's points, I believe, to a different model of femininity. Fanny, who calls herself a feminist and is committed to empowering women through her line of work, resists a more traditional performance of femininity, one that hinges on weakness, helplessness, and cluelessness.[8] If the price of having other people do things for you is appearing disempowered and incapable, she is, unlike her mother, not willing to pay it. The putative gains derived from that kind of flirting would not compensate for what is lost: the opportunity to be acknowledged as an autonomous, competent woman. Hence, the degree of one's adherence to a mainstream performance of femininity must be modulated against the risk of being devalued as a lightweight. As Beverly Skeggs writes with regard to young women, when engaging in flirtatious behavior a woman exposes herself to the "frequent daily humiliations of sexism."[9]

When men are the recipients of the flirtatious interaction, as they often are, there is an additional danger: that of being misunderstood and ending up in unpleasant situations. Again according to Fanny, that is when physical beauty can turn into a liability. Depending on the context, it can be wise to limit the room for ambiguity so as to minimize the risk of being misread: "I may not want to open an encounter to any type of flirtation or [imply that] 'I'm being sexy' because I'm uncomfortable [. . .] depending on who it might be," says Fanny. Women are generally aware of the need to protect themselves from potential aggression and harassment in everyday encounters with men. In addition, they are aware of the factors that may increase the risk of sexual harassment, such as time of day (night being perceived as more dangerous), place (bars being qualified as sites of increased ambiguity), activity (women drinking alcohol are judged according to their sexuality more than their "humanity"),[10] and neighborhood (urban dwellers can identify "bad" parts of town). As criminologist Elizabeth Stanko claims, the need to constantly negotiate their safety and assess risk in public and private spaces is part of women's subjectivity and gender performance.[11] Historically constructed as entailing danger and demanding male protection, femininity and beauty require the daily management of risk. The way Fanny evaluates the situations in which flirtation would make her uncomfortable takes all the above-mentioned factors into account. Similarly, Lena says she avoids short skirts and high heels when she goes to bars in downtown Montreal.[12] Hence, the advantages of using attractiveness to facilitate positive interactions, say, or to obtain better service, must be evaluated against the costs, as they are only obtainable in certain contexts and according to certain conditions; in addition to enabling sexist responses and humiliations, in many situations, women's attractiveness can easily be mistaken for sexual availability.

Zoe highlights an additional limitation of seductiveness and appearance as a female "power": when you obtain something through your appearance, you'll be stigmatized for it and not taken seriously as a person. According to Zoe's experience, in her line of work—radio, TV, and public relations—a man can be deemed both physically attractive and professionally or intellectually competent, but a beautiful woman, especially when younger, cannot. Zoe is not wrong. Indeed, research shows that men and women accrue different and unequal advantages from beauty, especially in work-related matters. When making assumptions on the basis of appearance, people combine inferences about looks with inferences based on the gender, race, and age of the person they evaluate. For instance, attractive men are rated more intellectually capable than attractive women. Also, since attractive individuals are perceived as more gender stereotypical, attractive women are seen as having more traditionally feminine qualities, which represents an additional obstacle for women in traditionally masculine jobs or work environments.[13] As condensed in the power paradox, and as we will discuss in more detail in the following sections, any attempt to use attractiveness as a power can have a quite disempowering effect on women.

WORKING WITH BEAUTY

Aware of the potential drawbacks of her attractiveness in the workplace, especially when she was a younger, less experienced professional, Zoe has learned to aim for what she calls "the right dosage" when getting ready for work. The goal is to look good but not sexy. So she applies makeup but is careful not to overdo it. Ideally, she says, the result is a version of "good-looking" that "it isn't too distracting."

I gather from Zoe's explanation that she does not simply mean that a woman's looks should not divert her colleagues from their tasks (an echo of the criticism commonly leveled at high school girls, who are publicly reprimanded for dressing in a fashion that might "distract" their ostensibly helpless male classmates).[14] She also means that it is in your best interest as a woman to avoid an appearance that would prevent other people from seeing *your real worth*. Indeed, it would seem that a fair and impartial recognition of one's skills and value in the workplace is not equally accessible across the spectrums of gender and race. Women, as well as racialized people of all genders, are subjected to more severe scrutiny with regard to their attire and physical comportment in the workplace, and they are often targeted by specific restrictions governing what is considered an appropriate appearance.[15] But even when no explicit workplace dress code is enforced, a look deemed "too feminine" or "too ethnic" might affect the perception of a woman's or a racialized person's competence. For example, in Glick and colleagues' experimental study, working women whose appearance was thought to be more sexualized were perceived as less competent when holding a higher-ranking job (as a manager, say), whereas this same characteristic tended not to matter for those in a lower-status position (like secretaries).[16] Attractiveness might bear advantages for working women, but only within very specific parameters.

As I mentioned in the previous section, there is a body of research demonstrating the social and economic advantages of attractiveness in the workplace. The preference for attractive individuals is generally explained as a form of trait inference, whereby a series of qualities are attributed to an individual on the basis of his or her looks, without the need for any further evidence.[17] However, women's attractiveness must be carefully managed to produce such advantages, as Zoe rightly believes. Female attractiveness must be framed in such a way that the negative bias attached to female beauty is defused. When you're young and attractive, says Zoe, they give you "small stuff" to do, because everybody assumes that you're a lightweight. Hence, impression management through aesthetic work is a crucial skill for any working woman.

Again, this claim is supported by qualitative research. As Paustian-Underdahl and Walker demonstrate, women's attractiveness is generally considered a liability in situations where they apply for "male-typed jobs," as their beauty symbolizes femininity and feminine qualities such as lack of agency. These results validate the core theoretical proposal of this book: that beauty upholds the difference between masculine and feminine (bodies, identities, activities, social spheres, etc.), which makes it both validating and belittling for women, regardless of whether or not they are deemed physically attractive.[18] Neil Howlett and colleagues, in addition, found that small manipulations of a woman's outfit can significantly change the way she is assessed and judged by her colleagues. The authors measured how women whose shirts were unbuttoned to varying degrees (one button vs. two), but who otherwise looked the same, were perceived with regard to their intelligence, responsibility, confidence, trustworthiness, organization, and authority. Women with two buttons undone were judged more negatively than those thought to be dressing more conservatively (with just one button undone); in addition, women in more prestigious positions (e.g., senior managers) were judged more negatively than their counterparts in lower-status positions (like receptionist).[19] However, when

Gurung and colleagues repeated a similar experiment while introducing a new independent variable (a camisole under the shirt), they found that women with unbuttoned shirts and no camisole (a more "provocative" look) indeed received the most negative ratings on all criteria save for one: they were deemed more *powerful*. The experiment's authors speculated that professional women dressing more provocatively are seen as being "high in confidence."[20]

In other words, a sexualized appearance is not univocal; rather, it can be taken to mean different things. For this reason, women have to learn to master this complicated language if they are to succeed in highly competitive professional environments. Lena, for instance, when she recalls her previous career as a broker in a very male-dominated field, is certain that her being an attractive woman, and—this is crucial—often the *only* woman "under thirty," enabled her "to stand out in a crowd" and thereby obtain more business from clients. While, in her opinion, she never consciously used this to gain any specific advantages, she's always recognized the more general benefit she's derived from this fact, if for no other reason than people always knew who she was, which was key in a business based on competition for contracts. Hence, she would "dress up" for events and emphasize her looks to make herself more recognizable, to "stand out." And yet, the very thing that enabled her to make a positive first impression on prospective clients—her looks—would also garner a lot of unwanted attention from men at informal business events. In defining her appearance and her self-presentation, then, Lena had to walk the very thin line between being "acknowledged" and being "drooled over."

Some work environments are indeed more demanding. In her magazine report on the (largely unspoken) dress code for women politicians in the United States, Magdalena Puniewska shows that candidates and elected representatives feel obliged to comply with strict rules governing their appearance. This requires careful attention to things like color, shape, and style in the choice of one's wardrobe, hairstyle, accessories, and makeup. Or, to put this differently, adherence to these rules requires a high degree of competence vis-à-vis the complexities of beautification, which, as we saw in chapter 3, requires time, money, energy, and lots of planning. Covering shoulders and arms, indeed, avoiding any type of revealing clothing, appears to be a pivotal aspect of the woman politician's dress code: in this sense, politics is clearly representative of a host of work environments in which, to achieve legitimacy, women must downplay any hint of sexualized femininity. However, even when they comply with the rules, women are not shielded from harsh scrutiny, and they are constantly reminded that appearance is a decisive factor in the assessment of their competence. Like their counterparts in show business, women politicians are criticized for wearing an outfit more than once. The contrast with male politicians is of course glaring. In a 2012 interview, US president Barack Obama explained that he would have a "blue or a gray suit"[21] already laid out for him the night before; clearly, lack of sartorial variety is no problem for male politicians, and indeed may even be seen as a smart trick to improve productivity.[22] A woman who wears the same outfit twice, or who reduces her choice of clothes to a single style (think of Hillary Rodham Clinton with her famous pantsuits), is called out for being poorly groomed, lazy, sloppy, and robotic. And when that woman politician belongs to a marginalized gender category or a visible minority, then the scrutiny is even harsher.[23]

This ability to manage one's appearance in order to be considered reliable and competent, while it is perhaps more visible among high-profile politicians or celebrities, is nonetheless key in lower-status jobs as well, as I learned from some of the younger women I talked to. The ability to effectively use one's appearance as an asset, then, does not mean exhibiting a stereotypical, hyper-feminine, or overtly sexualized beauty independent of a larger consideration of context and the importance of identity management; it consists, rather, in understanding what style of feminine beauty is required in each individual situation in order to derive the desired benefits. Eva, for instance, attributes her ability to secure student jobs while working toward her degrees to her pleasant but "unthreatening appearance." She believes that potential employers would perceive her as trustworthy and confident, but without being overbearing. To Eva, "unthreatening" basically means not sexualized; she explains, for example, that her breasts are small, which means that she looks like a woman, just a very harmless one. She found this appearance particularly advantageous while working in a children's shoe store.

But for all her acuity when it comes to understanding how men will see her in various professional settings, Eva's experience has also taught her to be aware of the dangers of being perceived as "competition" by women coworkers or superiors. She recalls once working for an older woman and having the clear sense that she felt threatened by Eva's youth. Looking "harmless"—that is, performing a plain, unchallenging femininity—is therefore often insufficient to navigate an additional hierarchy of feminine appearances in the workplace. As a subordinate, lower-status worker, or as a job applicant, Eva feels that putting too much emphasis on her looks would be like crossing a boundary in the eyes of other women. According to scholarship on the postfeminist culture that has thrived since the 2000s, a postfeminist sensibility encourages a fundamental ambiguity in relationships between women. Notwithstanding its superficial emphasis on female friendship and solidarity, postfeminist sensibility also enhances competition among women, specifically when it comes to appearance.[24] In this rivalry, where an attractive, overtly feminine appearance is treated as a sign of success and a marker of status, thinner trumps fatter, younger trumps older, and more traditionally feminine trumps more fluid gender presentations. Eva's self-presentation in the workplace might be grounded in the perception of the dangers of entering such a competition from an employee position.

As we'll see in chapter 6, where I analyze the role of selfies, Cassandra, who is older than Eva, offers her own variation on the theme of "harmlessness" when she comments on a picture taken at a special professional occasion. At the event, Cassandra was launching her first book, an achievement she describes with evident pride. Her appearance, she explains, was kept as simple as possible; she wanted to look pretty, but, most importantly, she wanted her book to occupy center stage. Had she emphasized her looks, or simply dressed as usual (you might remember Cassandra's love for conspicuous makeup, jewelry and accessories, wigs and elaborate outfits), this would have been distracting, or conveyed the wrong kind of self-promotion given the circumstances. Listening to Cassandra, I'm reminded of Zoe's idea of the "right dosage" of beautification for a professional setting.

However, adopting an ostensibly "harmless" femininity can sometimes mean trading self-respect for tranquility. Working in customer service, Eva observes that her "harmless" appearance evidently defines patrons' expectations regarding her behavior. Eva clearly sees that her male colleagues are permitted to treat clients with a degree of impoliteness that she, as a woman playing "kind" and harmless, is not allowed to match. Her unthreatening feminine persona binds her to a more limited set of reactions when facing, for instance, a client who is too demanding. Hence, she is sometimes forced to sacrifice her dignity to the unavoidable obligation to facilitate a polite and satisfying (for the customer) interaction. Eva is in this sense aware of performing what sociologist Arlie Hochschild called "emotional labor,"[25] a term that describes the effort, demanded as part of one's professional obligations, to display the appropriate feelings in a given work situation, and to reduce the gap between one's real and displayed feelings whenever the two might clash. Of course, Eva's willingness to show kindness and calm while dealing with a rude client can vary, and the difference between expressed and felt feelings fluctuates accordingly. However, she feels that appearance plays a role in her obligation to maintain the professional persona that her looks help to create. It is as though her feminine self-presentation as "harmless" automatically deprives her of a range of displayed feelings that are accessible to her male colleagues (or to different female professional personas). She must be kind, endure being treated as someone who doesn't have a clue, and reckon with the consequences of appearing harmless.

Yet another version of "harmless" attractiveness helps Emma, who is a twenty-two-year-old student, defuse potentially dangerous situations while working various part-time jobs. She often works in bars in downtown Montreal, and more specifically in an area characterized by a high prevalence of social problems such as substance abuse and homelessness, which means she often witnesses heavy alcohol consumption, drug addiction, sexual abuse, and fights. When her patrons get too drunk or violent, Emma jumps in to de-escalate the situation and help contain the damage. This is when she uses her "charms," as she calls them, to convince those in distress to calm down, and eventually to leave the venue. By playing the nice, cute, young girl, she "disarms" them; "it's like . . . [they know] I won't harm them," she says. However, this damage-control strategy is based purely on individual initiative, personal assets (age, gender, physical traits, manners, etc.), and the intuition that it will be effective, and Emma and her coworkers (mostly fellow waitresses) lament the total lack of formal training and information sharing that characterizes their conditions as employees. Feeling otherwise unequipped, Emma tries her best with what she has, but she holds her breath every time, unsure whether her strategy will continue to work.

It can be observed that Emma's employer's unwillingness to explicitly address this organizational inadequacy is yet another way of exploiting their employees' ability to perform emotional labor, as in Eva's case. However, Emma's description of her work points to an additional dimension of labor that work and employment scholars Chris Warhurst and Dennis Nickson call "aesthetic labour." This is certainly the more visible dimension of the relational and emotional labor performed by an employee, but it is also related to the employee's level of attractiveness and the ways in which that can serve organizational purposes and needs. Through the concept of "aesthetic labour," Warhurst and Nickson aim at foregrounding "embodiment [to reveal] how the corporeality, not just the feelings, of employees are organizationally appropriated and transmuted for commercial benefit."[26] In Emma's line of work, it's not just a matter of having the "right look" (it is well-known, after all, that bars try to hire good-looking staff to attract patrons); rather, employees are also encouraged, whether directly or indirectly, to convert the "right look" into an organizational tool to promote a particular corporate image. In Emma's case, then, aesthetic labor (which hinges on her being "cute," "nice," young, and good-looking) is performed both to boost profits, which could be considered part of her job description, and, in a form of well-intentioned improvisation, to maintain a manageable and livable environment, a task for which she has received no formal training but which, if not performed, could have consequences for her employment status.

As sociologist Miliann Kang observes on the basis of her work with nail salon workers and clients, "the power of beauty often derives and reinforces powerlessness in other areas of women's lives."[27] The women I talked to show their awareness of the risk of using a beautiful, overtly feminine appearance as a form of "power" in the workplace, as they expect to be perceived as threatening (as women who can't keep to their "place"), as superficial, or as incompetent. Hence, attractiveness can be downplayed and thereby rendered a "harmless" power—in which guise, attractiveness can have several advantages. However, it also confines women within the narrow boundaries of a feminine self-expression that excludes self-assertion, individual agency, and apparent self-confidence—qualities often demanded of employees in higher-status jobs and of self-employed workers in most lines of work. Primarily referring to her participants' description of the advantages and disadvantages that stem from the use of attractiveness (and, specifically, hair color and style) as a strategic tool to obtain social gains, Rose Weitz writes that "women often find that power obtained through these strategies is circumscribed, fragile, bittersweet, and limiting."[28] As the power paradox states, a women's power is powerless when her appearance remains the prime indicator of how much she can and must be taken seriously by her fellow social actors, coworkers, and employers.

FAVORS AND PRIVILEGES

As I showed in the previous sections, the association between attractiveness and material and symbolic advantage is as present in our folk sociology of beauty as it is demonstrated by a large body of scholarship. Knowing this, I was eager to learn how my interviewees might answer one question in particular: What does one get in return for being attractive? As we've already seen, research shows that more attractive people have a better chance of being hired and promoted, and in educational settings, they receive better grades when their physical features are visible to their instructor.[29] But what about people who already are employed or who hold a degree? What about circumstances that are perhaps more mundane than applying for a job or taking an exam? Does beauty bring tangible, albeit harder-to-measure, benefits that might make a difference in women's daily lives?

The majority of the women I talked to were able to provide specific examples of the material and symbolic advantages they derived from their beautiful appearance. In addition, they described a learning process related to exploiting one's appearance, a process that, as discussed in the previous sections, began during their youth. Younger participants reported experiencing the benefits of attractiveness, evidently coupled with those of youth, and gradually understanding how to effectively harness them. Older ones, too, recalled this youthful discovery, but were also able to shed a critical light on the alleged rewards of beauty and how these fluctuate throughout the course of one's life.

Like other participants, Audrey and Melissa clearly state their belief that better-looking people get superior treatment when shopping or trying to access a service. A sloppy look is disadvantageous for a customer in a store: the service will not be as prompt, as courteous, and the chances of receiving special treatment (as in, "Oh, I'll add this to your thing!" as Melissa says) shrink. This is why both women say they will go the extra mile when getting ready to go out shopping. To Audrey, this is also a strategy to compensate for the loss of visibility and recognition that comes with being a woman over forty, and a "bigger" woman, as we saw in chapter 4. Indeed, as mentioned in the previous section, studies in social psychology show that we share a folk sociology of beauty and ugliness, such that attractive people are generally perceived as having a higher social status. This would explain why they might get better customer service in stores and other venues: they appear to emanate a sort of unquestioned legitimacy and entitlement. Doing extra work to improve one's looks is therefore a way of regulating other people's perception of one's social status, which is expected to translate into access to opportunities, favors, and privileges. In other words, special treatment awaits people who present themselves as though they already belong among a privileged group deserving of such favor.[30] This is why, in the long run, investing in attractiveness and "beauty work" may even influence someone's social trajectory.

Aware of what she considers the power of attractiveness, Emma, who is constantly struggling to make ends meet, tries to get free drinks each time she goes to the bar. She uses her charms with male bartenders and patrons alike, and usually things go as planned. Her "charisma," she says, together with her young age and good looks, are a sufficient compensation for the men, who are content with her company and do not demand more. In stores and restaurants, Emma uses the same strategy to get rebates or free stuff, or an exchange to which she is otherwise not entitled, but bars remain the most common scenario. However, as we saw in the first section of this chapter, Emma also exploits her charms when she is on the other end of these interactions. Indeed, working as a bartender, her looks and her attitude are good for business to the extent that they allow her to sell more drinks. The learning process goes both ways, then: what she learns as a worker, she exploits as a customer, and vice versa.

Similar to Juliette, who emphasized the impact of beauty and youth, Zoe, among the older participants whom I interviewed, recounts discovering the power of youth and attractiveness when she started working in public relations. As an attractive young woman, and therefore someone who constantly ran the risk of being dismissed as incompetent, she would nevertheless obtain special treatment from her male coworkers. They would multiply gestures of chivalry, for example, to help her with the most trivial tasks, such as opening a door or carrying a box. However, whatever pleasure she initially derived from this discovery rapidly faded as she grew tired of putting herself in the position of the cute damsel (a reaction similar to Fanny's, as described in the first section of this chapter). On the other hand, Zoe understands the advantages of attractiveness as a fair compensation for all the "sweating" that goes into looking good as a woman.[31]

Cassandra recalls feeling the same "power" in her younger years, the power of obtaining something to which she was not entitled other than as a reward for her attractiveness. "A long time ago I was beautiful," she says, "and I just felt like you could have beauty and two dollars and get on the bus." Aging, however, had an enlightening effect, and Cassandra now understands that "there's no cheque in the mail for being beautiful, unless you're prostituting yourself." Different from other participants who receive free drinks in bars, Cassandra is emphatic on this point: "I don't get a free coffee for being beautiful." Her remarks point toward two different ways we might read the rewards for attractiveness. In the first reading, they depend on the situation, with bars and nighttime being framed as more propitious settings for more sexually ambiguous exchanges. In the second, the benefits of attractiveness might actually be negatively correlated with age. Cassandra recounts an experience that might bolster the latter claim. Asked whether her appearance has brought her any benefits in life, Cassandra, having just claimed that it does not, at least in the present, recalls a specific circumstance in which she believes that her beauty did indeed work in her favor, and for a sustained period of time no less. Back when her son was little (thus almost two decades prior to our interviews) and she was raising him as a single mother, Cassandra struggled financially. She was working as a professional dancer but was not making enough money to pay the bills. Specifically, she could not afford to pay the rent for her apartment on top of all her other expenses. Her landlord, an older "gentleman," came to the rescue by allowing her to keep the apartment for ten years without paying anything:

> He believed I had a dance studio, I believed that he believed in me, but I was never gonna make the money that I owed him. . . . I was raising my kid, and he just never asked for any money. He'd come in and have tea with me. He'd go upstairs and get rent from people upstairs, he'd complain about them to me, and he'd leave! So . . . I think that might have something to do with my looks. But I can't prove it. He could have just been a nice guy.

The landlord never asked for sexual favors; he seemed merely to enjoy her company and to want to help, says Cassandra. Like her, the landlord was a member of the Black community, which might have triggered an additional sense of solidarity. Nevertheless, she believes that her appearance made the difference, perhaps motivating her landlord to grant her certain privileges that she would not have enjoyed had she not been an attractive dancer. Cassandra acknowledges that her good looks and her personality might indeed have played the lead part in relieving her of a financial burden that she might otherwise have been unable to shoulder during a very challenging period of her life.

In her 2011 book *Erotic Capital*, economist Catherine Hakim variously describes sexiness, attractiveness, fitness, and beauty as powers that women can wield in the marriage market as well as in professional contexts. Such "erotic capital"[32] is rewarded in women more than in men because of what Hakim describes as the "male sex deficit." Simply put, women desire sex less than men, which bestows a higher market value on women's sexuality due to its scarcity. Hence, whoever controls access to this highly demanded good has power. Hakim encourages women to embrace this power and to use it to their advantage in all possible social situations, from the job market to the mating market. By exploiting their erotic capital, she argues, women might pursue a collective strategy whose end result is an increase in gender equality, since women would gain access to opportunities, resources, and profits that they might otherwise never obtain. Erotic capital, however, deteriorates and decreases over time if one does not try to preserve it, so it follows that beautification and bodywork are necessary investments to maintain one's assets. As a consequence, erotic capital also depends on one's ability to deploy other types of capital, each of which demands its own expenditure of finite resources. There is economic capital, for example, which requires a certain level of material affluence, or cultural capital, based on aesthetic knowledge and self-presentational know-how. Finally, there is social capital, which cannot be appreciated outside of one's social relations and exchanges—assuming these are available to the individual in question.[33]

This last observation already contains the most obvious refutation of the notion that "erotic capital" does indeed promote gender equality. First, women's access to resources such as money, education, prestige, and social status is regulated by structural inequalities and discriminations organized across gender, race, class, age, body size, and disability. Women's ability to exploit erotic capital therefore depends on a set of variables over which they have no control, especially at the individual level. Second, beauty and attractiveness are also organized by these inequalities. For instance, white beauty is more valued than racialized beauty, and as a consequence, racialized erotic capital appears to have, as it were, less market value. In her study of the "marketability" of women's erotic capital in the stripping industry, for instance, Siobhan Brooks shows that Black and Latina women enjoy considerably fewer rewards for their physical assets, both in material (e.g., money) and non-material terms (e.g., professional opportunities and social connections). Likewise, Tressie McMillan Cottom, in her powerful essay "In the Name of Beauty," argues that, notwithstanding the fact that beauty norms change over time (for instance, toward a lesser or greater appreciation of "curvier" bodies), such norms remain permanently exclusionary insofar as they seem always to either ignore or even penalize women belonging to visible minorities: "as long as beautiful people are white, what is beautiful at any given time can be renegotiated without redistributing capital from white to nonwhite people."[34]

The same is true in the case of older women, as we saw in chapter 4. Female beauty cannot work as a social equalizer so long as embodied attractiveness is assessed according to criteria that entail stratification and structural discrimination; the value of erotic capital is far from universal,[35] linked simply to the possession of one's female body (as the "male sex deficit" theory would encourage us to think). I'll not dwell further on the flaws in Hakim's theory, nor on the reasons why sexiness cannot be some magic wand that delivers us gender equality.[36] Suffice it to say that, despite its flaws, Hakim's book taps into a question with which feminist thinkers have long grappled—namely, whether it would advance women's cause to exploit the advantages provided by a patriarchal construction of sexuality and, as a consequence, of femininity. Or, to pose the question somewhat differently: Should women embrace or denounce the kind of power that they get from being objects of male desire in cultures organized by male sexual privilege?

The women I talked to struggle with similar questions. In addition, experience allows the older women I interviewed to see the limits of this alleged "power" and the problems that arise from attempts to wield it. Indeed, having interviewed both younger and older women, I came to appreciate the different perceptions that each age group has of the "power" of beauty. As I mentioned in chapter 4, younger participants still lack the hindsight that enables older women to assess the benefits and the drawbacks of beauty, as well as the limits of its profitability. For instance, Zoe knows well, having learned from experience, that the power to have a door held open by a man is actually no power at all. As for using attractiveness more generally, older participants tended to doubt the purported value of privileges acquired through it. Some women describe a feeling of disenchantment after repeatedly seeing the trick in action and finding it predictable, even tiring. Take Audrey and her girlfriends, for example: they are regular customers of a local bar, where she says they "constantly get free drinks." Audrey knows that the bartender's generosity, and all the fuss about their presence in the bar, is actually driven by a simple financial imperative: if women are in the room, the venue will do better business—men will stay longer, consume more, and possibly attempt to buy the women drinks. Audrey is under no illusions about this:

> I mean, it sounds really cynical, but I have a hard time figuring it out otherwise, 'cause the bar owner is like twenty-five years old, and they're good-looking kids, and they own a business—I mean, I don't think that it's because they're into us, you know what I mean? So . . . I think we are an advantage for them and therefore we get advantages. But I mean, it's just a theory; maybe they just think we're nice.

Years ago, Audrey would have believed in the authenticity of the favors she received, she would have felt gratified and "bent over backwards for that kind of attention." She would have felt genuinely liked. Now, she feels anything but flattered by the free drinks. "It's more, like—almost an exchange of business," she tells me. Audrey knows that women in a bar are a scarce, coveted good, and she accepts the free drinks brought to her because of this scarcity. But she also knows that her personality, her feelings, her *self*, are not part of the equation. Hence, she and her friends now know that "when men are being really nice to us, it's not because they're really nice to *us*."

Cassandra describes a different attitude, and a different learning process. To her, experience meant acquiring a skill that "every woman" should master: how to tailor one's appearance to fit into a specific situation and, more importantly, to achieve one's goals in it. Like Audrey, Cassandra has a fairly jaundiced view of the benefits of attractiveness. However, being more confident in her looks and in her ability to seduce, she starts by asking herself what she wants to happen in the context she's about to enter, and she defines her self-presentation accordingly. More specifically, she determines the level of "sexiness," the degree of artifice and self-transformation that she needs in order to manipulate the situation to her favor—whether it's a matter of just fitting in it, or standing out from others, or even trying to appeal to a potential partner. Audrey, on the other hand, is very self-conscious about the changes her body has undergone in the last couple of years. She is older, "as opposed to twenty-five," and "a bigger woman." This, she says, is when "people stop being nice to you, people stop wanting you, and therefore, they stop doing things to make you want them." Aware of the inevitability of the aging process, Cassandra is doing everything in her power to look younger than she is (she returns to this theme many times during our two interviews), to lose weight whenever she gains some, and to always look and feel her best (you might remember her insistence on a healthy lifestyle from the previous chapters). For beauty to remain a sort of currency, a considerable amount of work is required—planning, executing, managing, consuming, and so forth. Bodily changes, however, are often out of one's control, as is one's gradual exclusion from the category of women who can profit from their appearance and thereby wield it as a "power."

CONCLUSION: UNCERTAIN GAINS

The ability to derive benefits from one's attractiveness depends on individual characteristics as well as on the way these characteristics are perceived and appreciated by others in specific contexts. Hence, this ability is framed by differences of gender, age, ethnicity, education, disability, body size, and social class, and also by how others perceive these attributes. The intersection of these differences, which organize inequalities in the social sphere, influences the outcome of strategies aimed at profiting from one's beauty. Martina Cvajner's observations, discussed in the opening pages of this chapter, are an excellent example of the relative, context-specific character of attractiveness and femininity as strategic and symbolic resources. To begin with, aging significantly diminishes the rewards for beauty inasmuch as it reduces one's perceived attractiveness; the gap must be filled by additional beauty work, which may symbolize affluence and thereby regulate the perception of one's social status. Conversely, youth functions as a substitute for social status, since it is rewarded regardless, even in the *absence of*, signs of affluence or specific beauty work. Hence, attractiveness and youth can mitigate the effect of a lower social status in certain contexts. Performance of mainstream femininity through niceness, "harmlessness," smiling, and flirtatious self-presentation improves one's chances of being positively validated for one's presence and appearance. In this sense, cultural capital (as in education, access to information, manners), social capital (as in networks, contacts, social involvement), and some professional experience (such as in Emma's, Jeanne's, and Zoe's cases) can enhance attractiveness and ensure material and symbolic gains.

The complex intersection of the assessment variables I just presented refutes a voluntaristic conception of the power of attractiveness, like Hakim's, which claims that women can wield such power by sheer force of will and simply by overcoming the taboo linked to exploiting the male sex deficit. Not only bodily features, but, more importantly, bodily changes are largely beyond one's control. And so are the cultural frameworks regulating the aesthetic appreciation of different bodies, faces, and attitudes.[37] As the interviewees clearly stated, the advantages of attractiveness depend on a set of contextual variables, some of which can be taken into account and partially controlled, while others cannot. And idealized feminine appearance remains dominated by whiteness, social status (displayed by elegance), thinness, youth (or the preservation thereof in the case of older women), a subtly seductive femininity (achieved, for instance, through makeup and attire), sexiness without overt sexualization, a flirtatious attitude that flatters men without appearing threatening, and so on.[38] The extent to which a certain appearance can be traded as currency, can be "capitalized," cannot be determined by the individual; and for this reason, power based on appearance is tenuous and is further weakened by its dependence on the shifting, contextual appreciation of one's individual features.

As part of their primary and secondary socialization (family in the former case, education, peer, and group influences in the latter),[39] through which they are acclimatized to various situationally determined social expectations, women develop the ability to anticipate how their physical characteristics will be perceived in a specific situation. Hence, they learn to perform the necessary beautification and emotional work to enhance their assets and increase their odds of being positively acknowledged and validated. The benefits of beauty depend on this validation. However, women also learn—often at a considerable price—to simultaneously assess the situational risks associated with using beauty as a primary self-presentation cue. The most obvious risk is linked to harassment and aggression. More pervasive and ubiquitous, however, is the danger of being reduced to one's appearance and thereby judged as insubstantial.

As people, as workers, women walk the thin line between using femininity as an asset and being undervalued as feminine—and thus, as Rita Freedman observes, a deviation from the masculine norm. Freedman successfully summarizes these tensions when she claims that appearance is both an important source of women's sense of identity and a "serious threat" to it.[40] Avoiding a sexualized appearance, while still being subtly flirtatious, is, according to some of the interviewees, a good strategy—a good "balance"—for maximizing gains and minimizing risks, especially in professional contexts. As anticipated in chapter 1, the benefits of a beautiful appearance are regulated by paradoxical criteria. This is a second objection to a voluntaristic conception of beauty as "capital." The power of women's attractiveness reinforces a situational definition of gender difference as a hierarchical device, and, by reinforcing it, weakens women's actual power.

Chapter 6

SELFIES AND THE DIGITAL WORLD

As a result of the ongoing migration of traditional media to the Internet, the beauty culture analyzed in previous chapters is replicated with little difference in the digital sphere. This is particularly salient with regard to online platforms that are mainly devoted to the circulation of user-produced content. Social networking platforms (usually called "social media") such as Facebook, YouTube, Tumblr, Instagram, TikTok, Snapchat, and more, rely on users' willingness to display a seemingly limitless number of mundane aspects of their everyday lives: their families, partners, interests, jobs, meals, athletic performances, pets—the list is virtually inexhaustible. Self-presentation is at the center of this "digital participative culture,"[1] and the information shared by users is increasingly of a visual nature (pictures, videos), thanks in part to the relative affordability of portable connected devices—phones, tablets, laptops—equipped with digital cameras. Digital participative culture is of course entangled with various economic processes, including tech companies' reselling of user data and information to third-party commercial subjects, the sale of advertising on social media sites, and even celebrity culture, with its multilayered financial incentives and manifold professional profiles. In the latter case, celebrities use their substantial public platforms to create a visual self-narrative that can then be harnessed to the promotion of commercial goods and services. On Instagram, for example, the highest-ranking celebrities are often beautiful women advertising their own cosmetic brands, clothing lines, fitness programs, or lifestyle products.[2]

Selfies are a pivotal element of this landscape. Displaying a rather gender-stereotypical style of attractiveness often serves as a mark of one's belonging to the right visual conversation on social media. In addition to being a crucial aspect of women's social lives in general, as should now be clear from the previous chapters, beauty culture penetrates women's digital existence and helps set the norms, conventions, and values that govern it. This chapter will discuss the place that beauty holds in women's online visual self-representational practices. In particular, I will show how the paradoxes of beauty culture, having migrated to the digital sphere, translate into various paradoxical injunctions regarding women's appearance, visibility, and self-narrative in selfies.[3]

But before addressing the inherent tension between popular characterizations of women's selfies as narcissistic, on the one hand, and the insistence on the need for an "authentic" online persona, on the other, I will describe how the interviewees themselves situate beauty and beautification within their selfie-related practices. Despite being at the center of the popular discourse on selfies, the extent to which these images are about looking and feeling attractive goes, strangely enough, rather undiscussed in the scholarly literature. Hence, instead of taking it for granted, my aim is to provide evidence of the link between women's concern for beauty and their production and circulation of selfies.

THE PLACE OF BEAUTY IN SELFIES

The research participants and I did not only discuss selfie practices in general. Between our first and second interviews, I also assigned each woman some light homework. Specifically, I asked them to take several selfies and then send them to me. Before the second interview, I printed out each picture on an 8.5-by-11-inch piece of paper—which is merely to say that I reproduced them at a scale that is considerably bigger than the usual size of a selfie viewed on a portable device. I began each interview by asking what it had been like to take selfies for my project, and then we moved on to discussing the individual pictures. I wanted to record the various feelings, stories, and explanations each selfie triggered in its author.[4] Each participant's photo archive was—for me no less than for them—a rich source of memories, reflections, and judgments, and thus of insights into what it means to be a woman who takes selfies. Talking about a selfie entails putting one's past "self" into words, narrating the "who" that the selfie visually represents. This "self" played a tripartite role in our conversations and can be identified as follows: she who is portrayed in the picture, she who took the picture, and she who talks about and whose first-person perspective connects both subject and object. Such a posture binds the present to the past by situating the self vis-à-vis different contexts, life stages, commitments, and experiences. By situating them in the past, I reasoned, selfies would help the participants position themselves in the present and trace a biographical link between then and now—and sometimes project themselves into the future as well. Appearance played an active role in constructing these sorts of self-narratives, as it emerged as the primary site at which identity materializes and, in a sense, allows the observer to look back at another version of herself.[5]

Melissa's reaction to seeing her selfies during our second interview is an excellent example of this temporal self-construction. She says she sees two things when looking at the pictures I asked her to take of herself: the rough patch that she went through in her recent past, and the richness of her present life (that is, at the time of our second interview). When I first met with her, Melissa was having trouble dealing with the overwhelming combination of menopause, an injury, a career change, and her many family obligations. Coping with the physical changes wrought by menopause, and especially weight gain, was difficult, and the injury prevented her from keeping her weight in check by exercising at her usual intensity. She was facing the additional challenge of trying to establish herself in a new professional field, as we have seen in the previous chapters. Melissa did not like her body and felt the burden of fading beauty, seeing menopause as a symbolic threshold on the way to old age. She was very emotional during that first interview; at one point, while explaining that she no longer felt beautiful, strong, and attractive, as she did in the past, she started to cry.

Seven months later, however, Melissa is somewhere else, and she is able to *see* this change in her selfies. Her professional skills had been recognized and had gained a new visibility (this was also thanks to her efforts at self-promotion on social media). She resumed running and biking and was really enjoying the outdoors. The selfies she sent me capture some of the excitement she had derived from her life as of late, such as when traveling with her family, going out, meeting with clients, or playing with her beloved dogs. Looking at the selfies I've printed off, Melissa now sees a record of the beauty that she experienced: hers, that of the people she was with, of the places she visited, of the path she is now traveling. She tells me that, after talking with me the first time, she gave some thought to the reasons why she wants to take selfies. The answer is that those pictures comprise a visual journal of all this beauty. Melissa would like to preserve a record for when, in twenty years or so, her physical attractiveness will have left her forever. Turning fifty carries a symbolic meaning, she says: "just the number itself" reminds her of what is about to happen. Her recent experience of vulnerability taught her to seize the beauty that she enjoys in the here and now, and to treasure it.

Participants indeed reported that they are more likely to take selfies when they feel good, and particularly when they feel good about the way they look.[6] As discussed in chapter 2, feeling good is rooted in a combination of contextual circumstances in which personal beliefs, actions, and social interactions align to provide a sense of enthusiasm, legitimacy, serenity, or competence. The women I interviewed explain how feeling good motivates them to be more visible, notably through capturing their state of mind and their bodily appearance in a selfie. The good feelings can relate to specific surroundings (a nice sunset, for example), situations (being among friends), activities (leaving the hair salon, eating delicious ice cream), accomplishments (obtaining an important business deal), or a combination thereof, or they can just be part of a "good" day. By taking a selfie, one aims to preserve a memory not only of what one is doing, where, and with whom, but also of how one is feeling about these various factors; in this sense, a selfie is an act of visual self-expression through which one can say "who" one is—a mother, an older woman, a professional, someone who has access to leisure activities, someone who struggles with mental health, a feminist, a good friend, and so on. Since ordinary selfies are rarely planned in any formal sense (unless they are part of a professional practice, such as in the case of Instagram celebrities and so-called social media influencers), they are understood by their subjects as tokens of a felicitous concourse of circumstances (even including one's ability to successfully navigate one's technological devices and the various social platforms).[7]

It is important to highlight that this mode of visual self-expression hinges on what is visible, aims to capture something that is conspicuous, and can impress the viewers on an aesthetic level. The vast majority of the women I talked to drew a strong connection between having a certain appearance and taking a selfie. Some referred to their overall looks on a certain day, or in a certain picture. Most of them, however, pointed to more specific examples of one or other aesthetic feature that would make selfie-taking more likely—a new dress, for instance. But perhaps the most common feature—and this is consistent with what I presented in chapter 3—was good hair. Fully half of the interviewees linked their decision to take a selfie with having what they called a "good hair" day. Such a day can occur randomly, as a sort of "blessing," or can be facilitated through a visit to the hairdresser (with the selfie being shot right after). Beauty, then, feels like a sort of grace bestowed on us on certain days, for reasons beyond our control, accompanied by an exhilarating feeling and boosting our willingness to interact with and be seen by others.[8] But beauty can also be obtained through careful work, performed either by oneself or by professionals. Whatever its source, the presence of beauty at a specific moment in one's life is usually worth immortalizing and remembering. And as Melissa's example shows, selfies do exactly this.[9]

While they are a site for individual aesthetic self-expression, selfies circulated online and displaying one's attractiveness also tend to adhere to a rather circumscribed range of visual cues. This is one of the reasons Juliette expresses her annoyance with the genre. Thirty-five, single, and still completing her doctorate, she feels torn between the role of a young adult preparing for the "big" world and the desire to establish herself in a way that might be expected of someone her age. Her friends are starting to have kids, and their selfies are no longer about haircuts but rather babies. This is partly why Juliette stopped sharing selfies that, in her opinion, look facile and narcissistic, and has instead shifted to portraying herself in more "grown-up" ways. In order to be in tune with what she perceives as a more general transformation of selfie practices among her peers, she now feels the need to link her selfies to specific experiences, contexts, and activities that would qualify her as a more serious person, things like sightseeing, cultural events, work-related occasions, being with friends. She therefore felt that the homework I assigned for my study was meaningless and fake. Pretending to invest in her appearance for special occasions that do not occur in real life, as the other participants did, was out of question for her.

This had not been the case at the time of our first interview, when Juliette deemed selfies "narcissistic" overall, yet did not refrain from taking them to display a different hairstyle, a new necklace, or a nice dress. Nine months later, her feelings have changed. She recently spent several months abroad, in a country she loves, working as an intern for an organization related to her research field. Whereas writing her PhD is a lonely, isolated endeavor, her internship gave her the opportunity to reconnect with a busy work environment, a place where she could enjoy the company of colleagues and feel that she was part of something bigger. Also, being abroad, she felt freer and took advantage of every opportunity to have fun. Among the selfies that she sent me, there is a beautiful picture from that period: Juliette has a glass of wine in one hand, beams a contagious smile, and looks relaxed and happy. It is rare for her selfies to reveal much of her body, but in this one she wears an elegant tank top, which leaves her shoulders and upper chest bare. When I inquire about it, Juliette blames the wine: "I was drunk," she says candidly. She was attending a summer party on the rooftop of her residential complex, went back to her unit to refresh her drink, and took the picture to celebrate the good time she was having. Looking at it together, however, Juliette's reaction to the picture is quite negative. "I have big arms; I gained weight while I was there," she says. "I have broad shoulders." Finally, she tells me that she does not want to look at the picture anymore, which was first posted on Instagram and then immediately deleted. Even if Juliette intends to take selfies that are more than just about her looks, it is quite difficult for her to avoid foregrounding her physical appearance when assessing images of herself. Juliette's relationship to her own pictures points to the role that selfies play in enhancing and restructuring what Bernadette Wegenstein calls the "cosmetic gaze," which is a core aspect of the postfeminist female gaze: a way of gazing and seeing in which vision is privileged as a diagnostic tool for assessing individuals so as to improve, to transform, to produce "better" moral subjects by intervening in their bodily appearance—and thus, in their *selves*. By abetting this self-directed invocation of the cosmetic gaze, selfies enable an almost uninterrupted aesthetic self-scrutiny in the context of one's daily life, thus dramatizing the imperative of self-improvement.[10]

The extent to which selfies are about *looking good* is indeed a crucial aspect of their production and circulation. A selfie is generally a picture that the taker feels does justice to her looks and mood on a specific occasion, but it must also align more generally with her standards for looking her best in a picture. Melissa is very clear about this: she will not post a selfie if she feels she does not look good in it. But when she looks good, she will take a selfie and post it (as I mentioned, she finds that feeling beautiful is a rarer event in her everyday life, and so she feels that it is more important to immortalize it when it does occur). No doubt, like many other women, Fanny cannot stand the pictures that other people, and especially her husband, take of her. In her opinion, those pictures make her look uglier than she is in real life, and she resents them being "out there," circulating online. Selfies, which she often takes and shares, are a way of showing others—namely, her social media audience—how she sees herself. For Audrey, her appearance in a selfie "informs [her] decision whether or not to post." Sometimes, she feels the need to look her best, and therefore puts in the necessary effort. Other times, however, she posts selfies regardless of how they look (for instance, when her clothes are stained after a day of work), which in her mind is a way of challenging stereotypical selfie culture. This could take the form of pushing back against the invisibility of women over forty on social media, claiming a more visible place for "bigger" female bodies in the digital sphere, or showing her professional skills in a typically male work environment. The message she's trying to send, in her words, is that "I deserve to be here no matter what I look like." For her, this decision means having "complete control" over her image.

And yet in spite of this apparent confidence, Audrey is the first to admit feeling an enormous social pressure to comply with normative standards of feminine beauty, especially with regard to body size (she has gained weight in recent years), complexion (she is self-conscious about her skin), and grooming (a department in which she considers herself highly neglectful). To a certain extent, selfies have actually helped Audrey escape some of this pressure, to eschew the aesthetic surveillance: once her image, as out of step with mainstream beauty standards as it may be, is "out there," she feels empowered, shielded from negative judgments that cannot really hurt her. Audrey also uses selfies as a sort of "inoculation," deliberately posting unflattering pictures so as to familiarize herself with how she really looks; her hope is that the more often she sees a more or less candid picture of herself, the more comfortable she will be with her appearance in the long run. However, it takes courage to expose oneself while knowing very well that the dissonance between one's look and mainstream standards of online feminine comportment will be perceived and judged by others. On some days, she possesses such courage ("Sometimes I don't care, sometimes I'm like, 'Fuck it, this is reality, this is me'"), while on others it is in short supply ("I'm still [. . .] a woman, and I still occasionally get sensitive about what my skin looks like, or whether or not, you know, I've got more than one chin"). Regardless, Audrey is left navigating the ambiguities of the worth paradox, one selfie at the time.

With Eva, who is a decade younger, I discuss a selfie that she shared on Instagram and in which, contrary to most of her other pictures, she wears visible makeup, especially red lipstick. She tells me that the picture was shot on a day when she was getting ready for an important family celebration. Her choice to wear full makeup was part of the effort to comply with the norm in her family, according to which you are expected to put some work into looking proper and good for any family gathering (as you might remember from the discussion of the intergenerational gaze in chapter 4). In the last couple of years, Eva has willingly cut down on "the amount of stuff that I put on my face," especially compared to the sort of look she preferred in high school. Refusing to invest time in that sort of beautification, she now opts for a more natural presentation. Looking at the selfie, she says she felt "unnatural" with that much makeup on her face, not like "herself"; at the same time, she desired to preserve a memory of the day and of the effort she put into a more conventionally beautiful appearance, because she finds that, as a matter of fact, she did look quite beautiful.

The salience of appearance is particularly evident when women describe the use of selfies for professional self-promotion. None of the women who participated in my research works in the beauty industry as such, but for those who are self-employed, social media platforms are their main way of advertising their services and skills. While crafting her professional social media profiles on Instagram and Facebook, Melissa noticed that selfies in which she appeared *with* her work garnered more attention than pictures of her work alone. Her most effective method of professional self-promotion is putting her face next to her creations: that, she says, is when business opportunities arise. For her, selfies posted on social media accomplish what networking events such as parties would do if she chose to attend them. Images of herself with her work, she says, give people the impression that her creations are "coming alive," which in turn entices potential clients to retain her services. Hence, she intends to look good when she takes selfies for professional reasons.

The same is true of Lena. During both interviews, she talks extensively about her efforts to cultivate an interesting and consistent professional social media presence, especially by carefully planning her content and posting at a certain frequency (a task for which she uses a specific app), ideally every day or every other day. Like Melissa, selfies are Lena's main self-promotional tool because she, too, feels the need to put her face forward when advertising her work. She conducts her selfie practice in what she calls "batches." When she starts a selfie session (for which she uses semi-professional gear such as selfie stick, tripod, and timer) and the pictures look particularly good, she shoots plenty and archives them all. When, days or weeks later, she wants to post a certain piece of self-promotional content, she goes through her archive and picks a good-looking selfie. The image, taken in a wholly different context, is only remotely related, if at all, to the post with which it will be associated; its defining feature is that Lena looks particularly attractive (young, fresh) in it. In addition to the salience of beauty for this type of self-presentation, as well as the archival function of selfies, Lena's strategy also speaks to the reproducibility and versatility of these images: selfies from the same batch can be used at different times and for seemingly unrelated content (which, in fact, gave me the false impression that Lena had posted the same selfie twice to her Instagram feed).[11] Lena's reasoning as well as her techniques for enhancing her visibility on social media mirror what Brooke Erin Duffy calls "online aspirational labor," which refers to the performance of unpaid (or barely paid) self-promotional work online in the hope that one will be "paid to do what one loves" at some unspecified point in the future.[12] Viewed through the lens of this long-term strategy, even the very mundane gesture of trying to take a particularly good selfie is for Lena part of a more or less conscious business plan, of which a beautiful appearance is among the most important aspects. Lena hopes to increase the visibility of her posts, to build a large following, and, possibly, to strike up partnerships with companies that might see her growing Instagram presence as a worthwhile advertising vehicle.

If selfies are also a site for (partially) contesting normative injunctions regarding the online performance of femininity, this is not in spite of, but rather precisely *because of*, the centrality of beauty and femininity in women's selfie practices. Among the selfies that Lena sent me, one in particular aroused my curiosity ahead of our second interview. Unrelated to any of the situations that I asked the participants to portray or enact, this selfie shows Lena outdoors, biting into a beautiful doughnut, which occupies the foreground of the picture. Aware of Lena's passion for healthy living and clean eating, I found the picture odd to the extent that it does not demonstrate the same control, discipline, or quest for personal improvement that most of Lena's selfies tend to show. Rather, it seems to celebrate self-indulgence, the temporary loss of control, and the enjoyment of a "guilty" pleasure. "For me," Lena says during our second interview, "doughnut stands for treating yourself!" The selfie was taken at what she describes as "the best" doughnut place in town; she had visited the store with her kids and was just too excited and delighted by what she found.[13]

In addition to sending it to me, Lena is planning to use the selfie in an Instagram post about "why doughnuts are actually good for you, or not bad for you." In her Instagram posts devoted to health and fitness, she sometimes likes to "throw in something that doesn't make any sense," with the aim of releasing some of the pressure weighing on the women in her audience. The core message of the picture, once embedded in the planned post, will be the importance of allowing oneself small exceptions—a glass of wine, a pizza, or the best doughnut in town. Lena explains that this message of balance is particularly important for younger girls, like her daughters, who are the main target of the insistence on aesthetic perfection she finds circulating online. Seeing so many women obsessed with caloric intake and expenditure, Lena wants to promote balance and moderation, both in matters of self-discipline and in matters of self-presentation.

In the conclusion to chapter 3, I referred to Kate Cairns and Josée Johnston's book *Food and Femininity*, in which they introduce the concept of "calibration."[14] "Calibration," according to the authors, is a core quality of the contemporary female moral subject, as it allows her to competently distance herself from blueprints of "pathological" femininity. Lena aims to present an online persona that embodies a form of calibration; hence, she showcases both her strength and self-discipline and the occasional exception to the generally accepted rules of healthy living and fitness. She thereby presents herself as living proof of the virtues of balance, and of balance as a virtue: "obviously I'm in decent shape and I eat doughnuts," she says.

In Lena's case, the role attractiveness plays in her selfie practice allows it to assume the qualities of a visual language, and similar to its employment in offline contexts (as we saw in chapters 4 and 5), this visual language can function by subtraction as much as by addition. By modulating the conspicuousness of their beauty, women can display, and hence exploit, varying degrees of personal visibility in their selfies, thus enabling them to maintain a significant degree of ambivalence about what a picture is really about. Another good example comes from the stark contrast between the two sets of selfies that Cassandra shared with me. As we will see in the following sections, Cassandra loves staging photographic sessions in which she experiments with different wigs, types of makeup, clothing styles, and accessories. Throughout her life, Cassandra regarded her beauty as a tangible asset, and she is not shy in saying that she considers herself attractive—something that also comes through in the kinds of pictures she takes.

However, during our second interview, as we look over the "homework" that I'd assigned after our first meeting, Cassandra lingers on a series of three pictures that she recently shot on the same day. She picks the first one up and lets out a laugh: her hair is loose and naturally curly, she wears very light makeup, and she has a beautiful smile on her face. "I like this one," Cassandra says. "It's a natural selfie" (which, as she explains, means a selfie taken by hand with her phone, as opposed to camera and tripod). "I look more my age here; I like it. [. . .] My son would like this picture [too], he'd go 'That's my mum!'" "He wouldn't like the other one," she continues, pointing at one of the other shots from the series, this one showing her in a bikini. The three selfies that she likes were shot on an especially happy day, when Cassandra was about to launch her first book, which helps explain why she displays a different look than her usual, more formally curated selfies. She lingers on the thought, and adds, still looking at the first selfie:

I like being mum and not sexual [. . .] there's nothing pulled in on me. It's just normal, natural. My hair's normal, natural. Like today, I like just hiding—and not hiding. I like both sides.

By "hiding," Cassandra is referring to the fact that she is wearing a looser dress (one that conceals her figure), no jewelry, very light makeup, and undone hair. On the day of her book launch, while her appearance was relevant (of course, she wanted to look good), she was not particularly interested in flaunting her attractiveness: she wanted her work to have the spotlight, without her beauty distracting her audience from appreciating it. "Not hiding," on the other hand, refers to those times when Cassandra uses all that she has, "the boots, the makeup, the hair." While, in her younger years, she would relentlessly mobilize her aesthetic assets, aging has taught her that she needn't always be the center of other people's attention or desire. Her reward, instead, is feeling pride and joy for what she has accomplished, for what she has created. Interestingly, in Cassandra's description, this shift in focus is similar to the change she sees as part of maternity: in the more natural selfies, her son would recognize his "mum," because they express a different model of femininity—less "pulled," as she would say, and more contained, controlled, more welcoming and soft.

Since beauty holds a pivotal place in women's selfies, it undergoes the very same scrutiny, regulation, and policing that weigh on it in any other social or self-expressive context—a fact that should be fairly clear by now. As I will discuss in the next two sections, the production and circulation of selfies displaying embodied female identities are for this reason organized by the very paradoxes that condition women's experience of beauty, and which we've explored throughout this book. Where beauty culture converges with and intersects "selfie culture," there emerges specific normative frameworks that serve to organize practices of visibility. These frameworks can be analyzed through the lens of the four paradoxes discussed earlier, and especially in chapter 1. In what follows, I will focus in particular on the paradoxicality of two normative discourses targeting women's selfies and their visibility: the qualification of women's selfies as narcissistic, which I will present in the next section, followed by the authenticity discourse in selfie-related self-expression practices.

THE PARADOX OF THE "NARCISSISTIC" SELFIE

It would seem that there is a special place in hell, or rather in a psychiatric facility, for women who take selfies. In the public discourse, "selfie" is generally taken as a synonym for "facile," and the representational practice is perceived accordingly. Selfies posted on social media are evaluated more negatively by other users: for whatever reason, the same person portrayed in someone else's picture, when shown in a selfie, is more likely to be perceived as fake, narcissistic, in search of attention.[15] In addition, scholars have observed that selfies made by women are accompanied by a specific stigma, one constructed and reproduced by popular discourse purporting to explain why women take selfies and what these images say about them. Associating women's selfies with narcissism, lack of self-esteem, and the pathological need for attention has become commonplace in the last couple of years. As communication scholar Jessica Maddox notes, there seems to be a hierarchy of selfies according to which women's selfies are facile and meaningless, while, for instance, selfies taken by male astronauts from space are celebrated and revered.[16] In this section, I will discuss the association of women's selfies with problematic personality traits such as inauthenticity and narcissism, women's awareness of the risk of being considered superficial and self-centered while engaging in this form of visual self-expression, and the paradoxical injunctions that consequently target women's visibility through the production and circulation of selfies.

The early association, in popular and sometimes scholarly discourse, of selfies with narcissistic personality traits, has been particularly pervasive and has a wide influence on popular perceptions of women's selfie practices. Such discourse constructs the link between selfies and narcissistic personality traits in two ways: on the one hand, following a subject-to-practice form of inference, pathological needs associated with narcissistic traits are said to explain women's selfie-taking and -posting practices; on the other, following a practice-to-subject form of inference, selfie-taking women are portrayed as more likely to display narcissistic personality traits. An extreme example: narcissism, and the analogy with the Narcissus myth, in which the young, handsome boy falls into a pond in order to reunite with his beloved self-reflection, is evoked to condemn selfie-related deaths (which are often caused by fatal falls).[17] And this way of thinking about selfies is not only a dominant feature of media reports on the subject, it has also encouraged the production of a body of scholarly literature testing the correlation between selfie-related behaviors and personality traits identified as narcissistic. But what *is* narcissism, how is it assessed, and what is the evidence for its alleged correlation with selfie practices?

Narcissism is defined as "a pervasive pattern of grandiosity, need for admiration, and an exaggerated sense of self-importance. It is associated with positive self-views of agentic traits, including intelligence, physical attractiveness, and power."[18] Narcissism therefore "denotes excessive self-regard, grandiosity, and exhibitionism in the absence of genuine feelings for others."[19] Within the psychoanalytic tradition, narcissism is understood as rooted in feeble self-esteem, fragility, and fear; bold and grandiose behavior is thought to conceal feelings of inadequacy. Such an interpretation is often reproduced in lay presentations of narcissistic personalities, especially in popular media. Scholarly studies on the associations between selfie-taking and -sharing practices and narcissistic personality traits usually assess the latter through a validated scale, the Narcissistic Personality Inventory, or NPI, especially its shorter, sixteen-point version.[20] This scale contains sixteen forced-choice dyads, within which participants can choose between two statements, one constructed to reflect a narcissistic personality trait (and attributed a value of 1), the other constructed to reflect a non-narcissistic one (with a value of 0). Examples include "I think I am a special person" versus "I am no better or nor [*sic*] worse than most people"; "I insist upon getting the respect that is due me" versus "I usually get the respect that I deserve"; "I like to be the center of attention" versus "I prefer to blend in with the crowd."

On a personal level, if I had to take the test, I would probably answer "it depends" to every dyad. As a university professor, it is my job to be the center of attention while teaching, and I enjoy that. However, the couple of times that I decided to attend a spinning class (which I hated), I preferred to "blend in with the crowd" so as to prevent the trainer from noticing that I wasn't pedaling as hard as she expected. When targeted by a male coworker's sarcasm or discourteous comments during an official meeting (which happens to many women in academia), I might insist on receiving the respect that I feel is commensurate with my professionalism and competence. Generally speaking, though, I get the respect that I feel I deserve. My point is that, as a fairly extroverted and assertive female person whose job demands self-exposure and the ability to garner and retain attention, I might score pretty high on the NPI. Indeed, some authors have expressed concern about whether the NPI is really a reliable tool for measuring people's personality traits. According to Zeigler-Hill and Jordan, for instance, the NPI assesses "a subclinical form of 'normal' narcissism," that is, personality traits that are not considered worthy of clinical attention. This "normal" narcissism is "characterized by emotional resilience and extraversion" and "appears to be at least somewhat adaptive with its maladaptive aspects being largely limited to feelings of entitlement and the tendency to exploit others."[21] In layperson's terms, people with narcissistic personality traits are everywhere among us; they are able to live more or less ordinary lives, even if they are more outgoing than the average or are perhaps a bit show-offy (touché). People who score higher on the NPI could take the form of the uncle who loves telling interminable, self-centered stories at family gatherings, the infamous "mansplainer" and "manterruptor,"[22] or the bold coworker or fellow shopper who generates in us a light outrage and to whom we might want to ask, "Now who do *you* think you are?" In other words, the NPI does not assess a specific clinical condition or mental disorder so much as a range of personality traits that, much as they can be irritating, are not uncommon in our daily lives and that do not qualify someone as a social misfit. Establishing a correlation between high scores on the NPI and people's selfie-taking practices[23] (especially of oneself alone) is tantamount to stating the obvious—in this case, that extroverts are more likely than introverts to seek attention from an (online) audience through (visual) self-exposure. In addition, studies on the link between selfie-taking practices and narcissistic personality traits find a moderately positive correlation at best, and this moderate correlation (which is distinct from causation, mind you) occurs mainly with regard to individual selfie-taking (as distinct from group or partner selfie-taking), with no notable difference between male and female participants.[24]

Since the evidence is weak, the measurement tools are only partially reliable for clinical purposes, and scholars are particularly cautious about taking sides, why does the "narcissist" label continue to adhere to selfie-taking women?

Certainly, a great deal of social anxiety attends to the use of social media (or more precisely, *social networking sites*) in general, the dangers of online self-promotion, and its alleged corrosive effects on social relations. Long before the advent of social media, late-modern Western societies were accused by scholars and popular commentators alike of having taken a narcissistic turn: individual narcissistic self-absorption was seen for decades as the main cause of the decline of social bonds, the collapse of the family, the commercialization of people and social relations. Social media appears to fit perfectly into this narrative. What, after all, could be accused of being more isolating, self-celebrating, individualistic, and commercialized than social media? Never mind that extensive research shows that things are not so simple and that social media practices, even when they entail self-disclosure and the sharing of intimate details about oneself, are actually about connecting with people.[25] The label has nevertheless stuck. Narcissism is considered an ill in general, and social media are perhaps the greatest vehicle of all for narcissism: their merger is hence seen as dangerous and threatening.

In addition to the perceived threat of our increasing social media participation and practices, social anxiety is only heightened when we consider women's social media practices, and selfies in particular. As I've explained, at the center of selfie practice lies appearance, and beautiful appearance more often than not. In compliance with the worth paradox, women are encouraged to invest in their appearance, display their beauty, and, through it, demonstrate their value as competent feminine subjects. Historically speaking, in Western societies, women's self-presentation has become increasingly hinged on a beautiful, feminine appearance, and online self-presentation is no exception.[26] The other side of the paradox, however, affirms that women are unworthy *because* they are interested in beauty, invest in their appearance, and devote themselves to beautification practices. It is unsurprising that the so-called duck face selfie—a term that describes a self-portrait in which the subject (usually a young woman) purses their lips to form a stereotypical pout—became the epitome of the facile, distasteful, unworthy selfie. As Anne Burns notes, in a powerful echo of the worth paradox as I have defined it thus far, selfies are thereby targeted by a qualification that complies with the negative marking of female activities as meaningless: "Once the selfie is established as connoting narcissism and vanity, it perpetuates a vicious circle in which women are vain because they take selfies, and selfies connote vanity because women take them."[27] Hence, the depreciation of selfies, and of the central role that appearance plays in them, is political inasmuch as it participates in perpetuating a definition of gender difference that qualifies women as unworthy and inferior.

Consumer culture and beauty culture encourage women to expose themselves to the public gaze, to be bold, to think of themselves as special and worthy, to show off, to be "daring" when they feel beautiful and sexy. Beauty products and services are marketed (and have been for a long time) through a discourse in which noticeability is a reward for one's hard work or correct consumer choices: get a facelift, use lipstick, exercise, diet, dye your hair, get a tattoo, get a manicure, get hair extensions, buy flattering clothes—do all of that, the logic goes, and you will *feel* better because other people will notice that you *look* better. The cosmetic surgery industry thrives on this mantra.[28] Now, item 15.b of the long version of the NPI states, "I like to display my body."[29] Isn't bold self-display precisely what women's magazines, fashion ads, and beauty culture writ large have been encouraging women to do for decades? Item 29.a goes like this: "I like to look at myself in the mirror." As I have shown in the previous chapters, popular discourse around body positivity, self-acceptance, and self-esteem demands of women that they be more confident and assertive about their bodies and looks, that they stop being afraid of the mirror—or of the mirror-like device that is a self-directed camera. Should women take this as an invitation to be slightly narcissistic, self-absorbed, "positively" vain? It would seem so, since, when women seek attention and positive feedback on their appearance by posting selfies online, they are told that they *are* narcissistic. Women are given the message that they are "worth" everything, that they are right to spend every penny they spend on beautification, but when they want to be seen, well, then it's just their narcissism taking control——which directly disqualifies them and their voices. In her study on postfeminist digital cultures, Amy S. Dobson observes a similar tension in the way young girls' relationship to sexiness and sexuality is discursively constructed in Western societies today: encouraged to embody a confident femininity, one defiant of stereotypes and traditional gender norms, young women are nevertheless subjected to a strict public surveillance aimed at regulating the online expression of their sexuality and guarding the boundary between sexy and "slutty." Despite the shift toward a more "empowered" femininity, young women's respectability still depends on their ability to balance self-expression with a regulated, restrained sexual agency.[30]

Women who take selfies are familiar with these paradoxical injunctions—and I know this to be particularly true of the women I interviewed. This raises the question of "who" can legitimately take selfies, post them, and appreciate them.[31] On the one hand, as we've seen, my participants aspire to visibility by displaying a certain appearance and seek to increase their self-confidence and sense of worth through selfie-taking. On the other hand, as I will show, women are aware of the social stigma that attends to their selfie-taking. Hence, they practice a careful surveillance of their appearance in selfies, of the visibility they gain through these images, and of the frequency with which they post them online. Obviously, this same surveillance also applies to what they see appearing on their screens— namely, other women's selfies.

In addition to the content and frequency of one's selfie posts, self-surveillance applies to the ways in which one justifies the selfie to oneself and the intended audience, as well as to the question of how much discursive space the subject occupies in the image (in other words, how "self centered" the picture might appear to others). All these aspects of self-surveillance aim at negotiating the norms regulating the various "whos" of selfie-taking, norms that are organized around gender difference and whose transgression is particularly dangerous for women. Emma, for example, is relatively young and therefore particularly exposed to the stigma of the "young woman who does selfies." During our first interview, she repeatedly insists on the fact that each of her selfies is informed by her "artistic" thinking: she does not just take a selfie without reflection, simply to get likes, and she despises people who do ("it is impertinent," she insists). Even when she displays a part of her body, for instance her legs ("I have very beautiful legs!" she says) or her tattoos, she looks for some sort of "artistic" composition and framing so as to prevent an impression of triviality. Despite my questioning, Emma did not articulate further what "artistic" means to her. She also admits that she carefully "calculates" each selfie with regard to whether or not she might be perceived as expressing excessive self-satisfaction with her appearance. "Did I overdo it?" she usually asks herself. She wants to avoid the same disapproval that she addresses to other people.

Juliette, who is a bit older, while she deems the practice of selfie-taking in general "narcissistic," enjoys it nevertheless and uses it to communicate with friends and other audiences. This is why, when she must choose which selfie to post, she picks the one she feels is the "least narcissistic," which to her means the most "natural": since the medium itself encourages users to be self-centered and self-absorbed, one has either to appear as little self-satisfied as possible, or to "take a break"—by which Juliette means to reduce the frequency of one's selfie-taking, or at least selfie-posting. For similar reasons, Jeanne avoids taking selfies of "just [her] self alone" in public places, which she feels would make her appear self-absorbed and unconcerned with others around her. Indeed, the reason why she likes "bathroom selfies" (that is, a selfie capturing one's reflection in the bathroom mirror) is because she says they feel less vain: using a mirror, and thereby avoiding having to turn the camera toward oneself, mitigates the sense of self-absorption, and the resulting picture feels as if it was taken by someone else. Finally, Melissa, who is a more mature woman, explains that she refrains from posting selfies "just like that," for no apparent reason. Indeed, she disapproves of people posting pictures of themselves simply to be seen ("Why?" she asks rhetorically) and, like other interviewees, intends to abstain from practices that would garner a similar judgment. One needs a good reason to justify one's desire to be the subject of a selfie; for a woman, *too much me* is simply unacceptable.

As I discussed with regard to other aspects of aesthetic self-exposure, the selfie-taking woman must display specific qualities if she is to be recognized as a legitimate, worthy visual subject.[32] More specifically, she must display balance, which here means the right mix of self-confidence and self-restraint. When discussing her reasons for taking selfies, Audrey mentions feeling beautiful and confident. However, she also voices her prior reluctance to engage in the practice:

> When I'm feeling, like, really beautiful and really confident, then I want
> to take a picture of that. [. . .] Interestingly enough, I resisted for quite

a long time, 'cause there's also a counter-pressure for women not to be too vain, not to like themselves too much. Other people [might] find you attractive, but you're not allowed to find yourself attractive, right? So then it's, like, "No, I'm hot right now, *Ta-dah!!*"

Audrey recounts feeling this pressure even before starting to post selfies on social media platforms: she dared not claim the power to decide whether or not she deserved to be visible whenever she liked—especially when she liked *herself*. To her, no bodies should be made invisible or treated as unworthy, and she fights against the belittling, humiliating idea that women's view of themselves counts for less than other people's perceptions of them and their bodies. Nevertheless, Audrey must square her political stance with the widespread moral disapproval of and pathologizing around women's putative self-absorption—hazards of which she is well aware. When she describes her selfie-posting practices, she states more than once that she strives to be "interesting" in the eyes of her audience (for instance, when she embarks on a new professional project). She knows that she ought to avoid the social stigma of appearing facile and narcissistic, and that making her social media presence something more than a visual journal of her finding herself "hot" is a necessary step in this direction.

Of the different strategies the participants use to negotiate the maze of contradictory injunctions and legitimize their participation in selfie culture, Clarisse's and Fanny's are probably the most extreme. Clarisse accepts at face value the stigma attached to narcissism and its correlates in the public discourse—namely, that women's predisposition toward overexposure is grounded in a fundamental lack of self-confidence.[33] She says, "I've heard this so many times [. . .] women who take selfies, they're cuckoo, you know, they have . . . psychological problems." She is haunted by this idea because she knows that her own actions help to validate it: *she* posts selfies to boost her very low self-confidence with regard to her appearance. According to Clarisse, two categories of women participate in selfie culture, the "super confident ones, who believe they are beautiful and want to show it," and "people like me, more shy, less confident, who use [selfies] to feel better." By counting herself among the category of pathological selfie-takers, Clarisse justifies her practices by way of a psychological lens that disqualifies her as a competent feminine subject while simultaneously blaming her actions on something (her psychological needs) beyond her control. At the other end of the spectrum, we find Fanny, who recounts having written a blog post that reads like something of a selfie manifesto. In it, Fanny claims for herself the right to take selfies when and how she chooses; praises the fact that women are becoming the subjects (instead of the objects) of visual cultural production; and criticizes the war on selfies as yet another way of telling women that they should remain invisible unless other people decide to make them visible. Her text also borrows some of the themes and terms of the feminist discourse around women's images, objectification, and empowerment. Fanny feels that this open statement about her practice has conferred on her a somewhat unique status. During our conversation, she says,

> I'm also placing myself as a person who takes selfies, instead of just somebody who's, like, just quietly posting selfies of themselves but not making it into a thing, right? So I sort of made it into a thing. And I think I've done that kind of on purpose, because I think that it actually gives me more permission to take the pictures that I want to take, by saying, "I'm doing this," versus just doing it.

Through her discursive practice, Fanny openly fights the pathologization of women's selfies and its disempowering effect on their authors (she works with women, and she sees this firsthand). She enjoys taking selfies and she shoots them often. However, she is aware of being surrounded by criticism and disapproval; indeed, she speaks of people "rolling their eyes" when she suggests a selfie—starting with her husband, who she describes as "one of the[se] selfie eye-roller people." This awareness makes her feel uncomfortable. Hence, she only takes selfies when she feels at ease—either when she is with "selfie-friendly" people or when she is completely alone, enjoying some "me time." Self-surveillance, and specifically a competent negotiation of one's right to be considered a legitimate selfie-taker, is mandatory even for the proudest visual subjects. The road to social acceptance, it seems, is a long one.

THE AUTHENTICITY PARADOX AND THE SELFIE-TAKING ONLINE PERSONA

The negative judgment of women's "narcissistic" focus on appearance and self-contemplation in selfies is rooted in the cultural tradition condemning women's self-satisfaction. At the same time, women are encouraged to be *visually* available in the digital space, and indeed many feel the desire to conform to this expectation since they understand beauty to be a cardinal feature of the idealized female digital persona. The tensions between these two positions are clear enough when we consider cultural productions and commercial discourse pertaining to the female image, but they are also evident in the ways women negotiate norms around online visibility, as we saw in the previous section.

For some women, and in some public discourse, a self-presentation tied to "authenticity" can help to mitigate these tensions.[34] Being "authentic" means, on the one hand, presenting oneself without tricks, filters, or excessive editing. On the other hand, it means presenting oneself in one's "real," everyday life, engaging in ordinary activities and enduring the pleasures and problems we all face. Within the context of visual self-expression on social media, then, being authentic implies distancing oneself from idealization and "perfection," the latter being perceived as "fake" by social media users. But it also implies a successful staging of online authenticity, a convincing appearance as competent and worthy of attention: being oneself online entails showcasing the traits and activities that make one "special," that distinguish one's true self from everybody else's.

As I discussed in chapters 1 and 2, authenticity is at the core of one of the main paradoxes that structures women's experiences of beautification. The authenticity paradox states that a woman who pursues an ideal of perfect beauty is fake, and that a woman who wants to appear authentic must work to *create the impression* of authenticity (thus, in a certain sense, "faking it"). Moreover, women are traditionally conceived as naturally deceptive beings, and beauty regarded as their main device for deluding (men); this might explain why women's online presence and visibility, which so often depend on a beautiful appearance, are surrounded by a specific social anxiety, and have become, as a consequence, sites of political struggle.

In the last twenty years, advertising featuring idealized images of female beauty has increasingly become the target of widespread social criticism, political action, and even, somewhat ironically, advertising campaigns by big cosmetics companies (as presented in chapter 3). In addition, social media platforms in general have served to generate suspicion around the purported authenticity of users' self-presentation, especially, but not exclusively, on online dating platforms. As a consequence, authenticity has become a moral virtue of unique importance in the digital sphere, and a sort of authenticity contest has therefore arisen among social media users, not to mention platforms, to be recognized as the most trustworthy and truthful, as Salisbury and Pooley note.[35] The opportunity for self-embellishment and distinction, by which people seek to make themselves appear more interesting and attractive than they perhaps are, is limited by the authenticity injunction, which holds that it is crucial that one's online persona appear as trustworthy as one's real-world identity. Selfies are targeted by a specific scrutiny, then: generally considered more spontaneous than the images contained in advertising, they nevertheless entail, as I've mentioned, staging, "rehearsing," selecting, editing, and, more recently, the use of the many filters and editing features by which social media apps invite us to "improve" the images we post.

Every selfie-taker is aware of how this editing process is enabled and, to a certain extent, expected within social media affordances.[36] As the women I interviewed explained, taking a "good" selfie often requires some staging with regard to framing (e.g., avoiding "intruders"—that is, the unintentional presence of someone in the background of one's selfie—hiding embarrassing details such as a messy domestic background, using one's environment to enhance the intended visual effect, etc.), and, more importantly, staging with regard to oneself. It is important to choose the most flattering angle, to manage the lighting, to adjust one's facial expression, body posture, hair, accessories, clothing, sometimes makeup—you name it. This entails, in most cases, taking not one but several pictures, each containing one or more minor compositional variations. For her part, Lena runs through a sort of informal mental checklist of things that she does not want to see in her selfies. Hence, when examining the results of a selfie-taking session, she considers the "flaws" that might show in each picture: Am I cross-eyed? (she says this tends to happen when she is tired). Can you see the scar from my C-section? How do my abs look? (You may remember the crucial role this bodily feature plays in her feeling beautiful.) Would my skin look better with a black-and-white filter? The list goes on. Of the many selfies Lena shoots in one session, most are erased and only the best one(s) kept.[37] As Emma says, echoing Lena's concern for details, selfies are about taking a picture, but they are also about "making it beautiful" before presenting it to an audience.

Hence, appearing "natural" means enacting a ritualized posture,[38] one that expresses "authenticity" without compromising the ability to bestow other qualities on the online self—and, especially, to look good. In this sense, social media users maintain the authenticity of their selfies by qualifying their pictures as authentic, but also by policing the circulation of the inauthentic: limiting the amount of editing to what they perceive as acceptable, and collaborating at exposing selfies that reveal their inauthenticity by excessive staging or editing.[39] For women, this new social pressure around the authenticity of selfies merges with the traditional cultural suspicion targeting women as fake. With regard to combining authentic self-presentation with beauty, the stakes for the female selfie-taking online persona are, thus, definitely higher. During our second interview, I was intrigued by Melissa's description of her reaction to receiving a compliment from a friend. We were looking at a selfie that she took on a beach during a business trip, on a very happy day when she scored an important professional success. Wanting to keep a memory of that exhilarating day, she took a selfie and posted it:

> I had one friend who said, "Oh my god your skin is flawless!," and I had
> to literally comment on it, and [. . .] I said, "No, no, trust me, I have
> signs of . . . joy and of sadness and of . . . all the years that I've lived,
> so trust me, it must be the angle, but there is no filter on this." I just
> wanted people to know, I'm not filtering my shots because that's impor-
> tant, you know? A lot of people I know, it's like their camouflage is on.

Melissa, you might recall, is very conscious of her age. The part of our conversation I've just quoted follows one in which, as mentioned earlier in this chapter, she explains that she is aware of time passing and of her beauty fading with it, and that the selfies she takes therefore constitute an archive of memories of her appearance before the aging process alters it irrevocably. In the future, she will be able to look back at her younger self and appreciate those memories. Melissa sees her wrinkles increasing in depth and number, her complexion changing, and signs of fatigue appearing more obvious on her face. But she also knows that many selfie-takers try to appear with artificially "flawless skin," by using filters or manipulating camera angles. The urge to react to her friend's comment expresses her desire to appear authentic on social media, which can be as strong as the desire to appear beautiful. Melissa's comment is meant to reassure her friend and her wider social media audience, but also herself, that she is just like everybody else: she bears the signs of age and "experience" on her skin, and she does not intend to hide them. It just so happens that this was a good selfie; she is not guilty of pretending to be someone she is not (i.e., a fifty-year-old woman with flawless skin).

Melissa is aware of the cult(ure) of perfection haunting visual self-expression on social media, especially for women. In her view, the obsession with perfection motivates people to use filters and edit their selfies in an effort to rid them of perceived physical flaws. Going "authentic," by contrast, implies accepting one's flaws and the fact that they can be conspicuous. Embracing one's "ordinary ugliness"[40]—in other words, accepting the fact that nobody is truly flawless—is part of this version of the online commitment to "being ordinary." Authenticity therefore entails a considerable amount of self-surveillance and a constant process of comparing oneself with others. Take the next passage of my interview with Melissa, coming right after the one quoted above:

Chiara: Why is it so important, not to filter?

Melissa: To me? Because it's the real deal, you know, and I think that says a lot about you and, you know, probably in the future will be a little bit more necessary to mask just to . . . I don't know—yeah, you're right, to still look attractive, or to feel attractive, is also an important thing as you age, you know? You sort of . . . need that, that part of it. It's human nature to some of us, you know?

Melissa is committed to being and showing "the real deal," and she distances herself from the culture of perfection and inauthenticity: she draws a clear line between what she does and the appearance of perfection presented by some of her contacts on social media.[41] Reacting to my question, however, Melissa also observes that authenticity might come at too high a price in the future, when the effects of aging will be greater and therefore more apparent: Will she still be willing to sacrifice her desire to feel beautiful, less *imperfect*? Melissa clearly acknowledges such a desire as legitimate, understandable, especially in the context of aging. To paraphrase the title of a 2020 paper by Gun Peng, Melissa anticipates being torn, in the next couple of years, between the desire to feel attractive and the desire to feel authentic.[42] Aesthetic self-surveillance thus combines with moral self-surveillance, both of which are clearly connected to the norms regulating women's visual self-expression on social media.

Presenting oneself as an ordinary person living a real, ordinary life is another strategy for enacting authenticity. When asked what she tries to capture through her selfies, Eva declares that she wants to portray "authenticity. The natural character of [. . .] an image of myself at this exact moment in my life. Which is not more important than another moment." We are returned, once again, to paradoxicality: to be true, such selfies have to be ordinary, and yet achieving the ordinary here requires preparation, composition, and editing in order to express the notion that nothing special is going on—that one's life is like everybody else's. As sociologist Harvey Sacks argued in his insightful work on conversational analysis, "being ordinary" is the main work of people's everyday interactions and communications: it is something that people actively *do* through their utterances and self-presentation. As Sacks explains, in our everyday conversations, "the cast of mind of doing 'being ordinary' is essentially that your business in life is only to see and report the usual aspects of any possible usual scene." When people attempt to make their life seem "epic," Sacks claims, certain costs are exacted: in ordinary interactions, attempts to make the ordinary into the extraordinary are usually met with suspicion.

This same skepticism is part of the default attitude of social media users toward selfies; indeed, being skeptical about the purported reality of what one sees online is often presented as a basic competence of the savvy social media user. To draw on Sacks again, not everyone is entitled to extraordinary, and thus distinctive, experiences that are worth reporting and sharing with others.[43] Hence, Eva's performance of authenticity consists in not claiming this extraordinary entitlement and instead expressing the fact that a moment in her life captured in a selfie contains absolutely nothing that would set it apart from any other moment in her life, or in anyone else's for that matter. Obviously, the same criteria can apply to appearance. While looking at other people's visual self-presentations online, Eva appreciates images of ordinary subjects whose looks are not especially enhanced or represented in the most advantageous light or at the most flattering angle. To her, selfies presenting one's best looks are acceptable if part of a larger self-presentational stream that also includes ordinary, average-looking pictures— *this*, she feels, is authentic, since nobody can always be at the top. Hence, Eva deems it more authentic to show her followers a similarly multifaceted portrait of herself; sometimes, thanks to a special effort made for an event or a family celebration, she can show her best looks in her selfies, but, mostly, she is just her ordinary-looking self, more or less on par with everyone else.

Displaying and valuing authenticity as a quality of the female selfie-taking persona is part of proving one's competence as both a woman and a social media user. Critically responding to the cult(ure) of perfection and competitive femininity on social media, presenting oneself as "ordinary" (hence sometimes "ordinarily ugly") in appearance and context, and overtly refusing excessive self-surveillance are important components of this performance of competence. It follows that, using Goffman's concept, we can affirm that authenticity is "hyper-ritualized" in selfies: "standardized" (everyone must be able to detect it), "exaggerated" (the subject must express their intent to be authentic), and "simplified" (since "authenticity" in real life cannot be reduced to some simplistic either/or alternative).[44] Hence, authenticity is indissociable from appearance; moreover, it is not incompatible, but rather is combined with, self-surveillance, self-editing, and the work of self-improvement.

To illustrate this latter point, let us consider Cassandra's photographic practice. Cassandra is not a professional photographer, but she has years of experience organizing semi-professional selfie-shooting sessions, for which she has all the necessary equipment. Indeed, she does more than simply "taking" selfies—she picks a backdrop (e.g., an apartment that a girlfriend has just emptied out), creates a themed setting by way of objects and light, and fashions her physical appearance accordingly. Her looks are particularly salient, inasmuch as she foregrounds her beauty through a skillful combination of the authentic and the inauthentic. While she highlights the fact that her beauty is completely "natural" (which also means free from surgical enhancements), Cassandra experiments with her appearance and adopts a range of different looks for her pictures. She has a collection of wigs, for example, which she combines with makeup, clothing, accessories, colored contact lenses, and setting to create various "versions" of herself. Referring to this playful activity, which she greatly enjoys, together with the work it demands, Cassandra talks of "stretching the look": "It's just stretching the look to the limits of how I really look and taking a picture and having fun and not taking yourself seriously and not caring what other people think." Cassandra insists that she is still herself when she plays with her appearance; her intent is not deception, and people who know her are also aware that this is "my thing." She believes that this tacit understanding between her and her audience (social media followers, boyfriends) allows her to remain authentic while being playful, to pretend without deceiving. Viewed in this way, authenticity is a spectrum along which Cassandra allows herself a certain amount of mobility. The boundaries are established by her awareness of the social stigma associated with inauthenticity in matters of beauty, especially in the context of gender relationships. Cassandra makes it clear that "it is just, to me, accessories. I don't show up and take myself apart and have men go, 'Who are you?'" What she does in the secure, intimate setting she creates for her selfie-taking, Cassandra would not do for a date. It is that security that allows her to "stretch" authenticity too.

To conclude this discussion of the authenticity paradox in online visual practices, let me provide what I think is an interesting example of the way social media users who participate in the production of wellness- and beauty-related visual content have begun to question the contradictions that accompany the notion of "being oneself" online. In late summer 2021, a small controversy arose around the TikTok and Instagram hashtag #thatgirl. At the time, the most popular posts related to the hashtag on TikTok[45] were produced by young women promoting the virtues of a well-organized and healthy lifestyle. Essentially motivational, these videos sometimes reference the ongoing COVID-19 pandemic and the lack of social stimuli caused by the consequent curtailing of interactions and social activity, especially for younger people, during periods of lockdown and the move to online schooling. Partially reacting to this context (at least, this is my hypothesis), #thatgirl gets a grip on her life. Indeed, the TikTok posts show young women trying to become #thatgirl, a female person whose life, body, mind, and living space are perfectly organized, whose lifestyle involves daily exercise and healthy eating, who regularly sets and accomplishes her goals. To borrow fashion model and TikTok content producer Imran Rai's expression, #thatgirl is an expression of each woman's efforts to become "the best version of [her]self."[46] Using the hashtag, I found short videos on early morning workouts, on how to organize one's fridge, how to prepare a nutritious and healthy breakfast, how to pick a scented candle (apparently, a "must"), how to build a skin-care routine, and on the importance of keeping a daily journal of one's goals and accomplishments. As with similar inspirational trends, #thatgirl was criticized for its lack of diversity in terms of class, gender, body size, and ethnic background, thus setting goals that are unattainable for most young women.[47]

These criticisms perfectly illustrate the paradox inherent in the notion of "being oneself" and "appearing authentic" online. The "best version of oneself" must embody, and hence display the visible signs of, self-restraint, health, discipline, and competence. If your hair is dull, you're not doing enough to keep it shiny and strong. If you don't get up at six for an early morning workout, you are lazy, which doesn't go well with being #thatgirl. Hence, being the "best" version of oneself is in no way a matter of self-definition; one must instead bear all the visible marks of what fellow social media users can recognize and validate as the embodiment of #thatgirl. "Being oneself" thus boils down to a sort of symbolic sociocultural performance, the parameters of which are regulated by the visual definition of competent femininity. In this sense, it is less about being oneself than about imitating those who are publicly invested with the authority to determine just "who" #thatgirl is. The public criticism of the trend serves only to highlight this fact: online authenticity is an endeavor whose modalities are competitive, heavily scrutinized, and highly stereotyped, with mainstream feminine beauty serving as visible evidence of the hard work that women must undertake in order to become "the best version" of themselves.

CONCLUSION: NEGOTIATING VISIBILITY

A selfie is a gesture of contextual, dialogical, and embodied self-expression. As such, these images contribute to the creation of a larger visual self-narrative by providing an embedded and ongoing record of their author's appearance at a certain point in biographical time and space. Beauty plays a pivotal role in this self-expression for women, inasmuch as it motivates the selfie, is foregrounded by it, and its fluctuations traditionally participate in the individual and social definition of a woman's individual presentation and identity. However, the different aspects of presenting one's attractiveness must be negotiated against the normative injunctions governing women's online visibility; in this sense, the paradoxicality of Western beauty culture converges with the visual and self-expressive norms regulating the digital sphere. Thus, selfies can be regarded as a component of what Elana Levine defines as early twenty-first-century "feminized popular culture," inasmuch as the latter encompasses "areas of feminized concern that are simultaneously required of women and culturally dismissed as trifling."[48]

Decisions about when and how to take a selfie, and when and how to share it, are shaped by women's perceptions and judgments of their appearance and their sense of what constitutes an appropriate online self-presentation. My results clearly show that women want to look good in a selfie, but that this desire is very often motivated by a larger wish to convey the beauty, the attractiveness that they perceive in themselves. Selfie practices mobilize a range of skills to reproduce such an impression, whether for the subject or for her online audience. However, this raises for the selfie-taker the question of inauthenticity and narcissism, since, as we've seen, women are abundantly aware of the negative qualifications that adhere to female selfies in media and popular discourse, which tend to dismiss women's visual self-representational practices as superficial, facile, even pathological.

The charge of narcissism with regard to women's selfies stands in overt contradiction to some of the core elements of contemporary Western beauty culture. Western women are encouraged to seek approval and validation through attractiveness, to be confident and proud of their bodies, to expose themselves to other people's gaze. When they do so through their selfies, however, their behavior is interpreted as pathological and therefore ripe for stigmatization and ridicule. The women I interviewed try to juggle these paradoxical constraints; there aim is being visible without appearing too self-absorbed, to look good without appearing too "artificial" or staged. Aware of the moral risk of being perceived as inauthentic or self-absorbed, they also seek to enact authenticity in their selfies, and do so by planning, crafting, and assessing the images they might post. For instance, some explicitly reject the cult of aesthetic perfection that dominates on social media by displaying their natural, everyday imperfections and alternating between more and less flattering pictures; they moderate the amount of staging and editing that they regard as acceptable and unthreatening to the impression of authenticity; and they actively practice "being ordinary" to counter the stigma of falsity and self-absorption.

These contextual sociocultural constraints should not be overlooked when analyzing selfies and people's motives for taking and circulating them. There is no doubt that selfies are produced by an individual who decides to use a given set of skills and techniques to materialize an intention, and who aims to share it with a larger or smaller audience[49]—in this sense, self and self-expression lie at the core of the selfie (as the name would of course suggest). At the same time, however, selfies are contextual, situated in the larger social fabric, in time and space, with regard both to their material construction and their circulation (on a larger or smaller scale) and reception by different audiences. The sociological "where" and "when" of each selfie, and the history of its circulation, should be taken into account when analyzing these images. As a matter of fact, selfies are not just about oneself: endowed with the power of images to promote and make accessible various forms of meaning production, they are public, and as such they participate in the economies of visibility,[50] attention, legitimacy, and reputation, both online and off.

My results confirm the embeddedness of selfies in complex networks of social relations, normative injunctions, and economic processes. The place that women selfie-takers give to attractiveness and appearance in their selfies does not solely depend on the psychological features of each individual woman. Rather, it is connected to larger cultural and normative frameworks influencing the social appraisal of women's visibility and worth. Hence, selfies are sites where women's social legitimacy is negotiated with different audiences through practices of gazing and assessing. If selfies are also a site to (partially) contest normative injunctions regarding the performance of femininity online, this is not in spite of, but rather precisely *because* of the fact that beauty and femininity are expected to be foregrounded in them.

CONCLUSION

Beauty and the Paradoxes of Women's Subjectivity

> The situation is full of ironic contradictions: freedoms that create anxiety, empowerment that feels oppressive, individualism that leads to conformity.
>
> —Daniel Miller, *Stuff*

This book stems from my sociological interest in women's experience of beauty in their everyday lives. Throughout, I describe how individual women go about the business of being a woman, and presenting themselves as such, amid a matrix of paradoxical injunctions concerning their appearance, their visibility, and their social status as competent feminine subjects. A main claim of my book is that women outside of academia are in no way unaware of the stakes of beauty and of the contradictions of Western beauty culture. Each of the stories the interviewees told me, and which I recount and discuss from different angles in each chapter, is in essence a story about juggling the multiple, and usually contradictory, norms regulating women's appearance, whether online or in the physical world. Because women derive a sense of legitimacy and competence from being validated on the basis of their attractiveness (it makes them "feel good"), beauty is hardly a superficial matter in their everyday lives. As this book shows, it is therefore more than fair to apply to women's beauty the same observation made by Daniel Miller with regard to women's clothing choices: beautification is not just a series of surface gestures, disconnected from the depth and authenticity of the *real* self; rather, it "plays a considerable and active part in constituting the particular experience of the self, in determining what the self is."[1]

The entanglement of a beautified appearance and one's sense of self also goes some way toward explaining why women feel threatened when the validation they receive on the basis of their looks is revoked, and they are consequently scrutinized, judged, and/or marginalized for what people see on the surface of their bodies—or, in the most extreme scenario, when their bodies go completely unnoticed. Being invisible, as the withdrawal of visibility, is for human beings tantamount to being deemed unworthy; we are socialized to be exposed and to expose ourselves to other people's gaze, and to gaze at ourselves by anticipating the consequences of that "public" exposure. The centrality of this self-exposure in women's life was clearly shown by my fieldwork, in which gazing and being gazed at was also a pivotal element of mutual recognition between (woman) researchers and (women) participants during the data-collection process. Through mutual gazing during the interviews, looking at each interviewee's selfies with their author-subject, and exchanging stories about seeing other women and being seen by them, the participants and I recreated, within the relatively safe space of the research setting, women's entanglement in practices of evaluative visibility, and the anxieties that it engenders in all of us.

From childhood on, through peer surveillance, images of other women in media and social media, and through what I describe as the "intergenerational gaze," women learn to look at themselves and at one another, to judge and compare, and to situate themselves on the spectrum of acceptable feminine appearance. Through their socialization to the appraising female gaze, women also learn two additional social competencies linked to the performance of feminine identity. The first is that of acting as a gatekeeper of appropriate feminine aesthetic self-presentation: for the most part unwittingly, women's judgments of their and other women's looks reproduce stereotypes and norms of acceptability in aesthetic matters. Hence, they also reproduce the paradoxical injunctions that regulate women's appearance. The second, however, is the ability to question such norms and stereotypes in the search for greater freedom of expression for diverse individual identities and diverse bodies. Far from being the monopoly of militant feminists and social scientists, such criticism of the normative framework governing women's beauty informs emotions, reflections, bodily practices, consumer choices, and aesthetic judgments in ordinary women's lives. An excellent example can be found in the interviewees' attitude toward the cult of perfection on social media (and on Instagram especially, as the most explicitly pictorial of them). If women wish to share flattering selfies, they also insist on remaining faithful to themselves, to avoid "stretching the look" (to use Cassandra's evocative expression) to the point of blindly conforming to stereotypical norms of feminine beauty. In addition, women build and foster networks of mutual solidarity, both online and off, to support and be supported by other women who express a similar resistance to some of the normative elements of contemporary beauty culture.

It is my firm conviction that this partial rejection is due to the more generalized assimilation of feminist ideas into Western social reflexivity, as other scholars also point out in their criticisms of a postfeminist sensibility.[2] In other words, women (often unintentionally) reject the disempowering effect that beautification and stereotypical femininity bring about in their everyday interactions. Feminism is, generally speaking, a critique and ultimately a rejection of the difference between the masculine and the feminine as a source of hierarchical social divisions, of socioeconomic inequalities, and of obstacles to women's access to opportunities and resources. In most Western societies, and notably in North America, feminism has been absorbed within social reflexivity, by which I mean the way society observes itself, understands itself, and talks about itself. Feminist claims and demands penetrate the social and digital spheres: they are a lens through which society understands social processes and social relations between men and women—even when such claims and demands are rejected, ridiculed, and violently challenged. Governments are criticized for under-representing women, organizations and companies are called out for not granting women the same opportunities as men, and recurrent attacks on reproductive rights are (generally speaking) met with scorn and opposition—the examples are legion. These same feminist claims have also entered marketing strategies and corporate branding, to the (paradoxical) point where products and services that reinforce stereotypes and traditional norms of femininity are sold through a pseudofeminist rhetoric of empowerment, equality, and free agency.

Of course, the general awareness of the injustices caused by the enforcement of a hierarchical difference between masculine and feminine includes beauty culture. For a couple of centuries now, beauty and beautification practices have been criticized as a "prison" for women, as a device to keep them in a subordinate position in which they are simultaneously objectified as objects of aesthetic admiration and erotic desire and condemned for that very fact. The history and pervasiveness of feminist criticisms of beauty culture makes it almost impossible, in Western societies at least, to show an interest or engage in beautification without taking into account its drawbacks. My book describes how interviewees understand and apply the difference between empowering and disempowering, oppressive and emancipating, authentic and inauthentic to orient their choices and to position themselves in a landscape in which an awareness of gender injustice is now promoted, and marketed, as part of being a competent Western female subject. Awareness of both sides of beauty culture, and of two interconnected aspects of women's individual experiences of this culture—the rewarding and the penalizing one—has practical, emotional, and material consequences for the way women engage in beautification, sociability, their careers, motherhood, wellness, and so on.

These tensions and oppositions constitute what I call the *paradoxicality* of Western beauty culture, which, as I claim, is for ordinary women a matter of everyday negotiation vis-à-vis their decision-making, assessing, gazing, and judging. Choices about how much time and money to invest in beauty, what look to adopt, what pictures to post, whom to listen to— these are processed according to discursive patterns and a sensibility that increasingly frames constraints in terms of contradictions, obstacles in terms of inescapable discrimination, and oppression in terms of a restriction of women's ability to make worthy, legitimate choices about their bodies and identities. My contribution, in this book, is to bring together the voices of women who embody the paradoxes of beauty culture through their ways of looking at each other and at themselves, as well as their feelings about what they see and their ability, to some extent, to point out those contradictions and denounce them.

The book begins with a presentation of the four main paradoxes of beauty culture that I observed and formulated by way of the available literature, as well as some of my own experiences and conclusions drawn from a variety of popular sources. The four paradoxes define the attribution of worth to women's choices with regard to beauty, the attribution of authenticity to women's aesthetic identities, the attribution of power to women as attractive social actors, and the validation of women's commitment to beautification. As such, these paradoxes qualify women's engagement with beauty culture through a reinforcement of the perceived differences between worthy and unworthy, natural and artificial, power and impotence, commitment and negligence. Far from clearly identifying a set of behaviors that could be easily avoided, these dyads frame a matrix of judgments through which every behavior could be discredited; being "too artificial" can, after all, be as bad as being "too natural," just as "too much commitment" could be frowned upon as much as "not enough commitment." The paradoxes do not function in an either/or fashion; their paradoxicality, as I argue, depends on the "re-entry" of the difference between masculine and feminine in each dyad. In layperson's terms, it depends on the persisting negative bias that inevitably threatens to penalize all that bears the signs of "femininity," despite the idealization and celebration of feminine beauty. Beautification upholds the difference between the feminine (the category of those who need to beautify themselves) and the masculine (the category of those who do not need to undertake such work), and at the same time replicates it as a qualitative distinction creating a hierarchy. Beauty at once qualifies and disqualifies women as feminine. Women's involvement in beauty culture is both rewarding—which explains its persistence and pervasiveness—and penalizing—which explains the resistance, the generalized criticism, and the discursive somersaults that cosmetic brands must perform in order to market their products as empowering and "feminist."

My discussion of the participants' lived experience of these paradoxes starts with an exploration of the connection between "feeling good" and "feeling beautiful." A long-standing trope posits female beauty as emanating from a healthy body and from a morally blameless soul. In contemporary Western "wellness" rhetoric, this supposed correspondence between interior and exterior beauty is translated into the language of self-care and natural beauty. However, in today's marketing strategies, no less than in the past, it is claimed that these can only be achieved by way of an ongoing commitment to self-care rituals involving specific products and services— the opposite of something that would come "naturally." In addition, the idea, supported by the participants, of an immediate link between well-being and feeling beautiful yields considerable insight when submitted to a thorough sociological analysis. When recounting situations in which they felt or tend to feel good and beautiful, the women I interviewed evoked genuine *social* contexts, in which they feel validated, competent, and at the "right" place. Beauty is not situated exclusively on the inside or on the outside, then; its experience manifests a successful, embodied negotiation of norms, interactions, and criteria that determine the situational recognition of one's social worth. This is why, sociologically speaking, the experience of "feeling beautiful" and "feeling good" must not be dismissed as if it were a superficial aspiration.

Since an idealized beauty is not some accidental, natural occurrence, but rather must be achieved, produced, and maintained on a daily basis through skillful work and competent self-assessment, women face the challenge of determining the right amount of time, energy, and money to be invested in beautification. Through her well-crafted appearance, a woman does not show but rather *embodies* her commitment to being a competent female subject. Facing contradictory injunctions that make it impossible to determine when "enough" is truly enough, women navigate a panoply of advice, products, instructions, techniques, and competing looks circulating around them; in this maze of competing messages, they must search for reference points to help them make their decisions. Their criteria and strategies differ depending on their individual socioeconomic profiles, but they often involve a form of skepticism with regard to the marketing and consumption of various beauty products. Based on their experiences as informed consumers, the participants voiced mistrust and disbelief vis-à-vis companies and the generalized incitation to "excessive" spending and consumption. In this sense, their goal is to strike a balance (to walk the tightrope, as it were) between always doing more and doing too much.

Hair and makeup, as we've seen, have a specific salience in this framework. Hair remains for some a symbol of feminine beauty and sexiness, but it is also, on a daily basis, a crucial factor that women must take into account when determining how much work will be necessary to achieve an acceptable look. Hair needs to be "fixed"; one can wake up in the morning and find oneself with either "good" or "bad" hair, which for many interviewees is a harbinger of either a better or worse day ahead. Makeup is virtually a stand-in for beautification, requires specific skills, and is marketed by cosmetic companies as an indispensable part of any woman's successful self-care. In addition—or perhaps as a consequence—it functions as a mood booster on days when participants have trouble feeling beautiful. At the same time, makeup demands investments: mental investments aimed at acquiring know-how and the necessary information, and financial investments to secure the necessary products. It also requires competence with regard to choosing the appropriate makeup style for different situations (a topic that no issue of any women's magazine dares to neglect). Again, the act of looking at each other and at each other's selfies, in friendly and less-than-friendly situations, is crucial training in the endless learning process that beauty culture and consumption demand from women.

Time is as important a commodity as money for the women I interviewed. Defined by contemporary neoliberal discourse as a chronically scarce resource, particularly for successful people, time must be competently allocated to the right activities, but also to getting ready for them "offstage" (as sociologist Erving Goffman would have put it). One must constantly make decisions about one's allocation of time based on what the day has "in store" and what identity one intends to project. Hence, the day is a measure of beauty inasmuch as the work of beauty must start anew each day, as we are daily presented with new and different challenges (encounters, commitments, errands), and as we wake up each day with different emotions and self-perceptions. Time, however, is a measure of beauty not only as the temporal framework of the day—it is first and foremost an index of beauty's fading over time. As a constant worry over the course of a woman's biographical path, beauty is thought to peak in youth and decline with age, a trajectory that demands planning and investment according to the rhetoric of "anti-aging" beautification. The prevention of aging is a pivotal element of the "successful aging" rhetoric dominating in North American societies. The paradoxical injunctions of beauty culture intersect with its temporal aspects and articulate their contradictions differently at each stage of a woman's life. If youth is celebrated as the age of perfect beauty, younger women are nevertheless faced with paradoxical norms regarding the supposed association between their beauty and their worth. Older women, on the other hand, are torn between contradictory demands to embrace aging and love their bodies, and to fight aging through specific know-how, discipline, and consumer choices and practices. Specific normative claims targeting certain ethnic groups, such as the "Black don't crack" rhetoric explored in chapter 4, might relieve part of the burden of managing aging while also strengthening surveillance and self-surveillance for specific categories of women.

Selfies occupy a central place in the interviewees' attempts to grapple with aging and the cultural ambivalence toward it. These images can be used to create a journal of one's appearance throughout the aging process, in order to tame it, to resist it by setting the bar for an ideal appearance against which one can measure their future self, or to oscillate between the two. Since women are also exposed to what I call the "intergenerational gaze," they look at one another from different positions within their respective life spans. Younger women are initiated into the challenges of cultural ambivalence by the gaze of their female family members, and by watching them deal with those same issues. Advice and criticism, encouragement and surveillance can be exchanged between generations. This places a particular emphasis on motherhood as a specific stage in the life of beauty, for several reasons. First, motherhood is accompanied by physical changes that often go against the dominant ideals of feminine appearance. Second, the mother's body is at once de-sexualized and sexualized in postfeminist beauty culture, again creating contradictory expectations. Third, being the mother of a daughter comes with additional pressure to determine the right messages to pass on to members of the next generation regarding their engagement with beauty culture and the scrutiny to which they subject their physical selves.

But what about the advantages of beauty? According to the power paradox, beauty bestows a form of power on women. Indeed, interviewees reported using beauty as a facilitator in everyday situations, from the casual (such as buying a coffee or using public transit) to the more structured (such as dealing with colleagues or patrons in a work setting). Also, as I mentioned above, feeling attractive boosts self-confidence and self-assurance, which is perceived as increasing the chances that one will be able to direct interactions to one's advantage—hence the "flirting" that some women can use to ensure smooth interactions in their everyday lives. In a highly aestheticized economy in which "looking the part" is increasingly treated as an (often unspoken) element of any number of job descriptions, attractiveness and appropriate appearance are precious resources in the competition for jobs and promotions. As such, they must be used wisely. To this end, some interviewees report either emphasizing or downplaying feminine attractiveness in order to competently perform tasks in their working lives—especially, but not exclusively, in the service sector. The other side of the power paradox, however, states that attractiveness has concrete drawbacks for women in the different spheres of their lives, as it exposes them to the risk that they will be reduced to their appearance and divested of their professional competence and expertise, and hence of their worth as social actors. The awareness of this contradiction forces women to carefully balance different aspects of their self-presentation, and to retain their femininity while also avoiding its disqualifying effects.

Such a balance is crucial in matters of online sociability as well. This is why selfies present such a rich research material. Selfies circulating on online platforms are themselves a site for the convergence of paradoxical injunctions regulating women's appearance and visibility, which are in turn enforced through the affordances and the specific ideologies materialized by our digital devices and by social networking platforms. As with women's visibility in the public sphere throughout history, women's selfies are objects of considerable scrutiny and social anxiety in that they are regarded as a "feminine" (and thus unworthy) practice, one motivated by narcissism, vanity, or a pathological lack of self-confidence. At the same time, women are encouraged by postfeminist media and marketing discourse to expose themselves to the public gaze, to be proud of their attractiveness, to enhance it and make it visually available. A further contradiction in online visibility arises from the authenticity paradox, which, ambivalently, requires self-editing and an embrace of authenticity, the pursuit of acceptable appearance and of a "natural" beauty. My exploration of selfie-taking and -sharing practices begins with a description of what is, according to the women I interviewed, the role that beauty plays in the production and circulation of their selfies. The paradoxical injunctions pertaining to the visibility of feminine beauty influence women's assessment of the right time and context in which to take a picture, of the appropriate identity it should convey, and of which audience to address—in other words, their assessment of what should be visible, when, and for whom. Attractiveness plays a huge role, as each of these decisions often depends on aesthetic self-appraisal and the management of one's visibility. Hence, my book makes a contribution to our understanding of the place of beauty and appearance in women's selfie practices, a topic on which the relevant literature is in many ways silent. Similar to a more general type of decision-making in matters of beauty, decision-making in the context of one's selfies appears to be informed by the awareness of the contradictory injunctions regulating, quantitatively and qualitatively, women's visibility through attractiveness and the performance of femininity.

★ ★ ★

The question of appropriate appearance is a constant worry—it generates anxiety and is connected to all the major and minor events in a woman's life: from education to work, from motherhood to aging, from daily interactions to consumer practices, friendship, dating, parenting, and online activities. In each of the bigger and smaller "tests" to which a woman must submit her social identity in order to be validated, her bodily appearance projects and signifies that identity, but at the same time it serves as a device by which to "control" its projection, its expression, its daily unfolding. Due to the particular cultural emphasis placed on attractiveness as a mark of competent femininity, it is unlikely that women will be able to eschew their obligation to pursue beauty. Hence, beautification is far from being a superficial occupation of frivolous individuals or a hindrance to authentic womanhood: it is a commitment that the Western female subject must demonstrate and embody if she is to receive validation and be acknowledged as legitimate. Managing one's attractiveness serves the purpose of increasing one's chances of belonging among those who can legitimately demand recognition for their self-presentation as female subjects in diverse social contexts.

As I intend to show in this book, these ongoing efforts are thwarted by the paradoxicality of Western beauty culture, whose injunctions act as an inexhaustible matrix of negative judgments on women's actions and self-presentational choices. If picking one side of the paradox does not allow one to avoid the sanction stemming from its opposite, then women's choices appear to be undermined from the start, no matter what. It is here that the tightrope metaphor, evoked by one of the participants, reveals its particular salience: if achieved, balance can be maintained only for a short time before the challenge begins again. This observation concerning the social nature of women's ability to choose and act—their *agency*—has major consequences for feminist critiques of Western (beauty) culture. "Choice," understood here as the right to choose, to practice self-determination, to enjoy full autonomy, has indeed been a major theme of feminist thought and action throughout the twentieth century. Despite the dominance of the idea of individual choice, however, feminist movements past and present insist on the fact that social and political changes are necessary preconditions for securing individuals' ability to make their own decisions. In other words, access to agency is not simply a matter of willpower, of wanting something badly enough and bringing it about through sheer determination (as Western beauty discourse claims).

In recent decades, postfeminist discourse has inculcated in the general populace the idea that women have secured complete freedom, agency, and self-determination, especially in matters of individual identity, career, maternity, and, more importantly, bodily appearance. Through such rhetoric, beauty has been divested of its political dimensions, and systemic injustices are widely trivialized insofar as women are depicted as being in control of their bodies (a crucial feminist theme, by the way) and able to engage in beautification and related consumer practices for the pure sake of their own pleasure (as opposed to male desire and the male gaze). The results described in this book serve to undermine these claims in two main ways. They show, first, that women still perceive and use attractiveness as a resource to obtain social validation and legitimacy, notably in social situations (work, school, consumption, friendly sociability online and off) in which the appraisal of one's appearance is not the main theme of the interaction (as it could be, for instance, while dating or searching for a sexual partner). Hence, the social and political dimension of attractiveness as a source of inequality has not been overcome in contemporary Western societies, and women do not engage in beautification exclusively for the sake of their own pleasure (even if they embrace the corresponding rhetoric, as I've discussed).

Second, my observations point to the fact that women's choices in matters of appearance do not go unquestioned, as postfeminist discourse would claim, but, rather, are framed by paradoxical injunctions that variously sanction and disqualify them, precisely because they are made by women, as superficial, vain, lacking in intelligence, lacking in self-confidence, deceitful, psychologically unbalanced, inauthentic—even if it is conceded that the results are often nice to look at. Such observations could be extended to the sociopolitical status of women's choices in matters of motherhood, work-family conciliation, career, mating, and so forth. And the picture is even more complicated if we take into account ever-present axes of inequality, such as age, race, socioeconomic status, education, disability, and body size.

Here, then, is the great irony of postfeminist culture: to begin with, despite assumptions about women's empowerment and agency, women's ability to choose is conditioned by the paradoxes explored in this book. Moreover, as a consequence, "balance," which is a core component of the postfeminist discourse around successful, "emancipated" female subjectivity, reveals itself to be unattainable in any practical sense. Women do not choose, as neoliberal consumer rhetoric would have us believe, between equally available opportunities that allow them to create a harmonious network of commitments and to fulfill their ambitions; rather, they choose between contradictory obligations whose effects on their social legitimacy are equally deleterious. If women's "bad decisions" are usually attributed to their psychological issues—their lack of self-confidence, their selfishness, their narcissistic personality traits, and so on—my book is a plea for a return to a thoroughly sociological and political explanation of the collective scrutiny of women's agency. It is crucial that we return to a collective discussion of the specific sociopolitical conditions that prescribe women's choices, as well as the discursive practices that force them to walk the tightrope of paradoxical injunctions.

APPENDIX A

Introducing the Participants

Audrey is forty years old at the time of our first interview; she is a white Canadian woman and defines herself as "big." She has an undergraduate degree, but her current self-employment is only tangentially related to her educational path. She works full-time in a rather masculine environment, and she mentions a couple of times that this is an important element in her relationship to her appearance and sense of femininity. Audrey is married and has one young daughter. Due to her husband's health issues, she is the only breadwinner in the household, and she explicitly situates herself and her family in the low-income bracket,[1] with virtually no disposable income. She defines herself as a feminist. Her use of selfies is mainly recreational, but she also promotes her work through Instagram and Facebook.

Cassandra is a Black woman, born in Canada but not originally from Quebec. A single mother of a son in his late teens, she is forty-nine years old at the time of our first interview. She completed high school, worked in a variety of different jobs, and struggled to make ends meet when her son was younger. At the time of our interviews, Cassandra has no job, practically no income, and lives on her boyfriend's modest salary. She is an advocate of a healthy lifestyle, has artistic aspirations, and particularly loves photography. Interestingly, she was an avid selfie-taker years before this was even a "thing." Sometimes she uses Instagram and Facebook to promote her artwork. When I inquire about her relationship status, she says that she is a polyamorous woman in a committed relationship with her boyfriend.

Clarisse is a white woman born in Quebec; she is thirty-five at the time of our first interview. She holds an undergraduate degree and works full-time in a secretarial job, which gives her a personal yearly salary of around $45,000. She is in a long-term committed relationship with the father of her three young sons. Her frequent references to shopping and beautification services give the impression that her double-income household leaves her with enough disposable income for pleasurable personal expenses. Clarisse also struggled with mental health problems in the year before her participation in my research, which had a marked influence on her relationship with beauty. She describes her selfie practices as recreational.

Emma is twenty-two years old at the time of our first interview. She is a white, heterosexual woman born in Quebec, and is not in a relationship while participating in my study. She is completing her undergraduate degree in performing arts and supports herself with different student jobs, mainly in the service and hospitality industries. Her income level is therefore quite low at the time of our interviews (around $20,000 a year). While she shoots selfies for the pleasure of it, sometimes her pictures are also related to modelling gigs.

Eva is a white woman born in Quebec, and she is completing her master's degree while she participates in my research (when we meet for the second interview, she announces the successful completion of her graduate education). Twenty-nine years old at the time of our first interview, she holds a student job in the retail sector, having changed jobs at various points throughout her time in university in order to support herself. Situated in the low-income bracket (less than $20,000 a year in personal income), she mentions that she lacks the disposable income needed to shop for new clothes (she frequents thrift stores instead). Single at the time of the first interview, she alludes to her being in a heterosexual relationship during our second conversation. She takes selfies simply for the pleasure of it.

Fanny is a thirty-five-year-old white woman from Quebec who is very vocal about the emancipatory and pleasurable aspects of her selfie-taking and selfie-sharing practice, a pursuit that predates her participation in my research. Having read my recruitment announcement on a local Facebook group, a friend of Fanny's tagged her in the comment section—and she subsequently talked to me. Fanny is self-employed, works full-time (with women), and wears t-shirts with feminist messages. A mother of two young sons who lives with her male partner in a double-income household, she mentions her occasional difficulties balancing family and work.

Jeanne is a twenty-five-year-old white heterosexual woman from Quebec. She completed an undergraduate degree in performing arts, and at the time of our interviews, she works as a childhood educator while auditioning for different performance gigs. With a yearly personal income of less than

$20,000, she is financially precarious, and during our interviews, she sometimes refers to different tricks she uses to save money on beauty treatments—mainly dying her hair at home, which she greatly enjoys. She is in a committed relationship, loves to travel, and has a pet, which features often in her selfies. These are almost exclusively shot for personal and recreational reasons.

Juliette is a thirty-five-year-old white heterosexual woman from Quebec who is completing her PhD while participating in my study. She is the only participant whom I knew before embarking on this research: she was a student at my university and, years ago, took one of my courses. Her income is rather low (about $25,000 a year), which she mentions more than once when discussing the economics of beautification. Juliette states explicitly that she resents being single and stuck in a student lifestyle while friends her age are more affluent and already creating families. She is ambivalent toward selfies, which she uses to share her life experiences with friends.

Lena is a thirty-seven-year-old heterosexual white woman born outside of Canada, and is married with two young daughters. Her husband is the main breadwinner in their relatively affluent household. After working as a broker for years in a male-dominated environment, and then taking time off to care for her young children, she is attempting a career change and trying to establish herself in the fitness sector at the time of our first interview. Hence, her use of selfies is highly self-promotional and almost exclusively connected to her new line of work. She encourages her followers to adopt a reasonably healthy lifestyle but is also critical of the obsession with perfection she sees exhibited on social media.

Like Lena, **Melissa** is also going through a career change at the time of our first interview. Fifty years old, from Quebec, she is white, married, and lives with her husband, her two teenage children, and her beloved dogs. Melissa holds a bachelor's degree and worked for years as a project supervisor in a male-dominated field. Now relying on her husband as the sole breadwinner, she recently decided to indulge her lifelong passion and become a full-time artist (her annual personal income averages $30,000). At the time of our second interview, she is pleased to report that her work is receiving some attention from buyers and gallerists. Melissa also loves sports and stays very active.

Zoe is a fifty-year-old white heterosexual woman from Quebec. She worked in communications and media for a long time before resuming her education and embarking on a PhD. As a young woman, she also took modelling gigs. While participating in my research, she is completing her doctoral degree and is well-read in the social sciences (our research interests are situated in related fields). She is in a long-term, live-in relationship and has a personal income of about $45,000 a year.

APPENDIX B

Methodological Design and Procedure

This book is rooted in a three-year (2017–2020) qualitative research project generously funded by the Fonds de recherche du Québec—Société et culture. The research was carried out by myself as a principal investigator in collaboration with Catherine Lavoie Mongrain, a PhD student under my supervision who served as a graduate research assistant (2017–2019).

When I first submitted the grant application, I mainly wanted to tackle women's self-representational practices through selfie-taking and selfie-sharing. In 2016, this topic had not received much attention from Canadian scholars, despite the interest evident in media and popular discourse. My conversations with the participants during my eighteen months of fieldwork transformed my initial project into a deeper probe of women's experience of beautification, beauty culture, and its transposition into selfie culture. What began as an exploratory research project on digital visual habits produced a rich and wide-ranging set of data on women's lives and the place of appearance and femininity in them. This book is an attempt to do justice to the observations, feelings, and experiences that the participants generously shared with me.

Following insights by Mira Crouch and Heather McKenzie,[1] and aiming to gather substantial and heterogeneous data on each participant so as to fulfill the requirements of my exploratory research, I constituted a small convenience sample of eleven women aged twenty-two to fifty (ages are calculated based on the time of each participant's first interview), living in Montreal, either professionally active or completing post-secondary education, and who actively post selfies to their accounts on Instagram and/or Facebook. Readers can refer to appendix A for a description of the participants and their sociodemographic profiles. Drawing on Haridimos Tsoukas's epistemological observations on sampling strategies, my small-sample study aimed to "strike a balance" between, on the one hand, the desire to account for singularities and "cases" in a phenomenological sense, and on the other the ambition to reach a higher degree of generalization by organizing the narratives around strong theoretical concepts[2]—in the first place, that of "paradox." I aimed at achieving a general, overarching, and theoretical description of the phenomenon I was studying (namely, women's experience of beauty and their participation in beauty culture) through a careful account of the particular occurrences of such phenomenon which I could observe within singular cases (each participant's own verbal and visual storytelling) and the convergences emerging across multiple cases.

Ethics certification for this research was issued by the Ethics Committee of the Faculté des sciences humaines at Université du Québec à Montréal (certification # 1978_e_2017). The eleven women (a twelfth withdrew from the study after the first interview and demanded that her data be erased, which I promptly did) were recruited by word of mouth in the researcher's and graduate assistant's personal and professional networks (three participants), as well as through announcements pinned on boards in different public spaces in Montreal and circulated in local Facebook groups (eight participants). Due to the length and the complexity of their involvement in the study, I requested ongoing consent from the participants: an informed consent form was signed prior to the beginning of data collection and after a detailed explanation of the research protocol, and consent was renewed verbally after a presentation and a brief discussion at each of the four stages of data collection. Data were carefully anonymized. Participants were first assigned a code, which served to connect data items to each of them, then a pseudonym for the sake of a more palatable presentation of results in articles and in this book. To protect the participants' privacy, selfies were collected and stored for recurrent analysis but never used in the dissemination of results.

The first stage of data collection consisted in studying each participant's Facebook and Instagram accounts, to which I was granted access after each individual signed their consent form. The main focus of this initial exploration was to analyze the last ten selfies shared by each participant, the associated hashtags (if any), and more generally to take note of pages they liked or followed, such as women's magazines, celebrities, companies, or products related to self-care and beauty. In order to "thicken" the data,[3] and to understand them within their cultural context online, the observations conducted on Instagram and Facebook were discussed with each participant during the first semi-directed interview. The first round of interviews took place between January and May 2018. Participants were questioned about their pictures, their selfie-related habits, practices, and reflections, their understanding of the cultural features of social networking platforms, but also about their relationship with their appearance, gender stereotypes of beauty and femininity, and beautification practices. Interviews were transcribed in their entirety and coded for emerging themes through open and iterative codification,[4] after establishing inter-judge reliability.[5] Codification memos served to inform further data collection as well as analyses and theorization.[6] More generally, at each stage of data collection, the available data set (depending on the stage: memos, notes, interview transcriptions, or pictures) was globally analyzed and triangulated to inform further data gathering and analyses.

After this first interview, each participant was asked to take seven selfies connected to five predetermined situations (namely, a first date, a job interview, a presentation at work or school, a night out with girlfriends, and a "bathroom" selfie), plus two situations chosen by the participant. The choice of this visual data-collection technique, called photo-elicitation,[7] had a threefold goal. First, pictures were displayed to facilitate conversations and trigger memories with participants during interviews.[8] Second, they were used both by participants and the research team to exemplify the reflections, techniques, and behaviors described by participants (with regard to themselves or to other women in their circles). Lastly, they provided me with additional insights into patterns of behavior, visual choices, and personal experience discussed with the participants or inferred from subsequent data, and this from the point of view of the participant herself.[9] Before the second follow-up interview with each participant (which took place between September and December 2018), I printed out all the selfies they sent me in color on US Letter–size paper (8.5 by 11 inches, or 22 by 28 centimeters). The printed pictures—considerably larger in size than selfies viewed on a mobile phone, and hence magnifying details that would hardly be noticeable in a smaller format—were placed on the table in front of the participant at the beginning of the interview, and I would begin by questioning my interlocutor about two or three of these images, pre-selected for their particular salience. However, participants were also invited during the discussion to browse their phones, their social media accounts, and printed pictures to pick other relevant images. The five predetermined situations were chosen in order to document participants' visual languages in connection to formal (work, school), informal (leisure time), and private contexts (bathroom). By asking all participants to take selfies connected to the same situations, I was able to obtain a "controlled" variety, which allowed me to observe similarities as well as differences in visual language. I left participants the choice of two additional situations in order to ease whatever pressure might arise from this bit of "homework" and to enhance the resemblance to ordinary, spontaneous selfie-taking. If the selfies taken before the interviews testify to the ordinary labor entailed by "doing selfies," this labor was not necessarily reflected, contextualized, or criticized by the participants. Thus, compared to elicited selfie-taking, ordinary selfie-taking struck the participants as more spontaneous, less artificial than producing self-portraits "on demand." Methodologically speaking, this contrast helped generate awareness (in myself as well as the participants) of the "hows" and the "whys" of selfie-taking. This awareness was pointed out and discussed by most participants during the second semi-directed interview. Within the whole research design, selfies were thus used as data proper, as illustrations of practices and feelings, and as a fieldwork device to enhance participants' reflexivity vis-à-vis practices of visual self-expression.

Once transcribed, the second set of interviews was coded using the same coding grid created while processing the first set of interview transcripts. The grid consisted of overarching categories that mainly replicated the structure of the interview grid (e.g., selfies, appearance and self-presentation, feeling beautiful) and a three-level coding tree for each category (grandparent nodes, parent nodes, child nodes). As expected on the basis of the sample size,[10] "grandparent" and "parent" themes in each overarching category were rapidly saturated, sometimes even after the first round of interviews. Comprehensive analysis of the data set was carried out through a theory-oriented grouping of coded themes—especially child and parent nodes[11]—analytic memo writing on grouped themes, and increasingly general theorization of observed phenomena. All data were archived and processed with QSR International's NVivo 12 qualitative data analysis software. As I mentioned in the Introduction, I arrived at the concept of "paradoxicality" inductively, during the analytic phase: recurrent observations of interview passages in which participants would spell out or gesture at the "contradictions" of the perceived beauty injunctions generated questions on the centrality of this experience. The overarching category of "paradox" was then obtained through targeted analysis of the relevant interview extracts, rereading the entirety of transcripts to highlight relevant, albeit less explicit, formulations, analysis of popular media contents, and a recursive back-and-forth between analytic material and scholarly literature. The presentation of each paradox in chapter 1 is meant to reproduce as much as possible this thought process and my ongoing engagement with different materials.

Throughout the data analysis—and, as a consequence, throughout the writing of this book—I devoted particular attention to a pivotal aspect of the experience of beauty (as highlighted by feminist literature)—namely, its variability along axes of gender, age, class, race, and body size. Individuals are situated at the intersection of multiple axes of inequality, which causes normative injunctions to variously target, with either more or less intensity, social actors with different individual characteristics. The racial homogeneity of my sample (ten out of eleven women are white) did not allow for a detailed analysis of how experiences of beauty culture vary across races. However, my sample allowed for an analytical foregrounding of the intersections of axes of inequality that are less often explored and discussed, in this case age, class (or socioeconomic status), and body size.[12] Hence, as recommended by intersectionality scholar Sirma Bilge,[13] my empirical work allowed the overlap between observed inequalities to emerge, rather than presupposing the primacy of certain inequality axes over others. In addition, as highlighted in the introduction, sample homogeneity, while it often represents a limitation, can sometimes be turned into a methodological device. As Sarah Riley and colleagues observe, postfeminist beauty culture revolves around an idealized blueprint for femininity: white, heterosexual, upper middle class, and thin.[14] It is therefore relevant to document how white heterosexual women respond to its normativity and its imagery, and, I would add, how they reflect on its intrinsic neglect of (body) diversity. Documenting mainstream culture, and the way directly targeted subjectivities and bodies respond to it, also allowed me to appreciate continuities and differences in the experience of the only racialized participant. Despite the fact that her account of beauty culture cannot be extended to bearers of the same racialized identity without further data, it nevertheless added a layer of complexity to my analysis of North American beauty culture.

As previously stated, my observations and conclusions apply to the Western (postfeminist) cultural framework, especially to urban North American contexts, and cannot be generalized beyond these boundaries without additional research.

A final note on the presentation of data in this book. Montreal being a city where both French and English are widely spoken, I circulated my recruitment announcements in both languages. Anglophone and francophone participants were therefore recruited for the study, and, as a consequence, the interviews took place in both French and English, depending on each interviewee's preference. Excerpts from interviews conducted in

French are presented here in my own translations, conducted to the best of my abilities and with the hope that they convey as accurately as possible and with the necessary nuance the specific ideas and feelings that the participants wished to express. I assume full responsibility for any (inadvertent) failures in this regard. Finally, in an effort to further protect participants' privacy, I do not provide unnecessary details regarding their line of work or specific jobs, unless such details are relevant and can help to situate their experiences and claims.

NOTES

INTRODUCTION

1. Angelique Serrano, "All the Celebrity Beauty Pros Giving Their Expert Tips Away for Free on Instagram," *InStyle*, May 18, 2020, https://www.instyle .com/beauty/quarantine-hair-makeup-pro-tips.

2. As recommended by Kathy Davis in her 1991 paper on feminist approaches to beauty, "Remaking the She-Devil: A Critical Look at Feminist Approaches to Beauty," *Hypathia* 6, no. 2 (1991): 21–43.

3. *Cambridge English Dictionary*, s.v. "paradox," accessed June 30, 2020, https:// dictionary.cambridge.org/dictionary/english/paradox.

4. Assuming that happiness can be a feminist aspiration in a patriarchal society—a premise that both Sara Ahmed and Erin Wunker emphatically dispute. See Ahmed, *Living a Feminist Life* (Durham, NC: Duke University Press, 2017), and Wunker, *Notes from a Feminist Killjoy* (Toronto: BookThug, 2016).

5. Paul Watzlawick, John H. Weakland, and Richard Fisch, *Change: Principles of Problem Formation and Problem Resolution* (New York, Norton, 1974), especially chapter 3.

6. Christian Schneickert, Leonie C. Steckermeier, and Lisa-Marie Brand, "Lonely, Poor, and Ugly? How Cultural Practices and Forms of Capital Relate to Physical Unattractiveness," *Cultural Sociology* 14, no. 1 (2020): 80–105.

7. Angela McRobbie, *The Aftermath of Feminism: Gender, Culture and Social Change* (London: Sage, 2009), 57.

8. Sarah Riley, Adrienne Evans, and Martine Robson, *Postfeminism and Health: Critical Psychology and Media Perspective* (Oxon, UK: Routledge, 2019), 1.

9. McRobbie, *The Aftermath*, 55. An excellent example of this discursive tension can be found in Hannah Rosin's bestseller *The End of Men: And the Rise of Women* (New York: Riverhead Books, 2012).

10. Sarah Riley, Adrienne Evans, and Alison Mackiewicz, "It's Just Between Girls: Negotiating the Postfeminist Gaze in Women's 'Looking Talk,'" *Feminism & Psychology* 26, no. 1 (2016): 100. See Appendix B: Methodological Design and Procedure at the back of the book for a more detailed discussion of the methods, procedures, limitations, and overall design of my research. An analysis of how dominant, Western standards of beauty are negotiated in non-Western sociocultural contexts can be found in Meeta Ravi Jha, *The Global Beauty Industry* (London: Routledge 2016).

11. Riley, Evans, and Robson, *Postfeminism and Health*, 1. See also Amélie Keyser-Verreault, "The Continuum of Regaining One's Body: Childbirth and Reproductive Choice under Beauty Pressure in Taiwan," *European Journal of Cultural Studies*, June 28, 2022, https://doi.org/10.1177/13675494221104145.

12. On aesthetic economy and aesthetic labor, see Chris Wahrhurst and Dennis Nickson, *Aesthetic Labour* (Los Angeles: Sage, 2020). Arlie Hochschild's research is presented in her seminal book *The Managed Heart: Commercialization of Human Feeling* (Berkeley: University of California Press, 1983).

13. See Katrin Tiidenberg, *Selfies: Why We Love (and Hate) Them* (Bigley, UK: Emerald Publishing, 2018), 12: "selfie culture means people's way of taking, sharing, posting, filtering, liking and deleting selfies, the norms and values that guide it and our collective ways of speaking about selfies."

14. Greg Smith, "Reconsidering Gender Advertisements: Performativity, Framing and Display," in *The Contemporary Goffman*, ed. Michael H. Jacobsen (New York: Routledge, 2010), 175.

15. Claire Tanner, JaneMaree Maher, and Suzanne Fraser, *Vanity: 21st Century Selves* (Basingstoke, UK: Palgrave Macmillan, 2013), 2.

CHAPTER 1

1. *Oxford English Dictionary*, s.v. "paradox," A.2.b., accessed July 13, 2021, https://www.oed.com/oed2/00170984.

2. Camille Rainville, "Be a Lady They Said," *Writing of a Furious Woman* (blog), December 9, 2017, https://writingsofafuriouswoman.wordpress.com/2017/12/09/be-a-lady-they-said.

3. The video was shared via the *Girls Girls Girls* Instagram account: https://www.instagram.com/p/CMK8KrAAeLk (accessed July 13, 2021).

4. Jo Chappel, "Be Provocative They Said. A Serious Message from *Girls. Girls. Girls.* Magazine," *Creative Moment*, March 5, 2020, https://www.creativemoment.co/be-provocative-they-said-a-serious-message-from-girls-girls-girls-magazine-with-a-cultural-currency-with-real-value.

5. Amanda Mull, "Americans Have Baked All the Flour Away," *The Atlantic*, May 12, 2020, https://www.theatlantic.com/health/archive/2020/05/why-theres-no-flour-during-coronavirus/611527.

6. Le HuffPost, "La Une de Elle sur les kilos et le confinement déclenche les critiques," *Le HuffPost*, June 1, 2020, https://www.huffingtonpost.fr/entry/la-une -de-elle-sur-les-kilos-et-le-confinement-declenche-les-critiques_fr_5ed4a8f9c5b 6adee41bc4ae9.

7. Laure Botella (@LaureBotella), Twitter, May 30, 2020, https://twitter.com /LaureBotella/status/1266663823722909696/photo/3. Unless otherwise noted, all translations are my own.

8. See Jennifer Padjemi, "Le maquillage, une affaire de classe," episode 27 of *Miroir miroir* (podcast), November 18, 2019, https://www.binge.audio/podcast/ miroirmiroir/le-maquillage-une-affaire-de-classe. On the same topic, see Mona Chollet's discussion of the contradictions to be found in French women's magazines: *Beauté fatale: Les nouveaux visages d'une aliénation féminine* (Paris: La Découverte, 2012).

9. Please note: When quoting from these unpublished interviews, I use bracketed ellipses to indicate where I've omitted a portion of the interviewee's original statement (as opposed to interrupted or faltering speech on the part of the speaker, the occasional instance of which is indicated by unbracketed ellipses). When quoting from published sources (books, articles, online sources, etc.), I've retained the convention of using unbracketed ellipses to indicate similar elisions.

10. Here, I'm drawing on Efrat Tseëlon, *The Masque of Femininity* (London: Sage, 1995), 91; Dean MacCannell and Juliet Flower MacCannell, "The Beauty System," in *The Ideology of Conduct*, ed. Nancy Armstrong and Leonard Tennenhouse (New York: Methuen, 1987), 214.

11. See Bruno Remaury, *Le beau sexe faible. Les images du corps féminin entre cosmétique et santé* (Paris: Grasset, 2000), 31ff.

12. See Elena Gianini Belotti, *What Are Little Girls Made Of?* (New York: Schocken, 1978); Peggy Orenstein, *Cinderella Ate My Daughter* (New York: Harper Collins, 2011).

13. Colette Guillaumin, *Racism, Sexism, Power and Ideology* (London: Routledge, 1995), chap. 6.

14. For a similar argument, see Sandra Lee Bartky's seminal work "Foucault, Femininity, and the Modernization of Patriarchal Power," in *Femininity and Domination: Studies in the Phenomenology of Oppression* (New York: Routledge, 1990), 63–82. I quote the relevant passage below in note 63 of this chapter. See also Beverly Skeggs, *Formations of Class & Gender: Becoming Respectable* (London: SAGE Publications, 1997), 109.

15. Bartky, "Foucault, Femininity, and the Modernization of Patriarchal Power," 73. In his ethnographic research on clothing, Daniel Miller puts in perspective the Western cultural framework according to which "philosophers and saints" are seen as profound because they do not care for appearance, while those who do—mainly women—are superficial. This cultural understanding of the opposition between surface and depth, which places clothing (and other adornments) on the side of superficiality, is historically disqualifying for women in the West. See Daniel Miller, *Stuff* (Cambridge: Polity Press, 2010), 16.

16. Max Beerbohm, "A Defence of Cosmetics," *The Yellow Book* 1 (April 1894), available at https://archive.org/stream/defenceofcosmeti00beer/defenceofcosmet i00beer_djvu.txt. For a reconstruction of the historical context, see Madeleine Marsh, *Compacts and Cosmetics: Beauty from Victorian Times to the Present Day* (Barnsley, UK: Pen & Sword History, 2018), 45. For a discussion of the cultural trope of women's vanity, see Tseëlon, *The Masque of Femininity*, 16.

17. Catherine Fouquet and Yvonne Knibiehler, *La beauté pour quoi faire? Essai sur l'histoire de la beauté féminine* (Paris: Temps Actuels, 1982), especially 104. See also Sarah Maza's insightful studies of public women's progressive exclusion from the political sphere before and during the French Revolution, which was justified on the basis of the power that these women, from the king's mistresses to Marie Antoinette herself, would allegedly exert on mighty political men—including the king—through their sexuality and sex appeal. Sarah Maza, "The Diamond Necklace Affair Revisited: The Case of the Missing Queen," in *Eroticism and the Body Politics*, ed. Lynn Hunt (Baltimore: Johns Hopkins University Press, 1991), 63–89, and "L'image de la souveraine: Féminité et politique dans les pamphlets de l'affaire du collier," *Studies on Voltaire and the Eighteenth Century* 287 (1991): 363–78.

18. Marion Braizaz, "Le 'problème' de la beauté: Quand la sociologie s'intéresse au travail esthétique de soi," *Strathèse* 6 (2017), https://strathese.unistra.fr:443/ strathese/index.php?id=1139.

19. Interestingly, as reported by Kristina Holmqvist and Carolina Lunde, the worth paradox seems to remain pervasive even in sociocultural and political contexts characterized by higher gender equality, as is the case, for example, in Sweden. A collective commitment to promoting gender equality might in some cases negatively impact the severity of the worth paradox for women: according to recent data, Holmqvist and Lunde explain, Swedish women feel that admitting their participation in beautification practices could expose them to negative judgment to the extent that their behavior would not only be seen as superficial but also as failing to promote gender equality. Kristina Holmqvist and Carolina Lunde, "Appearance-Related Practices," in *Body Positive: Understanding and Improving Body Image in Science and Practice*, ed. Elizabeth A. Daniels, Meghan M. Gillen, and Charlotte H. Markey (Cambridge: Cambridge University Press, 2018), 128. See also Johanna Kling, Kristina Holmqvist Gattario, and Ann Frisén, "Swedish Women's Perceptions of and Conformity to Feminine Norms," *Scandinavian Journal of Psychology* 58, no. 3 (2017): 238–48.

20. *Inside Amy Schumer*, season 3, episode 2, "Cool with It," directed by Ryan McFaul, aired April 25, 2015, on Comedy Central.

21. See Tseëlon, *The Masque of Femininity*, chapter 2, which provides an extensive analysis of the place of women in religious traditions, mythical tales, and modern understandings of the role of female inauthenticity in social bonds (such as psychoanalysis).

22. Kathy Peiss, *Hope in a Jar: The Making of America's Beauty Culture* (New York: Owl Books, 1998), 55. A notice regarding the bill can be found in the

Weekly Drug Markets, February 17, 1915, available on Google Books: https://books .google.ca/books?id=5zJl7kP7WjoC&lpg=RA18-PA14-IA4&dq=kansas%20anti -cosmetics%20law%201915&pg=RA18-PA14-IA4#v=onepage&q=kansas%20anti -cosmetics%20law%201915&f=false. I am indebted to Kathy Peiss for providing me with this reference.

23. Remaury, *Le beau sexe faible*, 102. As Remaury notes, the language of advertising praises "natural makeup," but never speaks of an "artificial makeup, unless to depreciate it. Beauty is always natural" (103).

24. See Peiss, *Hope in a Jar*, 26: "Nineteenth-century moralists continued to view face paint as 'corporal hypocrisy,' a mask that did not conceal female vice and vanity."

25. Philippe Perrot, *Le travail des apparences. Le corps féminin XVIIIe–XIXe siècle* (Paris: Éditions du Seuil, 1984), chaps. 2 and 3.

26. Peiss, *Hope in a Jar*, 28.

27. Tseëlon, *The Masque of Femininity*, 91.

28. A contradiction of beauty culture that Rita Freedman phrases as follows: "First beauty is worshiped as an innate quality that cannot be artificially contrived; next it is packaged and peddled as an illusion than anyone can cultivate." Freedman, *Beauty Bound: Why Women Strive for Perfection* (Lexington, MA: Lexington Books, 1986), 5.

29. See Remaury, *Le beau sexe faible*, especially the book's conclusion, where this point is effectively summarized.

30. MacCannell and MacCannell, "The Beauty System," 215.

31. For a discussion of online authenticity, see Meredith Salisbury and Jefferson Pooley, "The #Nofilter Self: The Contest for Authenticity among Social Networking Sites, 2002–2016," *Social Sciences* 6, no. 1 (2017), https://doi.org/10 .3390/socsci6010010.

32. "How to Simplify Your Beauty Routine" (blog post), Marcelle.com, accessed July 13, 2021, https://www.marcelle.com/en/simplify-your-beauty -routine.

33. Liam Stack, "Trump, in France, Tells Brigitte Macron, 'You're in Such Good Shape,'" *New York Times*, July 13, 2017, https://www.nytimes.com/2017 /07/13/world/europe/trump-france-brigitte-macron.html. See also the footage of the encounter posted on YouTube by the *Washington Post*: "Trump to Brigitte Macron: 'You're in Such Great Shape,'" YouTube, July 13, 2017, https://www .youtube.com/watch?v=Q5wpa14ORW4.

34. Kristina Rodulfo, "Alexandria Ocasio-Cortez Details Her Skincare Routine and Offers Tips on Oration in the Same IG Story," *Elle*, January 28, 2019, https://www.elle.com/beauty/makeup-skin-care/a26062012/alexandria-ocasio -cortez-skincare-makeup-beauty-routine; Eliza Relman, "Outgoing Democratic Sen. Claire McCaskill Dismisses Alexandria Ocasio-Cortez as a 'Shiny New Object' and Says Her 'Rhetoric Is Cheap,'" *Business Insider*, December 26, 2018, https://www.businessinsider.com/sen-claire-mccaskill-dismisses-alexandria-ocasio

-cortez-as-shiny-new-object-2018-12; Megan Garber, "How Alexandria Ocasio-Cortez's Plain Black Jacket Became a Controversy," *The Atlantic*, November 16, 2018, https://www.theatlantic.com/entertainment/archive/2018/11/alexandria-ocasio-cortezs-clothes-a-tedious-backlash/576064; Sangeeta Singh-Kurtz, "The Powerful Feminist Statement in Alexandria Ocasio-Cortez's Instagram Beauty Tips," *Quartz*, January 29, 2019, https://qz.com/quartzy/1535649/aocs-instagram-beauty-tips-are-a-powerful-feminist-statement.

35. Singh-Kurtz, "The Powerful Feminist Statement."

36. The quote is taken from Paul Solotaroff, "Trump Seriously: On the Trail with the GOP's Tough Guy," *Rolling Stone*, September 9, 2015, https://www.rollingstone.com/politics/politics-news/trump-seriously-on-the-trail-with-the-gops-tough-guy-41447.

37. Bill Pennington, "What Exactly Is 'Locker-Room Talk'? Let an Expert Explain," *New York Times*, October 20, 2016, https://www.nytimes.com/2016/10/11/sports/what-exactly-is-locker-room-talk-let-an-expert-explain.html.

38. See Tseëlon, *The Masque of Femininity*, 91. See also Renée Engeln, *Beauty Sick: How the Cultural Obsession with Appearance Hurts Girls and Women* (New York: Harper 2017), chap. 1, a section of which bears the subheading "Beauty Can Be Powerful for Women but It's a Weak and Temporary Power"—thereby pointing to the fragility of any power derived from attractiveness.

39. Maxine Leeds Craig, "Race, Beauty, and the Tangled Knot of a Guilty Pleasure," *Feminist Theory*, 7, no. 2 (2006): 160.

40. For a portrayal of the cultural shift by which "girl power" and sexiness were merged, see Susan Douglas, *Enlightened Sexism: The Seductive Message That Feminism's Work Is Done* (New York: Times Books, Henry Holt and Company, 2010); Deborah Spar, *Wonder Women: Sex, Power and the Quest for Perfection* (New York: Sarah Crichton Books, 2013). An example of the criticism of feminist thinkers' alleged "anti-beauty" stance can be found in Catherine Hakim, *Erotic Capital: The Power of Attraction in the Boardroom and in the Bedroom* (New York: Basic Books, 2011). For a discussion of the postfeminist sensibility, see Rosalind Gill, "The Affective, Cultural and Psychic Life of Postfeminism: A Postfeminist Sensibility 10 Years On," *European Journal of Cultural Studies* 20, no. 6 (2017): 606–26; Rosalind Gill, "Postfeminist Media Culture: Elements of a Sensibility," *European Journal of Cultural Studies* 10, no. 2 (2007): 147–66; Sarah Banet-Weiser, *Empowered: Popular Feminism and Popular Misogyny* (Durham, NC: Duke University Press, 2018); and Angela McRobbie, "Notes on the Perfect: Competitive Femininity in Neoliberal Times," *Australian Feminist Studies* 30, no. 83 (2015): 3–20.

41. Alexandria Ocasio Cortez (@AOC), Twitter, January 28, 2019, https://twitter.com/AOC/status/1089916535601287170?s=20.

42. Cheryl Wischhover, "Talking to Chimamanda Ngozi Adichie, the Beauty Brand Ambassador We All Need Right Now," *Racked*, November 22, 2016, https://www.racked.com/2016/11/22/13714228/chimamanda-ngozi-adichie-boots-beauty.

43. Roberta Cavaglià, "Il curioso caso del 'Festival della bellezza' senza donne (e con problemini di copyright)," *Wired.it*, September 9, 2020, https://www.wired.it /attualita/politica/2020/09/09/festival-bellezza-maschi-maggie-taylor.

44. Data retrieved from "Popolazione residente al 1° gennaio," I.Stat, accessed July 13, 2021, http://dati.istat.it/Index.aspx?QueryId=18460.

45. Historical examples can be found in many sources, but the following are especially useful: for developments from the sixteenth through to the nineteenth century, see Remaury, *Le beaux sexe faible*, 99–108; on the Victorian age, see Peiss, *Hope in a Jar*, 26. On women's efforts to retain a visible respectability, and thus their social legitimacy, see Beverly Skeggs, *Formations of Class & Gender: Becoming Respectable*. (London: SAGE, 1997). On contemporary postfeminist "makeover culture," which also entails a classist tendency to enact style and body shaming, see Angela McRobbie, "Notes on 'What Not to Wear' and Post-feminist Symbolic Violence," *Sociological Review* 52, no. 2 (2004): 99–109, and Katherine Sender, *The Makeover: Reality Television and Reflexive Audiences* (New York: NYU Press, 2012).

46. Peiss, *Hope in a Jar*, 155.

47. See Chollet, *Beauté fatale. Les nouveaux visages d'une aliénation féminine* (Paris: La Découverte, 2012); McRobbie, "Notes on 'What Not to Wear'"; Naomi Wolf, *The Beauty Myth: How Images of Beauty Are Used against Women* (London: Vintage, 1991).

48. British sociologists Ana Sofia Elias, Rosalind Gill, and Christina Scharff already discussed this allegedly newly discovered issue of the interaction between technology and the female body in their edited collection *Aesthetic Labour: Rethinking Beauty Politics in Neoliberalism* (London: Palgrave Macmillan, 2017) (see p. 30 in particular). On the specific dangers of modern life for women's appearance, see Michelle Henning, "Don't Touch Me (I'm Electric): On Gender and Sensation in Modernity," in *Women's Bodies: Discipline and Transgression*, ed. Jane Arthurs and Jean Grimshaw (London and New York: Cassell, 1999), 17–47, and Amina Mire, *Wellness in Whiteness: Biomedicalization and the Promotion of Whiteness and Youth among Women* (London: Routledge, 2020). An example of instructions on how to "capitalize" on beauty—an idea that is usually related to the selling of cosmetics or beauty services (such as surgery)—can be found in Alain Lajeunie, *Capital Jeunesse. Apprendre à le gérer grâce à la médecine anti-âge et à la médecine esthétique* (Paris: Ellipses, 2004). For a critical discussion of the "skin-care routine" recommended to women, see Bartky, "Foucault, Femininity, and the Modernization of Patriarchal Power."

49. See, for instance, Camille Sweeney, "Seeking Self-Esteem through Surgery," *New York Times*, January 14, 2009, https://www.nytimes.com/2009/01/15/fashion/15skin.html.

50. In fact, the scholarly interest in aesthetic judgment long predates Bourdieu. The idea that the desire to differentiate oneself aesthetically is driven more by the logic of social distinction than by the love of beauty can already be found in Alfred Binet's *Le fétichisme dans l'amour*, published for the first time in 1887.

51. McRobbie, "Notes on 'What Not to Wear,'" 105.

52. McRobbie, 107.

53. Paradoxes are central to some non-Western traditions too, such as Zen Buddhism, which uses the koan as a tool to facilitate insight during meditation. Since my general discussion of paradoxical thinking aims mainly at clarifying its role in Western culture and society, I will not get into these other examples.

54. On the liar paradox, see J. C. Beall, Michael Glanzberg, and David Ripley, "Liar Paradox," *Stanford Encyclopedia of Philosophy*, ed. Edward N. Zalta (Fall 2020 Edition), https://plato.stanford.edu/archives/fall2020/entries/liar-paradox. For a discussion of Russell's paradox, see Paul Watzlawick, Janet B. Beavin, and Don D. Jackson, *Pragmatics of Human Communication: A Study of Interactional Patterns, Pathologies, and Paradoxes* (London: Faber and Faber, 1967), chaps. 6 and 7.

55. See Paul Watzlawick, "Components of 'Ideological Realities,'" in *The Invented Reality: How Do We Know What We Believe We Know?*, ed. Paul Watzlawick (New York: W. W. Norton, 1984), 206–56, and Jurgen Ruesch and Gregory Bateson, *Communication: The Social Matrix of Psychiatry* (New York: W. W. Norton, 1968).

56. See Gregory Bateson, "Double Bind (1969)," in *Steps to an Ecology of Mind* (Northvale, NJ: Jason Aronson, 1987), 199–204.

57. See Watzlawick, "Components of 'Ideological Realities,'" 230.

58. Niklas Luhmann, "The Paradoxy of Observing Systems," *Cultural Critique* 31 (1995): 39.

59. Within power relationships, for instance, authority and privilege can dissuade dominated individuals from questioning the terms of the relationship. The voice of subordinates can be dismissed as pointless or "crazy." Just think about the way "hysterical" has been used to disqualify women's perspectives since the end of the nineteenth century. For more, see Watzlawick, Beavin, and Jackson, *Pragmatics of Human Communication*, chapter 6.

60. In other words, while observing the differentiation of a form, the paradox arises as the unity of medium and form. See Niklas Luhmann, *Die Gesellschaft der Gesellschaft* (Frankfurt am Main: Suhrkamp, 1997), 1:59, and "Meaning as Sociology's Basic Concept," in *Essays on Self-Reference* (New York: Columbia University Press, 1990), 21–79.

61. As shown by anthropologist Françoise Héritier in *Masculin/feminin. La pensée de la différence* (Paris: Odile Jacob, 1996), the difference between masculine and feminine is almost a universal feature in both present-day and historical societies. Such difference does not just distinguish men from women; rather, it structures a whole vision of the world: spaces, activities, rituals, relationships, institutions, and so on.

62. Guillaumin, *Racism, Sexism, Power and Ideology*.

63. In his classic work on the arrangement between the sexes, Erving Goffman analyzed the systems of courtship and courtesy as evidence of the high regard in which women appear to be held in society. However, as Goffman shows, such "high regard" is based on the assumption of women's (natural) difference and

inferiority. See Goffman, "The Arrangement between the Sexes," *Theory and Society* 4, no. 3 (1977): 301–31. This apparent inferiority is inscribed on women's bodies through beautification work; as Sandra Bartky puts it, the "disciplinary practices" of beautification produce "a body in which an inferior status has been inscribed." See Bartky, "Foucault, Femininity, and the Modernization of Patriarchal Power," 71.

64. Among the first, classical feminist critiques of beauty culture as a form of oppression for women are Mary Wollstonecraft, *A Vindication of the Rights of Woman* (London: Joseph Johnson, 1792), and Simone de Beauvoir, *Le Deuxième sexe* (Paris: Gallimard, 1949). Denunciations of beauty culture as a source of discipline and delusion for women can be found in Wolf, *The Beauty Myth*; Chollet, *Beauté fatale*; Bartky, "Foucault, Femininity, and the Modernization of Patriarchal Power"; Susan Bordo, *Unbearable Weight: Feminism, Western Culture, and the Body*, 10th ann. ed. (Berkeley: University of California Press: 2003). In addition to Wolf, Bartky, and Bordo, see the following authors for discussions of the beauty as an industry and form of consumption: Sheila Jeffreys, *Beauty and Misogyny: Harmful Cultural Practices in the West* (London: Routledge, 2005); Paula Black, *The Beauty Industry: Gender, Culture, Pleasure* (London: Routledge, 2004); Laurie Essig, *American Plastic: Boob Jobs, Credit Cards, and Our Quest for Perfection* (Boston: Beacon Press, 2010); and Ana Sofia Elias and Rosalind Gill, "Beauty Surveillance: The Digital Self-Monitoring Cultures of Neoliberalism," *European Journal of Cultural Studies* 21, no. 1 (2018): 59–77.

65. For a discussion of beautification as a source of pleasure, sociability, and a sense of dignity, see Debra Gimlin, *Body Work: Beauty and Self-Image in American Culture* (Oakland: University of California Press, 2002); Ann Cahill, "Feminist Pleasure and Feminine Beautification," *Hypathia* 18, no. 4 (2004): 42–64; Black, *The Beauty Industry*; and Martina Cvajner, "Hyper-Femininity as Decency: Beauty, Womanhood and Respect in Emigration," *Ethnography* 12, no. 3 (2011): 356–74.

66. I'm paraphrasing here from Remaury, *Le beau sexe faible*, 39.

67. Ori Schwarz, "Cultures of Choice: Towards a Sociology of Choice as a Cultural Phenomenon," *British Journal of Sociology* 69, no. 3 (2017): 845–64.

68. Similar results are reported by Paula Black and Ursula Sharma in their fieldwork on the beauty therapy industry, "Men Are Real, Women Are 'Made Up': Beauty Therapy and the Construction of Femininity," *Sociological Review* 49, no. 1 (2001): 100–16, and especially 105.

69. See, in particular, chapter 4 of Bourdieu's *Méditations pascaliennes* (Paris: Seuil, 1997), available in English translation as *Pascalian Meditations* (Stanford, CA: Stanford University Press, 2000).

70. In addition to the work of Tseëlon and MacCannell and MacCannell, discussed above, references to the paradoxical, contradictory, or ambiguous nature of beauty culture can be found, among others places, in Freedman, *Beauty Bound*; Bartky, "Foucault, Femininity, and the Modernization of Patriarchal Power"; Peiss, *Hope in a Jar*; Black and Sharma, "Men Are Real, Women Are 'Made Up'";

Engeln, *Beauty Sick*; Holmqvist and Lunde, "Appearance-Related Practices"; Joan J. Brumberg, *The Body Project: An Intimate History of American Girls* (New York: Vintage Books, 1997); Amy S. Dobson, *Postfeminist Digital Cultures: Femininity, Social Media, and Self-Representation* (New York: Palgrave Macmillan, 2015); and Sophie Cheval, *Belle autrement! Pour en finir avec la tyrannie de l'apparence* (Paris: Armand Colin, 2013). The idea that some cultural blueprints targeting woman are intrinsically paradoxical is discussed in scholarly literature that goes beyond the study of beauty culture. Discussing the Japanese cultural and artistic movement *kawaii*, for example, Dilton Ribeiro writes that "as a cultural-aesthetical enterprise, *kawaii* is paradoxical. On one side, it is a women-driven movement that questions previous gender and sexual paradigms. On a different side, it could pressure women into acting in accordance with the *kawaii* aesthetics when they will reproduce behaviors and consume products that are submissive and childish." See Ribeiro, "Sexuality and Femininity: The Paradox of the Cultural-Aesthetical *Kawaii* Movement," *Cadernos Pagu* 62 (2021), https://www.scielo.br/j/cpa/a/Yvr x8GfcZ7rYXkd3vznKV5h/?lang=en&format=pdf. The embodiment and negotiation of the tensions between contradictory norms of beauty and femininity was also observed among young Korean women in Yuri Seo, Angela Gracia B. Cruz, and 'Ilaisaane M. E. Fifita, "Cultural Globalization and Young Korean Women's Acculturative Labor: K-Beauty as Hegemonic Hybridity," *International Journal of Cultural Studies* 23, no. 4 (2020): 600–18.

71. Bari Weiss, "The Bikini Contest Is Over, but We Are Living Inside the Beauty Pageant," *New York Times*, June 5, 2018, https://www.nytimes.com/2018 /06/05/opinion/miss-america-bikini-contest.html.

72. Beauty culture's paradoxical injunctions also affect women's self-perception inasmuch as they constantly destabilize women's sense of self-worth and legitimacy. According to Frida Kerner Furman, in *Facing the Mirror: Older Women and Beauty Shop Culture* (New York: Routledge, 1997), this explains women's reluctance to talk about beauty, and also the fact that, when they do talk about it, they apologize for their good looks or for their interest in beauty. Being met with suspicion and criticism when they appear too invested in their beautification practices, and at the same time blamed for relinquishing a "proper" amount of feminine self-care, women oscillate between self-interest and self-deprecation. As Liz Frost suggests, "there is no language of physical self-appreciation, no discursive space for self-admiration" for women. See Frost "'Doing Looks': Women, Appearance and Mental Health," in *Women's Bodies: Discipline and Transgression,* ed. Jane Arthurs and Jean Grimshaw (London: Cassell, 1999), 128. I would argue that this also explains why the "body-positive" movement often takes the form of a learning process during which one embraces a posture of elf-admiration that opposes the more self-deprecating attitudes women normally internalize as part of their socialization in Western societies. The findings I describe here and in subsequent chapters are consistent with Kerner Furman's and Frost's.

CHAPTER 2

1. Bruno Remaury, *Le beau sexe faible. Les images du corps féminin entre cosmétique et santé* (Paris: Grasset, 2000), 74–85.

2. Yvonne Knibiehler and Catherine Fouquet, *La femme et les médecins* (Paris: Hachette, 1983). See also Georges Vigarello, *Histoire de la beauté. Le corps et l'art d'embellir de la Renaissance à nos jours* (Paris: Seuil, 2004), especially part 3, chap. 1.

3. Originating in France, the idea of *décadence* circulated in Europe at the end of the nineteenth century. See Chiara Piazzesi, *Nietzsche: Fisiologia dell'arte e décadence* (Lecce, IT: Conte, 2003). The German philosopher Friedrich Nietzsche, who would later unwittingly inspire some aspects of Nazi ideology, made *décadence* into the main feature of modern Western civilization. Giuliano Campioni, *Les lectures françaises de Nietzsche* (Paris: Presses universitaires de France, 2001).

4. Michelle Henning, "Don't Touch Me (I'm Electric): On Gender and Sensation in Modernity," in *Women's Bodies: Discipline and Transgression*, ed. Jane Arthurs and Jean Grimshaw (London: Cassell, 1999), 17–47.

5. See Gina Lombroso Ferrero, *Criminal Man, According to the Classification of Cesare Lombroso* (New York: G. P. Putnam's Sons, 1911).

6. See especially Michel Foucault, *"Il faut défendre la société." Cours au Collège de France, 1976* (Paris: Gallimard, 1997). See also the introduction to Chiara Piazzesi, *Vers une sociologie de l'intime* (Paris: Hermann 2017).

7. Sabrina Strings, *Fearing the Black Body: The Racial Origins of Fat Phobia* (New York: NYU Press, 2019), 73.

8. Strings, 73.

9. See George L. Mosse, *The Image of Man: The Creation of Modern Masculinity* (Oxford: Oxford University Press, 1996); Sander L. Gilman, *Making the Body Beautiful: A Cultural History of Aesthetic Surgery* (Princeton, NJ: Princeton University Press, 1999).

10. Mosse, *The Image of Man*, 59.

11. See, for instance, Sophia Efstathiou, "The Nazi Cosmetic: Medicine in the Service of Beauty," *Studies in History and Philosophy of Science Part C: Studies in History and Philosophy of Biological and Biomedical Sciences* 43, no. 3 (2012): 634–42.

12. See Gilman, *Making the Body Beautiful*, for a cultural history of aesthetic surgery.

13. See Alvaro Jarrín, *The Biopolitics of Beauty: Cosmetic Citizenship and Affective Capital in Brazil* (Oakland: University of California Press, 2017).

14. Knibiehler and Fouquet, *La femme et les médecins*, 9.

15. As Wendy Parkins has argued, in the first decades of the twentieth century this form of exclusion from the public sphere through a reduction of women to their body and physiology has been employed to delegitimize the voices and even the "presence" of British suffragettes in public spaces (women were deemed too emotional and unable to display the appropriate demeanor). The suffragettes' recourse to embodied political actions—from smashing windows to engaging in

hunger strikes—represented an attempt to highlight the impossibility of having their voices heard as citizens. Hence, "deliberately drawing attention to their bodies has been an important strategy for women engaged in dissident citizenship." Wendy Parkins, "Protesting Like a Girl: Embodiment, Dissent and Feminist Agency," *Feminist Theory* 1, no. 1 (2000): 73.

16. Simone de Beauvoir, *Le deuxième sexe* (Paris: Gallimard, 1949).

17. Carroll Smith-Rosenberg, *Disorderly Conduct: Visions of Gender in Victorian America* (New York: Alfred A. Knopf, 1985), 258.

18. Smith-Rosenberg, 258. Discouraging women from pursuing intellectual education was yet another way of "correcting" the dangerous inclinations of changing womanhood. As Claire Tanner, JaneMaree Maher, and Suzanne Fraser note, early twentieth-century exercise regimes were marketed to women as a means of improving their fitness for maternity and focusing their interest away from the frivolity of fashion. In the same period, exercise was promoted among men for the mere purpose of achieving muscular strength and fitness, without further benefits for the common good. Tanner, Maher, and Fraser, *Vanity: 21st Century Selves* (Basingstoke, UK: Palgrave Macmillan, 2013), especially 43 and 58.

19. Catherine Fouquet and Yvonne Knibiehler, *La beauté pour quoi faire? Essai sur l'histoire de la beauté féminine* (Paris: Temps Actuels, 1982), 135.

20. See Rita Freedman's observation about fitness culture in the second half of the 1980s: "Health reformers of the nineteenth century argued that activity, not cosmetics, was the natural key to beauty. . . . Today's heavy emphasis on fitness is motivated by a desire for beauty as well as for health." Freedman, *Beauty Bound*, 164.

21. See, for instance, Joan J. Brumberg's essay on American girls' "body projects" in the nineteenth and twentieth centuries, where she writes: "In the nineteenth century, young women were commonly taught that the face was a 'window on the soul' and that facial blemishes indicated a life that was out of balance." Brumberg, *The Body Project: An Intimate History of American Girls* (New York: Vintage Books, 1997), 62. See also Remaury, *Le beau sexe faible*, 132–44. Bernadette Wegenstein discusses the traditional interrelatedness of female beauty and ugliness in myth and literature, where ugliness—of both the aesthetic and moral varieties—constantly threatens to resurface due to the fundamental (moral) ambiguity of female nature. Such ideas, Wegenstein argues, are still present in the rhetoric of contemporary beauty advertising and are at the core of popular makeover-related television shows. See Wegenstein, *The Cosmetic Gaze: Body Modification and the Construction of Beauty* (Cambridge, MA: MIT Press, 2012), chap. 2.

22. See Catherine Rottenberg, *The Rise of Neoliberal Feminism* (New York: Oxford University Press, 2018).

23. Peiss, *Hope in a Jar: The Making of America's Beauty Culture* (New York: Owl Books, 1998), 140.

24. Pond's advertisement "An Interview with Mrs. O.H.P. Belmont on the care of the skin," reproduced in Peiss, 138.

25. As Claire Tanner, JaneMaree Maher, and Suzanne Fraser recount, beauty played an additional political role within the British suffragist movement. An important aspect of the suffrage militants' battle was indeed negotiating their political engagement while convincing society that they could still be "real" women, hence beautiful (and proud of that fact), and able to take on feminine domestic and reproductive duties. Curating their beautiful appearance and staying up-to-date on fashion were at once a vindication of their dignity and an immediate demonstration of their willingness to uphold the gender difference while deliberately trespassing into a sphere of public life, such as politics, usually restricted to men. Tanner, Maher, and Fraser, *Vanity*, 56.

26. See Leigh Stein's novel *Self Care: A Novel* (New York: Penguin Books, 2020).

27. Such postfeminist "cleansing" is simultaneously physiological and emotional. This becomes evident when we consider the rhetoric developed by best-selling wellness and self-help books such as *The Clarity Cleanse* by Habib Sadeghi (New York: Goop Press/Grand Central Life & Style, 2017), which claim that we can heal our bodies and prevent illness by promoting emotional unclogging and "clarity."

28. See Brianna Wiens and Shana MacDonald, "Living Whose Best Life? An Intersectional Feminist Interrogation of Postfeminist #Solidarity in #Selfcare," *NECSUS European Journal of Media Studies* 10, no. 1 (2021): 219–42. For a short history of Black movements' demands for a more inclusive beauty culture and market, see Maxine Leeds Craig, *Ain't I a Beauty Queen? Black Women, Beauty and the Politics of Race* (New York: Oxford University Press 2002).

29. See Wikipedia, s.v. "Pamela Anderson," last modified October 8, 2020, 20:40, https://en.wikipedia.org/w/index.php?title=Pamela_Anderson&oldid =982547074.

30. On wellness as a total life regime, see also chapter 6, in which I discuss the trending hashtag #ThatGirl on TikTok.

31. For a discussion, see Peter Conrad, "Wellness as Virtue: Morality and the Pursuit of Health," *Culture, Medicine, and Psychiatry* 18, no. 3 (1994): 385–401.

32. Rachel O'Neill, "'Glow from the Inside Out': Deliciously Ella and the Politics of 'Healthy Eating,'" *European Journal of Cultural Studies* 24, no. 6 (2021): 1295. In a short but powerful discussion of public and corporate discourse on "self-care" and "care of others" during the COVID-19 pandemic, Chatzidakis and colleagues use the term "carewashing" to capture the discursive strategies through which "corporations [are] trying to increase their legitimacy by presenting themselves as socially responsible 'citizens' while really contributing to inequality and ecological destruction." See Andreas Chatzidakis et al., "From Carewashing to Radical Care: The Discursive Explosions of Care during Covid-19," *Feminist Media Studies* 20, no. 6, 2020: 891. See also Fariha Róisín, *Who Is Wellness For? An Examination of Wellness Culture and Who It Leaves Behind* (New York: Harper Wave, 2022).

33. "I don't believe in women with gray hair, I'm sorry, I know, I just, honestly on a very objective level, I don't think it looks . . . I don't think it looks beautiful

and that's really my bias, unfortunately, but that's it," says Melissa during our second interview. On the "body positive" philosophy, see Céline Leboeuf, "What Is Body Positivity? The Path from Shame to Pride." *Philosophical Topics* 47, no. 2 (2019): 113–27.

34. Laura Martínez-Jiménez, "Postfeminist Neoliberalization of Self-Care: A Critical Discourse Analysis of Its Representation in *Vogue, Cosmopolitan* and *Elle*," *Feminist Media Studies*, June 29, 2022, 10, https://doi.org/10.1080/14680777.2022.2093936.

35. This rhetoric can still be found on the website of Goop (the beauty and wellness company founded by Gwyneth Paltrow in 2008)—including in articles written by Aarona Lea. See, for instance, Lea, "Aligning with the Four Phases of the Moon," Goop.com, accessed July 27, 2021, https://goop.com/wellness/spirituality/how-to-align-with-the-moon.

36. Martínez-Jiménez, "Postfeminist Neoliberalization of Self-Care," 14.

37. In one of our interviews, Eva refers to "the Swedish version of well-being," which might allude to the more Instagrammable aspects of *hygge*, or the Danish recipe for coziness, well-being, and self-care. For a description of *hygge*'s popularity in mainstream media, see Anna Altman, "The Year of Hygge, the Danish Obsession with Getting Cozy," *New Yorker*, December 18, 2016, https://www.newyorker.com/culture/culture-desk/the-year-of-hygge-the-danish-obsession-with-getting-cozy.

38. Strings, *Fearing the Black Body*, 84.

39. Strings, chaps. 4 and 5.

40. See Richard Kestenbaum, "The Biggest Trends in the Beauty Industry," *Forbes*, September 9, 2018, https://www.forbes.com/sites/richardkestenbaum/2018/09/09/beauty-industry-biggest-trends-skin-care-loreal-shiseido-lauder/#5893074f6982.

41. This rhetoric of clean cosmetics and "miraculous substances" is thoroughly discussed by Bruno Remaury in *Le beau sexe faible*, especially part 2, chapter 1. It would be interesting to reflect more broadly on our complicated relationship—characterized simultaneously by a sense of belief as well as skepticism—to the "miraculous" effect expected from beauty treatments altogether. Within current Western beauty culture, "miracles" can be hoped for when choosing clean beauty, but also when engaging in high-tech, non-surgical cosmetic treatments, such as those that consist in injecting the skin with different substances. For a sociological discussion of the moral panic triggered by the widespread recourse to "injectables," see Anna Dowrick and Ruth Holliday, "Tweakments: Non-surgical Beauty Technologies and Future Directions for the Sociology of the Body." *Sociology Compass*, September 27, 2022, https://doi.org/10.1111/soc4.13044.

42. See Rebecca Herzig, *Plucked: A History of Hair Removal* (New York: NYU Press, 2015), for a discussion of the strength of the norms governing hair removal for women, even for those who harshly criticize mainstream beauty regimes.

43. Social media, where participants are most likely to see these hairy women, have become a site of resistance against the norm of hairlessness, as Erica Åberg

and Laura Salonen point out in their analysis of the #januhairy trend on Instagram, "Well-Behaved Women Rarely Make History," in *Appearance as Capital: The Normative Regulation of Aesthetic Capital Accumulation and Conversion*, ed. Outi Sarpila et al., 149–64 (Bingley, UK: Emerald Publishing, 2022).

44. On the commercial rhetoric of a "skin stomach," according to which skin must be nourished with the same care and ingredients that we use to nourish our bodies, see again Remaury, *Le beau sexe faible*, 109–10. Indeed, contemporary homemade cosmetics are often crafted using fresh edible ingredients.

45. Elsie Rutterford and Dominika Minarovic, *Clean Beauty: Recipes to Manage Your Beauty Routine, Naturally* (London: Square Peg, 2017). The copy from which I am reading is an e-book; the quotation in this paragraph comes from the section entitled "What Is This Clean Beauty Lark?"

46. Rutterford and Minarovic develop the same narrative in *Clean Beauty*. As they point out, pharmacy and drugstore products might look reliable, but a closer look reveals "questionable" ingredients and deceitful commercial strategies. More of the same rhetoric can be found in Gwyneth Paltrow's Foreword to *Goop Clean Beauty*, by the Editors of Goop (New York: Goop Press/Grand Central Life & Style, 2016).

47. Remaury, *Le beau sexe faible*, 108–9.

48. In *Clean Beauty*, their plea for "natural" cosmetics (quoted above), Rutterford and Minarovic are very clear about the fact that clean beauty and home-made beauty products are "bloody expensive."

49. Based on a Google search with the terms "natural makeup tutorial" ran on October 26, 2020, at 10:19 a.m. EST. I took the first five results below the adver-tised links, excluding videos and aggregating platforms such as Pinterest.

50. The "courage" of going without makeup is widely celebrated and promoted as universally accessible in social media trends like the #nomakeupchallenge and magazine articles on celebrities who choose to forego makeup in their official pictures. See Stephanie Petit, "Princess Eugenie Is Embracing This Natural Beauty Look during Coronavirus Lockdown," *People*, April 27, 2020, https://people.com/royals/princess-eugenie-is-embracing-this-natural-beauty-look-during-coronavirus-lockdown. However, having a flawless, makeup-less appearance requires regular access to high-quality aesthetic services, hence disposable income and leisure time. "Natural" beauty does not mean effortless or inexpensive beauty. See Brianna Arps, "Here's the Major Problem behind Celebrities' 'No Makeup' Selfies that No One Is Talking About," *Insider*, August 1, 2017, https://www.insider.com/no-makeup-selifes-are-a-problem-this-is-why-2017-7. Considerable media attention has been devoted, for instance, to Lady Gaga's performance in Bradley Cooper's 2018 movie *A Star Is Born*, in which the actress wears no makeup. Meg Storm's interview with Gaga's personal "facialist" highlights the amount of work and money that this "natural" performance demanded. Meg Storm, "Lady Gaga's Facialist Spills the Skincare Secrets that Allowed the Singer to Go Makeup-Free in 'A Star Is Born,'" *Us Weekly*, March 8, 2019, https://www.usmagazine.com/stylish/news/lady-gagas-skin-secrets-for-makeup-free-a-star-is-born-scenes-details.

51. Victoria Jowett, "9 Ways to Ensure Your Makeup Always Looks Natural," *Cosmopolitan*, October 12, 2020, https://www.cosmopolitan.com/uk/beauty-hair/makeup/g18192402/natural-makeup-look.

52. Beth Gillette, "10 Hacks to Achieving the 'No Makeup' Makeup Look," *The Everygirl*, July 9, 2018, https://theeverygirl.com/10-hacks-to-achieving-the-no-makeup-makeup-look.

53. Skeggs, *Formation of Class and Gender*, 104.

54. For more general information on the cultural and social undergirding of the "sense of place," see the literature review in Gerard Kyle and Garry Chick, "The Social Construction of a Sense of Place," *Leisure Sciences* 29 (2007): 209–25.

55. For a synthesis of Bourdieu's conception of the social space, see Pierre Bourdieu, "Social Space and Symbolic Power," *Sociological Theory* 7, no. 1 (1989): 14–25. A more detailed discussion can be found in *La distinction. Critique sociale du goût* (Paris: Les éditions de minuit, 1979).

56. Bourdieu, "Social Space and Symbolic Power," 20.

57. Erving Goffman, "Symbols of Class Status," *British Journal of Sociology* 2, no. 4 (1951): 297.

58. For an analysis of how the (originally mainly religious) practice of confession contributed from late antiquity onward to shaping the constitution of modern, self-expressing subjectivities, Michel Foucault's work surely is a foundational reference. See in particular Foucault, *Les aveux de la chair* (Paris: Gallimard, 2018), 70–75. In our days, media and scholars often employ the term "confessional culture" to define the self-disclosing and allegedly "shameless" posture of social media users who share the most intimate details about their everyday lives. For an example of such criticism, see Firmin DeBrabander, *Life after Privacy: Reclaiming Democracy in a Surveillance Society* (Cambridge: Cambridge University Press, 2020), especially chapter 1. For a more nuanced reading of the importance of self-disclosure for the joint construction of shared intimacy and personal relationships online, see Deborah Chambers, *Social Media and Personal Relationships* (Basingstoke, UK: Palgrave Macmillan, 2013); Lee Humphreys, *The Qualified Self: Social Media and the Accounting of Everyday Life* (Cambridge, MA: MIT Press, 2018); Cristina Miguel, "Visual Intimacy on Social Media: From Selfies to the Co-construction of Intimacies through Shared Pictures," *Social Media + Society* 2, no. 2 (April 2016), https://doi.org/10.1177/2056305116641705.

59. Diana T. Meyers speaks in this respect of a "synecdochic psychology," that is, the "tendency to fixate on a single flaw and to condense the whole monstrous problem into that flaw." See Meyers, "Miroir, Mémoire, Mirage: Appearance, Aging, and Women," in *Mother Time: Women, Aging, and Ethics*, ed. Margaret Urban Walker (Lanham, MD: Rowman & Littlefield, 1999), 25. See also Frida Kerner Furman, *Facing the Mirror: Older Women and Beauty Shop Culture* (New York: Routledge, 1997), and Kathy Davis, *Reshaping the Female Body: The Dilemma of Cosmetic Surgery* (New York: Routledge, 1995), for a description of similar attitudes in the women they interviewed.

60. See Conrad, "Wellness as Virtue," and Roberta Villa, "For Media, 'Women's Health' Often Stands for 'Beauty,'" in *Health and Gender: Resilience and Vulnerability Factors for Women's Health in Contemporary Society*, ed. Ilaria Tarricone and Anita Riecher-Rössler (Cham, CH: Springer, 2019), 69–73.

61. Kathy Charmaz and Dana Rosenfeld, "Reflections of the Body, Images of Self: Visibility and Invisibility in Chronic Illness and Disability," in *Body/Embodiment: Symbolic Interaction and the Sociology of the Body*, ed. Dennis Waskul and Phillip Vannini (Burlington, VT: Ashgate, 2006): 38.

62. See Peiss, *Hope in a Jar*; Joan J. Brumberg, *The Body Project: An Intimate History of American Girls* (New York: Vintage Books, 1997), 70; Philippe Perrot, *Le travail des apparences. Le corps féminin XVIIIe–XIXe siècle* (Paris: Éditions du Seuil, 1984). Brumberg observes that, starting in the 1950s, the injunction to bodily self-scrutiny for young girls was considered part of successful mothering (see Brumberg, *The Body Project*, chapter 3 in particular). On the impact of advertising, see Susan Bordo, *Unbearable Weight: Feminism, Western Culture, and the Body*, 10th ann. ed. (Berkeley: University of California Press: 2003). Beginning in the early 2010s, YouTube became the locus for an updated form of bodily self-surveillance for young girls, specifically through the phenomenon of "Am I pretty or ugly" videos. In such videos, young girls would share images of themselves and ask viewers to assess their appearance and deliver them from self-doubt and suffering. For a discussion of this trend, see Sarah Banet-Weiser, "Am I Pretty or Ugly? Girls and the Market for Self-Esteem," *Girlhood Studies* 7, no. 1 (2014): 83–101, and Dobson, *Postfeminist Digital Cultures*, especially chapter 6.

63. Claire Tanner, JaneMaree Maher, and Suzanne Fraser explain that the mirror became a symbol of feminine vanity in the popular imagination of the late nineteenth century. See Tanner, Maher, and Fraser, *Vanity*, 35. See also Sabine Melchoir-Bonnet, *The Mirror: A History* (London: Routledge, 2002).

64. See Brumberg, *The Body Project*.

65. For a critical, feminist discussion of the pleasure of beautification for women, see Ann J. Cahill, "Feminist Pleasure and Feminine Beautification," *Hypathia* 18, no. 4 (2004): 42–64.

66. See Miliann Kang, *The Managed Hand: Race, Gender, and the Body in Beauty Service Work* (Berkeley: University of California Press, 2010), which also examines the intersection between race, class, and gender in the beauty service industry in the U.S., where working-class immigrant women provide body work for more affluent, mainly white women.

67. O'Neill, "'Glow from the Inside Out,'" 1284.

68. See Ruth Williams, "*Eat, Pray, Love*: Producing the Female Neoliberal Spiritual Subject," *Journal of Popular Culture* 47, no. 3 (2011): 613–33.

69. In 2018, Goop's value was estimated at US$250 million. See Wikipedia, s.v. "Goop (Company)," last modified December 8, 2020, 02:09, https://en.wikipedia.org/w/index.php?title=Goop_(company)&oldid=992965605.

70. Gwyneth Paltrow, Foreword to *The Clarity Cleanse: 12 Steps to Finding Emotional Healing, Spiritual Fulfillment, and Renewed Energy*, by Habib Sadeghi (New York: Goop Press/Grand Central Life & Style, 2017).

71. I will return to the question of women's "self-confidence" in chapters 4 and 6. For a discussion of some of the cultural antecedents of the wellness discourse promoting self-care and self-pampering as a path to female empowerment, see Dana Becker, *The Myth of Empowerment: Women and the Therapeutic Culture in America* (New York: NYU Press, 2005). Becker argues that, from the 1960s onward, the growth of therapeutic culture in North America increasingly framed women's problems (stress, anxiety, etc.) as psychological issues, the solution to which was to be found individually, through a therapeutic approach, instead of collectively, through broader social change directed at providing women with social support and resources.

72. Also known as "the makeover paradigm." See Gill, "The Affective, Cultural and Psychic Life of Postfeminism," 606–26, and "Postfeminist Media Culture," 147–66. As Gill notes, self-surveillance is extended to all aspects of life, "yet, in an extraordinary ideological sleight of hand, this labour must be understood nevertheless as 'fun,' 'pampering' or 'self-indulgence'" ("Postfeminist Media Culture," 155). See also Katherine Sender, *The Makeover: Reality Television and Reflexive Audiences* (New York: NYU Press, 2012).

73. In her very popular Instagram post form June 16, 2020, chef and civil rights advocate Sophia Roe criticizes the mainstream wellness culture in which wellness rituals have no purpose other than "self-optimization." Roe claims that real wellness is that which better equips us to support our community and give back. Sophie Roe (@sophie_roe), Instagram, June 16, 2020, https://www.instagram.com/tv/CBf_O7nFoVl. In my view, Roe highlights a feature of beauty and wellness that is already constitutive of "feeling good," but that is concealed by mainstream wellness discourse and marketing.

CHAPTER 3

1. Quoted from Peiss, *Hope in a Jar*, 153.

2. See Elias, Gill, and Scharff, "Aesthetic Labour," 28–30.

3. While looking at a different set of activities—specifically household and care labor and its division within heterosexual couples—Allison Daminger provides a useful conceptualization of the cognitive dimension of such activities: "Cognitive labor is best defined as the work of (1) anticipating needs; (2) identifying options for meeting those needs; (3) deciding among the options; and (4) monitoring the results." Allison Daminger, "The Cognitive Dimension of Household Labor," *American Sociological Review* 84, no. 4 (2019): 610. In my opinion, such a definition can be extended to the cognitive work that my interviewees described with regard to beautification practices.

4. As Kathy Peiss's historical study of the emergence of beauty culture shows (*Hope in a Jar*, 176–82 in particular), Clarisse's father was not alone in resenting and ridiculing his wife for her womanly concerns and investments. The masculine dismissal of women's beautification practices as useless, superficial, and artificial is an impressively resilient trope of Western beauty discourse (you might remember the song "What Makes You Beautiful" by the British-Irish boy band One Direction, discussed in chapter 1).

5. Billur Akdeniz, Roger J. Calantone, and Clay M. Voorhees, "Effectiveness of Marketing Cues on Consumer Perceptions of Quality: The Moderating Roles of Brand Reputation and Third-Party Information," *Psychology & Marketing* 30, no. 1 (2013): 76–89.

6. See Riley, Evans, and Alison Mackiewicz, "It's Just between Girls," 94–113.

7. Brooke Erin Duffy, *(Not) Being Paid to Do What You Love* (New Haven, CT: Yale University Press, 2017), especially chapter 2.

8. Claire Tanner, JaneMaree Maher, and Suzanne Fraser, *Vanity: 21st Century Selves* (Basingstoke, UK: Palgrave Macmillan, 2013), 33–40; Geoffrey Jones, *Beauty Imagined: A History of the Global Beauty Industry* (Oxford: Oxford University Press, 2010), chapter 8.

9. For a discussion of examples drawn from the sphere of family life, see Stephanie Coontz, "Gender Equality and Economic Inequality: Impact on Marriage," in *Gender and Couple Relationships*, ed. S. M. McHale et al. (Cham, CH: Springer, 2016), 79–90.

10. On the logics, feelings, and decision-making processes involved in women's clothing choices, see Sophie Woodward, *Why Women Wear What They Wear* (London: Bloomsbury, 2007). For a study of the discursive regulation of women's consumer practices in matters of fashion in times of economic recession (thus of private and public "austerity"), see Elizabeth Nathanson, "Dressed for Economic Distress: Blogging and the 'New' Pleasures of Fashion," In *Gendering the Recession: Media and Culture in an Age of Austerity*, ed. Diane Negra and Yvonne Tasker (Durham, NC: Duke University Press, 2014), 136–60.

11. See McRobbie, "Notes on 'What Not to Wear,'" and Elias, Gill, and Scharff, "Aesthetic Labour." For an earlier criticism of the fashion-beauty complex as tying women's social worth to their ability to follow beautification trends, see Bartky, "Foucault, Femininity, and the Modernization of Patriarchal Power."

12. See S. Michael Kalick, "Physical Attractiveness as Status Cue," *Journal of Experimental Social Psychology* 24, no. 6 (1987): 469–80; Tonya K. Frevert and Lisa S. Walker, "Physical Attractiveness and Social Status," *Sociology Compass* 8, no 3 (2014): 313–23.

13. See Peiss, *Hope in a Jar*, 155–6: "In the 1930s, an explicitly therapeutic language began to pervade cosmetic promotions. . . . Women's mental health and feminine development depended on continually embracing new looks and beauty products."

14. For Canadian statistics on time use, see Melissa Moyser and Amanda Burlock, "Time Use: Total Work Burden, Unpaid Work, and Leisure," *Women in Canada: A Gender-Based Statistical Report*, Statistics Canada, July 30, 2018, https://www150.statcan.gc.ca/n1/pub/89-503-x/2015001/article/54931-eng.htm.

15. Cheryl Thompson, "Black Women, Beauty, and Hair as a Matter of Being," *Women's Studies* 38, no. 8 (2009): 851. As we saw in chapter 2, in the discussion of Sabrina Strings's work on the historical construction of Black beauty as inferior to white beauty and its association with lower social and moral status, the "implications" Thompson refers to are closely tied to the history of colonialism and slavery in North America. This legacy, and its later development into more or less overtly racist social structures after the legal abolition of slavery, still affects Black women's sense of self and is materialized in what Shirley A. Tate aptly calls "Black beauty shame." See Tate, *The Governmentality of Black Beauty Shame* (London: Palgrave Macmillan, 2018), especially chapter 1.

16. Kristin Denise Rowe, "'Nothing Else Mattered After That Wig Came Off': Black Women, Unstyled Hair, and Scenes of Interiority," *Journal of American Culture* 42, no. 1 (2019): 22. See also Brina Hargro, "Hair Matters: African American Women and the Natural Hair Aesthetic" (MA thesis, Georgia State University, 2011); Deborah Rhode, *The Beauty Bias: The Injustice of Appearance in Life and Law* (New York: Oxford University Press, 2010).

17. Thompson, "Black Women, Beauty, and Hair," 848–9.

18. Rowe, "'Nothing Else Mattered After That Wig Came Off,'" 33.

19. See Susan Brownmiller, *Femininity* (New York: Linden Press/Simon and Schuster, 1984), and Freedman, *Beauty Bound*.

20. In her work on women's nail polish blogging, Michele White quotes a blogger who relates a very similar experience: she uses conspicuous, hyper-feminine nail polish to affirm her femininity in a male-dominated work environment. White, "Women's Nail Polish Blogging and Femininity," in *Cupcake, Pinterest and Ladyporn: Feminized Popular Culture in the Early Twenty-first Century*, ed. Elena Levine (Urbana: University of Illinois Press, 2015), 138–56. See also Samantha Kwan and Mary Nell Trautner, "Beauty Work: Individual and Institutional Rewards, the Reproduction of Gender, and Questions of Agency," *Sociology Compass* 3, no. 1 (2009): 57.

21. See Deborah Spar, *Wonder Women*; Elias and Gill, "Beauty Surveillance," 59–77; Gill, "The Affective, Cultural and Psychic Life of Postfeminism," 606–26; McRobbie, "Notes on the Perfect," 3–20.

22. See Attwood's 1985 dystopic novel *The Handmaid's Tale* (Toronto: McClelland and Stewart, 1985).

23. Freedman, *Beauty Bound*, 82.

24. For a description, see Larry Elliott, "Into the Red: 'Lipstick Effect' Reveals the True Face of the Recession," *The Guardian*, December 22, 2008, https://www.theguardian.com/business/2008/dec/22/recession-cosmetics-lipstick, and Sarah Butler, "'The Lipstick Effect': Britons Treat Themselves as Budgets Tighten," *The*

Guardian, July 15, 2017, https://www.theguardian.com/business/2017/jul/15/the
-lipstick-effect-britons-treat-themselves-as-budgets-tighten. For comprehensive
data on global beauty industry retail sales from 2005 to 2019, see Emily Gerstell et
al., "How COVID-19 Is Changing the World of Beauty," McKinsey & Company,
May 5, 2020, https://www.mckinsey.com/industries/consumer-packaged-goods/
our-insights/how-covid-19-is-changing-the-world-of-beauty.

25. Sarah E. Hill et al., "Boosting Beauty in an Economic Decline: Mating,
Spending, and the Lipstick Effect," *Journal of Personality and Social Psychology* 103,
no. 2 (2012): 275–91.

26. Jessica Schiffer, "The Beauty Trends Customers Are Buying during Covid-
19." *Vogue Business*, August 12, 2020, https://www.voguebusiness.com/beauty/
the-beauty-trends-customers-are-buying-during-covid-19; Zoe Wood, "Sleeping
Beauty Halls: How Covid-19 Upended the 'Lipstick Index,'" *The Guardian*,
December 18, 2020, https://www.theguardian.com/business/2020/dec/18/how
-covid-19-upended-the-lipstick-index-pandemic-cosmetic-sales-makeup-skincare;
Gerstell et al., "How COVID-19 is Changing the World of Beauty."

27. Many social scientists have interpreted women's recourse to beautification in
times of personal or collective hardship more generally as a manifestation of a desire
for dignity, self-worth, pleasure, or self-care. See, for example, Martina Cvajner's
analysis of the beautification practices of Eastern European women immigrants
living in northern Italy: "Hyper-Femininity as Decency: Beauty, Womanhood
and Respect in Emigration," *Ethnography* 12, no. 3 (2011): 356–74. (I will discuss
Cvajner's research in more detail in chapter 5.) As Kathy Peiss has shown, since the
early twentieth century the burgeoning beauty advertising industry has insisted on
the "beauty duty" as a way of bestowing worth and credibility on women. During
the Depression, and later during World War II, the availability and affordability of
makeup in the United States were framed by advertisers as a key element in the
maintenance of national morale. As I discussed in chapter 2, in recent decades beautification has increasingly been marketed as a form of self-care or self-pampering,
and as a key element in the effort to regain control over one's life, either through
mini-rituals and "treats" (such as a manicure) or through drastic changes in one's
look (such as aesthetic surgery). You might remember Clarisse's story from chapter
2: she considers investing in aesthetic self-care (beautification treatments, clothes,
etc.) as her main form of therapy in her struggle with depression and burnout.
Her visits to the nail salon and hairdresser changed the way that she manages her
personal and family time, as well as her feelings of guilt as a mother and partner.
On beauty advertising during the Depression and World War II, see Peiss, *Hope
in a Jar*, chapter 8. For an analysis of the postfeminist rhetoric of spirituality as a
consumer practice in the Eat, Pray, Love brand (tied to Elizabeth Gilbert's best-
selling memoir of the same name), see Williams, "Eat, Pray, Love," 613–33. On
the specific "therapeutic" effect of manicures, see Kang, *The Managed Hand*. On
aesthetic surgery, see Davis, *Reshaping the Female Body*, and Essig, *American Plastic*.

28. See Davis, *Reshaping the Female Body*, and "Remaking the She-Devil."

29. Christina Scharff, "The Psychic Life of Neoliberalism: Mapping the Contours of Entrepreneurial Subjectivity," *Theory, Culture & Society* 33, no. 6 (2016): 107–22.

30. Gill, "Postfeminist Media Culture."

31. Riley, Evans, and Mackiewicz, "It's Just between Girls"; Alison Winch, "Brand Intimacy, Female Friendship and Digital Surveillance Networks," *New Formations* 84 (2015): 228–45.

32. Peiss, *Hope in a Jar,* chapter 7. See also Cheryl Thompson, "Black Women, Beauty, and Hair as a Matter of *Being,*" *Women's Studies* 38, no. 8 (October 15, 2009): 831–56.

33. Take hair, for example. In February 2021, during Black History Month, CBC News featured an interview with Nancy Falaise, a Black hairdresser whose services targeting curly hair aim at filling a gap in Montreal and increasing Black women's love for their hair. Kamila Hinkson, "This Hairdresser Is Helping Black Women Embrace Their Hair, Curls and All," CBC News, February 15, 2021, https://www.cbc.ca/news/canada/montreal/black-changemakers-nancy-falaise-1 .5912485. The urban segregation of hair salons catering to Black women in North America is also a topic in Chimamanda Angozi Adichie's novel *Americanah* (New York: Alfred A. Knopf, 2013), the first chapter in particular.

34. As sociologist Jo Littler wrote in 2013, "treatments like facials that would 20 years ago have only been the preserve of the very rich are now advised as necessary and routine." Littler, "The Rise of the 'Yummy Mummy': Popular Conservatism and Neoliberal Maternal in Contemporary British Culture," *Communication, Culture and Critique* 6, no. 2 (2013): 230.

35. Scharff, "The Psychic Life of Neoliberalism," and Micki McGee, *Self Help, Inc.: Makeover Culture in American Life* (New York: Oxford University Press, 2007).

36. The concept of a "male gaze" as organizing cultural representations of femininity was forged by Laura Mulvey, "Visual Pleasure and Narrative Cinema," *Screen* 16, no. 3 (1975): 6–18.

37. Gill, "Postfeminist Media Culture."

38. Riley, Evans, and Mackiewicz, "It's Just between Girls," 108.

39. Winch, "Brand Intimacy."

40. Michel Foucault, *Surveiller et punir: Naissance de la prison* (Paris: Gallimard, 1975).

41. Instagram is home to countless aspiring fashion influencers, ranging from professional digital entrepreneurs to style and glamour enthusiasts, like Clarisse, who share curated selfies of their outfit of the day (a.k.a. #ootd, and variations thereof). A pre-existing discourse promoting clothing style as the material out of which one crafts one's original identity has felicitously merged with a framing of social media as enabling authentic visual self-expression. In seeking to find one's own beauty and fashion style, one participates in the joint injunction to authenticity and exceptionality, according to which careful evaluations, investments, and strategies coexist with the produced illusion of effortless self-revelation through style and

clothing. A demonstrated savvy in expressing one's identity through well-chosen outfits is a much-admired feminine competence. Indeed, Clarisse feels that she enjoys a certain authority among friends and followers thanks to her ability to muster such skill. For a discussion of fashion inspiration online, and of its multiple logics and their incorporation in the performance of competent femininity, see Duffy, "(Not) Being Paid to Do What You Love," especially chapter 6, and Nathanson, "Dressed for Economic Distress."

42. Elias and Gill, "Beauty Surveillance."

43. "In this gynaeopticon they all turn their eyes on each other in tightly bound networks where they gaze and are gazed upon." Winch, "Brand Intimacy," 232.

44. Mardi Schmeichel, Stacey Kerr, and Chris Linder, "Selfies as Postfeminist Pedagogy: The Production of Traditional Femininity in the US South," *Gender and Education* 32, no. 3 (2020): 363–81.

45. Kate Cairns and Josée Johnston, *Food and Femininity* (London: Bloomsbury Academic, 2015), 32.

CHAPTER 4

1. For a discussion of feminist criticism of women's choices in matters of beauty, see Davis, "Remaking the She-Devil."

2. Gill, "Postfeminist Media Culture," 153.

3. For an analysis of this discourse, see Sarah Banet-Weiser, "'I'm Beautiful the Way I Am': Empowerment, Beauty, and Aesthetic Labour," in *Aesthetic Labour: Rethinking Beauty Politics in Neoliberalism*, ed. Ana Sofia Elias, Rosalind Gill, and Christina Scharff (London: Palgrave Macmillan, 2017), 265–82.

4. See Sheryl Sandberg, *Lean In: Women, Work, and the Will to Lead* (New York: Knopf, 2013). Sandberg's self-help book, and the connected initiatives to support women, have been harshly criticized for their rather neoliberal spirit. According to Sandberg, women are "doing it to themselves": the system of power relations and gendered exclusion is not at fault—rather, it is women's self-diminishing psychology. In this way, *Lean In* depoliticizes women's struggles in the workplace and elsewhere, reducing them to something like a "wrong" perspective. For a critique of this view, see Catherine Rottenberg, *The Rise of Neoliberal Feminism* (New York: Oxford University Press, 2018); Rosalind Gill and Shani Orgad, "The Confidence Cult(ure)," *Australian Feminist Studies* 30, no. 86 (2015): 324–44.

5. Gill and Orgad, "The Confidence Cult(ure)." On the discursive strategies through which corporations market themselves as capable of concern and solidarity, even as embracing feminist struggles, see Chatzidakis et al., "From Carewashing to Radical Care: The Discursive Explosions of Care during Covid-19," *Feminist Media Studies* 20, no. 6 (August 2020): 889–95, which specifically discusses the role of corporations during the COVID-19 pandemic.

6. Elias and Gill, "Beauty Surveillance," 30.

7. Abigail I. Brooks, "Opting In or Opting Out? North American Women Share Strategies for Aging Successfully with (and without) Cosmetic Intervention," in *Successful Aging as a Contemporary Obsession: Global Perspectives*, ed. Sarah Lamb (New Brunswick, NJ: Rutgers University Press, 2017), 47.

8. The ambivalence that I could notice is consistent with observations of Isabelle Wallach and colleagues pertaining to a sample of Montreal women aged sixty-four and up. See Isabelle Wallach et al., *Normes de beauté, perceptions de l'apparence et vie intime des femmes âgées hétérosexuelles et lesbiennes au Québec: Une étude qualitative exploratoire.* Rapport de recherche (Montreal: Chaire de recherche sur l'homophobie, Université du Québec à Montréal, 2019).

9. Sarah Lamb, Jessica Robbins-Ruszkowski, and Anna I. Corwin, "Introduction: Successful Aging as a Twenty-First-Century Obsession," in *Successful Aging as a Contemporary Obsession: Global Perspectives*, edited by Sarah Lamb (New Brunswick, NJ: Rutgers University Press, 2017), 1–23.

10. Lamb, Robbins-Ruszkowski, and Corwin, "Successful Aging." For a discussion of the salience of the body in the aging process, see Julia Twigg, "The Body, Gender, and Age: Feminist Insights in Social Gerontology," *Journal of Aging Studies* 18, no. 1 (2004): 59–73.

11. See for instance Toni Calasanti and Neil King, "Successful Aging, Ageism, and the Maintenance of Age and Gender Relations," in *Successful Aging as a Contemporary Obsession: Global Perspectives*, ed. Sarah Lamb (New Brunswick, NJ: Rutgers University Press, 2017), 27–40.

12. On women's struggle with the cultural ambivalence around aging, see Sara M. Hofmeier et al., "Body Image, Aging, and Identity in Women Over 50: The Gender and Body Image (GABI) Study," *Journal of Women & Aging* 29, no. 1 (2017): 3–14. An interesting discussion of women's hesitation when it comes to choosing the right stance can also be found in chapters 1 and 8 of Martha Holstein's *Women in Late Life: Critical Perspectives on Gender and Age* (Lanham, MD: Rowman & Littlefield, 2015). On aging women on social media, see Katrin Tiidenberg, "Visibly Ageing Femininities: Women's Visual Discourses of Being Over-40 and Over-50 on Instagram," *Feminist Media Studies* 18, no. 1 (2018): 61–76. Kathy Pilcher and Wendy Martin ("Forever 'Becoming'? Negotiating Gendered and Ageing Embodiment in Everyday Life," *Sociological Research Online* 25, no. 4 [2020]: 698–717) also look at the way cultural ambiguities around aging are lived and negotiated by older women. Notably, they define the main contradiction as the "in\visibility paradox": older women "might be visible as 'older' women (read by others as such from visual markers, such as grey hair), but this often meant that they would be deemed invisible as competent beings" (714).

13. Steven Petrow, "What the '10-Year Challenge' Might Say about You, and Me," *New York Times*, January 31, 2019, https://www.nytimes.com/2019/01/31/well/mind/10-year-challenge-facebook-instagram.html.

14. See Geniece Crawford Mondé, "#BlackDontCrack: A Content Analysis of the Ageing Black Woman in Social Media," *Feminist Media Studies* 18, no. 1

(2018): 47–60. More recently, a 2019 medical study empirically "proving" the claim that "black don't crack" caused the hashtag to be in vogue again on social media. See David Buziashvili et al., "Long-term Patterns of Age-Related Facial Bone Loss in Black Individuals," *JAMA Facial Plastic Surgery* 21, no. 4 (2019): 292–7. #BlackDontCrack could also be read as a way of reclaiming dignity and positive qualities for non-white skin: as Shirley Ann Tate highlights, skin itself is for Black women the materialization of the undesirability of their beauty, as opposed to the white-skinned kind. See Shirley Ann Tate, *The Governmentality of Black Beauty Shame* (London: Palgrave Macmillan, 2018).

15. Tamara A. Baker et al., "Reconceptualizing Successful Aging among Black Women and the Relevance of the Strong Black Woman Archetype," *The Gerontologist* 55, no. 1 (2015): 51–7.

16. Maria S. Johnson, "#BlackGirlMagic and Its Complexities," in *Black Feminist Sociology*, ed. Zakiya Luna and Whitney N. Laster Pirtle (New York: Routledge, 2022), 111.

17. Johnson, 118.

18. The impact of gestational weight gain on health outcomes for both fetus and mother is a current medical concern, one that has generated an array of studies directed at evaluating strategies to influence women's perception of healthy weight gain and subsequent behaviors. See Meredith Vanstone et al., "Pregnant Women's Perceptions of Gestational Weight Gain: A Systematic Review and Meta-Synthesis of Qualitative Research," *Maternal and Child Nutrition* 13, no. 4 (2017), https://doi.org/10.1111/mcn.12374. Medical and popular discourse on gestational weight gain also induce a greater demand for professional guidance from women during and after pregnancy. See Hara Nikolopoulos et al., "Women's Perceptions of Discussions about Gestational Weight Gain with Health Care Providers during Pregnancy and Postpartum: A Qualitative Study," *BMC Pregnancy and Childbirth* 17, no. 1 (2017): 97. According to a 2013 study, in the United States there is still a lack of professional support from health-care providers on this issue. See Tammy Chang et al., "Perspectives about and Approaches to Weight Gain in Pregnancy: A Qualitative Study of Physicians and Nurse Midwives," *BMC Pregnancy and Childbirth* 13, no. 47 (2013), https://doi.org/10.1186/1471-2393-13-47.

19. According to a 2004 Italian study, changes in breast size and shape are reported almost equally by women who breastfed and by women who didn't, an observation that has led researchers to exclude a causal relationship between such physical changes and breastfeeding. See Alfredo Pisacane and Paola Continisio, "Breastfeeding and Perceived Changes in the Appearance of the Breasts: A Retrospective Study," *Acta Pædiatrica* 93, no. 10 (2004): 1346–48.

20. In Canada, a persistently unequal division of unpaid child care and housework weighs on women. See Moyser and Burlock, "Time Use." Not only do women statistically carry most of the burden of caring for a young child (Dwenda K. Gjerdingen and Bruce A. Center, "First-Time Parents' Postpartum Changes in Employment, Childcare, and Housework Responsibilities," *Social Science Research*

34, no. 1 [2005]: 103–16; Jonathan Gershuny, "Time, through the Life Course, in the Family," in *The Blackwell Companion to the Sociology of Families*, ed. Jacqueline L. Scott, Judith Trees, and Martin Richards [Malden, MA: Blackwell Publishing, 2004], 159–77): the transition to parenthood also appears to trigger a shift toward a more traditionally gendered division of domestic labor, with women performing a greater portion of it. This also occurs in couples who hold non-traditional views of gender difference and divisions of labor *prior* to the birth of their first child (Pia S. Schober, "The Parenthood Effect on Gender Inequality: Explaining the Change in Paid and Domestic Work When British Couples Become Parents," *European Sociological Review* 29, no. 1 [2013]: 74–85; Gill Cappuccini and Raymond Cochrane, "Life with the First Baby: Women's Satisfaction with the Division of Roles," *Journal of Reproductive and Infant Psychology* 18, no. 3 [2000]: 189–202).

21. May Friedman, "Beyond MILF: Exploring Sexuality and Feminism in Public Motherhood," *Atlantis* 36, no. 2 (2014): 49–60.

22. Littler, "The Rise of the 'Yummy Mummy.'"

23. For examples of this type of self-help literature, see Sarah Maizes, *Got MILF? The Modern Mom's Guide to Feeling Fabulous, Looking Great, and Rocking a Minivan* (New York: Berkeley Books, 2011), and Jessica Porter, *The MILF Diet: Let the Power of Whole Foods Transform Your Body, Mind, and Spirit . . . Deliciously!* (New York: Atria/Emily Bestler Books, 2013).

24. Littler, "The Rise of the 'Yummy Mummy,'" 230.

25. Christina Malatzky, "Australian Women's Complex Engagement with the Yummy Mummy Discourse and the Bodily Ideals of Good Motherhood," *Women's Studies International Forum* 62 (2017): 28.

26. As Amélie Keyser-Verreault's work with women in Taiwan shows, the impact of beauty norms on women's aesthetic self-discipline before and after childbirth is felt not just in Western societies and cultural contexts. See Keyser-Verreault, "The Continuum of Regaining One's Body: Childbirth and Reproductive Choice under Beauty Pressure in Taiwan," *European Journal of Cultural Studies*, June 28, 2022, https://doi.org/10.1177/13675494221104145.

27. According to the National Household Survey, in Quebec in 2011 (that is, during Eva's younger years), the vast majority of people claimed to belong to the Roman Catholic religion. See Statistics Canada, *National Household Survey* (Statistics Canada Catalogue no. 99-010-X2011032 [2011]), accessed October 8, 2021, https://www12.statcan.gc.ca/nhs-enm/2011/dp-pd/prof/index.cfm?Lang=E.

28. Aside from being a part of Canadian national symbolism, "rougher" outdoor experiences in the wilderness, such as attending a summer camp or going canoeing and camping, are an important component of youth socialization in Canada. See Rebecca J. Purc-Stephenson et al., "We Are Wilderness Explorers: A Review of Outdoor Education in Canada," *Journal of Experiential Education* 42, no. 4 (2019): 364–81.

29. According to sociologists Maya Maor and Julie Cwikel, "filtering" one's language and messages pertaining to body image is one of the main strategies by

which mothers promote a healthy body image in their daughters. Other strategies include "transmitting awareness of the dangers of eating disorders," "positive reinforcements," and critical "discussion." See Maor and Cwikel, "Mothers' Strategies to Strengthen Their Daughters' Body Image," *Feminism & Psychology* 26, no. 1 (2016): 19–20 in particular.

30. In this context, I adopt Laura Hurd Clarke's definition of body image as "how a woman perceives and feels about her body and how much of her sense of feminine identity and self-esteem are invested in her appearance." Hurd Clarke, *Facing Age: Women Growing Older in Anti-aging Culture* (Lanham, MD: Rowman & Littlefield, 2011), 6.

31. Holstein, *Women in Late Life*, 43.

CHAPTER 5

1. Each of the quotations in this opening passage come from Martina Cvajner, "Hyper-Femininity as Decency: Beauty, Womanhood and Respect in Emigration," *Ethnography* 12, no. 3 (2011): 360, 358, 362, and 363.

2. As does the average North American person. See Daniel S. Hamermesh, *Beauty Pays: Why Attractive People Are More Successful* (Princeton, NJ: Princeton University Press, 2011), chapter 1. Iida Kukkonen defines it as the belief "in *appearance as currency*," which is more strongly entertained by women due to the normative framework compelling them to invest in their appearance to enhance their visibility and their social success. Kukkonen, "Who Performs Appearance Work, and Who Believes Appearance Works?," in *Appearance as Capital: The Normative Regulation of Aesthetic Capital Accumulation and Conversion*, ed. Outi Sarpila, Iida Kukkonen, Tero Pajunen, and Erica Åberg, p. 41 (Bingley, UK: Emerald Publishing, 2022), 41.

3. See MacCannell and MacCannell, "The Beauty System," 220–2.

4. Consider this excerpt from model and actress Emily Ratajkowski's memoir: "In my early twenties, it had never occurred to me that the women who gained their power from beauty were indebted to the men whose desire granted them that power in the first place. . . . Facing the reality of the dynamics at play would have meant admitting how limited any woman's power is when she survives and even succeeds in the world as a thing to be looked at." Ratajkowski, *My Body* (New York: Metropolitan, 2021), 47.

5. The association between "beautiful" and "good" has been already discussed in chapter 2. For an overview of research on social preference for attractive individuals (or "the beauty bias"), see Deborah Rhode, *The Beauty Bias: The Injustice of Appearance in Life and Law* (New York: Oxford University Press, 2010), chap. 2. See also Freedman, *Beauty Bound*; Megumi Hosoda, Eugene F. Stone-Romero, and Gwen Coats, "The Effects of Physical Attractiveness on Job-Related Outcomes: A Meta-Analysis of Experimental Studies," *Personnel Psychology* 56, no. 2 (2003): 431–62; and Tonya K. Frevert and Lisa S. Walker, "Physical Attractiveness and

Social Status," *Sociology Compass* 8, no. 3 (2014): 313–23. For an overview of classic research about quality attribution to physically attractive individuals, see Gordon L. Patzer, *The Power and Paradox of Physical Attractiveness* (Boca Raton, FL: BrownWalker Press, 2006), 178–82. In a recent discussion of returns to attractiveness, Ellis P. Monk and colleagues also offer an overview of current relevant literature on common attribution and inferences on the basis of physical appearance. See Ellis P. Monk Jr., Michael H. Esposito, and Hedwig Lee, "Beholding Inequalities: Race, Gender, and Returns to Physical Attractiveness in the United States," *American Journal of Sociology* 127, no. 1 (2021): 194–241.

6. Gordon L. Patzer (*The Power and Paradox of Physical Attractiveness*, chapter 6) presents a summary of results from studies in experimental psychology: people who score higher in physical attractiveness appear more likely to be trusted by strangers, to receive the help they demand from strangers, to make friends in a new environment, and to succeed when attempting to persuade others through verbal communication.

7. David D. Henningsen, Mary Braz, and Elaine Davies, "Why Do We Flirt? Flirting Motivations and Sex Differences in Working and Social Contexts," *Journal of Business Communication* 45, no. 4 (2008): 483.

8. As Rita Freedman writes, this model replicates "the paradox of climbing onto a pedestal to gain power by perfecting the art of signalling submission" (*Beauty Bound*, 81).

9. Skeggs, *Formations of Class and Gender*, 128.

10. Abigail R. Riemer et al., "She Looks Like She'd Be an Animal in Bed: Dehumanization of Drinking Women in Social Contexts," *Sex Roles* 80 (2019): 617–29.

11. Elizabeth A. Stanko, "Safety Talk: Conceptualizing Women's Risk Assessment as a 'Technology of the Soul,'" *Theoretical Criminology* 1, no. 4 (1997): 479–99. For a discussion of women's strategies to avoid street harassment, see Carol B. Gardner, *Passing By: Gender and Public Harassment* (Berkeley: University of California Press 1995).

12. Lena's caution might appear unfounded considering that Montreal is one of the safest large cities in North America (see Roberto Rocha, "How Many Crimes Happen Near You," CBC News, accessed October 8, 2021, https://news-interactives.cbc.ca/montreal-crime). However, a negative labeling of downtown Montreal as dangerous and louche still lingers among those who live there, and it might be rooted in history. Starting with American Prohibition in the 1920s, and throughout the twentieth century, Montreal bore the reputation of being one of the most sinful, dangerous, and corrupt cities in North America. The downtown area, with its red-light district full of bars, gambling venues, and brothels, hosted a wild nightlife and presented endless challenges for law enforcement (see Catherine Charlebois and Mathieu Lapointe, eds., *Scandale! Le Montréal illicite 1940–1960* [Montreal: Cardinal, 2016], and William Weintraub, *City Unique: Montreal Days and Nights in the 1940s and '50s* [Toronto: Robin Brass Studio, 2004]). Despite

changes in the area since the 1960s, and the progressive eradication of illicit activities, the negative perception of the downtown nightlife remains.

13. See Hamermesh, *Beauty Pays*; Linda A. Jackson, John E. Hunter, and Carole N. Hodge, "Physical Attractiveness and Intellectual Competence: A Meta-Analytic Review," *Social Psychology Quarterly* 58, no. 2 (1995): 108–22; Hosoda, Stone-Romero, and Coats, "The Effects of Physical Attractiveness on Job-related Outcomes."

14. For one example out of many occurrences of this rather misogynist narrative, see Karen Bartko, "Note Telling Girls to 'Dress Conservatively' in School to Avoid Distracting Boys Sparks Concern in Alberta Village," *Global News*, June 5, 2017, https://globalnews.ca/news/3503389/note-telling-girls-to-dress-conservatively-in-school-to-avoid-distracting-boys-sparks-outrage-in-alberta-village.

15. See Rhode, *The Beauty Bias*, chap. 5.

16. See Peter Glick, Sadie Larsen, Cathryn Johnson, and Heather Branstiter , "Evaluations of Sexy Women in Low- and High-Status Jobs," *Psychology of Women Quarterly* 29, no. 4 (2005): 389–95.

17. This is why scholarship explains the preference for attractiveness in the workplace as a form of discrimination (see, for instance, Rey Hernández-Julián and Christina Peters, "Student Appearance and Academic Performance," *Journal of Human Capital* 11, no. 2 (2017): 260, but also their review of the relevant literature). Prejudice, rather than evidence-based belief, is the best explanation for the widespread opinion that more attractive individuals are *better* (e.g., better employees, better managers, better students) than supposedly average-looking ones. See Michael Kalick's seminal work (cited above), "Physical Attractiveness as Status Cue." See Rhode, *The Beauty Bias*, and Hamermesh, *Beauty Pays*, for an overview of relevant scholarship on the role of attractiveness in the workplace. Rhode's book also presents an analysis of the legal framework of discrimination based on appearance.

18. Samantha C. Paustian-Underdahl and Lisa Slattery Walker, "Revisiting the Beauty Is Beastly Effect: Examining When and Why Sex and Attractiveness Impact Hiring Judgments," *International Journal of Human Resource Management* 27, no. 10 (2016): 1034–58.

19. Neil Howlett et al., "Unbuttoned: The Interaction between Provocativeness of Female Work Attire and Occupational Status," *Sex Roles* 72, no. 3 (2015): 105–16.

20. Regan A. Gurung et al., "Power and Provocativeness: The Effects of Subtle Changes in Clothing on Perceptions of Working Women," *Journal of Social Psychology* 158, no. 2 (2017): 254.

21. Michael Lewis, "Obama's Way," *Vanity Fair*, September 11, 2012, https://www.vanityfair.com/news/2012/10/michael-lewis-profile-barack-obama. It's worth recalling, however, the considerable hot water Obama found himself in when he dared to deviate from these two color choices. See, for example, Leanne Italie, "Obama's Tan Suit Buzzed Around the World," *Associated Press*, August 29, 2014, https://apnews.com/article/e912379e95ab41588a39e4e53ec20f93.

22. See Melanie Pinola, "President Obama's Productivity Tactics," *LifeHacker*, September 18, 2012, https://lifehacker.com/president-obamas-productivity-tactics -5944198. Debora Rhode's compelling account of her experience as a woman in academia who did not care for a stylized appearance is representative of the sloppiness stigma for women's minimalist self-grooming choices (see especially Rhode's preface to *The Beauty Bias*).

23. Magdalena Puniewska, "Inside the Strict, Unspoken Dress Code for Women Political Candidates," *Racked*, June 4, 2018, https://www.racked.com /2018/6/4/17417386/political-candidates-women-female-dress-code.

24. See McRobbie "Notes on 'What Not To Wear'"; Gill, "Postfeminist Media Culture"; Alison Winch, *Girlfriends and Postfeminist Sisterhood* (Basingstoke, UK: Palgrave Macmillan, 2013).

25. Arlie Hochschild, *The Managed Heart: Commercialization of Human Feeling* (Berkeley: University of California Press, 1983).

26. Chris Warhurst and Dennis Nickson, "'Who's Got the Look?' Emotional, Aesthetic and Sexualized Labour in Interactive Services," *Gender, Work and Organization* 16, no. 3 (2009): 386.

27. Miliann Kang, *The Managed Hand: Race, Gender, and the Body in Beauty Service Work* (Berkeley: University of California Press, 2010), 240.

28. Rose Weitz, "Women and Their Hair," *Gender and Society* 15, no. 5 (October 2001): 675.

29. See Hernández-Julián and Peters, "Student Appearance and Academic Performance"; Patzer, *The Power and Paradox of Physical Attractiveness*, chapter 8 in particular.

30. As Lois Banner observes, beauty requires affluence, but it also symbolizes it. Banner, *American Beauty* (New York: Alfred A. Knopf, 1983), 24–7. For a discussion of the association between physical attractiveness and the accumulation of economic, cultural, and social capital, and hence impacting one's social trajectory, see Christian Schneickert, Leonie C. Steckermeier, and Lisa-Marie Brand, "Lonely, Poor, and Ugly? How Cultural Practices and Forms of Capital Relate to Physical Unattractiveness," *Cultural Sociology* 14, no. 1 (2020): 80–105.

31. Zoe also evokes the discriminating double standard for men and women in show business and in public relations. Generally speaking, not as stigmatized for aging or for gaining some weight, men are also allowed certain aesthetic faux pas that would be considered outrageous if done by women: "You will never see a triple-chinned girl as spokesperson for [a big company]," says Zoe.

32. The concept of a social actor's resources as forms of "capital" comes from French sociologist Pierre Bourdieu's expansion of classic Marxist theory. According to Bourdieu, a social actor's position and trajectory in society are strongly influenced (if not determined) by the amount of different embodied resources that he or she possesses and can wield: economic, cultural, social, and symbolic capital. For a synthesis, see Bourdieu, "The Forms of Capital," in *Handbook of Theory and Research for the Sociology of Education*, edited by John Richardson (New York: Greenwood,

1986), 241–58. Bourdieu's concept of "capital" has been further applied to the sociological description of different social spheres and interactional frameworks, thus "multiplying" the forms of capital and, according to Neveu, considerably diminishing its conceptual power. See Érik Neveu, "Les sciences sociales doivent-elles accumuler les capitaux? A propos de Catherine Hakim, Erotic Capital, et de quelques marcottages intempestifs de la notion de capital," *Revue française de science politique* 63, no. 2 (2013): 337–58.

33. See Schneickert, Steckermeier, and Brand, "Lonely, Poor, and Ugly?," for a discussion of the association between attractiveness and the accumulation of different forms of capital. Not only does attractiveness facilitates access to all forms of capital, but one's perceived attractiveness is also higher when economic, social, and especially cultural capital increase.

34. Tressie McMillan Cottom, *Thick, and Other Essays* (New York: New Press, 2019), 32, EPUB. See also Siobhan Brooks, *Unequal Desires: Race and Erotic Capital in the Stripping Industry* (New York: SUNY Press, 2010). Another notable essay on racial inequalities in matters of beauty is Maxine Leeds Craig, "Race, Beauty, and the Tangled Knot of a Guilty Pleasure," *Feminist Theory* 7, no. 2 (2006): 159–77.

35. "Physical appearance has no social value per se but rather has to be recognized, perceived, evaluated, and classified in social practice by social agents to produce social effects" (Schneikert, Steckermeier, and Brand, "Lonely, Poor, and Ugly?," 82). Among the most recent work on beauty as a form of capital, the multiauthor volume edited by Outi Sarpila and colleagues develops an analysis of aesthetic capital in contemporary Western societies: *Appearance as Capital: The Normative Regulation of Aesthetic Capital Accumulation and Conversion*, ed. Outi Sarpila, Iida Kukkonen, Tero Pajunen, and Erica Åberg (Bingley, UK: Emerald Publishing, 2022).

36. For a critical discussion of Hakim's theoretical proposal, see Adam I. Green, "'Erotic Capital' and the Power of Desirability: Why 'Honey Money' Is a Bad Collective Strategy for Remedying Gender Inequality," *Sexualities* 16, nos. 1–2 (2013): 137–58; Julie Lavigne and Chiara Piazzesi, "Femmes et pouvoir érotique," *Recherches féministes* 32, no. 1 (2019): 1–18; Neveu, "Les sciences sociales doivent-elles accumuler les capitaux?"; Schneikert, Steckermeier, and Brand, "Lonely, Poor, and Ugly?" Critics of postfeminist culture actually argue the opposite. The idea of a "girl power" hinged on sexiness and beauty reinforces existing inequalities among women (race, class, age, ability), depoliticizes feminist struggles, increases pressure and competition for "perfection" among women, and encourages a misogynist reduction of women's identities to their sexualities and body shape and size. See McRobbie, "Notes on 'What Not to Wear'"; Spar, *Wonder Women*; Winch, *Girlfriends and Postfeminist Sisterhood*; and Banet-Weiser, *Empowered*.

37. As Rita Freedman writes, paraphrasing the work of Elizabeth Janeway, women "cannot count on male preference for pretty to grant security to women as a group, nor they can they allow male contempt for ugly women to block their ambitions" (Freedman, *Beauty Bound*, 95).

38. See Rhode, *The Beauty Bias*; Amina Mire, *Wellness in Whiteness: Biomedicalization and the Promotion of Whiteness and Youth among Women* (London: Routledge, 2020).

39. For a discussion of the influence of primary and secondary socialization on adult attitudes, see Marcel Lubbers, Eva Jaspers, and Wout Ultee, "Primary and Secondary Socialization Impacts on Support for Same-Sex Marriage after Legalization in the Netherlands," *Journal of Family Issues* 30, no. 12 (2009): 1714–45.

40. Freedman, *Beauty Bound*, 24.

CHAPTER 6

1. For an overview of the convergence between traditional and digital media, as well as a discussion of what a "participative culture" is, see Henry Jenkins, *Convergence Culture: Where Old and New Media Collide* (New York: NYU Press, 2008).

2. In February 2021, all four women who made the list of the world's ten most followed Instagram accounts fell into this category: Kylie Jenner (number 5), Selena Gomez (6), Kim Kardashian West (7), and Beyoncé (9). For the full ranking, see H. Tankovska, "Instagram Accounts with the Most Followers Worldwide as of February 2021," *Statista*, accessed March 18, 2021, https://www.statista.com/statistics/421169/most-followers-instagram. Regarding the construction of a mundane self-narrative by Instagram celebrities through selfies, see Rocio Palomeque Recio, "Postfeminist Performance of Domesticity and Motherhood during the COVID-19 Global Lockdown: The Case of Chiara Ferragni," *Feminist Media Studies*, October 12, 2020, https://doi.org/10.1080/14680777.2020.1830147.

3. See Nicola Döring, Anne Reif, and Sandra Poeschl, "How gender Stereotypical Are Selfies? A Content Analysis and Comparison with Magazine Adverts," *Computers in Human Behavior* 55 (2016): 955–62, for a discussion of the role of stereotypical female attractiveness in selfies. On the role and circulation of selfies as a commodity within forms of digital consumption, see Mehita Iqani and Jonathan E. Schroeder, "#Selfie: Digital Self-Portraits as Commodity Form and Consumption Practice," *Consumption Markets and Culture* 19, no. 5 (2016): 405–15.

4. For further details on my methodological approach, see appendix B in this volume, "Methodological Design and Procedure." See also Chiara Piazzesi and Catherine Lavoie Mongrain, "Selfies de femmes, négociation normative et production de culture visuelle sur Instagram et Facebook," *Recherches féministes* 33, no. 1 (2020): 135–51, and "Women 'Doing Selfies': Reflexivity and Norm Negotiation in the Production and Circulation of Digital Self-Portraits," *Sociologia e Politiche sociali* 22, no. 3 (2019): 95–111. In her research on older women and beauty carried out in the 1990s, Frida Kerner Furman (*Facing the Mirror*) used a similar heuristic approach while interviewing aging women on their appearance, although the pictures were taken by her (selfie-taking being a later cultural practice).

5. See Humphreys, *The Qualified Self,* for a comprehensive discussion of the place of *selves* in the production of digital traces.

6. As I mentioned, the importance of perceived appearance in selfie-taking practices is generally neglected in the literature. However, my observations are consistent with findings of other studies focusing on selfie-taking behavior. In their research on people's motivations for taking selfies while traveling, for example, Prokopis Christou and colleagues report: "The vast majority of the interviewees stated that they take selfies when they feel good; specifically, when they feel good about themselves (appearance), or when they are experiencing positive emotions such as 'joy' and 'happiness.'" See Prokopis Christou et al., "Travel Selfies on Social Networks, Narcissism and the 'Attraction-Shading Effect,'" *Journal of Hospitality and Tourism Management* 43 (2020): 290.

7. This is why many of the participants in my research experienced an additional challenge in taking selfies for the study. To them, taking selfies on demand felt inauthentic, artificial, too calculated. Some participants had to "stage" situations that do not occur in their daily lives (like first dates in the case of married women) or force situations in order to make them selfie-worthy ("I should take a selfie here"). Participants who did not face this challenge reported that taking selfies for the study was just the same as their usual selfie-taking practices: the timing and situation felt right, and they could do their homework at the same time.

8. For a study of the connection between a *good hair day* and a feeling of empowerment, see Rose Weitz, "Women and Their Hair," *Gender and Society*, 15, no. 5 (October 2011): 667–86. Weitz, whom I quoted in chapter 3 as well, also discusses the fragile, unstable character of such power, and women's strategies for coping with the tensions that are intrinsic to what I call the *power paradox.*

9. For this reason, I disagree with Rebecca Coleman and Monica Moreno Figueroa's view of the temporality of beauty, according to which beauty is either a memory of the past or a hope for the feature, but "beauty in the present is a difficult, if not impossible, experience" (Coleman and Moreno Figueroa, "Past and Future Perfect? Beauty, Affect and Hope," *Journal for Cultural Research* 14, no. 14 [2010]: 365). For the women I interviewed, selfies function as the evidence of their "present" beauty, when they are shot with the purpose of capturing the event of beauty. But selfies are not just the "past" experience of beauty: by archiving and browsing selfies in their devices or on their social media profiles, women establish a relationship with their beauty that is not just one of longing and loss, but rather one of pleasure, pride, and ownership as well.

10. Wegenstein, *The Cosmetic Gaze.*

11. This also speaks to the changing balance between the salience of the picture and the salience of the text that is associated with it, especially on Instagram. Depending on the message and on the topic at hand, the picture can be regarded by its author as a complement to an important written statement, or as the core of the post. For a discussion of these dynamics, see Émilie Zaoré-Vanié, "#Strongissexy: Empowerment et sexiness dans les selfies ayant pour thème le fitness chez les

femmes sur Instagram" (MA thesis, Université du Québec à Montréal, 2021), 117–18, 124.

12. See Duffy, *(Not) Getting Paid to Do What You Love*, especially chap. 2.

13. An analysis of postfeminist representations of women treating themselves with sweets and baked goods (e.g., pink cupcakes) can be found in Elizabeth Nathanson, "Sweet Sisterhood: Cupcakes as Sites of Feminized Consumption and Production," in *Cupcakes, Pinterest and Ladyporn: Feminized Popular Culture in the Early Twenty-first Century*, ed. Elana Levine (Urbana: University of Illinois Press, 2015), 249–67.

14. See also Strings, *Fearing the Black Body*, especially chap. 5, for a discussion of the discursive construction in nineteenth-century North America of women as primarily responsible for enforcing domestic moderation and moral temperance within the family. "Moderation" here refers mainly to consumption, both in terms of acquiring goods and consuming them, hence eating and drinking. Strings connects this moral ideal with the celebration of its symbolic materialization in women's slenderness.

15. Nicole C. Krämer et al. "Beware of Selfies: The Impact of Photo Type on Impression Formation Based on Social Networking Profiles," *Frontiers in Psychology* 8 (2017), https://doi.org/10.3389/fpsyg.2017.00188.

16. See Jessica Maddox, "'Guns Don't Kill People . . . Selfies Do': Rethinking Narcissism as Exhibitionism in Selfie-Related Deaths," *Critical Studies in Media Communication* 34, no. 3 (2017): 193–205. On the specific stigmatization of women's selfies, see Amy S. Dobson, *Postfeminist Digital Cultures: Femininity, Social Media, and Self-Representation* (New York: Palgrave Macmillan, 2015). According to Anne Burns ("Self(ie)-Discipline: Social Regulation as Enacted Through the Discussion of Photographic Practice," *International Journal of Communication*, 9 [2015]: 1716–33), in the general discourse, selfies are interpreted as symptoms of the mental health problems and pathological needs of the women who take them. A similar analysis, specifically focused on selfie-takers' alleged narcissism, is provided by Derek C. Murray ("Selfie Consumerism in a Narcissistic Age," *Consumption Markets & Culture* 23, no. 1 [2020]: 21–43). As Murray writes elsewhere, "there is a concerted effort to characterize selfie-taking as a disorder" ("Introduction: The Selfie as Visual Culture: A Methodological Quandary," in *Visual Culture Approaches to the Selfie*, ed. by Derek C. Murray [New York: Routledge, 2022], 3).

17. Maddox, "Guns Don't Kill People . . . Selfies Do."

18. Soraya Mehdizadeh, "Self-Presentation 2.0: Narcissism and Self-Esteem on Facebook," *Cyberpsychology, Behavior, and Social Networking* 13, no. 4 (2010): 358.

19. Elizabeth N. Lima, *The Association between Narcissism and Implicit Self-Esteem: A Test of the Fragile Self-Esteem Hypothesis* (PhD diss., Florida State University, 2007), 1.

20. See Robert Raskin and Calvin S. Hall, "The Narcissistic Personality Inventory: Alternative Form Reliability and Further Evidence of Construct Validity," *Journal of Personality Assessment* 45, no. 2 (1981): 159–62, and "A

Narcissistic Personality Inventory," *Psychological Reports* 45, no. 2 (1979): 590. See also Lima, *The Association between Narcissism and Implicit Self-Esteem*, Appendix A, and Daniel R. Ames, Paul Rose, and Cameron P. Anderson, "The NPI-16 as a Short Measure of Narcissism," *Journal of Research in Personality* 40, no. 4 (2006): 440–50.

21. Virgil Zeigler-Hill and Christian H. Jordan, "Behind the Mask: Narcissism and Implicit Self-Esteem," in *The Handbook of Narcissism and Narcissistic Personality Disorder: Theoretical Approaches, Empirical Findings, and Treatments*, ed. William K. Campbell and Joshua D. Miller (Hoboken, NJ: Wiley, 2011), 110. See also Jennifer Bosson and Jonathan Weaver's description of the NPI as "a self-report scale that measures seven key components of narcissistic personality including authority, entitlement, exhibitionism, exploitativeness, self-sufficiency, superiority, and vanity" ("'I Love Me Some Me': Examining the Links between Narcissism and Self-Esteem," in Campbell and Miller, eds., *The Handbook of Narcissism and Narcissistic Personality Disorder*, 262).

22. See Jessica Bennett, *Feminist Fight Club: An Office Survival Manual for a Sexist Workplace* (New York: Harper Wave, 2016).

23. As, for instance, McCain and colleagues do using the NPI ("Personality and Selfies: Narcissism and the Dark Triad," *Computers in Human Behavior* 64 [2016]: 126–33).

24. See Evita March and Tayla McBean, "New Evidence Shows Self-Esteem Moderates the Relationship between Narcissism and Selfies," *Personality and Individual Differences* 130 (2018): 107–11; Roberta Biolcati and Stefano Passini, "Narcissism and Self-Esteem: Different Motivations for Selfie Posting Behaviors," *Cogent Psychology* 5, no. 1(2018): 1–12. Agnieszka Sorokowska and colleagues found a moderately positive correlation between selfie-taking and narcissism (see Sorokowska et al., "Selfies and Personality: Who Posts Self-Portrait Photographs?," *Personality and Individual Differences* 90 [2016]: 119–23). Piotr Sorokowski and colleagues found no correlation among women, but a significative correlation among men (Sorokowska et al., "Selfie Posting Behaviors Are Associated with Narcissism among Men," *Personality and Individual Differences* 85 [2015]: 123–27). Daniel Re and colleagues found no difference in NPI scoring between selfie-takers and non-selfie-takers (Re et al., "Selfie Indulgence: Self-Favoring Biases in Perceptions of Selfies," *Social Psychological and Personality Science* 7, no. 6 [2016]: 588–96). Using observational methods instead of self-reporting methods, Christopher Barry and colleagues found no correlation, which, they add, raises the question as to why some studies using self-reporting methods establish even a moderate correlation between narcissism and selfie-taking (Barry et al., "'Let Me Take Another Selfie': Further Examination of the Relation between Narcissism, Self-Perception, and Instagram Posts," *Psychology of Popular Media Culture* 8, no. 1 [2017]: 22–33). Christina Shane-Simpson and colleagues found that grandiose narcissism predicts selfie-posting frequency. However, it might not influence a high frequency of selfie-posting: 92 percent of participants in their sample reported posting a selfie

between zero and two times a month (Shane-Simpson et al., "I Love My Selfie! An Investigation of Overt and Covert Narcissism to Understand Selfie-Posting Behaviors within Three Geographic Communities," *Computers in Human Behavior* 104 [2020]: 106158).

25. On social anxiety around the negative effects of social media on the social bond, see Murray, "Selfie Consumerism in a Narcissistic Age." For the history of how late-modern Western societies have been negatively characterized as "narcissistic," see Greg Goldberg, "Through the Looking Glass: The Queer Narcissism of Selfies," *Social Media + Society* 3, no. 1 (2017), https://doi.org/10 .1177/2056305117698494. Several scholars have deconstructed the commonplace association between social media and self-absorption, arguing that social media users are indeed interested in interaction and sociability. See, for instance, Deborah Chambers, *Social Media and Personal Relationships* (Basingstoke, UK: Palgrave Macmillan, 2013); Humphreys, *The Qualified Self*; Claire Balleys, "L'incontrôlable besoin de contrôle. Les performances de la féminité par les adolescentes sur YouTube," *Genre, sexualité & société* 17 (2017), https://doi.org/10.4000/gss.3958; Amy Dobson, Brady Robards, and Nicholas Carah, eds., *Digital Intimate Publics and Social Media* (Cham, CH: Palgrave Macmillan, 2012); Zizi Papacharissi, ed., *A Networked Self* (New York: Routledge, 2011).

26. In 1986, in tune with de Beauvoir's observations on narcissism in *The Second Sex*, Rita Freedman noted: "While many roles are denied to females, that of beauty object is subtly as well as overtly encouraged. To enact femininity is to become a kind of exhibitionist, to display oneself as a decorative object" (*Beauty Bound*, 37). Research on a sample of college students has found that female Facebook users are more inclined to self-promote through images (as opposed to text, information, or self-description) than male Facebook users. See Mehdizadeh, "Self-Presentation 2.0." This finding is unsurprising when we consider the many ways consumer and beauty cultures encourage young and less young women to garner other people's attention through their (attractive) looks.

27. Burns, "Self(ie)-Discipline," 1720. See also Murray "Selfie Consumerism in a Narcissistic Age." Drawing on Stanley Cohen's work, Theresa Senft and Nancy Baym see the emergence of a moral panic around selfie practices, especially when "adopted by young people, women, or people of color." See Senft and Baym, "What Does the Selfie Say? Investigating a Global Phenomenon," *International Journal of Communication* 9 (2015): 1592.

28. For an extensive discussion, see Laurie Essig, *American Plastic: Boob Jobs, Credit Cards, and Our Quest for Perfection* (Boston: Beacon Press, 2010).

29. Lima, *The Association between Narcissism and Implicit Self-Esteem*, Appendix A, also for item 29.a quoted in the next sentence.

30. Dobson, *Postfeminist Digital Cultures*, chap. 2.

31. My results are consistent with Marijke Naezer's findings in her analysis of girls' reflections on and considerations of sexiness while taking and sharing selfies. According to Naezer, girls navigate sexiness in selfies by partially rejecting and

partially embracing it—hence trying to find a balance between invisibility and overexposure through sexiness ("Sexy Selves: Girls, Selfies, and the Performance of Intersectional Identities," *European Journal of Women's Studies* 27, no. 1 [2018]: 41–56). For a discussion of the careful negotiation of selfie practices by women on Instagram, see also Zaoré-Vanié, *#Strongissexy: Empowerment et sexiness*, 125–7 and 139.

32. Audrey clearly formulates the double standard through which it is decided "who" can take selfies: "It's funny, because women get criticized all the time for taking selfies, then the selfie generation gets criticized, we're all absorbed in ourselves and so, and I'm like, 'Really? Are we that much more absorbed than van Gogh, who spent literally hundreds of hours on his own face? Why are men's self-portraits so much more valued than the picture we can take of ourselves? Anyway, it's, finally—it's accessible, we have control over our image and we get slammed for it all the time."

33. Following the traditional conception of narcissism as a mask for insecurity, public discourse depicts selfie-taking women as both narcissist and lacking in self-esteem (see, for example, Murray, "Selfie Consumerism in a Narcissistic Age"). This is contradictory, since studies show that narcissists usually score high in tests measuring self-esteem. In a study conducted by Roberta Biolcati and Stefano Passini ("Narcissism and Self-Esteem"), which measured the correlation of selfie practices with narcissism and self-esteem, narcissistic personality traits and self-esteem are "moderately positively correlated" to one another. Narcissism and an explicitly positive self-view are generally linked. How do these findings reconcile with the traditional view of narcissism as a "mask" for fragility and low self-esteem? To answer this question, recent research has introduced a distinction between explicit self-esteem (the reflexive expression of a positive self-view) and implicit self-esteem (implicit attitudes toward oneself, rooted in previous experiences and their processing, that, while not uttered explicitly, nonetheless influence behavior). Narcissistic personality, according to some studies, is positively correlated to low implicit self-esteem and high explicit self-esteem. However, other studies invalidate these results. For a discussion, see Lima, *The Association between Narcissism and Implicit Self-Esteem*, and Zeigler-Hill and Jordan, "Behind the Mask." There still is no conclusive evidence for the correlation between narcissistic personality and low implicit self-esteem, and no theoretical framework to explain data showing a possible correlation. See Bosson and Weaver, "I Love Me Some Me." In addition, there is no evidence pointing toward a relation between women's self-esteem and selfie-posting behaviors. See Sorokowska et al., "Selfies and Personality."

34. For an interdisciplinary and more general discussion of the modern and contemporary Western discourse on authenticity as moral imperative, see Godehard Brüntrup, Michael Reder, and Liselotte Gierstl, eds., *Authenticity. Interdisciplinary Perspectives from Philosophy, Psychology, and Psychiatry* (Wiesbaden, DE: Springer, 2020). In a discussion of the distinctive features of the online consuming self, Jefferson Pooley argues that the widespread performance of "calculated

authenticity" online can be interpreted as a response to the "cocktail" of cultural and moral injunctions that encourage individuals to simultaneously practice online self-expression and online self-promotion. Hence, a curated display of authenticity allows the online self to balance "being oneself" with being remarkable enough to garner attention and recognition from online audiences. See Pooley, "The Consuming Self: From Flappers to Facebook," in *Blowing Up the Brand*, ed. Melissa Aronczyk and Devon Powers (New York: Peter Lang, 2010), especially 78, 79, and 83.

35. On the qualification of the self through digital traces and self-expression online, see Humphreys, *The Qualified Self*. For a discussion of self-presentation and the issue of authenticity in online dating, see Kun Peng, "To Be Attractive or to Be Authentic? How Two Competing Motivations Influence Self-Presentation in Online Dating," *Internet Research* 30, no. 4 (2020): 1143–65. As Salisbury and Pooley demonstrate, not only users but social media platforms themselves aspire at being recognized as the main locus for online authenticity: as in the case of users, the contest usually entails publicly denouncing competitors' inauthenticity. See Meredith Salisbury and Jefferson Pooley, "The #nofilter Self: The Contest for Authenticity among Social Networking Sites, 2002–2016," *Social Sciences* 6, no. 1, 10 (2017), https://doi.org/10.3390/socsci6010010.

36. According to Michael J. Walsh and Stephanie A. Baker, "although the face presented is one that appears spontaneous and casual in appearance, it is actually the result of crafting, deliberate framing and ultimately embodied practices." Walsh and Baker, "The Selfie and the Transformation of the Public-Private Distinction," *Information, Communication and Society* 20, no. 8 (2017): 1191. For a discussion of selfie as a "gestural image," entailing reflection and decision-making, see Paul Frosh, "The Gestural Image: The Selfie, Photographic Theory, and Kinesthetic Sociability," *International Journal of Communication* 9 (2015): 1607–28. Walsh and Baker note that the selfie's "ostensibly spontaneous and casual nature . . . embedded in everyday life" has become a main feature of our understanding of selfie-taking, "notwithstanding [that] its production may require 20 photographs before capturing the 'right' presentation worthy of dissemination" ("The Selfie and the Transformation," 1189).

37. In addition to being part of her efforts at online professional self-promotion, Lena's attention to detail in her selfies is also grounded in her idea of what a "real" Instagrammer should be. With a good dose of irony, she describes the distinction as follows: "It's, like, the people who have like real photoshoots with their husbands, they have an Instagram husband who likes to take pictures of them, you know, in front of the brick walls . . . Look it up, seriously [. . .]." As instructed, I did look it up, and found out that the "Instagram husband" and the "brick wall" are indeed standard tropes by which the Internet tends to ridicule the semi-professional female Instagrammer who performs aspirational labor in the hopes of acquiring visibility and perhaps, one day, a certain amount of celebrity and revenue. See Duffy, *(Not) Getting Paid to Do What You Love*, especially chap. 6.

38. Ritualized inasmuch as it is collectively recognizable as participating in the representation of authenticity as a mode of self-presentation. As Erving Goffman observes, such performance is indeed part of a larger photographic culture, which involves advertising images too: "Commercial photographs, of course, involve carefully performed poses presented in the style of being 'only natural.'" See Goffman, *Gender Advertisements* (Cambridge, MA: Harvard University Press, 1979), 84. With regard to selfies specifically, Walsh and Baker point out the centrality of "the *suggestion* or successful performance of authenticity" for selfies ("The Selfie and the Transformation of the Public-Private Distinction," 1193).

39. See Aaron Hess, "The Selfie Assemblage". *International Journal of Communication* 9 (2015): 1629-46.

40. "Ordinary ugliness is what we all experience: stretch marks, cellulite, wrinkles, the downward pull of gravity, the realization that our bodies are not and can never be really perfect" (Essig, *American Plastic*, 84. See also MacCannell and MacCannell, "The Beauty System"). On the cult of perfection, see Elias and Gill, "Beauty Surveillance." Angela McRobbie provides an analysis of "perfection" as being an aspirational ideal for women in neoliberal societies: such an ideal enforces self-regulation, enhances competition among women, and encourages an increasing participation in aesthetic consumer culture (McRobbie, "Notes on the Perfect"). According to Ana Sofia Elias and Rosalind Gill, beauty apps dramatize this form of self-surveillance and the cult of bodily perfection (Elias and Gill, "Beauty Surveillance"). On aesthetic perfection as being an ethical ideal in contemporary beauty culture, see Heather Widdows, *Perfect Me: Beauty as an Ethical Ideal* (Princeton, NJ: Princeton University Press, 2018).

41. Like the advertisement photos studied by Erving Goffman, celebrity and commercial selfies also "present a dolled-up, affluent version of reality" (*Gender Advertisements*, 22), where "everyone is better dressed and has straighter teeth than we find in our ordinary experience" (Greg Smith, "Reconsidering Gender Advertisements: Performativity, Framing and Display," in *The Contemporary Goffman*, ed. Michael H. Jacobsen [New York]: Routledge, 2010], 177). However, this stylization and enhancement of reality is also a frequent compositional feature of selfies that are disconnected from commercial purposes, or at least such is the perception that social media users have (as discussed in this and previous chapters).

42. See Peng, "To Be Attractive or to Be Authentic?" The criteria through which users anticipate appraisal correspond to the criteria through which users appraise other users' pictures. In their study of the perceived authenticity of selfies, Katharina Lobinger and Cornelia Brantner found that selfies are indeed perceived as inauthentic by other users when they present facial or bodily expressions imitating pictures of celebrities; this is also the case when the situation in which the selfie is taken appears staged *in order to* take a picture. Lobinger and Brantner, "In the Eye of the Beholder: Subjective Views on the Authenticity of Selfies," *International Journal of Communication* 9 (2015): 1848–60.

43. Harvey Sacks, "On Doing 'Being Ordinary,'" in *Structures of Social Action: Studies in Conversation Analysis*, ed J. Maxwell Atkinson and John Heritage

(Cambridge: Cambridge University Press, 1984), 416, 419, and 424–5. See also 428: "although lots of people figure that experience is a great thing, and apparently at least some people are eager to have experiences, they are extraordinary carefully regulated sort of things."

44. Goffman, *Gender Advertisements*, 84.

45. I base my claims on the results of a query using the term "#thatgirl" that I ran on TikTok on September 7, 2021, around 10:00 a.m. EST, consulted at the url https://www.tiktok.com/tag/thatgirl.

46. I take the expression from Imran Rai's YouTube video "Becoming 'THAT Girl' TikTok's New GLOW UP Trend! How to Become the Best Version of Yourself FOR YOU," YouTube, May 30, 2021, https://www.youtube.com/watch?v=5jdkPMx87CY&t=6s, which attempts to promote the idea according that anyone can be "That Girl" provided they become the best version of themselves. Different formulations of a similar mantra can be found in the captions of various TikTok videos.

47. Jessica Singer, "TikTok's That Girl Is Meant to Promote Wellness, but Some Say It Does the Opposite," CBC News, August 15, 2021, https://www.cbc .ca/news/entertainment/that-girl-tiktok-trend-wellness-1.6139284.

48. Elana Levine, "Introduction," in Levine, ed., *Cupcakes, Pinterest and Ladyporn*, 7.

49. See Gabriel Faimau, "Towards a Theoretical Understanding of the Selfie: A Descriptive Review," *Sociology Compass* 14 (2020): 1–12.

50. For a discussion of online and offline visibility as both currency and risk, see Andrea M. Brighenti, *Visibility in Social Theory and Social Research* (Basingstoke, UK: Palgrave Macmillan, 2010), and "Visibility: A Category for the Social Sciences," *Current Sociology* 55, no. 3 (2010): 323–42. On the ability of digital traces to "qualify" (instead of just "quantifying") both the real and the digital self, see Humphreys, *The Qualified Self*.

CONCLUSION: BEAUTY AND THE PARADOXES OF WOMEN'S SUBJECTIVITY

1. Miller, *Stuff*, 40.

2. See, notably, Rosalind Gill, "Postfeminist Media Culture: Elements of a Sensibility," *European Journal of Cultural Studies* 10, no. 2 (2007): 150–55.

APPENDIX A: INTRODUCING THE PARTICIPANTS

1. My use of the term "low-income" is based on the definition of the "low income measure," or LIM, according to which a household is determined to be low

income if its after-tax income is less than half of the median after-tax income for households. In 2018, when interviews for this research were conducted, the median after-tax income of Canadian families and unattached individuals was $61,400. See Statistics Canada, "Canada Income Survey 2018," last modified February 24, 2020, https://www150.statcan.gc.ca/n1/daily-quotidien/200224/dq200224a-eng .htm. This gives an upper limit of $30,700 for the low-income bracket. In Quebec, according to 2016 data, the upper threshold of the low-income bracket after tax was $21,290 for unattached individuals, $30,110 for single-parent households with children, and $42,582 for bi-parental households with children. See Centre d'étude sur la pauvreté et l'exclusion, *La pauvreté, les inégalités et l'exclusion sociale au Québec. État de la situation 2019* (Quebec City: Ministère du Travail, de l'Emploi et de la Solidarité sociale, 2020), https://www.mtess.gouv.qc.ca/publications/pdf/CEPE _Etat-situation-2019.pdf.

APPENDIX B: METHODOLOGICAL DESIGN AND PROCEDURE

1. See Mira Crouch and Heather McKenzie, "The Logic of Small Samples in Interview-Based Qualitative Research," *Social Science Information* 45, no. 4 (2006): 483–99.

2. Haridimos Tsoukas, "Craving for Generality and Small-N Studies: A Wittgensteinian Approach towards the Epistemology of the Particular in Organization and Management Studies," in *The SAGE Handbook of Organizational Research Methods*, ed. David A. Buchanan and Alan Bryman, 285–301 (Los Angeles: Sage, 2009), 298.

3. See Guillaume Latzko-Toth, Claudine Bonneau, and Mélanie Millette, "Small Data, Thick Data: Thickening Strategies for Trace-Based Social Media Research," in *The SAGE Handbook of Social Media Research Methods*, ed. Luc Sloan and Anabel Quan-Haase (London: Sage, 2017), 199–241.

4. See Dennis A. Gioia, Kevin G. Corley, and Aimee L. Hamilton, "Seeking Qualitative Rigor in Inductive Research: Notes on the Gioia Methodology," *Organizational Research Methods* 16, no. 1 (2013): 15–31.

5. See Chris Cope, "Ensuring Validity and Reliability in Phenomenographic Research Using the Analytical Framework of a Structure of Awareness," *Qualitative Research Journal* 4, no. 2 (2004): 5–18, and Martin Drapeau, "Les critères de scientificité en recherche qualitative," *Pratiques Psychologiques* 10, no. 1 (2004): 79–86.

6. See Kathy Charmaz, *Constructing Grounded Theory* (London: Sage, 2006).

7. See Gillian Rose, *Visual Methodologies* (London: Sage, 2016).

8. See Wendy J. Wills, Angela M. Dickinson, Angela Meah, and Frances Short, "Reflections on the Use of Visual Methods in a Qualitative Study of Domestic Kitchen Practices," *Sociology* 50, no. 3 (2016): 470–85.

9. As described by Angela Bolton, Christopher Pole, and Phillip Mizen in "Picture This: Researching Child Workers," *Sociology* 35, no. 2 (2001): 501–18.

10. See Greg Guest, Arwen Bunce, and Laura Johnson, "How Many Interviews Are Enough? An Experiment with Data Saturation and Variability," *Field Methods* 18, no. 1 (2006): 59–82, and Ashley K. Hagaman and Amber Wutich, "How Many Interviews Are Enough to Identify Metathemes in Multisited and Cross-Cultural Research?," *Field Methods* 29, no. 1 (2017): 23–41.

11. See Gioia, Corley, and Hamilton, "Seeking Qualitative Rigor in Inductive Research."

12. For a legal discussion of discrimination on the basis of body size, see Deborah Rhode, *The Beauty Bias: The Injustice of Appearance in Life and Law* (New York: Oxford University Press, 2010).

13. In Fanny Gallot, "Enjeux et défis de l'intersectionnalité. Entretien avec Sirma Bilge," *Contretemps: Revue de critique communiste*, April 30, 2012.

14. See Sarah Riley, Adrienne Evans, and Alison Mackiewicz. "It's Just between Girls: Negotiating the Postfeminist Gaze in Women's 'Looking Talk,'" *Feminism & Psychology* 26, no. 1 (2016): 94–113.

BIBLIOGRAPHY

Abecassis, Tally, and Kim France. "We Love to Talk Beauty." Episode 13 of *Everything Is Fine* (Podcast), May 19, 2020. https://play.acast.com/s/everythingisfine/welovetotalkbeauty.

Åberg, Erica, and Laura Salonen. "Well-Beshaved Women Rarely Make History." In *Appearance as Capital: The Normative Regulation of Aesthetic Capital Accumulation and Conversion*, edited by Outi Sarpila, Iida Kukkonen, Tero Pajunen, and Erica Åberg, 149–64. Bingley, UK: Emerald Publishing, 2022.

Adichie, Chimamanda Ngozi. *Americanah*. New York: Alfred A. Knopf, 2013.

Ahmed, Sara. *Living a Feminist Life*. Durham, NC: Duke University Press, 2017.

Akdeniz, Billur, Roger J. Calantone, and Clay M. Voorhees. "Effectiveness of Marketing Cues on Consumer Perceptions of Quality: The Moderating Roles of Brand Reputation and Third-Party Information." *Psychology & Marketing*, 30, no. 1 (2013): 76–89.

Allen, Margaret. *Selling Dreams: Inside the Beauty Business*. New York: Simon and Schuster, 1981.

Altman, Anna. "The Year of Hygge, the Danish Obsession with Getting Cozy." *New Yorker*, December 18, 2016. https://www.newyorker.com/culture/culture-desk/the-year-of-hygge-the-danish-obsession-with-getting-cozy.

Ames, Daniel R., Paul Rose, and Cameron P. Anderson. "The NPI-16 as a Short Measure of Narcissism." *Journal of Research in Personality* 40, 4 (2006): 440–50.

Anderson, Patricia J. *When Passion Reigned: Sex and the Victorians*. New York: Basic Books, 1995.

Arps, Brianna. "Here's the Major Problem behind Celebrities' 'No Makeup' Selfies that No One Is Talking About." *Insider*, August 1, 2017. https://www.insider.com/no-makeup-selifes-are-a-problem-this-is-why-2017-7.

Attwood, Margaret. *The Handmaid's Tale*. Toronto: McClelland and Stewart, 1985.

Baker, Tamara A., NiCole T. Buchanan, Chivon A. Mingo, Rosalyn Roker, and Candace S. Brown. "Reconceptualizing Successful Aging among Black Women and the Relevance of the Strong Black Woman Archetype." *The Gerontologist* 55, no. 1 (2015): 51–7.

Balleys, Claire. "L'incontrôlable besoin de contrôle. Les performances de la féminité par les adolescentes sur YouTube." *Genre, sexualité & société* 17 (2017). https://doi.org/10.4000/gss.3958.

Banet-Weiser, Sarah. "Am I Pretty or Ugly? Girls and the Market for Self-Esteem." *Girlhood Studies* 7, no. 1 (2014): 83–101.

———. *Empowered: Popular Feminism and Popular Misogyny*. Durham, NC: Duke University Press, 2018.

———. "'I'm Beautiful the Way I Am': Empowerment, Beauty, and Aesthetic Labour." In *Aesthetic Labour: Rethinking Beauty Politics in Neoliberalism*, edited by Ana Sofia Elias, Rosalind Gill, Christina Scharff, 265–82. London: Palgrave Macmillan, 2017.

Banner, Lois W. *American Beauty*. New York: Alfred A. Knopf, 1983.

Barry, Christopher T., Shari R. Reiter, Alexandra C. Anderson, Mackenzie L. Schoessler, and Chloe L. Sidoti. "Let Me Take Another Selfie": Further Examination of the Relation between Narcissism, Self-Perception, and Instagram Posts. *Psychology of Popular Media Culture* 8, no. 1 (2017): 22–33.

Bartko, Karen. "Note Telling Girls to 'Dress Conservatively' in School to Avoid Distracting Boys Sparks Concern in Alberta Village." *Global News*, June 5, 2017. https://globalnews.ca/news/3503389/note-telling-girls-to-dress-conservatively-in-school-to-avoid-distracting-boys-sparks-outrage-in-alberta-village.

Bartky, Sandra L. "Foucault, Femininity, and the Modernization of Patriarchal Power." In *Femininity and Domination: Studies in the Phenomenology of Oppression*, 63–82. New York: Routledge, 1990.

Bateman, Justine. *Face: One Square Foot of Skin*. New York: Akaschic Books, 2021.

Bateson, Gregory. "Double Bind (1969)." In *Steps to an Ecology of Mind*, 199–204. Northvale, NJ: Jason Aronson, 1987.

Beall, J. C., Michael Glanzberg, and David Ripley. "Liar Paradox." In *The Stanford Encyclopedia of Philosophy*, edited by Edward N. Zalta (Fall 2020 Edition). https://plato.stanford.edu/archives/fall2020/entries/liar-paradox.

Beauvoir, Simone de. *Le Deuxième sexe*. Paris: Gallimard, 1949.

Becker, Dana. *The Myth of Empowerment: Women and the Therapeutic Culture in America*. New York: NYU Press, 2005.

Beckman, Christine M., and Melissa Mazmanian. *Dreams of the Overworked: Living, Working and Parenting in the Digital Age*. Stanford, CA: Stanford University Press, 2020.

Beerbohm, Max "A Defence of Cosmetics." *The Yellow Book* 1 (April 1894). First Published 1896 by Dodd, Mead and Company (New York). https://archive.org/stream/defenceofcosmeti00beer/defenceofcosmeti00beer_djvu.txt.

Belmi, Peter, and Margaret Neale. "Mirror, Mirror on the Wall, Who's the Fairest of Them All? Thinking that One Is Attractive Increases the Tendency to Support Inequality." *Organizational Behavior and Human Decision Processes* 124, no. 2 (2014): 133–49.

Bennett, Jessica. *Feminist Fight Club: An Office Survival Manual for a Sexist Workplace.* New York: Harper Wave, 2016.

Binet, Alfred. *Le fétichisme dans l'amour.* 1887. Reprint, Paris: Payot Rivages, 2001.

Biolcati, Roberta, and Stefano Passini. "Narcissism and Self-Esteem: Different Motivations for Selfie Posting Behaviors." *Cogent Psychology* 5, no. 1(2018): 1–12.

Biskind, Peter. *Seeing Is Believing: How Hollywood Taught Us to Stop Worrying and Love the Fifties.* New York: Pantheon Books, 1983.

Black, Paula. *The Beauty Industry: Gender, Culture, Pleasure.* London: Routledge, 2004.

Black, Paula, and Ursula Sharma. "Men Are Real, Women Are 'Made Up': Beauty Therapy and the Construction of Femininity." *Sociological Review* 49, no. 1 (2001): 100–16.

Bolton, Angela, Christopher Pole, and Phillip Mizen. "Picture This: Researching Child Workers." *Sociology* 35, no. 2 (2001): 501–18.

Bordo, Susan. *Unbearable Weight: Feminism, Western Culture, and the Body.* 10th ann. ed. Berkeley: University of California Press, 2003.

Bosson, Jennifer K., and Jonathan R. Weaver. "'I Love Me Some Me': Examining the Links between Narcissism and Self-Esteem." In *The Handbook of Narcissism and Narcissistic Personality Disorder: Theoretical Approaches, Empirical Findings, and Treatments,* edited by William K. Campbell and Joshua D. Miller, 261–71. Hoboken, NJ: Wiley, 2011.

Bourdieu, Pierre. *La distinction. Critique sociale du goût.* Paris: Les éditions de minuit, 1979. [Engl. trans.: *Distinction: A Social Critique of the Judgement of Taste.* London: Routledge and Kegan Paul, 1986.]

———. "The Forms of Capital." In *Handbook of Theory and Research for the Sociology of Education,* edited by John Richardson, 241–58. New York: Greenwood, 1986.

———. *Méditations pascaliennes.* Paris: Seuil, 1997. [Engl. trans.: *Pascalian Meditations.* Stanford, CA: Stanford University Press, 2000.]

———. "Social Space and Symbolic Power." *Sociological Theory* 7, no. 1 (1989): 14–25.

Braizaz, Marion. "Le 'problème' de la beauté: Quand la sociologie s'intéresse au travail esthétique de soi." *Strathèse* 6 (2017). https://strathese.unistra.fr:443/strathese/index.php?id=1139.

Brighenti, Andrea M. "Visibility: A Category for the Social Sciences." *Current Sociology* 55, no. 3 (2007): 323–42.

———. *Visibility in Social Theory and Social Research.* Basingstoke, UK: Palgrave Macmillan, 2010.

Brooks, Abigail I. "Opting In or Opting Out? North American Women Share Strategies for Aging Successfully with (and without) Cosmetic Intervention." In *Successful Aging as a Contemporary Obsession: Global Perspectives,* edited by Sarah Lamb, 41–54. New Brunswick, NJ: Rutgers University Press, 2017.

Brooks, Siobhan. *Unequal Desires: Race and Erotic Capital in the Stripping Industry.* New York: SUNY Press, 2010.

Brownmiller, Susan. *Femininity*. New York: Linden Press/Simon and Schuster, 1984.

Brumberg, Joan J. *The Body Project: An Intimate History of American Girls*. New York: Vintage Books, 1997.

Brüntrup, Godehard, Michael Reder, and Liselotte Gierstl, eds. *Authenticity: Interdisciplinary Perspectives from Philosophy, Psychology, and Psychiatry*. Wiesbaden, DE: Springer, 2020.

Burns, Anne. "Self(ie)-Discipline: Social Regulation as Enacted through the Discussion of Photographic Practice." *International Journal of Communication* 9 (2015): 1716–33.

Butler, Sarah. "'The Lipstick Effect': Britons Treat Themselves as Budgets Tighten." *The Guardian*, July 15, 2017. https://www.theguardian.com/business /2017/jul/15/the-lipstick-effect-britons-treat-themselves-as-budgets-tighten.

Buziashvili, David, Jacob I. Tower, Neel R. Sangal, Aakash M. Shah, and Bordi Paskhover. "Long-Term Patterns of Age-Related Facial Bone Loss in Black Individuals." *JAMA Facial Plastic Surgery* 21, no. 4 (2019): 292–7.

Cahill, Ann J. "Feminist Pleasure and Feminine Beautification." *Hypathia* 18, no. 4 (2004): 42–64.

Cairns, Kate, and Josée Johnston. *Food and Femininity*. London: Bloomsbury Academic, 2015.

Calasanti, Toni. "Bodacious Berry, Potency Wood and the Aging Monster: Gender and Age Relations in Anti-aging Aids." *Social Forces* 86, no. 1 (2007): 335–55.

Calasanti, Toni, and Neil King. "Successful Aging, Ageism, and the Maintenance of Age and Gender Relations." In *Successful Aging as a Contemporary Obsession: Global Perspectives*, edited by Sarah Lamb, 27–40. New Brunswick, NJ: Rutgers University Press, 2017.

Campioni, Giuliano. *Les lectures françaises de Nietzsche*. Paris: Presses universitaires de France, 2001.

Cappuccini, Gill, and Raymond Cochrane. "Life with the First Baby: Women's Satisfaction with the Division of Roles." *Journal of Reproductive and Infant Psychology* 18, no. 3 (2000): 189–202.

Cavaglià, Roberta. "Il curioso caso del 'Festival della bellezza' senza donne (e con problemini di copyright)." *Wired.it*, September 9, 2020. https://www.wired.it/ attualita/politica/2020/09/09/festival-bellezza-maschi-maggie-taylor.

Centre d'étude sur la pauvreté et l'exclusion. *La pauvreté, les inégalités et l'exclusion sociale au Québec. État de la situation 2019*. Quebec City: Ministère du Travail, de l'Emploi et de la Solidarité sociale, 2020. https://www.mtess.gouv.qc.ca/ publications/pdf/CEPE_Etat-situation-2019.pdf.

Chambers, Deborah. *Social Media and Personal Relationships*. Basingstoke, UK: Palgrave Macmillan, 2013.

Chang, Tammy, Mikel Llanes, Katherine J. Gold, and Michael D. Fetters. "Perspectives about and Approaches to Weight Gain in Pregnancy: A Qualitative Study of Physicians and Nurse Midwives." *BMC Pregnancy and Childbirth* 13, no. 47 (2013). https://doi.org/10.1186/1471-2393-13-47.

Chappel, Jo. "Be Provocative They Said. A Serious Message from *Girls. Girls. Girls. Magazine.*" *Creative Moment*, March 5, 2020. https://www.creativemoment .co/be-provocative-they-said-a-serious-message-from-girls-girls-girls-magazine -with-a-cultural-currency-with-real-value.

Charlebois, Catherine, and Mathieu Lapointe, eds. *Scandale! Le Montréal illicite 1940–1960.* Montreal: Cardinal, 2016.

Charmaz, Kathy. *Constructing Grounded Theory.* London: Sage, 2006.

Charmaz, Kathy, and Dana Rosenfeld. "Reflections of the Body, Images of Self: Visibility and Invisibility in Chronic Illness and Disability." In *Body/Embodiment: Symbolic Interaction and the Sociology of the Body*, edited by Dennis Waskul and Phillip Vannini, 35–50. Burlington, VT: Ashgate, 2006.

Chatzidakis, Andreas, Jamie Hakim, Jo Littler, Catherine Rottenberg, and Lynne Segal. "From Carewashing to Radical Care: The Discursive Explosions of Care during Covid-19." *Feminist Media Studies* 20, no. 6 (August 2020): 889–95.

Cheval, Sophie. *Belle autrement! Pour en finir avec la tyrannie de l'apparence.* Paris: Armand Colin, 2013.

Chollet, Mona. *Beauté fatale. Les nouveaux visages d'une aliénation féminine.* Paris: La Découverte, 2012.

Christou, Prokopis, Anna Farmaki, Alexi Saveriades, and Marios Georgiou. "Travel Selfies on Social Networks, Narcissism and the 'Attraction-Shading Effect.'" *Journal of Hospitality and Tourism Management* 43 (2020): 289–93.

Coleman, Rebecca, and Monica Moreno Figueroa. "Past and Future Perfect? Beauty, Affect and Hope." *Journal for Cultural Research* 14, no. 14 (2010): 357–73.

Conrad, Peter. *The Medicalization of Society: On the Transformation of Human Conditions into Treatable Disorders.* Baltimore: Johns Hopkins University Press, 2007.

———. "Wellness as Virtue: Morality and the Pursuit of Health." *Culture, Medicine, and Psychiatry* 18, no. 3 (1994): 385–401.

Coontz, Stephanie. "Gender Equality and Economic Inequality: Impact on Marriage." In *Gender and Couple Relationships*, edited by Susan M. McHale, Valarie King, Jennifer Van Hook, and Alan Booth, 79–90. Cham, CH: Springer 2016.

Cope, Chris. "Ensuring Validity and Reliability in Phenomenographic Research Using the Analytical Framework of a Structure of Awareness." *Qualitative Research Journal* 4, no. 2 (2004): 5–18.

Coulter, Kristi. *Nothing Good Can Come from This.* New York: MCD x FSG Originals, 2018.

Crawford Mondé, Geniece. "#BlackDontCrack: A Content Analysis of the Ageing Black Woman in Social Media." *Feminist Media Studies* 18, no. 1 (2018): 47–60.

Crépeau, Catherine, Catherine Couturier, and Kathleen Couillard. "Gwyneth Paltrow: Rigorous Health Claims? False." Quebec Chief Scientist, Gouvernement du Québec, November 3, 2020. http://www.scientifique-en-chef.gouv.qc .ca/en/impacts-of-research-cat/gwyneth-paltrow-rigorous-health-claims-false -french-version-only.

Criddle, Cristina. "Girl Guides: Enhanced Photos Need Labels on Social Media." *BBC News*, September 2, 2020. https://www.bbc.com/news/technology-54003536.

Crouch, Mira, and Heather McKenzie. "The Logic of Small Samples in Interview-Based Qualitative Research." *Social Science Information* 45, no. 4 (2006): 483–99.

Cvajner, Martina. "Hyper-Femininity as Decency: Beauty, Womanhood and Respect in Emigration." *Ethnography* 12, no 3 (2011): 356–74.

Daminger, Allison. "The Cognitive Dimension of Household Labor." *American Sociological Review* 84, no. 4 (2019): 609–33.

Daniels, Elizabeth A., Meghan M. Gillen, and Charlotte H. Markey, eds. *Body Positive: Understanding and Improving Body Image in Science and Practice.* Cambridge: Cambridge University Press, 2018.

Davis, Kathy. "Remaking the She-Devil: A Critical Look at Feminist Approaches to Beauty." *Hypathia* 6, no. 2 (1991): 21–43.

———. *Reshaping the Female Body: The Dilemma of Cosmetic Surgery.* New York: Routledge, 1995.

DeBrabander, Firmin. *Life after Privacy: Reclaiming Democracy in a Surveillance Society.* Cambridge: Cambridge University Press, 2020.

Dobson, Amy S. *Postfeminist Digital Cultures: Femininity, Social Media, and Self-Representation.* New York: Palgrave Macmillan, 2015.

Dobson, Amy S., Brady Robards, and Nicholas Carah, eds. *Digital Intimate Publics and Social Media.* Cham, CH: Palgrave Macmillan, 2012.

Döring, Nicola, Anne Reif, and Sandra Poeschl. "How Gender Stereotypical Are Selfies? A Content Analysis and Comparison with Magazine Adverts." *Computers in Human Behavior* 55 (2016): 955–62.

Douglas, Susan. *Enlightened Sexism: The Seductive Message that Feminism's Work Is Done.* New York: Times Books, Henry Holt and Company, 2010.

Dowrick, Anna, and Ruth Holliday. "Tweakments: Non-surgical Beauty Technologies and Future Directions for the Sociology of the Body." *Sociology Compass*, September 27, 2022. https://doi.org/10.1111/soc4.13044.

Drapeau, Martin. "Les critères de scientificité en recherche qualitative." *Pratiques Psychologiques* 10, no. 1 (2004): 79–86.

Duffy, Brooke Erin. *(Not) Getting Paid to Do What You Love: Gender, Social Media, and Aspirational Work.* New Haven, CT: Yale University Press, 2017.

Efstathiou, Sophia. "The Nazi Cosmetic: Medicine in the Service of Beauty." *Studies in History and Philosophy of Science Part C: Studies in History and Philosophy of Biological and Biomedical Sciences* 43, no. 3 (2012): 634–42.

Ehrenreich, Barbara. *Natural Causes: An Epidemic of Wellness, the Certainty of Dying, and Killing Ourselves to Live Longer.* New York: Twelve, 2018.

Elias, Ana Sofia, and Rosalind Gill. "Beauty Surveillance: The Digital Self-Monitoring Cultures of Neoliberalism." *European Journal of Cultural Studies* 21, no. 1 (2018): 59–77.

Elias, Ana Sofia, Rosalind Gill, Christina Scharff. "Aesthetic Labour: Rethinking Beauty Politics in Neoliberalism." In *Aesthetic Labour: Rethinking Beauty Politics in Neoliberalism*, edited by Ana Sofia Elias, Rosalind Gill, and Christina Scharff, 3–50. London: Palgrave Macmillan, 2017.

Elliott, Larry. "Into the Red: 'Lipstick Effect' Reveals the True Face of the Recession." *The Guardian*, December 22, 2008. https://www.theguardian.com/business/2008/dec/22/recession-cosmetics-lipstick.

Engeln, Renee. *Beauty Sick: How the Cultural Obsession with Appearance Hurts Girls and Women*. New York: Harper 2017

Ensler, Eve. *The Good Body*. New York: Villard, 2004.

Essig, Laurie. *American Plastic: Boob Jobs, Credit Cards, and Our Quest for Perfection*. Boston: Beacon Press, 2010.

Etcoff, Nancy, Susy Orbach, Jennifer Scott, and Heidi D'Agostino, H. (2004). *The Real Truth About Beauty: A Global Report*. Findings of the Global Study on Women, Beauty and Well-Being, Commissioned by Dove/Unilever. September 2004. http://www.clubofamsterdam.com/contentarticles/52%20Beauty/dove_white_paper_final.pdf.

Faimau, Gabriel. "Towards a Theoretical Understanding of the Selfie: A Descriptive Review." *Sociology Compass* 14 (2020): 1–12.

Felder, Rachel. *Red Lipstick. An Ode to a Beauty Icon*. New York: HarperCollins, 2019.

Foucault, Michel. *Les aveux de la chair*. Paris: Gallimard, 2018.

———. *"Il faut défendre la société." Cours au Collège de France, 1976*. Paris: Gallimard, 1997.

———. *Surveiller et punir: Naissance de la prison*. Paris: Gallimard, 1975. [Engl. trans.: *Discipline and Punish: The Birth of the Prison*. New York: Random House, 1977.]

Fouquet, Catherine, and Yvonne Knibiehler. *La beauté pour quoi faire? Essai sur l'histoire de la beauté féminine*. Paris: Temps Actuels, 1982.

Freedman, Rita. *Beauty Bound*. Lexington, MA: Lexington Books, 1986.

Frevert, Tonya K., and Lisa S. Walker. "Physical Attractiveness and Social Status." *Sociology Compass* 8, no. 3 (2014): 313–23.

Friedman, May. "Beyond MILF: Exploring Sexuality and Feminism in Public Motherhood." *Atlantis* 36, no. 2 (2014): 49–60.

Frosh, Paul. "The Gestural Image: The Selfie, Photographic Theory, and Kinesthetic Sociability." *International Journal of Communication* 9 (2015): 1607–28.

Frost, Liz. "'Doing Looks': Women, Appearance and Mental Health." In *Women's Bodies: Discipline and Transgression*, edited by Jane Arthurs and Jean Grimshaw, 117–36. London: Cassell, 1999.

Gallot, Fanny. "Enjeux et défis de l'intersectionnalité. Entretien avec Sirma Bilge." *Contretemps : Revue de critique communiste*, April 30, 2012. www.contretemps.eu/enjeux-et-defis-de-lintersectionnalite-entretien-avec-sirma-bilge.

Garber, Megan. "How Alexandria Ocasio-Cortez's Plain Black Jacket Became a Controversy." *The Atlantic*, November 16, 2018. https://www.theatlantic.com/entertainment/archive/2018/11/alexandria-ocasio-cortezs-clothes-a-tedious-backlash/576064.

Gardner, Carol B. *Passing By: Gender and Public Harassment*. Berkeley: University of California Press, 1995.

Gershuny, Jonathan. "Time, through the Life Course, in the Family." In *The Blackwell Companion to the Sociology of Families*, edited by Jacqueline L. Scott, Judith Trees, and Martin Richards, 159–77. Malden, MA: Blackwell, 2004.

Gerstell, Emily, Sophie Marchessou, Jennifer Schmidt, and Emma Spagnuolo. "How COVID-19 Is Changing the World of Beauty." McKinsey & Company, May 5, 2020. https://www.mckinsey.com/industries/consumer-packaged -goods/our-insights/how-covid-19-is-changing-the-world-of-beauty#.

Gianini Belotti, Elena. *What Are Little Girls Made Of?* New York: Schocken Books, 1978.

Gill, Rosalind. "The Affective, Cultural and Psychic Life of Postfeminism: A Postfeminist Sensibility 10 Years On." *European Journal of Cultural Studies* 20, no. 6 (2017): 606–26.

———. "Postfeminist Media Culture: Elements of a Sensibility." *European Journal of Cultural Studies* 10, no. 2 (2007): 147–66.

Gill, Rosalind, and Shani Orgad. "The Confidence Cult(ure)." *Australian Feminist Studies* 30, no. 86 (2015): 324–44.

Gillette, Beth. "10 Hacks to Achieving the 'No Makeup' Makeup Look." *The Everygirl*, July 9, 2018. https://theeverygirl.com/10-hacks-to-achieving-the-no -makeup-makeup-look.

Gilman, Sander L. *Making the Body Beautiful: A Cultural History of Aesthetic Surgery*. Princeton, NJ: Princeton University Press, 1999.

Gimlin, Debra. *Body Work: Beauty and Self-Image in American Culture*. Oakland: University of California Press, 2002.

Gioia, Dennis A., Kevin G. Corley, and Aimee L. Hamilton. "Seeking Qualitative Rigor in Inductive Research: Notes on the Gioia Methodology." *Organizational Research Methods* 16, no. 1 (2013): 15–31.

Gjerdingen, Dwenda K., and Bruce A. Center. "First-Time Parents' Postpartum Changes in Employment, Childcare, and Housework Responsibilities." *Social Science Research* 34, no. 1 (2005): 103–16.

Glick, Peter, Sadie Larsen, Cathryn Johnson, and Heather Branstiter. "Evaluations of Sexy Women in Low- and High-Status Jobs." *Psychology of Women Quarterly* 29, no. 4 (2005): 389–95.

Goffman, Erving. "The Arrangement between the Sexes." *Theory and Society* 4, no. 3 (1977): 301–31.

———. *Gender Advertisements*. Cambridge, MA: Harvard University Press, 1979.

———. "Symbols of Class Status." *British Journal of Sociology* 2, no. 4 (1951): 294–304.

Goldberg, Greg. "Through the Looking Glass: The Queer Narcissism of Selfies." *Social Media + Society* 3, no. 1 (2017). https://doi.org/10.1177/2056305117698494.

Green, Adam I. "'Erotic Capital' and the Power of Desirability: Why 'Honey Money' Is a Bad Collective Strategy for Remedying Gender Inequality." *Sexualities* 16, nos. 1–2 (2013): 137–58.

Guest, Greg, Arwen Bunce, and Laura Johnson. "How Many Interviews Are Enough? An Experiment with Data Saturation and Variability." *Field Methods* 18, no. 1 (2006): 59–82.

Guillaumin, Colette. *Racism, Sexism, Power and Ideology*. London: Routledge, 1995.

Gupta, Alisha H. "Why Did Hundreds of Thousands of Women Drop Out of the Workforce?" *New York Times*, October 3, 2020. https://www.nytimes

.com/2020/10/03/us/jobs-women-dropping-out-workforce-wage-gap-gender .html.

Gurung, Regan A., Elizabeth Punke, Michaella Brickner, and Vincenzo Badalamenti. "Power and Provocativeness: The Effects of Subtle Changes in Clothing on Perceptions of Working Women." *Journal of Social Psychology* 158, no. 2 (2017): 252–5.

Hagaman, Ashley K., and Amber Wutich. "How Many Interviews Are Enough to Identify Metathemes in Multisited and Cross-Cultural Research?" *Field Methods* 29, no. 1 (2006): 23–41.

Hakim, Catherine. *Erotic Capital: The Power of Attraction in the Boardroom and in the Bedroom.* New York: Basic Books, 2011.

Hamermesh, Daniel S. *Beauty Pays: Why Attractive People Are More Successful.* Princeton, NJ: Princeton University Press, 2011.

Hargro, Brina. "Hair Matters: African American Women and the Natural Hair Aesthetic." MA thesis, Georgia State University, 2011. https://scholarworks.gsu .edu/art_design_theses/95.

Henning, Michelle. "Don't Touch Me (I'm Electric): On Gender and Sensation in Modernity." In *Women's Bodies: Discipline and Transgression*, edited by Jane Arthurs and Jean Grimshaw, 17–47. London: Cassell, 1999.

Henningsen, David Dryden, Mary Braz, and Elaine Davies. "Why Do We Flirt? Flirting Motivations and Sex Differences in Working and Social Contexts." *Journal of Business Communication* 45, no. 4 (2008): 483–502.

Héritier, Françoise. *Masculin/feminin. La pensée de la différence.* Paris: Odile Jacob, 1996.

Hernández-Julián, Rey, and Christina Peters. "Student Appearance and Academic Performance." *Journal of Human Capital* 11, no. 2 (2017): 247–62.

Herzig, Rebecca M. *Plucked: A History of Hair Removal.* New York: NYU Press, 2015.

Hess, Aaron. "The Selfie Assemblage." *International Journal of Communication* 9 (2015): 1629–46.

Hill, Sarah E., Christopher D. Rodeheffer, Vlakas Griskevicius, Kristina Durante, and Andrew E. White. "Boosting Beauty in an Economic Decline: Mating, Spending, and the Lipstick Effect." *Journal of Personality and Social Psychology* 103, no. 2 (2012): 275–91.

Hinkson, Kamila. "This Hairdresser Is Helping Black Women Embrace Their Hair, Curls and All." CBC News, February 15, 2021. https://www.cbc.ca/news/ canada/montreal/black-changemakers-nancy-falaise-1.5912485.

Hochschild, Arlie. *The Managed Heart: Commercialization of Human Feeling.* Berkeley: University of California Press, 1983.

Hofmeier, Sara M., Cristin D. Runfola, Margarita Sala, Danielle A. Gagne, Kimberly A. Brownley, and Cynthia M. Bulik. "Body Image, Aging, and Identity in Women Over 50: The Gender and Body Image (GABI) Study." *Journal of Women & Aging* 29, no. 1 (2017): 3–14.

Holmqvist, Kristina, and Carolina Lunde. "Appearance-Related Practices." In *Body Positive: Understanding and Improving Body Image in Science and Practice*, edited by

Elizabeth A. Daniels, Meghan M. Gillen, and Charlotte H. Markey, 111–34. Cambridge: Cambridge University Press, 2018.

Holstein, Martha. *Women in Late Life: Critical Perspectives on Gender and Age.* Lanham, MD: Rowman & Littlefield, 2015.

Hosoda, Megumi, Eugene F. Stone-Romero, and Gwen Coats. "The Effects of Physical Attractiveness on Job-Related Outcomes: A Meta-Analysis of Experimental Studies." *Personnel Psychology* 56, no. 2 (2003): 431–62.

Howlett, Neil, Karen J. Pine, Natassia Cahill, İsmail Orakçıoğlu, and Ben Fletcher. "Unbuttoned: The Interaction between Provocativeness of Female Work Attire and Occupational Status." *Sex Roles* 72, no. 3 (2015): 105–16.

HuffPost. "La Une de Elle sur les kilos et le confinement déclenche les critiques." *Le HuffPost*, June 1, 2020. https://www.huffingtonpost.fr/entry/la-une-de-elle -sur-les-kilos-et-le-confinement-declenche-les-critiques_fr_5ed4a8f9c5b6ade e41bc4ae9.

Humphreys, Lee. *The Qualified Self: Social Media and the Accounting of Everyday Life.* Cambridge, MA: MIT Press, 2018.

Hurd Clarke, Laura. *Facing Age: Women Growing Older in Anti-aging Culture.* Lanham, MD: Rowman & Littlefield, 2011.

Iqani, Mehita, and Jonathan E. Schroeder. "#Selfie: Digital Self-Portraits as Commodity Form and Consumption Practice." *Consumption Markets and Culture* 19, no. 5 (2016): 405–15.

Italie, Leanne. "Obama's Tan Suit Buzzed Around the World." Associated Press, August 29, 2014, https://apnews.com/article/e912379e95ab41588a39e4e53ec20f93.

Jackson, Linda A., John E. Hunter, and Carole N. Hodge. "Physical Attractiveness and Intellectual Competence: A Meta-Analytic Review." *Social Psychology Quarterly* 58, no. 2 (1995): 108–22.

Jain, Andrea R. *Peace, Love, Yoga: The Politics of Global Spirituality.* New York: oxford University Press, 2020.

Jarrín, Alvaro. *The Biopolitics of Beauty: Cosmetic Citizenship and Affective Capital in Brazil.* Oakland: University of California Press, 2017.

Jeffreys, Sheila. *Beauty and Misogyny: Harmful Cultural Practices in the West.* London: Routledge, 2005.

Jenkins, Henry. *Convergence Culture: Where Old and New Media Collide.* Updated ed. New York: NYU Press, 2008.

Jha, Meeta Ravi. *The Global Beauty Industry.* London: Routledge, 2016.

Johnson, Maria S. "#BlackGirlMagic and Its Complexities." In *Black Feminist Sociology*, edited by Zakiya Luna and Whitney N. Laster Pirtle, 110–20. New York: Routledge, 2022.

Jones, Geoffrey. *Beauty Imagined: A History of the Global Beauty Industry.* Oxford: Oxford University Press, 2010.

Jowett, Victoria. "9 Ways to Ensure Your Makeup Always Looks Natural." *Cosmopolitan*, October 12, 2020. https://www.cosmopolitan.com/uk/beauty -hair/makeup/g18192402/natural-makeup-look.

Kalick, S. Michael. "Physical Attractiveness as Status Cue." *Journal of Experimental Social Psychology* 24, no. 6 (1987): 469–80.

Kang, Miliann. *The Managed Hand: Race, Gender, and the Body in Beauty Service Work*. Berkeley: University of California Press, 2010.

Kerner Furman, Frida. *Facing The Mirror: Older Women and Beauty Shop Culture*. New York: Routledge, 1997.

Kestenbaum, Richard. "The Biggest Trends in the Beauty Industry." *Forbes*. September 9, 2018. https://www.forbes.com/sites/richardkestenbaum/2018/09/09/beauty-industry-biggest-trends-skin-care-loreal-shiseido-lauder/#5893074f6982.

Keyser-Verreault, Amélie. "The Continuum of Regaining One's Body: Childbirth and Reproductive Choice under Beauty Pressure in Taiwan." *European Journal of Cultural Studies*, June 28, 2022. https://doi.org/10.1177/13675494221104145.

Khazan, Olga. "The Makeup Tax." *The Atlantic*, August 5, 2015. https://www.theatlantic.com/business/archive/2015/08/the-makeup-tax/400478.

———. Why Do So Many Women Wear So Much Makeup? *The Atlantic*, April 28, 2014. https://www.theatlantic.com/health/archive/2014/04/women-wear-too-much-makeup-because-they-mistakenly-think-men-want-them-to/361264.

Kling, Johanna, Kristina Holmqvist Gattario, and Ann Frisén. "Swedish Women's Perceptions of and Conformity to Feminine Norms." *Scandinavian Journal of Psychology* 58, no. 3 (2017): 238–48.

Knibiehler, Yvonne, and Catherine Fouquet. *La femme et les médecins*. Paris: Hachette, 1983.

Krämer, Nicole C., Markus Feurstein, Jan P. Kluck, Yannic Meier, Marius Rother, and Stephan Winter. "Beware of Selfies: The Impact of Photo Type on Impression Formation Based on Social Networking Profiles." *Frontiers in Psychology* 8 (2017). https://doi.org/10.3389/fpsyg.2017.00188.

Kukkonen, Iida. "Who Performs Appearance Work, and Who Believes Appearance Works?" In *Appearance as Capital: The Normative Regulation of Aesthetic Capital Accumulation and Conversion*, edited by Outi Sarpila, Iida Kukkonen, Tero Pajunen, and Erica Åberg, 39–55. Bingley, UK: Emerald Publishing, 2022.

Kyle, Gerard, and Garry Chick. "The Social Construction of a Sense of Place." *Leisure Sciences* 29 (2007): 209–25.

Kwan, Samantha, and Mary Nell Trautner. "Beauty Work: Individual and Institutional Rewards, the Reproduction of Gender, and Questions of Agency." *Sociology Compass* 3, no. 1 (2009): 49–71.

Lajeunie, Alain. *Capital Jeunesse. Apprendre à le gérer grâce à la médecine anti-âge et à la médecine esthétique*. Paris: Ellipses, 2004.

Lamb, Sarah, Jessica Robbins-Ruszkowski, and Anna I. Corwin. "Introduction: Successful Aging as a Twenty-First-Century Obsession." In *Successful Aging as a Contemporary Obsession: Global Perspectives*, edited by Sarah Lamb, 1–23. New Brunswick, NJ: Rutgers University Press, 2017.

Latzko-Toth, Guillaume, Claudine Bonneau, and Mélanie Millette. "Small Data, Thick Data: Thickening Strategies for Trace-Based Social Media Research." In *The SAGE Handbook of Social Media Research Methods*, edited by Luc Sloan and Anabel Quan-Haase, 199–241. London: Sage, 2017.

Lavigne, Julie, and Chiara Piazzesi. "Femmes et pouvoir érotique." *Recherches féministes* 32, no. 1 (2019): 1–18.

Lea, Aarona. "Aligning with the Four Phases of the Moon." Goop.com, accessed July 27, 2021. https://goop.com/wellness/spirituality/how-to-align-with-the -moon.

Leboeuf, Céline. "What Is Body Positivity? The Path from Shame to Pride." *Philosophical Topics* 47, no. 2 (2019): 113–27.

Lee, Soohyung, and Keunkwan Ryu. "Plastic Surgery: Investment in Human Capital or Consumption?" *Journal of Human Capital* 6, no. 3 (2012): 224–50.

Leeds Craig, Maxine. *Ain't I a Beauty Queen? Black Women, Beauty and the Politics of Race.* New York: Oxford University Press, 2002.

———. "Race, Beauty, and the Tangled Knot of a Guilty Pleasure." *Feminist Theory* 7, no. 2 (2006): 159–77.

Lemieux, Cyril. "De la théorie de l'habitus à la sociologie des épreuves: Relire L'expérience concentrationnaire. In *Michaël Pollak. De l'identité blessée à une sociologie des possibles*," edited by Liora Israël and Danièle Voldman, 179–205. Paris: Éditions Complexe, 2008.

Levine, Elana. "Introduction." In *Cupcakes, Pinterest and Ladyporn: Feminized Popular Culture in the Early Twenty-first Century*, edited by Elana Levine, 1–12. Urbana: University of Illinois Press, 2015.

Lewis, Michael. "Obama's Way." *Vanity Fair*, September 11, 2012. https://www .vanityfair.com/news/2012/10/michael-lewis-profile-barack-obama.

Lima, Elizabeth N. *The Association between Narcissism and Implicit Self-Esteem: A Test of the Fragile Self-Esteem Hypothesis.* PhD dissertation, Florida State University, 2007.

Littler, Jo. "The Rise of the 'Yummy Mummy': Popular Conservatism and the Neoliberal Maternal in Contemporary British Culture." *Communication, Culture and Critique* 6, no. 2 (2013): 227–43.

Lobinger, Katharina, and Cornelia Brantner. "In the Eye of the Beholder: Subjective Views on the Authenticity of Selfies." *International Journal of Communication* 9 (2015): 1848–60.

Lombroso Ferrero, Gina. *Criminal Man, According to the Classification of Cesare Lombroso.* New York: G. P. Putnam's Sons, 1911.

Löwy, Ilana. *L'emprise du genre.* Paris: La Dispute, 2006.

Lubbers, Marcel, Eva Jaspers, and Wout Ultee. "Primary and Secondary Socialization Impacts on Support for Same-Sex Marriage after Legalization in the Netherlands." *Journal of Family Issues* 30, no. 12 (2009): 1714–45.

Luhmann, Niklas. *Die Gesellschaft der Gesellschaft.* 2 vols. Frankfurt am Main: Suhrkamp, 1997.

———. "Meaning as Sociology's Basic Concept." In *Essays on Self-Reference*, 21–79. New York: Columbia University Press, 1990.

———. "The Paradoxy of Observing Systems." *Cultural Critique* 31 (1995): 37–55.

MacCannell, Dean, and Juliet Flower MacCannell. "The Beauty System." In *The Ideology of Conduct*, edited by Nancy Armstrong and Leonard Tennenhouse, 206–38. New York: Methuen, 1987.

Maddox, Jessica. "Guns Don't Kill People . . . Selfies Do": Rethinking Narcissism as Exhibitionism in Selfie-Related Deaths." *Critical Studies in Media Communication* 34, no. 3 (2017): 193–205.

Maizes, Sarah. *Got MILF? The Modern Mom's Guide to Feeling Fabulous, Looking Great, and Rocking a Minivan.* New York: Berkeley Books, 2011.

Malatzky, Christina. "Australian Women's Complex Engagement with the Yummy Mummy Discourse and the Bodily Ideals of Good Motherhood." *Women's Studies International Forum* 62 (2017): 25–33.

Maor, Maya, and Julie Cwikel. "Mothers' Strategies to Strengthen Their Daughters' Body Image." *Feminism & Psychology* 26, no. 1 (2016): 11–29.

Marandola, Sabrina. "'It's Something to Celebrate': Flash Mobs, Private Screenings of Black Panther Hit Montreal." CBC News, February 15, 2018. https://www.cbc.ca/news/canada/montreal/black-panther-montreal-1.4537988.

March, Evita, and Tayla McBean. "New Evidence Shows Self-Esteem Moderates the Relationship between Narcissism and Selfies." *Personality and Individual Differences* 130 (2018): 107–11.

Marsh, Madeleine. *Compacts and Cosmetics: Beauty From Victorian Times to the Present Day.* London: Remember When, 2009. Reprint, Barnsley, UK: Pen and Sword History, 2018.

Martínez-Jiménez, Laura. "Postfeminist Neoliberalization of Self-Care: A Critical Discourse Analysis of Its Representation in *Vogue, Cosmopolitan* and *Elle.*" *Feminist Media Studies*, June 29, 2022. https://doi.org/10.1080/14680777.2022.2093936.

Martuccelli, Danilo. "Les deux voies de la notion d'épreuve en sociologie." *Sociologie* 6, no. 1 (2015): 43–60.

Maza, Sarah. "The Diamond Necklace Affair Revisited: The Case of the Missing Queen." In *Eroticism and the Body Politics*, edited by Lynn Hunt, 63–89. Baltimore: Johns Hopkins University Press, 1991.

———. "L'image de la souveraine: Féminité et politique dans les pamphlets de l'affaire du collier." *Studies on Voltaire and the Eighteenth Century* 287 (1991): 363–78.

McCain, Jessica L., Zachary G. Borg, Ariel H. Rothenberg, Kristina M. Churillo, Paul Weiler, and W. Keith Campbell. "Personality and Selfies: Narcissism and the Dark Triad." *Computers in Human Behavior* 64 (2016): 126–33.

McCann, H. "Look Good, Feel Good." *Overland Literary Journal*, December 8, 2019. https://overland.org.au/previous-issues/issue-237/feature-look-good-feel-good.

McGee, Micki. *Self Help, Inc.: Makeover Culture in American Life.* New York: Oxford University Press, 2007.

McMillan Cottom, Tressie. *Thick, and Other Essays.* New York: New Press, 2019. EPUB.

McRobbie, Angela. *The Aftermath of Feminism: Gender, Culture and Social Change.* London: Sage, 2009.

———. "Notes on the Perfect: Competitive Femininity in Neoliberal Times." *Australian Feminist Studies* 30, no. 83 (2015): 3–20.

———. "Notes on 'What Not to Wear' and Post-Feminist Symbolic Violence." *Sociological Review* 52, no. 2 (2004): 99–109.

Mehdizadeh, Soraya. "Self-Presentation 2.0: Narcissism and Self-Esteem on Facebook." *Cyberpsychology, Behavior, and Social Networking* 13, no. 4 (2010): 357–64.

Melchoir-Bonnet, Sabine. *The Mirror: A History*. London: Routledge, 2002.

Meyers, Diana T. "Miroir, Mémoire, Mirage: Appearance, Aging, and Women." In *Mother Time: Women, Aging, and Ethics*, edited by Margaret Urban Walker, 23–41. Lanham, MD: Rowman & Littlefield, 1999.

Miguel, Cristina. "Visual Intimacy on Social Media: From Selfies to the Co-construction of Intimacies through Shared Pictures." *Social Media + Society* 2, no. 2 (April 2016). https://doi.org/10.1177/2056305116641705.

Miller, Daniel. "The Little Black Dress Is the Solution, but What Is the Problem?" In *Elusive Consumption*, edited by Karin M. Ekström and Helene Brembeck, 113–28. Oxford: Berg, 2004.

———. *Stuff*. Cambridge: Polity Press, 2010.

Mire, Amina. *Wellness in Whiteness. Biomedicalization and the Promotion of Whiteness and Youth among Women*. London: Routledge, 2020.

Monk, Ellis P. Jr, Michael H. Esposito, and Hedwig Lee. "Beholding Inequalities: Race, Gender, and Returns to Physical Attractiveness in the United States." *American Journal of Sociology* 127, no. 1 (2021): 194–241.

Mosse, George L. *The Image of Man: The Creation of Modern Masculinity*. Oxford: Oxford University Press, 1996.

Moyser, Melissa, and Amanda Burlock. "Time Use: Total Work Burden, Unpaid Work, and Leisure." *Women in Canada: A Gender-Based Statistical Report*. Statistics Canada, July 30, 2018. https://www150.statcan.gc.ca/n1/pub/89-503 -x/2015001/article/54931-eng.htm.

Mull, Amanda. "Americans Have Baked All the Flour Away." *The Atlantic*, May 12, 2020. https://www.theatlantic.com/health/archive/2020/05/why-theres -no-flour-during-coronavirus/611527.

Mulvey, Laura. "Visual Pleasure and Narrative Cinema." *Screen* 16, no. 3 (1975): 6–18.

Murray, Derek C. "Introduction: The Selfie as Visual Culture: A Methodological Quandary." In *Visual Culture Approaches to the Selfie*, edited by Derek C. Murray, 1–19. New York: Routledge, 2022.

———. "Selfie Consumerism in a Narcissistic Age." *Consumption Markets & Culture* 23, no. 1 (2020): 21–43.

Nadkarni, Ashwini, and Stefan G. Hoffman. "Why Do People Use Facebook?" *Personality and Individual Difference* 52 (2012): 243–9.

Naezer, Marijke. "Sexy Selves: Girls, Selfies, and the Performance of Intersectional Identities." *European Journal of Women's Studies* 27, no. 1 (2018): 41–56

Nash, Rebecca, George Fieldman, Trevor Hussey, Jean-Luc Lévêque, and Patricia Pineau. "Cosmetics: They Influence More than Caucasian Female Facial Attractiveness." *Journal of Applied Social Psychology* 36, no. 2 (2006): 493–504.

Nathanson, Elizabeth. "Dressed for Economic Distress: Blogging and the 'New' Pleasures of Fashion." In *Gendering the Recession: Media and Culture in an Age of*

Austerity, edited by Diane Negra and Yvonne Tasker, 136–60. Durham, NC: Duke University Press, 2014.

————. "Sweet Sisterhood: Cupcakes as Sites of Feminized Consumption and Production." In *Cupcakes, Pinterest and Ladyporn: Feminized Popular Culture in the Early Twenty-first Century*, edited by Elana Levine, 249–67. Urbana: University of Illinois Press, 2015.

Neveu, Érik. "Les sciences sociales doivent-elles accumuler les capitaux? A propos de Catherine Hakim, Erotic Capital, et de quelques marcottages intempestifs de la notion de capital." *Revue française de science politique* 63, no. 2 (2013): 337–58.

Nikolopoulos, Hara, Maria Mayan, Jessica MacIsaac, Terri Miller, and Rhonda C. Bell. "Women's Perceptions of Discussions about Gestational Weight Gain with Health Care Providers during Pregnancy and Postpartum: A Qualitative Study." *BMC Pregnancy and Childbirth* 17, no. 1 (2017): 97.

O'Neill, Rachel. "'Glow from the Inside Out': Deliciously Ella and the Politics of 'Healthy Eating.'" *European Journal of Cultural Studies* 24, no. 6 (2021): 1282–1303.

Orenstein, Peggy. *Cinderella Ate My Daughter: Dispatches from the Front Lines*. New York: HarperCollins, 2011.

Padjemi, Jennifer. "Le maquillage, une affaire de classe." Episode 27 of *Miroir miroir* (podcast), November 18, 2019. https://www.binge.audio/podcast/miroirmiroir/le-maquillage-une-affaire-de-classe.

Paltrow, Gwyneth. Foreword to *The Clarity Cleanse: 12 Steps to Finding Emotional Healing, Spiritual Fulfillment, and Renewed Energy*, by Habib Sadeghi. New York: Goop Press/ Grand Central Life & Style, 2017.

————. Foreword to *Goop Clean Beauty*, by the Editors of Goop. New York: Goop Press/ Grand Central Life & Style, 2016.

Parkins, Wendy. "Protesting Like a Girl. Embodiment, Dissent and Feminist Agency." *Feminist Theory* 1, no. 1 (2000): 59–78.

Papacharissi, Zizi, ed. *A Networked Self*. New York: Routledge, 2011.

Patzer, Gordon L. *The Power and Paradox of Physical Attractiveness*. Boca Raton, FL: BrownWalker Press, 2006.

Paustian-Underdahl, Samantha C., and Lisa Slattery Walker. "Revisiting the Beauty Is Beastly Effect: Examining When and Why Sex and Attractiveness Impact Hiring Judgments." *International Journal of Human Resource Management* 27, no. 10 (2016): 1034–58.

Peiss, Kathy. *Hope in a Jar: The Making of America's Beauty Culture*. New York: Owl Books, 1998.

Peng, Kun. "To Be Attractive or to Be Authentic? How Two Competing Motivations Influence Self-Presentation in Online Dating." *Internet Research* 30, no. 4 (2020): 1143–65.

Pennington, Bill. "What Exactly Is 'Locker-Room Talk'? Let an Expert Explain." *New York Times*, October 20, 2016. https://www.nytimes.com/2016/10/11/sports/what-exactly-is-locker-room-talk-let-an-expert-explain.html.

Perrot, Philippe. *Le travail des apparences. Le corps féminin XVIIIe–XIXe siècle*. Paris: Éditions du Seuil, 1984.

Petit, Stephanie. "Princess Eugenie Is Embracing This Natural Beauty Look during Coronavirus Lockdown." *People*, April 27, 2020. https://people.com/royals/princess-eugenie-is-embracing-this-natural-beauty-look-during-coronavirus-lockdown.

Petrow, Steven. "What the '10-Year Challenge' Might Say about You, and Me." *New York Times*, January 31, 2019. https://www.nytimes.com/2019/01/31/well/mind/10-year-challenge-facebook-instagram.html.

Piazzesi, Chiara. *Nietzsche: Fisiologia dell'arte e décadence*. Lecce, IT: Conte, 2003.

———. *Vers une sociologie de l'intimité*. Paris: Hermann, 2017.

Piazzesi, Chiara, and Catherine Lavoie Mongrain. "Selfies de femmes, négociation normative et production de culture visuelle sur Instagram et Facebook." *Recherches féministes* 33, no. 1 (2020): 135–51.

———. "Women 'Doing Selfies': Reflexivity and Norm Negotiation in the Production and Circulation of Digital Self-Portraits." *Sociologia e Politiche sociali* 22, no. 3 (2019): 95–111.

Pilcher, Katy, and Wendy Martin. "Forever 'Becoming'? Negotiating Gendered and Ageing Embodiment in Everyday Life." *Sociological Research Online* 25, no. 4 (2020): 698–717.

Pinola, Melanie. "President Obama's Productivity Tactics." *LifeHacker*, September 18, 2012. https://lifehacker.com/president-obamas-productivity-tactics-5944198.

Pisacane, Alfredo, and Paola Continisio. "Breastfeeding and Perceived Changes in the Appearance of the Breasts: A Retrospective Study." *Acta Pædiatrica* 93, no. 10 (2004): 1346–8.

Poitevin, Kimberly. "Inventing Whiteness: Cosmetics, Race, and Women in Early Modern England." *Journal for Early Modern Cultural Studies* 11, no. 1 (2011): 59–89.

Pooley, Jefferson. "The Consuming Self: From Flappers to Facebook." In *Blowing Up the Brand*, edited by Melissa Aronczyk and Devon Powers, 71–89. New York: Peter Lang, 2010.

Porter, Jessica. *The MILF Diet: Let the Power of Whole Foods Transform Your Body, Mind, and Spirit . . . Deliciously!* New York: Atria/Emily Bestler Books, 2013.

Puniewska, Magdalena. "Inside the Strict, Unspoken Dress Code for Women Political Candidates." *Racked*, June 4, 2018. https://www.racked.com/2018/6/4/17417386/political-candidates-women-female-dress-code.

Purc-Stephenson, Rebecca, Mikaela Rawleigh, H. Kemp, and Morten Asfeldt. "We Are Wilderness Explorers: A Review of Outdoor Education in Canada." *Journal of Experiential Education* 42, no. 4 (2019): 364–81.

Pylypa, Jen. "Power and Bodily Practice." *Arizona Anthropologist* 13 (1998): 21–36.

Rainville, Camille. "Be a Lady They Said." *Writing of a Furious Woman* (blog), December 9, 2017. https://writingsofafuriouswoman.wordpress.com/2017/12/09/be-a-lady-they-said.

Raskin, Robert, and Calvin S. Hall. "A Narcissistic Personality Inventory." *Psychological Reports* 45, no. 2 (1979): 590.

———. "The Narcissistic Personality Inventory: Alternative Form Reliability and Further Evidence of Construct Validity." *Journal of Personality Assessment* 45, no. 2 (1981): 159–62.

Ratajkowski, Emily. *My Body*. New York: Metropolitan, 2021.

Re, Daniel E., Sylvia A. Wang, Joyce C. He, and Nicholas O. Rule. "Selfie Indulgence: Self-Favoring Biases in Perceptions of Selfies." *Social Psychological and Personality Science* 7, no. 6 (2016): 588–96.

Recio, Rocio P. "Postfeminist Performance of Domesticity and Motherhood during the COVID-19 Global Lockdown: The Case of Chiara Ferragni." *Feminist Media Studies*, October 12, 2020. https://doi.org/10.1080/14680777.2020.1830147.

Relman, Eliza. "Outgoing Democratic Sen. Claire McCaskill Dismisses Alexandria Ocasio-Cortez as a 'Shiny New Object' and Says Her 'Rhetoric Is Cheap.'" *Business Insider*, December 26, 2018. https://www.businessinsider.com/sen-claire-mccaskill-dismisses-alexandria-ocasio-cortez-as-shiny-new-object-2018-12.

Remaury, Bruno. *Le beau sexe faible. Les images du corps féminin entre cosmétique et santé*. Paris: Grasset, 2000.

Rhode, Deborah L. *The Beauty Bias: The Injustice of Appearance in Life and Law*. New York: Oxford University Press, 2010.

Ribeiro, Dilton. "Sexuality and Femininity: The Paradox of the Cultural-Aesthetical Kawaii Movement." *Cadernos Pagu* 62 (2021). https://doi.org/10.1590/18094449202100620013.

Riemer, Abigail R., Sarah J. Gervais, Jeanine L. M. Skorinko, Sonya Maria Douglas, Heather Spencer, Katherine Nugai, Anastasia Karapanagou, and Andreas Miles-Novelo. "She Looks Like She'd Be an Animal in Bed: Dehumanization of Drinking Women in Social Contexts." *Sex Roles* 80 (2019): 617–29.

Riley, Sarah, Adrienne Evans, and Alison Mackiewicz. "It's Just Between Girls: Negotiating the Postfeminist Gaze in Women's 'Looking Talk.'" *Feminism & Psychology* 26, no. 1 (2016): 94–113.

Riley, Sarah, Adrienne Evans, and Martine Robson. *Postfeminism and Health: Critical Psychology and Media Perspectives*. London: Routledge, 2019.

Rocha, Roberto. "How Many Crimes Happen Near You." CBC News, accessed October 8, 2021. https://newsinteractives.cbc.ca/montreal-crime.

Rodulfo, Kristina. "Alexandria Ocasio-Cortez Details Her Skincare Routine and Offers Tips on Oration in the Same IG Story." *Elle*, January 28, 2019. https://www.elle.com/beauty/makeup-skin-care/a26062012/alexandria-ocasio-cortez-skincare-makeup-beauty-routine.

Rose, Gillian. *Visual Methodologies*. London: Sage, 2016

Róisín, Fariha. *Who Is Wellness For? An Examination of Wellness Culture and Who It Leaves Behind*. New York: Harper Wave, 2022.

Rosin, Hanna. *The End of Men. And the Rise of Women*. New York: Riverhead Books, 2012.

Rottenberg, Catherine. *The Rise of Neoliberal Feminism*. New York: Oxford University Press, 2018.

Rowe, Kristin Denise. "'Nothing Else Mattered After That Wig Came Off': Black Women, Unstyled Hair, and Scenes of Interiority." *Journal of American Culture* 42, no. 1 (2019): 21–36.

Ruesch, Jurgen, and Gregory Bateson. *Communication: The Social Matrix of Psychiatry*. New York: Norton, 1968.

Rutterford, Elsie, and Dominika Minarovic. *Clean Beauty: Recipes to Manage Your Beauty Routine, Naturally.* London: Square Peg, 2017.

Sacks, Harvey. "On Doing 'Being Ordinary.'" In *Structures of Social Action: Studies in Conversation Analysis,* edited by J. Maxwell Atkinson and John Heritage, 413–29. Cambridge: Cambridge University Press, 1984.

Sadeghi, Habib. *The Clarity Cleanse: 12 Steps to Finding Emotional Healing, Spiritual Fulfillment, and Renewed Energy.* New York: Goop Press/Grand Central Life & Style, 2017.

Salisbury, Meredith, and Jefferson Pooley. "The #nofilter Self: The Contest for Authenticity among Social Networking Sites, 2002–2016." *Social Sciences* 6, no. 1 (2017). https://doi.org/10.3390/socsci6010010.

Sandberg, Sheryl. *Lean In: Women, Work, and the Will to Lead.* New York: Knopf, 2013.

Sarpila, Outi, Iida Kukkonen, Tero Pajunen, and Erica Åberg, eds. *Appearance as Capital: The Normative Regulation of Aesthetic Capital Accumulation and Conversion.* Bingley, UK: Emerald Publishing, 2022.

Scharff, Christina. "The Psychic Life of Neoliberalism: Mapping the Contours of Entrepreneurial Subjectivity." *Theory, Culture & Society* 33, no. 6 (2016): 107–22.

Schiffer, Jessica. "The Beauty Trends Customers Are Buying during Covid-19." *Vogue Business,* August 12, 2020. https://www.voguebusiness.com/beauty/the -beauty-trends-customers-are-buying-during-covid-19.

Schmeichel, Mardi, Stacey Kerr, and Chris Linder. "Selfies as Postfeminist Pedagogy: The Production of Traditional Femininity in the US South." *Gender and Education* 32, no. 3 (2020): 363–81.

Schneickert, Christian, Leonie C. Steckermeier, and Lisa-Marie Brand. "Lonely, Poor, and Ugly? How Cultural Practices and Forms of Capital Relate to Physical Unattractiveness." *Cultural Sociology* 14, no. 1 (2020): 80–105.

Schober, Pia S. "The Parenthood Effect on Gender Inequality: Explaining the Change in Paid and Domestic Work When British Couples Become Parents." *European Sociological Review* 29, no. 1 (2013): 74–85.

Schwarz, Ori. "Cultures of Choice: Towards a Sociology of Choice as a Cultural Phenomenon." *British Journal of Sociology* 69, no. 3 (2017): 845–64.

Sender, Katherine. *The Makeover: Reality Television and Reflexive Audiences.* New York: NYU Press, 2012.

Senft, Theresa M., and Nancy K. Baym. "What Does the Selfie Say? Investigating a Global Phenomenon." *International Journal of Communication* 9 (2015): 1588–1606.

Seo, Yuri, Angela Gracia B. Cruz, and 'Ilaisaane M. E. Fifita. "Cultural Globalization and Young Korean Women's Acculturative Labor: K-Beauty as Hegemonic Hybridity." *International Journal of Cultural Studies* 23, no. 4 (2020): 600–18.

Serrano, Angelique. "All the Celebrity Beauty Pros Giving Their Expert Tips Away for Free on Instagram." *InStyle,* May 18, 2020. https://www.instyle.com /beauty/quarantine-hair-makeup-pro-tips.

Shane-Simpson, Christina, Anna M. Schwartz, Rudy Abi-Habib, Pia Tohme, and Rita Obeid. "I Love My Selfie! An Investigation of Overt and Covert

Narcissism to Understand Selfie-Posting Behaviors within Three Geographic Communities." *Computers in Human Behavior* 104 (2020): 106158. https://doi .org/10.1016/j.chb.2019.106158.

Singer, Jessica. "TikTok's That Girl Is Meant to Promote Wellness, but Some Say It Does the Opposite." CBC News, August 15, 2021. https://www.cbc.ca/news /entertainment/that-girl-tiktok-trend-wellness-1.6139284.

Singh-Kurtz, Sangeeta. "The Powerful Feminist Statement in Alexandria Ocasio-Cortez's Instagram Beauty Tips." *Quartz*, January 29, 2019. https://qz .com/quartzy/1535649/aocs-instagram-beauty-tips-are-a-powerful-feminist -statement.

Skeggs, Beverly. *Formations of Class & Gender: Becoming Respectable*. London: SAGE, 1997.

Smith, Greg. "Reconsidering Gender Advertisements: Performativity, Framing and Display." In *The Contemporary Goffman*, edited by Michael H. Jacobsen, 165–84. New York: Routledge, 2010.

Smith-Rosenberg, Carroll. *Disorderly Conduct: Visions of Gender in Victorian America*. New York: Alfred A. Knopf, 1985.

Solotaroff, Paul. "Trump Seriously: On the Trail with the GOP's Tough Guy." *Rolling Stone*, September 9, 2015. https://www.rollingstone.com/politics/poli-tics-news/trump-seriously-on-the-trail-with-the-gops-tough-guy-41447.

Sorokowska, Agnieszka, Anna Oleszkiewicz, Tomasz Frackowiak, Katarzyna Pisanski, Anna Chmiel, and Piotr Sorokowski. "Selfies and Personality: Who Posts Self-Portrait Photographs?" *Personality and Individual Differences* 90 (2016): 119–23.

Sorokowski, Piotr, Agnieszka Sorokowska, Anna Oleszkiewicz, Tomasz Frackowiak, Anna Maria Huk, and Katarzyna Pisanski. "Selfie Posting Behaviors Are Associated with Narcissism among Men." *Personality and Individual Differences* 85 (2015): 123–27.

Spar, Deborah. *Wonder Women: Sex, Power and the Quest for Perfection*. New York: Sarah Crichton Books, 2013.

Spencer Brown, George. *Laws of Form*. London: Allen and Unwin, 1939.

Stack, Liam. "Trump, in France, Tells Brigitte Macron, 'You're in Such Good Shape.'" *New York Times*, July 13, 2017. https://www.nytimes.com/2017/07 /13/world/europe/trump-france-brigitte-macron.html.

Stanko, Elizabeth A. "Safety Talk: Conceptualizing Women's Risk Assessment as a 'Technology of the Soul.'" *Theoretical Criminology* 1, no. 4 (1997): 479–99.

Statistics Canada. *Canada Income Survey 2018*. Statistics Canada, February 24, 2020. https://www150.statcan.gc.ca/n1/daily-quotidien/200224/dq200224a -eng.htm.

———. *National Household Survey*. Statistics Canada Catalogue no. 99-010-X2011032 (2011), accessed October 8, 2021. https://www12.statcan.gc.ca/nhs -enm/2011/dp-pd/prof/index.cfm?Lang=E.

Stein, Leigh. *Self Care: A Novel*. New York: Penguin Books, 2020.

Storm, Meg. "Lady Gaga's Facialist Spills the Skincare Secrets that Allowed the Singer to Go Makeup-Free in 'A Star Is Born.'" *Us Weekly*, March 8, 2019.

https://www.usmagazine.com/stylish/news/lady-gagas-skin-secrets-for-makeup
-free-a-star-is-born-scenes-details.

Strings, Sabrina. *Fearing the Black Body: The Racial Origins of Fat Phobia.* New York: NYU, 2019.

Sweeney, Camille. "Seeking Self-Esteem through Surgery." *New York Times,* January 14, 2009. https://www.nytimes.com/2009/01/15/fashion/15skin.html.

Tankovska, H. "Instagram Accounts with the Most Followers Worldwide as of February 2021." *Statista,* accessed March 18, 2021. https://www.statista.com/statistics/421169/most-followers-instagram.

Tanner, Claire, JaneMaree Maher, and Suzanne Fraser. *Vanity: 21st Century Selves.* Basingstoke, UK: Palgrave Macmillan, 2013.

Tate, Shirley Ann. *The Governmentality of Black Beauty Shame.* London: Palgrave Macmillan, 2018.

Thomas, William I., and Dorothy S. Thomas. *The Child in America: Behavior Problems and Programs.* New York: Knopf, 1928.

Thompson, Cheryl. "Black Women, Beauty, and Hair as a Matter of Being." *Women's Studies* 38, no. 8 (2009): 831–85.

Tiidenberg, Katrin. *Selfies: Why We Love (and Hate) Them.* Bigley, UK: Emerald Publishing, 2018.

———. "Visibly Ageing Femininities: Women's Visual Discourses of Being Over-40 and Over-50 on Instagram." *Feminist Media Studies* 18, no. 1 (2018): 61–76.

Travers, Lea V., Edin T. Randall, Fred B. Bryant, Colleen S. Conley, and Amy M. Bohnert. "The Cost of Perfection with Apparent Ease: Theoretical Foundations and Development of the Effortless Perfectionism Scale." *Psychological Assessment* 27, no. 4 (2015): 1147–59.

Tseëlon, Efrat. *The Masque of Femininity.* London: Sage, 1995.

Tsoukas, Haridimos. "Craving for Generality and Small-N Studies: A Wittgensteinian Approach towards the Epistemology of the Particular in Organization and Management Studies." In *The SAGE Handbook of Organizational Research Methods,* edited by David A. Buchanan and Alan Bryman, 285–301. Los Angeles: SAGE, 2009.

Twigg, Julia. "The Body, Gender, and Age: Feminist Insights in Social Gerontology." *Journal of Aging Studies,* 18, no. 1 (2004): 59–73.

Vanstone, Meredith, Sujane Kandasamy, Mita Giacomini, Deirdre DeJean, and Sarah D. McDonald. "Pregnant Women's Perceptions of Gestational Weight Gain: A Systematic Review and Meta-synthesis of Qualitative Research." *Maternal and Child Nutrition* 13, no. 4 (2017). https://doi.org/10.1111/mcn.12374.

Vigarello, Georges. *Histoire de la beauté. Le corps et l'art d'embellir de la Renaissance à nos jours.* Paris: Seuil, 2004.

Villa, Roberta. "For Media, 'Women's Health' Often Stands for 'Beauty.'" In *Health and Gender: Resilience and Vulnerability Factors for Women's Health in Contemporary Society,* edited by Ilaria Tarricone and Anita Riecher-Rössler, 69–73. Cham, CH: Springer, 2019.

Wallach, Isabelle, Julie Beauchamp, Sabrina Maiorano, Julie Lavigne, and Line Chamberland. *Normes de beauté, perceptions de l'apparence et vie intime des femmes âgées hétérosexuelles et lesbiennes au Québec: Une étude qualitative exploratoire.* Rapport de recherche. Montreal: Chaire de recherche sur l'homophobie, Université du Québec à Montréal, 2019.

Walsh, Michael J., and Stephanie A. Baker. "The Selfie and the Transformation of the Public-Private Distinction." *Information, Communication and Society* 20, no. 8 (2017): 1185–1203.

Warhurst, Chris, and Dennis Nickson. *Aesthetic Labour.* Los Angeles: Sage, 2020.

———. "Employee Experience of Aesthetic Labour in Retail and Hospitality." *Work, Employment & Society* 21, no. 1 (2007): 103–20.

———. "'Who's Got the Look?' Emotional, Aesthetic and Sexualized Labour in Interactive Services." *Gender, Work and Organization* 16, no. 3 (2009): 385–404.

Watzlawick, Paul. "Components of 'Ideological Realities.'" In *The Invented Reality: How Do We Know What We Believe We Know?*, edited by Paul Watzlawick, 206–56. New York: W. W. Norton and Co., 1984.

Watzlawick, Paul, Janet B. Beavin, and Don D. Jackson. *Pragmatics of Human Communication: A Study of Interactional Patterns, Pathologies, and Paradoxes.* London: Faber and Faber, 1967.

Watzlawick, Paul, John H. Weakland, and Richard Fisch. *Change: Principles of Problem Formation and Problem Resolution.* New York: W. W. Norton and Co., 1974.

Wegenstein, Bernadette. *The Cosmetic Gaze: Body Modification and the Construction of Beauty.* Cambridge, MA: MIT Press, 2012.

Weintraub, William. *City Unique: Montreal Days and Nights in the 1940s and '50s.* Toronto: Robin Brass Studio, 2004.

Weiss, Bari. "The Bikini Contest Is Over, but We Are Living Inside the Beauty Pageant." *New York Times*, June 5, 2018. https://www.nytimes.com/2018/06/05/opinion/miss-america-bikini-contest.html.

Weitz, Rose. "Women and Their Hair: Seeking Power through Resistance and Accommodation." *Gender and Society* 15, no. 5 (October 2001): 667–86.

Wellington, Elizabeth. "It's Official: Science Has Proven that Black Doesn't Crack." *Philadelphia Inquirer*, June 12, 2019. www.inquirer.com/life/black-doesnt-crack-rutgers-study-20190612.html.

White, Michele. "Women's Nail Polish Blogging and Femininity." In *Cupcakes, Pinterest and Ladyporn: Feminized Popular Culture in the Early Twenty-first Century*, edited by Elana Levine, 138–56. Urbana: University of Illinois Press, 2015.

Whitefield-Madrano, Autumn. *Face Value: The Hidden Ways Beauty Shapes Women's Lives.* New York: Simon and Schuster, 2016.

Widdows, Heather. *Perfect Me: Beauty as an Ethical Ideal.* Princeton, NJ: Princeton University Press, 2018.

Wiens, Brianna, and Shana MacDonald. "Living Whose Best Life? An Intersectional Feminist Interrogation of Postfeminist #Solidarity in #Selfcare." *NECSUS European Journal of Media Studies* 10, no. 1 (2021): 219–42.

Williams, Ruth. "*Eat, Pray, Love*: Producing the Female Neoliberal Spiritual Subject." *Journal of Popular Culture* 47, no. 3 (2011): 613–33.

Wills, Wendy J., Angela M. Dickinson, Angela Meah, and Frances Short. "Reflections on the Use of Visual Methods in a Qualitative Study of Domestic Kitchen Practices." *Sociology* 50, no. 3 (2016): 470–85.

Winch, Alison. "Brand Intimacy, Female Friendship and Digital Surveillance Networks." *New Formations* nos. 84–5 (2015): 228–45.

———. *Girlfriends and Postfeminist Sisterhood.* Basingstoke, UK: Palgrave Macmillan, 2013.

———. "'I Just Think It's Dirty and Lazy': Fat Surveillance and Erotic Capital." *Sexualities* 19, no. 8 (2016): 898–913.

Wischhover, Cheryl. "Talking to Chimamanda Ngozi Adichie, the Beauty Brand Ambassador We All Need Right Now." *Racked*, November 22, 2016. https://www.racked.com/2016/11/22/13714228/chimamanda-ngozi-adichie-boots-beauty.

Wolf, Naomi. *The Beauty Myth: How Images of Beauty Are Used against Women.* London: Vintage, 1991.

Wollstonecraft, Mary. *A Vindication of the Rights of Woman.* London: Joseph Johnson, 1792.

Wood, Zoe. "Sleeping Beauty Halls: How Covid-19 Upended the 'Lipstick Index.'" *The Guardian*, December 18, 2020. https://www.theguardian.com/business/2020/dec/18/how-covid-19-upended-the-lipstick-index-pandemic-cosmetic-sales-makeup-skincare.

Woodward, Sophie. *Why Women Wear What They Wear.* London: Bloomsbury, 2007.

Wunker, Erin. *Notes from a Feminist Killjoy.* Toronto: BookThug, 2016.

Zaoré-Vanié, Émilie. "#Strongissexy: Empowerment et sexiness dans les selfies ayant pour thème le fitness chez les femmes sur Instagram." MA thesis, Université du Québec à Montréal, 2021.

Zeigler-Hill, Virgil, and Christian H. Jordan. "Behind the Mask: Narcissism and Implicit Self-Esteem." In *The Handbook of Narcissism and Narcissistic Personality Disorder: Theoretical Approaches, Empirical Findings, and Treatments*, edited by William K. Campbell and Joshua D. Miller, 101–15. Hoboken, NJ: Wiley, 2011

INDEX

ABOUT THE AUTHOR

Chiara Piazzesi is full professor of sociology at the Université du Québec à Montréal (UQAM), Canada. Born in Florence, Italy, she received her education at the prestigious Scuola Normale Superiore di Pisa and at the Università del Salento, where she earned her PhD. She has taught and done research in France, Germany, and Brazil before moving to Canada to start her career at UQAM, in Montreal, in 2013. Her research interests span love relationships, feminist issues, gender relations, digital practices, and the place of beauty in women's lives. Trained in philosophy and sociology, she has published several books, peer-reviewed articles, book chapters, and participated in many international conferences and events. Among her publications are the books: *Grammatiche dell'amore [Love Grammars]* (2019); *Vers une sociologie de l'intime. Éros et socialisation* (2017); *Nietzsche* (2015); *La verità come trasformazione di sé. Terapie filosofiche in Pascal, Kierkegaard e Wittgenstein [Truth as Self-tranformation: Philosophical Therapies in Pascal, Kierkegaard and Wittgenstein]* (2009); *Abitudine e potere. Da Pascal a Bourdieu [Habit and Power. From Pascal to Bourdieu]* (2003). Chiara is also strongly committed to disseminating ideas and knowledge among the general public, and she has well-established contacts with some of the biggest media outlets in Canada. You can find her and her work on her official page at UQAM, on Facebook, Twitter, Academia.edu, LinkedIn, and ResearchGate. When she is not writing, teaching, or doing research, Chiara loves spending time with her family, and friends, reading novels, watching superhero movies, and playing classical guitar.